Artificial Intelligence and the Value Alignment Problem

ARTIFICIAL INTELLIGENCE

and the Value Alignment Problem

A PHILOSOPHICAL INTRODUCTION

Travis LaCroix

broadview press

BROADVIEW PRESS
Peterborough, Ontario, Canada

Founded in 1985, Broadview Press is a fully independent academic publishing house owned by approximately twenty-five shareholders—almost all of whom are either Broadview employees or Broadview authors. Broadview is supported by a collaboration with Trent University, a liberal arts university located in Peterborough, Ontario—the city where Broadview was founded and continues to operate. Broadview is committed to environmentally responsible publishing and fair business practices.

Library and Archives Canada Cataloguing in Publication

Title: Artificial intelligence and the value alignment problem : a philosophical introduction / Travis LaCroix.
Names: LaCroix, Travis, author.
Description: Includes bibliographical references and index.
Identifiers: Canadiana (print) 20250165376 | Canadiana (ebook) 20250165384 | ISBN 9781554816293 (softcover) | ISBN 9781460409459 (EPUB) | ISBN 9781037700361 (PDF)
Subjects: LCSH: Artificial intelligence—Moral and ethical aspects—Textbooks. | LCSH: Artificial intelligence—Philosophy—Textbooks.
| LCSH: Values—Philosophy—Textbooks. | LCSH: Computers and civilization—Textbooks. | LCGFT: Textbooks.
Classification: LCC Q334.7 .L33 2025 | DDC 006.301—dc23

Broadview Press handles its own distribution in Canada and the United States:
PO Box 1243, Peterborough, Ontario K9J 7H5, Canada
555 Riverwalk Parkway, Tonawanda, NY 14150, USA
Tel: (705) 482-5915
customerservice@broadviewpress.com

Broadview Press books are imported and distributed in the United Kingdom and European Union by:
Gazelle Book Services Ltd.
White Cross Mills, Hightown, Lancaster, Lancashire, LA1 4XS
sales@gazellebookservices.co.uk

European Union – Responsible Person (for official use only):
eucomply OÜ
Pärnu mnt 139b14
11317 Tallinn, Estonia
hello@eucompliancepartner.com
+33757690241

Canada

Broadview Press acknowledges the financial support of the Government of Canada for our publishing activities.

Edited by Michel Pharand
Interior Design by Travis LaCroix
Cover Design by Em Dash Design

PRINTED IN CANADA

1 2 3 4 5 6 7 8 9 10   25 26 27 28 29 30

For you—
the only one to whom this could belong.

For your wild mind,
your fierce heart,
your mad, beautiful, infuriating way of seeing.

Contents

List of Figures

List of Tables

List of Cases

Preface

This book is something of a strange beast, sitting, perhaps uneasily, between an introductory text and an original philosophical manuscript. I want to take a moment to explain myself.

Beginning in Winter 2022, I regularly taught a first-year course for the Faculty of Computer Science at Dalhousie University, required for undergraduates in the Bachelor of Computer Science and Bachelor of Applied Computer Science programs. The course, Case Studies in Computing and Society, was paired with a companion course offered in the Fall, History of Computing and Society, taught by my colleague Aaron Wright. For my section, I chose to focus on Artificial Intelligence and the Value Alignment Problem—a topic central to my research. I had already taught an advanced undergraduate seminar on the subject in the philosophy department at the University of Toronto the previous summer. However, since no centralised text on the topic exists, I assigned recent journal and conference articles as course readings.

Although the course went reasonably well, it became clear that these readings were pitched at too high a level for first-year CS undergraduates in their second term. To bridge the gap, I provided lecture notes each week, which eventually became the foundation for this book. As a result, this book is designed to be used as a teaching text.

Through researching and teaching courses on value alignment, I came to believe two things. First, discussions of the value alignment problem in the literature were often frustratingly vague—so much so that they offered little practical guidance on addressing or mitigating the issue. Second, and perhaps because of this vagueness, many topics under the broader umbrella of AI ethics—bias, fairness, transparency, and others—could be understood as manifestations of value misalignment (although they are not typically described as such).

In Winter 2024, I beta-tested a draft manuscript while teaching Case Studies in Computing and Society for the third (and final) time at Dalhousie. Here's how I envisioned the text being used, in case this is helpful for instructors who are interested in using this text for teaching: roughly one chapter was assigned per week, with lectures providing additional details, examples, and explanations over two hours of class time. The first four weeks covered foundational material, drawing from Chapters 1, 2, and 3. The next two weeks focused on Part III (Chapters 7 and 8), followed by Part II in the final six weeks (Chapters 4, 5, and 6). I also drew from some of the material in Chapter 11 for the final lecture of the term—in part because it tries to end on an optimistic note. However, the order of parts II and III could be reversed depending on the instructor's preference, emphasis, or scheduling constraints. (The original draft of this book reversed parts II and III.)

As mentioned, I have used this text for an introductory undergraduate course for computer science students. Given my intended audience—undergraduates in philosophy and computer science, as well as professional researchers—I have aimed to make the technical exposition clear for philosophers by using concrete examples, and the philosophical insights clear for computer scientists by avoiding jargon (or describing it plainly when introduced).

Part IV is pitched at a slightly higher level, intended more for opening avenues for future research than for direct teaching. (However, as mentioned, Chapter 11 could be assigned as optional reading or incorporated into a final lecture to close the course on a slightly more optimistic note than what is presented throughout the rest of the text.) For an advanced undergraduate or graduate seminar in philosophy, all 12 chapters would be suitable, with one chapter assigned per week. These could easily be paired with additional readings on relevant topics—some of which are suggested at the end of each chapter as a starting point.

This likely explains the "introductory text" features of this book. On the side of the "original philosophical manuscript", the presentation revolves around a novel approach to conceptualising value alignment. The reason for presenting an original philosophical argument in what is intended as an introductory text lies in the lack of comprehensive works addressing the value alignment problem. (The two exceptions are both "popular press" books.) Meanwhile, the professional research on value alignment still relies on an unsatisfactory formulation of the problem. As a result, each chapter in Part II serves a dual purpose: it introduces key topics in AI ethics that are useful for teaching, while also making original philosophical contributions that explain how these topics can be understood within the framework of the value alignment problem.

There are many possible ways to structure a course around this book; and there is much more research that can follow from the proposals that I start to characterise here. I would be delighted to hear if anyone finds it useful for their teaching or research.

Travis LaCroix
March 27, 2025
Halifax / Toronto / Durham

Acknowledgements

I would like to begin by acknowledging the deep intellectual debt I owe to the many thoughtful and outspoken researchers in this field. In particular, the socio-technical and politically engaged work on AI that has emerged over the past five years has been invaluable. It has shed light on the costs of AI and made an understanding of its harms more concrete and unavoidable in public discourse.

I am grateful to Gillian K. Hadfield and Sheila McIlraith for providing office space at the Schwartz Reisman Institute (University of Toronto) during the summers of 2023, when much of this book was written in its first draft, and 2024, when the final edits were completed.

I extend my sincere thanks to Michael Noukhovitch, Sasha Luccioni, Dom Rosati, Yoshua Bengio, Atoosa Kasirzadeh, Karina Vold, Simon J. D. Prince, and Lynn LaCroix for their insightful conversations, which greatly influenced my thinking.

Portions of this book have been presented at various venues, where audience feedback has been invaluable. Early ideas were introduced at a symposium on AI and value alignment, co-organized by Atoosa Kasirzadeh and me, at the 2023 meeting of the Canadian Philosophical Association. I also shared parts of this work with audiences at Dalhousie University (December 2023), the University of Illinois at Chicago (February 2024), and Durham University (March 2024). Additionally, I was invited to lead a tutorial discussion at the 2024 Responsible AI Research component of the Canadian AI Conference in Guelph, ON (May 2024). Many thanks to Ebrahim Bagheri for the invitation and to Calvin Hillis for his work in organizing the event.

In a more structured setting, discussing these ideas with students proved immensely valuable. I am grateful to the advanced undergraduate philosophy students at the University of Toronto (Summer 2021), who engaged with the earliest version of this book's structure and ideas. Likewise, I appreciate the undergraduate students in computer science and the teaching assistants for my Case Studies in Computing and Society courses at Dalhousie University (Winter 2022, 2023, and 2024) for their engagement and feedback.

I would also like to express my gratitude to Stephen Latta, Archie Fields III, and Broadview Press for their support in bringing this project to completion. The anonymous reviewers who provided early feedback on the book proposal were especially encouraging. Once the project was approved, much of the writing took place in solitude, with little opportunity to refine the exposition in conversation. Given this, I was particularly grateful—and perhaps pleasantly surprised—to receive highly positive feedback from two anonymous reviewers. Their kind words were especially motivating in the final stages of completion. Thanks as well to Michel Pharand for attentive copy editing and indexing suggestions.

Chapter 9 is an extension of my prior work, published in *AI and Ethics*, in addition to research co-authored with Sasha Luccioni; Chapter 10 is adapted from an earlier paper published in *Philosophical Studies*. Additional acknowledgements for feedback on those works can be found in published articles.

Introduction

I am interested in cinema. Film, in general, and science fiction, in particular, is a wonderful medium for exploring philosophical questions. It can be used as a resource, providing examples that illuminate philosophical ideas, or it can be understood as a form of philosophical enquiry in its own right.[1] For example, Michel Gondry's (2004) *Eternal Sunshine of the Spotless Mind*, written by Charlie Kaufman, provides an extended meditation on memory, minds, identity, persons, relationships, and love. Pixar's industry-changing *Toy Story* (1995, dir. John Lasseter) is an existential nightmare about the meaning and meaninglessness of existence. Denis Villeneuve's (2016) *Arrival* explores deep questions surrounding communication, language, culture, understanding, perception, time, and the Sapir-Whorf hypothesis.[2]

Science fiction in cinema and literature has a unique and somewhat pernicious place in present-day discussions about artificial intelligence (AI). In part, this is because imagination often outruns reality. This fact is somewhat unfortunate since it implies that a general cultural or popular understanding of "artificial intelligence" is predominantly shaped by science *fiction* narratives rather than science. Consider that Samuel Butler's 1872 satirical novel, *Erewhon: or, Over the Range*, is regarded as one of the first works of fiction to explore the idea of machine intelligence even though the programmable electronic computer would not be invented for another 71 years. The phrase "artificial intel-

[1] There is an ongoing debate about the philosophical character of cinema beyond mere heuristic or pedagogic function; see discussion in Wartenberg (2015).

[2] The Sapir-Whorf hypothesis (sometimes referred to as the *linguistic relativity hypothesis*) posits that language *determines*—or, in a weaker version, *influences*—a speaker's perception of the world (Sapir, 1921; Whorf, 1940).

ligence" would not be coined for another 12 years after that.[3] In the intervening time, numerous fictional and speculative narratives have been created that contain hypothetical depictions of artificial intelligence. As a result, popular knowledge about the actual science and technology surrounding present-day artificial intelligence is limited.[4] Hence, it should be relatively unsurprising that philosophical thought about artificial intelligence is often coloured by fiction and metaphor rather than being informed by real-world systems.

Crawford (2021) highlights that any choice of definition for AI determines a frame for how the technology is "understood, measured, valued, and governed" (7). This point is further complicated by the fact that "artificial intelligence" may refer to several distinct (non-mutually-exclusive) ideas, systems, fields, etc. Moreover "artificial intelligence" denotes both a property (of a system) and a research method for achieving that property.

To complicate things further, an answer to the question of what artificial intelligence is (as a property of an artificial system), requires understanding what *intelligence* consists of. Already, we are in conceptually murky territory insofar as any notion of intelligence is highly contested.[5] Some key (if imprecise) features of intelligence include common sense, effective learning, planning, reasoning, and handling complex information across various natural and abstract domains. Even so, thinking about the nature of intelligence is historically bound with eugenics and race "science". Moreover, standard metrics of intelligence, like the intelligence quotient (IQ), serve more of an ideological function than a scientific one.[6] These are the sort of goalposts that AI research has sought to surpass since its inception.

That said, "artificial intelligence" is something of a *misnomer* (i.e., an inaccurate name or designation). On the one hand, several scholars have pointed out that artificial intelligence, as it exists today, is not particularly artificial; it is created using natural resources and fuel as well as human labour, infrastructures, logistics, histories, and classifications. Hence, AI depends upon and is deeply embedded within the natural world (Crawford, 2021, 8). At the same

[3]The *Colossus Mark 1*, regarded by some as the first programmable, electronic, digital computer, was operational at Bletchley Park in the United Kingdom by December 1943 (Sale, 2000). Much earlier than this, in the mid-19th century, Charles Babbage invented (though never produced) a *mechanical* general-purpose computer called the *analytical engine* (Menabrea and Lovelace, 1843). The term "artificial intelligence" in the present-day sense is attributed to John McCarthy in 1956; see Chapter 1.

[4]See further discussion in Cave et al. (2018).

[5]Legg and Hutter (2007) discuss more than 70 distinct definitions.

[6]See discussion in Richardson (2017).

time, AI is not particularly intelligent—at least to the extent that intelligence involves autonomy or rationality. AI systems currently require computationally intensive training, with pre-defined (human-defined) rewards or objectives, based upon huge datasets. Nonetheless, some conceptual distinctions can be clarified.

Narrow AI refers to AI systems designed to perform a specific task or limited range of tasks, such as recognising images, translating languages, or playing games. For example, Agent57 is a deep reinforcement learning model, created by researchers at DeepMind, which can play all 57 Atari video games.[7] When built well, these systems can achieve high performance (sometimes exceeding human performance) in narrow domains. Agent57 excels in a subset of the domain of *game-playing*. However, this model's ability does not transfer to other domains, like image recognition, natural language processing, or common-sense reasoning. This fact is unsurprising: Agent57 was not designed to perform tasks in these domains.

Weak AI is sometimes taken as a relative synonym for narrow AI. However, weak AI may also refer to artificial intelligence designed to simulate human intelligence in specific tasks or domains—which need not be true of narrow AI. It is commonly referred to as "weak" because it does not possess consciousness or self-awareness, unlike strong AI, which refers to (hypothetical) AI systems with human-level cognitive capabilities *and* consciousness.

In contrast to narrow AI, artificial general intelligence (AGI) is an (hypothetical) AI system that can achieve tasks in general (perhaps arbitrary) cognitive domains. Human intelligence (and some examples of non-human biological intelligence, more widely construed) is a prototypical example of *general* intelligence. Biological intelligence excels at myriad intellectual activities; it is not constrained to one specific task. That said, a notion of human-level artificial intelligence is not particularly well-defined insofar as any reference to an anthropocentric baseline presupposes that human intelligence is a "gold standard" for intelligence. In addition, it may seem like human-level AI implies AGI; however, this is unclear insofar as a game-playing (narrow) AI system may perform at "superhuman" levels (albeit in narrow domains). Context matters for clarifying these terms.

Note further that these various definitions of artificial intelligence are inherently vague insofar as there are no strict criteria for demarcating between these concepts. Narrow AI contrasts with AGI in terms of their domains of application; weak AI contrasts with strong AI concerning the property of phenomenal

[7] Technical details are given in Badia et al. (2020).

consciousness. Some researchers understand "weak AI" and "narrow AI" as basically synonymous. However, an artificial general intelligence lacking phenomenal consciousness would still be weak, by definition.

Finally, artificial superintelligence refers to a hypothetical form of AI that surpasses human intelligence in virtually all aspects. It represents an AI system with cognitive abilities that greatly exceed those of the most intelligent humans across multiple domains. Thus, the standard definition of superintelligence hinges upon understanding what human intelligence—or, perhaps, intelligence more generally—consists of: imagine *that* (whatever it is), but *super*.

Artificial superintelligence would, by definition, possess superior problem-solving skills, learning abilities, creativity, and decision-making capacities as compared with humans (or any other species for that matter). Superintelligence is usually supposed to be AGI (although it needs to be clarified whether there could be an AGI that is not superintelligent). However, superintelligence does not need to be strong AI since it is possible to imagine an artificial superintelligence that is not phenomenally conscious.[8] The concept of artificial superintelligence has received undue theoretical interest in research on AI safety because of concerns about such a system's potential impact and whether we could control it, as its capabilities could surpass human comprehension and potentially have far-reaching consequences. Table 0.1 provides a coarse-grained summary of various concepts falling under the heading of *artificial intelligence*.[9]

Ultimately, these coarse-grained distinctions are superficial and vague. Still, these (very rough) categories will be adequate for our purpose in light of the following. First, a lack of clarity about forms of intelligence underscores the conceptual issues surrounding superintelligence; second, the remainder of this book is concerned solely with present-day and near-future AI systems. It is worth noting that all present-day AI systems are examples of narrow AI. Thus, the naïve taxonomy should adequately distinguish these concepts. Let us put these issues aside for now.

When we think about artificial intelligence in the context of science fiction, it is usually a form of artificial general intelligence or artificial superintelligence. Sometimes these agents are embodied—e.g., the replicants of *Blade Runner* (1982), Ava (*Ex Machina*, 2014), or Yang (*After Yang*, 2021)—and sometimes they are not—e.g., Alpha 60 (*Alphaville*, 1965), HAL 9000 (*2001:*

[8]Thus, a weak AGI could be thought of as an instantiation of a "philosophical zombie" or a "p-zombie" from the thought experiment popularised by Chalmers (1996), which is sometimes considered to be evidence against physicalism (the philosophical view that rejects dualism about minds and brains). See discussion in Kirk (2023).

[9]See Van Rooij et al. (2023) for an alternative and more fine-grained list.

Table 0.1: Coarse-grained conceptions of types of artificial intelligence

Natural intelligence	The form of intelligence exhibited by biological species; includes human intelligence and non-human animal intelligence; contrasts with artificial intelligence
Artificial intelligence	The form of intelligence exhibited by non-biological entities, sometimes called machine intelligence; contrasts with biological or natural intelligence
Narrow AI	A form of AI that can apply intelligence to a narrow, limited domain rather than across general, distinct domains; similar to weak AI; contrasts with AGI, strong AI, Superintelligence
Weak AI	Simulates human cognition but lacks consciousness; contrasts with strong AI
Artificial general intelligence	A form of AI that can apply intelligence to a range of domains rather than one specific, narrow domain; similar to human-level artificial intelligence; contrasts with weak or narrow artificial intelligence
Human-level artificial intelligence	Not a useful concept
Strong AI	Artificial humans; phenomenally conscious
Artificial superintelligence	A hypothesised form of AI that greatly exceeds the cognitive or intellectual capacities of any living biological intelligence

A Space Odyssey, 1968), Skynet (*The Terminator*, 1984), or Samantha (*Her*, 2013). In many cinematic cases, the existence of superintelligent AI systems bodes poorly for the humans in those films.

However, the cultural and social impact of fictional works in shaping perceptions of artificial intelligence poses a risk insofar as it may lead to unfounded fears and misconceptions, thus diverting public debate (particularly, when the debate concerns a fictional version of AI). For example, these misapprehensions may lead to an unjustified or inefficient distribution of resources (like funding or attention) toward researchers and labs focusing on AGI and existential risk and away from groups who examine the real-world harms of extant systems (like algorithmic bias or power dynamics). Cave et al. (2018) highlight that fictional conceptions of artificial intelligence provide more compelling narratives than present-day issues surrounding algorithmic decision-making. As a result, undue emphasis on a fictive possible-future scenario overshadows pressing moral, social, and philosophical issues that already exist.

This book is not about science fiction. Instead, it is about social, ethical, philosophical, and practical problems that exist today in the context of extant real-world AI systems—i.e., the standard, boring type of models that suggest, for example, that one might be interested in Denis Villeneuve's 2013 film, *Enemy*, based on having watched David Cronenberg's (1988) *Dead Ringers*. These so-called *narrow* AI systems—i.e., models that can perform limited tasks and are embedded or integrated within larger applications—give rise to significant social harms despite the relative specificity of their operation.[10]

Part of the impetus for the analysis of the value alignment problem presented in this book is that these systems, narrow though they may be, are increasingly integrated into society. Thus, they are increasingly implicated in our interactions as human beings and autonomous agents. As these systems become more powerful, complex, sophisticated, integrated, embedded, etc., this problem will be exacerbated. But, to be clear, it is already a problem.

The value alignment problem for artificial intelligence may be one of the most pressing problems in the area of AI ethics. However, this statement will undoubtedly be controversial—surely anyone working on a particular research topic in a specific field (or set of fields, in the case of interdisciplinary research) thinks that *this* research topic is the most important in their area. Perhaps unsurprisingly, then, I happen to think that the value alignment problem *is* the most pressing problem in this area. (Never mind that the main focus of my research in the philosophy and ethics of artificial intelligence and machine learning has been on value alignment.)

However, I also believe that at least some of those who agree with me about the importance of value alignment do so for different reasons. Specifically, researchers who spend their time thinking about the existential risk posed by a possible future superintelligence may take value alignment to be uniquely important insofar as it is often approached as a *method* for solving a distinct

[10] Although recommending new films based on, e.g., one's viewing history and the viewing history of others appears to be a relatively innocuous application of algorithms, closeted queers have recounted anecdotes on Internet fora about how they have been "outed" (or nearly so) because Netflix recommended queer content based on viewing history. Moreover, a 2009 lawsuit in the United States alleged that Netflix had violated user privacy by running a contest to improve its recommendation algorithm. The company released "anonymised" training data which, Narayanan and Shmatikov (2006) demonstrated, could be de-anonymised, allowing two individuals to be identified explicitly. This latter example is an issue of privacy, which does not concern the model per se; however, the motivation for the contest was to design a better recommendation algorithm. Netflix settled the lawsuit in 2010 and cancelled a subsequent "Netflix Prize" (Hunt, 2023). In practice, issues surrounding, e.g., privacy, human-computer interaction, and technology ethics more generally, cannot always be disentangled from the algorithmic environment in which they occur.

problem; namely, the problem of maintaining control over such a superintelligent AI system. The importance, in this case, is obvious: failing to achieve robust value alignment before the advent of superintelligence could be catastrophic to our species. (Those who have seen James Cameron's (1984) *The Terminator* know how this story plays out.)

Finding effective solutions to the value alignment problem would help to ensure the maintenance of control over artificial systems whose intelligence far exceeds our own. At the very least, ensuring the values of a superintelligent system are aligned with our own values would provide a safety net in the event that we fail to maintain control over those systems. Of course, some sceptics think that it is very unlikely that we will ever create a superintelligent AI system. However, the argument goes that regardless of whether the advent of superintelligence is exceedingly unlikely, the outcome would be catastrophic, and so the negative expectation (i.e., the probability of an outcome multiplied by the utility of that outcome) of this possibility is still significant and thus worthy of inquiry.

I am not interested in superintelligence. Hence, I do not think that the value alignment problem is one of the most pressing problems in AI research in light of the possibility of a superintelligent AI system whose values are misaligned with our own. Superintelligent AI is not a necessary condition for the value alignment problem's import. Instead, I am interested in the present-day AI systems that already generate significant harm (particularly to already-marginalised groups) because of misaligned "values". The value alignment problem is pressing because it is already a significant problem, and we are beginning to see its effects as these systems become increasingly integrated in society.

However, making this claim requires clarifying what, precisely, the value alignment problem is. The intuitive gloss is that the value alignment problem is the problem of ensuring that AI systems are appropriately aligned with human values. Typical approaches to solving this problem involve normative work—which asks *what* the correct values are to encode in AI systems so that they are aligned with our own values—and technical work—which asks *how* we encode those values in such a system. This specification of the value alignment problem is reasonably simple to understand. However, it is only superficially useful in application because, as should be apparent, it raises many more questions than answers.

Therefore, the first objective of this book is to provide a clear, conceptual basis for understanding the value alignment problem in the context of artificial intelligence which is grounded in the actual functioning of real-world systems.

What I suggest is that the value alignment problem arises in the dynamic context of multi-agent interactions. This definition shifts the focus from the normative or technical to the *structural* and social. Conceiving of the value alignment problem in this way further underscores the fact that ensuring value alignment for AI systems—or, more loftily, designing robustly *beneficial*, provably *safe*, or *ethical* artificial agents—requires more than just translating our best normative theories into a programming language.

The second objective of this reconceptualisation is to clarify the ways in which the value alignment problem is already instantiated by present-day AI systems; this concept covers many of the key targets of analysis in the field of AI ethics. For example, it is now well known that credit-scoring models predict income-related outcomes, which include disparities in employment and salary (Blattner and Nelson, 2021). Predictive-policing models predict where to send police resources based on past instances of *measured* crime which can lead to a feedback loop of increased surveillance and policing of certain minority groups (Lum and Isaac, 2016; O'Neil, 2016). Models for hiring decisions are affected by racial and gender bias (Ajunwa, 2019). Retail pricing models penalise poorer households (DellaVigna and Gentzkow, 2017). Healthcare models discriminate against people of colour (Joynt Maddox et al., 2019a,b; Obermeyer et al., 2019).

One reason for these issues is because the data upon which these models are trained often contain labelling errors that reflect structural inequalities (Mullainathan and Obermeyer, 2017). The standard analysis of algorithmic bias typically focuses on biased, unrepresentative, or noisy data that are used for training models in a machine learning context. However, this is only part of the story. Even if data are unbiased, unreflective of social bias, and fully representative (if such an antecedent is even possible), learned models can still cause social harms when they optimise for the wrong thing—what I take to be a paradigmatic case of value misalignment.

For example, in the field of healthcare, models for measuring hospital performance that optimise for *mortality* or *readmission rates* will "learn" to penalise those hospitals that serve poorer or non-white populations (Joynt Maddox et al., 2019a,b). In this instance, it is not the data *per se*[11] that are the problem. Instead, the system uses a *proxy* (mortality rates or readmission rates) to stand in for the true target of analysis (performance). The problem, which we shall see defines present-day approaches to artificial intelligence research, is that the objective which the model optimises is misaligned with the *true* object-

[11] A fancy way of saying in and of itself; in essence.

ive. This is a value alignment problem. The normative aspects of this problem become more pressing when such misaligned systems are deployed in society. Thus, it is the dynamics of interactions between human agents (individuals or collections thereof) and algorithmic systems which generates the problem. Rather than being primarily technical or normative, we will see throughout that value alignment is a *social* problem above all else.

Part I: Basic Concepts

To ensure that the analysis of the value alignment problem presented in this book is grounded in the actual functioning of real-world systems, Part I begins by providing a conceptual foundation necessary for understanding the problem in the first place. We begin by exploring a brief history of artificial intelligence (Chapter 1) and some of the formal and technical underpinnings of artificial intelligence today (Chapter 2). With this foundation laid, the value alignment problem is introduced (Chapter 3).

A Brief History of Artificial Intelligence. Chapter 1 provides a brief and incomplete history of artificial intelligence research. Awareness of the history of booms and busts in the field is useful for contextualising the present-day AI spring (or summer) in which we currently find ourselves—not least because this context may help to temper expectations about the abilities of artificial intelligence systems. Additionally, this history lays the foundation for the (technical) presentation of artificial intelligence today. In particular, it is worth underscoring the fact that many of the technical approaches to AI today were invented decades prior to these techniques being useful, practical, or commercialisable.

Artificial Intelligence Today. Chapter 2 provides some technical background on present-day approaches to artificial intelligence. This chapter defines some technical language in the field and describes research methods for achieving artificial intelligence. The key driver of present-day AI systems is machine learning and particularly deep learning approaches to AI. In effect, machine learning models are sophisticated optimisation engines. A key concept introduced in this chapter is that of the *objective function*, which defines the target of optimisation for a machine learning model.

I begin by providing some technical background on model architectures, the data used to train and evaluate these models, and three key approaches to machine learning—supervised, unsupervised, and reinforcement learning. I then discuss the formal concept of the objectives, goals, or "values", of a machine learning model. In particular, I discuss loss and cost (in the context of supervised and unsupervised learning models) and rewards (in the context of reinforcement learning). Finally, I describe some key algorithms—particularly, backpropagation and stochastic gradient descent (SGD)—that are used to train these models to optimise their objective functions on the basis of training data. The chapter concludes by highlighting the importance of so-called *scaling laws*. The scaling hypothesis—that model performance can be improved simply by making the model bigger—has come to represent one of the motivating forces behind present-day AI research and application.

The Value Alignment Problem. With the necessary conceptual groundwork laid, Chapter 3 introduces and defines the *value alignment problem*.

I begin by discussing the standard description of value alignment, highlighting how current research on the subject suffers from two key weaknesses. On the one hand, many discussions of value alignment are unsystematic and vague. The value alignment problem, as it is typically stated, is only superficially useful for understanding the key components of the problem. This lack of clarity makes it difficult for researchers who are interested in the conceptual foundations of value alignment to engage with this research in a way that is grounded in real-world systems.

In addition, there has been relatively little interface between machine learning and philosophy on the subject of value alignment. Much work on the subject from a machine learning perspective tends to be overly formal, ignoring the conceptual difficulties that arise when considering the formalisation of human values; in contrast, much work from philosophical perspectives has tended to be overly abstract, focusing, again, on vague concepts, while not engaging with the actual instantiation of artificial intelligence systems today. This lack of clarity exacerbates the difficulty of devising robust approaches to mitigate value misalignment.

The key insight of this chapter—and indeed, this book—is that the value alignment problem for artificial intelligence can be reconceptualised in terms of the principal-agent framework from economics. The (structural) definition of the value alignment problem that I propose emphasises the conditions that give rise to value misalignment in the first place, thus providing the possibility for practical intervention and mitigation. According to the structural definition, there are three key axes along which value misalignment may arise: misspecified objectives, informational asymmetries, and relative principals. Each of these axes is treated separately in Part II. In addition to allowing for concrete approaches to mitigating value misalignment, redefining the value alignment problem in terms of its structure, and the dynamics arising as a result of that structure, opens the door to philosophically-interesting insights. I demonstrate how everything that is conceptually appealing about current research on value alignment can be captured by my definition; at the same time, this definition offers analytic possibilities that are not available under the standard conceptualisation of the problem.

Part II: Axes of Value Alignment

The second part of this book explores the three different axes of the value alignment problem on the structural definition described in Chapter 3—namely, *misaligned objectives* (Chapter 4), *informational asymmetries* (Chapter 5), and *relative principals* (Chapter 6). These chapters, together, highlight the robustness of the structural definition of value alignment, insofar as several pressing problems falling under the purview of AI ethics can be cashed out as a type of value misalignment along one or more of these axes.

Objectives. Chapter 4 focuses on misspecified objectives (what we might think of as misaligned values) as a key component of value alignment. The structural definition of the value alignment problem for artificial intelligence captures intuitions arising from the standard definition, that misaligned objectives can lead to value misalignment. In addition, the structural definition underscores that value misalignment can occur at effectively every stage of the algorithmic development pipeline. This chapter explores the commonalities between each of these distinct aspects of the creation and deployment of machine learning models; namely, that we use proxies to stand in for our actual goals or objectives.

I then proceed to discuss how re-orienting focus on the proxies that give rise to instances of the value alignment problem on the objectives axis helps to clarify other pressing concerns that fall under the heading of the value alignment problem which are not readily captured by the standard definition. The paradigmatic case of misalignment along the objectives axis arises from issues of bias and fairness. I then explore how value misalignment along the objectives axis is not solely a technical problem, as is implied by the standard definition of the value alignment problem.

Information. Chapter 5 focuses on information asymmetries as a key component of value alignment. I describe how informational asymmetries alone can give rise to value misalignment on the structural definition of the problem. This may occur when the agent's actions are concealed from the principal or when certain details about the AI system are unavailable to the principal. This chapter explores two specific examples of informational asymmetries that can be classified as instances of the value alignment problem. First, the size and complexity of model architectures can create an informational asymmetry, leaving the principal uninformed about how the system generated an output. This highlights issues of transparency and opacity as typical instances of value misalignment along the objectives axis. Second, informational asymmetries emerge from large and uncurated datasets used to train a model. This type of informational asymmetry is becoming more prevalent due to the trend toward ever-larger models requiring extensive training data.

Principals. Chapter 6 focuses on the inherent *principal*-relativity raised by the structural definition of the value alignment problem. In this sense, an AI model may be sufficiently aligned (no informational asymmetry; no misspecified objective function) for one principal (set of principals) while still failing to be aligned for a distinct set of principals. This component of the value alignment problem makes explicit the contextual and pragmatic character of value alignment. Although some may view such a consequence of the reconceptualisation of the value alignment problem as primarily negative—insofar as it becomes more difficult, if not impossible, to align values across all relevant principals—this chapter flirts with optimism about this difficulty. In particular, mapping the boundaries of the value alignment problem more clearly makes it easier to understand *when* such problem instances will arise.

Part III: Approaches to Value Alignment

The third part of this book reviews some extant approaches to "solving" the value alignment problem by aligning the values of AI system with the values of humanity (on the standard definition). Although this is somewhat vexed, I categorise two distinct "approaches" to value alignment, based on two (fuzzily-demarcated) sub-fields. The first is (technical) AI safety, which seeks to find purely formal means for creating "provably safe" AI systems; the second is machine ethics, which seeks to mitigate value misalignment through the creation of artificial moral agents.

AI Safety. Chapter 7 discusses technical approaches to value alignment that fall under the heading of AI safety, beginning with adversarial examples. I survey several "concrete problems" in AI safety, as described by Amodei et al. (2016), highlighting how these problems can be cashed out in the language of value alignment, on the structural definition offered in Chapter 3. I then move on to survey several proposals for ensuring *provably* safe artificial intelligence, including reward modelling, cooperative inverse reinforcement learning (CIRL), and reinforcement learning from human (or computational) feedback (RLHF/RLCF). This chapter then provides an analysis of how (purely) technical approaches to value alignment will not suffice for addressing this problem. This argument is made more clear on the structural definition of value alignment, highlighting one of its conceptual benefits.

Machine Ethics. Chapter 8 discusses normative approaches to value alignment that fall under the heading of machine ethics; in particular, the notion of artificial moral agency (AMA) as a method for ensuring that the values of AI systems are aligned with human values. I begin by surveying distinctions between levels of moral agency as well as normative theories that have been proposed in moral philosophy. I then discuss extant proposals for imbuing artificial agents with morality, as well as critiques of this approach. In particular, I highlight the ways in which machine ethics purports to focus on the normative aspects of the value alignment problem, but in reality, this approach ends up being primarily technical. Again, the reconceptualisation of the value alignment problem offered in Chapter 3 makes salient some of the shortcomings of this approach.

Part IV: Mitigating Misalignment

The final part of this book addresses the potential for mitigating instances of the value alignment problem on the basis of the structural definition. Part IV explores some of the logical implications of the structural definition of value alignment provided in Chapter 3 by exploring some key philosophical questions arising from the analysis given.

Each chapter in this section aligns (to some extent) with the axes of the value alignment problem described in Part II.

Measuring Degrees of Alignment. Chapter 9 examines how we might measure degrees of alignment. The structural definition, along with the analysis of its three axes, provides some guidance on this question. In particular, some researchers have proposed *benchmarking* as a useful tool for measuring how "ethical" the decisions made by an AI system are. However, several researchers have highlighted numerous weaknesses of the dataset-as-benchmark paradigm in machine learning even in the simple case where what we care about is mere *accuracy*. Several distinct arguments are forwarded to demonstrate that attempting to measure how ethical an AI system is by using benchmarks is incoherent.

Nonetheless, the structural definition of the value alignment problem offers a way forward for measuring degrees of alignment with respect to a given axis of the problem. However, the results of this analysis are primarily negative: in some cases, ensuring alignment along one or another axis is impossible. Furthermore, the structural definition allows us to differentiate between alignment with respect to a particular axis, and alignment *simpliciter*.[12] This chapter asserts that alignment *simpliciter* doesn't exist for most practical AI models based on the structural definition. The chapter concludes that achieving alignment becomes more challenging with widespread AI deployment—a result which I call the *scaling hypothesis for value-aligned AI*.

Normativity and Language. Chapter 10 examines the possibility of value alignment for artificial intelligence by observing that humans are capable of aligning their values. Thus, the starting point for this inquiry is to examine the question: *How do we align our values?* One of the key reasons proposed is that humans are capable of communicating linguistically. This chapter describes linguistic communication as a system evolved in *Homo sapiens* for conveying conventionally meaningful signals to share information and compares these robust communication systems with non-human animal communication. Some distinctive features of human linguistic communication are described in terms of compositionality, hierarchy, and recursion. This chapter highlights the relevance of language to moral behaviour on the basis of empirical studies.

The key insight is that linguistic communication is necessary for addressing the value alignment problem in artificial intelligence—at least in complex action spaces. In effect, value alignment can be cashed out as a type of coordination problem in multi-agent interactions, and communication systems are useful for coordination and cooperation. This insight highlights that the informational asymmetries that give rise to instances of the value alignment problem on the structural definition make the possibility of linguistic communication crucial for the very possibility of value alignment. However, in the context of aligning values with an artificial agent, we cannot take linguistic abilities for granted. Hence, the claim that linguistic communication is necessary for robust value alignment specifies a demanding lower bound on the very possibility of *ensuring* that complex AI systems are value-aligned.

Values and Value-Ladenness. Chapter 11 examines the question of whose values are considered in the context of the value alignment problem. To this end, I rehearse arguments against the value-free ideal of science and examine how these arguments apply to AI research—particularly when considering the principals axis of the value alignment problem. The value-ladenness of artificial intelligence research underscores that the values of stakeholders—

[12] A fancy way of saying "simply". In a legal context, to apply the adjective *simpliciter* to a word (or phrase) means that that word (or phrase) is intended to be read absolutely, unconditionally, and without any "shades of meaning" or ambiguity given to it by surrounding words or phrases.

communities affected by the deployment of AI systems—ought to be at the forefront when designing these systems.

In an uncharacteristically optimistic turn, I gesture toward some approaches for mitigating instances of the value alignment problem, drawing primarily on scholarship in social science surrounding community-based and participatory research, design justice, and democratic, anti-fascist, and decolonial AI.

The book concludes with a general overview of the advantages and implications of reconceptualising the value alignment problem as a structural problem.

I

Basic Concepts

1 A Brief History of Artificial Intelligence

Once men turned their thinking over to machines in the hope that this would set them free. But that only permitted other men with machines to enslave them.

— Frank Herbert (1965)
Dune

To contextualise artificial intelligence today—the subject of Chapter 2—we begin with a brief, incomplete, and somewhat false history of artificial intelligence research.[1] Part of the purpose of including such a history—which could easily occupy an entire volume instead of a meagre chapter—is to underscore several points that will be important to keep in mind throughout the discussion of value alignment in the remainder of this book.

On the one hand, many state-of-the-art techniques in artificial intelligence research today are not new. Instead, they are based on theoretical and practical advances as old as the field itself. On the other hand, it is worthwhile to contextualise the present-day "AI spring" (or summer) within the history of booms and busts that the research field has experienced since its inception. This framing helps to situate the "promise" of AI as historically cyclical, which is related to the fact that, despite AI (the technology) being ostensibly new, the development—and moreover, the conception—of AI is not. These insights may curtail some of the hype (and metaphors and falsehoods) surrounding discussions and analyses of AI systems today. Hence, this brief chapter emphasises those aspects of the history of AI research that are particularly relevant when considering recent advances in the field.

[1]For a more detailed and nuanced account of the first waves of AI, see Nilsson (2010).

The cyclic "seasons" of AI research and hype can be characterised as follows:[2]

Spring. New ideas create optimism. Optimism leads to the promise of breakthroughs. The promise of breakthroughs leads to extensive government funding for academic research and venture capital funding for new startups.

Summer. The popular media hype the promise of imminent breakthroughs. Funding abounds. Public awareness grows.

Autumn. Overpromising and media hype lead to disappointment in modest, overstated, or non-existent breakthroughs.

Winter. Funding dries up. Media interest dissipates. Companies fold. Those privileged few continue theoretical research. Theoretical research leads to new ideas. (A new spring dawns.)

Perusal of popular reporting on AI should make apparent that we are in the throes of an AI summer. Optimists think that AGI is around the corner; pessimists suggest that we are on the cusp of a third winter.

This chapter begins by exploring some theoretical precursors to modern-day AI research. It is easy to *imagine* artificial intelligence—as evidenced by folklore and works of science fiction. However, whether the creation of AI is plausible, or even possible, depends upon whether intelligence can arise from inanimate matter. Hence, we can trace the theoretical precursors of artificial intelligence research to 17th-century materialism and philosophical theories about the relationship between body and mind. Moreover, connections between reasoning, rationality, and calculation were advanced through the philosophical study of mathematical logic and theories of computation in the late 19th and early 20th centuries.

There are many different, equally arbitrary ways of conceptually demarcating the various epochs (periods) in the history of artificial intelligence research. On the account offered here, the first wave of artificial intelligence research encompasses the excitement of the 1950s and 1960s surrounding the newly minted field. This wave also sees fundamental competition between *symbolic* versus *connectionist* (or *subsymbolic*) approaches to artificial intelligence. The first AI winter occurred in the 1970s, followed by the second wave of AI research—characterised by expert systems and so-called "good old-fashioned artificial intelligence" (GOFAI).

---

[2]This seasonal description is adapted from Crawford (2021).

Excitement, again, was curtailed by a second (brief) AI winter in the 1990s. However, researchers were sowing the seeds of the present-day AI spring during this time. This third wave of AI is characterised by the return of connectionism, deep learning approaches to artificial intelligence, and the advent of big data.

1.1 The Idea of AI

Imagining artificial intelligence—in the literal rather than present-day computational sense of the phrase—is ancient. Historical and cross-cultural examples abound. In Western philosophy, the ancient Greeks already imagined creating artificial humans, and the notion of creating artificial life or intelligence from inanimate matter is present in creation stories from Sumerian, Chinese, Jewish, Christian, and Muslim traditions.[3]

For example, Hephaestus, the god of fire, crafted the golden attendants described in Homer's *Iliad*. The Golem in Jewish folklore is animated through ritual incantations and sequences of Hebrew letters.[4] In Estonian mythology, the kratt would be given a soul (thus animated) if one went to a crossroads on a Thursday night during a full moon and made a deal with the devil.[5] However, there is a fundamental difference between *artificial intelligence* and mere *automata*. Each case just mentioned refers to the latter—creatures *animated* through magic, religious ceremony, or mechanics.[6] These are not examples of artificial *intelligence*, per se.

True artificial intelligence depends, to some extent, upon the study of knowledge (epistemology), the nature of rational thought, a theory of action, and the structure of reasoning. Moreover, the very possibility of artificial intelligence depends on the nature of metaphysics and mind. For example, suppose a fundamental distinction exists between physical and mental states (i.e., mind $\neq$ brain).[7] In that case, how we could create artificial intelligence from physi-

[3] See further discussion in Mayor (2018); Coeckelbergh (2020).

[4] A golem may be created by inscribing אמת (*emét*; truth) into its forehead and then destroyed by removing the aleph to make the inscription מת (*mét*; death).

[5] See Sarnet (2017).

[6] See the contributions in Cave et al. (2020) for further and more detailed examples.

[7] This position is called *dualism*, which contends that the mental is distinct from the physical, and neither is reducible to the other. This position contrasts with *idealism*, which holds that physical states are actually mental, and *materialism* or *physicalism*, which holds that mental states are actually physical. See the discussions in Robinson (2023); Guyer and Horstmann (2023), and Stoljar (2023), respectively.

cal parts (like steel, glass, silica sand, iron ore, gold, bauxite, etc.) is unclear.[8] In contrast, if physicalism is true, and mental states are ultimately physical (i.e., mind = brain),[9] then it may be possible to instantiate those *cognitive* systems that give rise to intelligence in a physical computational system. Indeed, a guiding faith of *connectionist* approaches to artificial intelligence (discussed below) turns on the metaphor that the brain is like a computer; hence, human intelligence is instantiated by a physical computational system, meaning we could replicate or emulate such an instantiation.[10]

Materialism, or physicalism, has precursors in the atomism espoused by the pre-Socratic philosophers Leucippus and Democritus.[11] This view was reinvigorated in the 17th century by Thomas Hobbes and Pierre Gassendi, among others. In the introduction to *Leviathan*, Hobbes (1668/1994) writes:

> For seeing life is but a motion of limbs, the beginning whereof is in some principal part within, why may we not say that all automata (engines that move themselves by springs and wheels as doth a watch) have an artificial life? For what is the heart, but a spring; and the nerves, but so many strings; and the joints, but so many wheels, giving motion to the whole body.

In this book, he characterises the commonwealth as an "artificial man". Hence, Hobbes has been called the "grandfather" and "patriarch" of artificial intelligence.[12] In the 17th century, Hobbes, Gottfried Wilhelm Leibniz, and René Descartes explored the relationship between mathematics and rational thought. Hobbes wrote that "reason is nothing but reckoning".[13] Thus, perhaps the logic of thought could be as systematic as algebra or geometry. In this case, reasoning is thought to be like numerical calculation. This view makes possible the idea that an artificial computer could *reason*, which is an important precursor to present-day AI.

---

[8] Although it becomes less obvious how to instantiate intelligence if the mind is non-physical, dualism makes the view that biological brains are computers more coherent since the computer is characterised as dualistic between hardware and software (Bell, 1999). In this case, we might think the mind programs the brain (Penfield, 1975). See the discussion in Brette (2022).

[9] See Footnote 7 above.

[10] For example, Minsky (1956, III-17) suggested that "human beings are instances of certain kinds of very complicated machines". Of course, the price of a metaphor is eternal vigilance. Brette (2022) highlights that the brain-computer metaphor is a source of confusion in neuroscience (as well as computer science).

[11] Atomism is the philosophical view that all the physical universe is composed of indivisible components, called atoms. Democritus wrote that "all is atoms and the void". Versions of atomism also arise in Classical Indian philosophy as well as Buddhist and Jaina systems of philosophy. See the discussion in Berryman (2023).

[12] See Haugeland (1985) and Dyson (1997), respectively.

[13] See further discussion in McCorduck (1979); Buchanan (2005); Russell and Norvig (2021).

Inspired by Ramon Llull's *Ars generalis ultima*, which explored using mechanical means for generating new knowledge by combining concepts, Leibniz sought to create an "alphabet of human thought".[14] He envisioned a universal language of reasoning, the *characteristica universalis*, which would reduce argumentation to a simple calculation. Leibniz thought that if this were successful, "there would be no more need of disputation between two philosophers than between two accountants. For it would suffice to take their pencils in hand, down to their slates and say to each other (with a friend as a witness, if they liked): Let us calculate" (Leibniz, 1677/1951).

These philosophical views are forebears to the *physical symbol system hypothesis*—later expressed by Newell and Simon (1976)—that would become a driving force behind AI research in the mid-20th century. Essentially, this hypothesis proposes that a physical symbol system (i.e., a *formal* system) has all the necessary and sufficient features for intelligent behaviour. This claim implies that human thought is a form of symbol manipulation (since a symbol system is necessary for intelligence) and that machines can be intelligent (since a symbol system is sufficient for intelligence).

During the late 19th and early 20th centuries, the study of mathematical logic was crucial in making artificial intelligence *plausible.* This foundation had been set by George Boole's (1854) *Laws of Thought* and Gottlob Frege's (1879) *Begriffsschrift.* Building on this system of logic, Alfred North Whitehead and Bertrand Russell presented a formal treatment of the foundations of mathematics in the *Principia Mathematica* (Whitehead and Russell, 1910, 1912, 1913). The *logicist* programme sought to discover a set of (finite) laws that govern the operation of the mind.[15] Inspired by Russell's success (at least at the time), David Hilbert challenged mathematicians of the early 20th century to answer a fundamental question: *Can all mathematical reasoning be formalised?*[16] This question was answered by Kurt Gödel's (1931) incompleteness theorems, Alonzo Church's (1932) λ-calculus, and Alan Turing's (1937b) *universal Turing machine*.

The incompleteness theorems state that any consistent and sufficiently strong formal system is incomplete, which means there are statements in the language

[14]Ramon Llull was a Catalan poet. *Ars generalis ultima* was published in 1308. See discussion in Priani (2021).

[15]Logicism is a philosophical and foundational approach to mathematics that seeks to reduce mathematical truths (traditionally, arithmetic truths) to logical truths. It asserts that mathematics can be entirely derived from the principles of formal logic. See Tennant (2023) for further discussion.

[16]See Hilbert (1900); Hilbert and Ackermann (1928). This question is referred to as the *Entscheidungsproblem.* See the discussion in Zach (2023).

that cannot be proved or disproved (from within that system). Furthermore, any consistent system cannot prove its own consistency. Effectively, it is impossible to write down an axiomatic system that, while being consistent, is also complete.[17] These theorems prove that there are, in fact, limits to what mathematical logic (or any formal system) can accomplish.[18]

More importantly for AI, this work also suggested that, within these limits, any form of mathematical reasoning could be mechanised. According to the Church-Turing Thesis, a machine that manipulates symbols as basic as 0 and 1 could simulate any possible mathematical deduction process.[19] The key insight was the Turing machine—a simple, theoretical construct that captures the essence of abstract symbol manipulation. This model would inspire a handful of scientists to discuss the possibility of thinking machines.[20]

The question of whether a machine could "think" is made more precise by Turing's proposed *Imitation Game* (now called the "Turing Test"):[21]

> The new form of the problem can be described in terms of a game which we call the 'imitation game.' It is played with three people, a man (*A*), a woman (*B*), and an interrogator (*C*) who may be of either sex. The interrogator stays in a room apart from the other two. The object of the game for the interrogator is to determine which of the other two is the man and which is the woman. He knows them by labels *X* and *Y*, and at the end of the game he says either '*X* is *A* and *Y* is *B*' or '*X* is *B* and *Y* is *A*.' The interrogator is allowed to put questions to *A* and *B* thus:

---

[17] Consistency in a logical system means that all provable arguments are valid; completeness is the converse of this: all valid arguments are provable. More generally, a formal system is consistent if there is no statement of the system such that it and its negation are both derivable (provable) within the system. It is complete if, for every statement in the system's language, the statement or its negation can be derived within the system.

[18] Some philosophers have taken Gödel's incompleteness theorems to logically imply that the human mind is more than a Turing machine insofar as *understanding* cannot be reduced to mere calculation (Nagel and Newman, 1958; Lucas, 1961; Penrose, 1989, 1994). However, it is relatively well-accepted that anti-mechanist arguments from Gödelian incompleteness typically fail because of the conditional form of Gödel's theorem (Putnam, 1960; Boolos, 1968; Shapiro, 1998). See the discussion in Raatikainen (2022).

[19] See Church (1936); Kleene (1936); Turing (1937a,b). Note that this is a *thesis*, not a theorem. It has not been (and cannot be) formally proved, but it is generally believed to be true. See the discussion in Copeland (2020).

[20] Of course, it is difficult (impossible) to translate all real-world problems into symbolic form, which implies a limit on the abilities that follow from the Church-Turing Thesis. From a computational perspective, even if this were possible in theory, that would not imply that such a problem is computationally *tractable*.

[21] I quote Turing (1950) at length here because the sexed presuppositions of the Imitation Game are often forgotten or ignored. Some scholars have recently argued that treating the imitation of intelligence as similar to the imitation of sex has led discussions of machine intelligence astray; see, e.g., Kind (2022).

> *C*: Will *X* please tell me the length of his or her hair?
>
> Now suppose *X* is actually *A*, then *A* must answer. It is *A*'s object in the game to try and cause *C* to make the wrong identification. His answer might therefore be
>
> 'My hair is shingled, and the longest strands are about nine inches long.'
>
> In order that tones of voice may not help the interrogator the answers should be written, or better still, typewritten. The ideal arrangement is to have a teleprinter communicating between the two rooms. Alternatively the question and answers can be repeated by an intermediary. The object of the game for the third player (*B*) is to help the interrogator. The best strategy for her is probably to give truthful answers. She can add such things as 'I am the woman, don't listen to him!' to her answers, but it will avail nothing as the man can make similar remarks.
>
> We now ask the question, 'What will happen when a machine takes the part of *A* in this game?' Will the interrogator decide wrongly as often when the game is played like this as he does when the game is played between a man and a woman? These questions replace our original, 'Can machines think?' (Turing, 1950, 433–434)

Throughout this paper, Turing addresses several potential objections to the possibility of thinking machines and the adequacy of the Imitation Game.[22] In addition, he describes what we would now call machine learning, genetic algorithms, and reinforcement learning. Hence, despite the recent success and popularisation of machine learning, many present-day approaches are built on conceptual foundations as old as (or older than) the field itself.

1.2 The Invention of AI

The phrase "artificial intelligence" was not coined until 1955, when it was used in a funding proposal for a summer workshop organised by John McCarthy, in collaboration with Marvin Minsky, Nathaniel Rochester, and Claude Shannon. The purpose of introducing this terminology was twofold. On the one hand, McCarthy wanted to distance his approach from the burgeoning field of *cybernetics*, which studies how systems regulate themselves through feedback.[23] On the other hand, "artificial intelligence" provided a lucrative marketing term—i.e., a way of generating funding and hype—by tapping into a longstanding

[22] These objections include whether an individual with extrasensory perception (ESP), like telepathy, could cheat in the Imitation Game. In light of this objection, which is treated quite seriously, Turing (1950) suggests that the game should occur in a "telepathy-proof room". A summary of the objections and Turing's responses is given by Oppy and Dowe (2021).

[23] See Rosenblueth et al. (1943); McCulloch and Pitts (1943); Wiener (1948/1961).

artefact of imagination and culture. Hence, "AI" was coined as a buzzword. In their proposal, they wrote:

> We propose that a 2-month, 10-man study of artificial intelligence be carried out during the summer of 1956 at Dartmouth College in Hanover, New Hampshire. The study is to proceed on the basis of the conjecture that every aspect of learning or any other feature of intelligence can in principle be so precisely described that a machine can be made to simulate it. An attempt will be made to find how to make machines use language, form abstractions and concepts, solve kinds of problems now reserved for humans, and improve themselves. We think that a significant advance can be made in one or more of these problems if a carefully selected group of scientists work on it together for a summer. (McCarthy et al., 1955/2006, 12)

The workshop did not lead to any major breakthroughs.[24] But, on a sociological note, what the workshop *did* accomplish was introducing these individuals to one another. The workshop participants—McCarthy, Minsky, Rochester, Shannon, Arthur Samuel, Herbert A. Simon, Allen Newell, Ray Solomonoff, Oliver Selfridge, and Trenchard More—their colleagues, and their students at the Massachusetts Institute of Technology, Carnegie Mellon University (then called the Carnegie Institute of Technology), and IBM—in addition to military research centres—would dominate the field and effectively decide its direction for the next several decades.

Although the term "artificial intelligence" was not coined until 1955, significant technical and theoretical groundwork had already been laid for the new field. The first work now recognised as artificial intelligence research was presented by Warren McCulloch and Walter Pitts more than a decade earlier, in 1943. They proposed a mathematical model of a neuron which drew upon contemporary knowledge of the basic physiology and functioning of biological neurons, propositional logic, and Turing's theory of computation.

McCulloch and Pitts (1943) argued that because (biological) neural activity is "all-or-nothing", neural events and their relations can be modelled using propositional logic. In their model, an artificial neuron is characterised as being `on` or `off` (1 or 0, True or False), with a switch occurring in response to stimulation by a sufficient number of neighbouring neurons. The model takes binary inputs, $x_i \in \{0, 1\}$, and aggregates (sums) them. If the aggregated value exceeds the threshold specified by the discontinuous sigmoid function, the output is 1; otherwise, the output is 0. In mathematical notation,

[24] Russell (2019) highlights that each problem listed in their proposal is an open problem in the field today.

$$f(\mathbf{x}) = \begin{cases} 1 & \text{if } \sum_{i=1}^{n} x_i \geq t \\ 0 & \text{otherwise} \end{cases}, \tag{1.1}$$

for some specified threshold, t. See Figure 1.1.

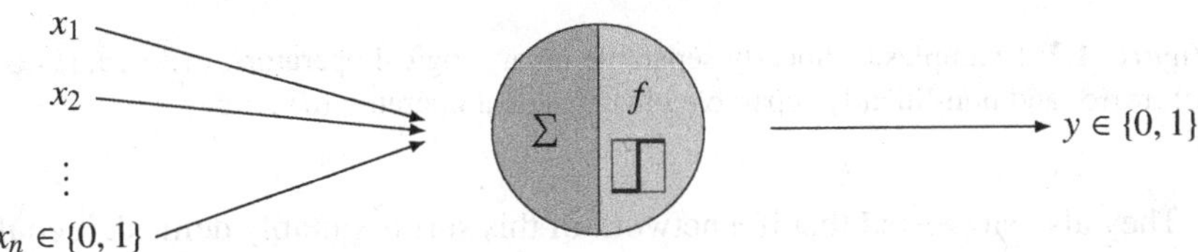

Figure 1.1: McCulloch-Pitts (MP) neuron model with n binary inputs, $x_1, \ldots, x_n \in \{0, 1\}$, and one binary output, $y = f(\mathbf{x}) \in \{0, 1\}$. The MP-neuron receives information as the sum of the inputs; this sum passes through a discontinuous threshold sigmoid function, f, to obtain the output, y.

The range of this model (the set of possible outputs) is identical to the domain (the set of allowable inputs). As such, individual MP-neurons could be connected in a network, so the output of one MP-neuron (or set of MP-neurons) could serve as the input of another. McCulloch and Pitts showed that *some* network of connected neurons can compute any computable function.[25] A *computable function* is a function whose value can be obtained by some *effective procedure*—i.e., an algorithm—where the solution is provided within a finite number of steps.[26] Furthermore, the logical connectives, `and` (∧), `or` (∨), `not` (¬), can be modelled by individual neurons, and more complex logical functions, like `xor` (⊕), could be modelled by simple network structures of these neurons; see Figure 1.2.

[25]Note that an existence proof does not specify *which* network of connected neurons can do so, just that one exists.

[26]The following gives a standard example of a function that is not computable. Let $H(p, x)$ be a function that takes as input the description of an arbitrary program, p, and an arbitrary input for that program, x; $H(p, x)$ outputs 1 if the program, p, halts on input x, and 0 otherwise. Hence,

$$H(p, x) = \begin{cases} 1, & \text{if program } p \text{ halts on input } x, \\ 0, & \text{otherwise.} \end{cases} \tag{1.2}$$

This function is called the *Halting problem* since there is no general algorithm that will determine whether an arbitrary program will halt on arbitrary input in finite time—i.e., as long as the program has not stopped with output 1, it cannot be differentiated whether the program will run forever, or halt on some future iteration with output 0.

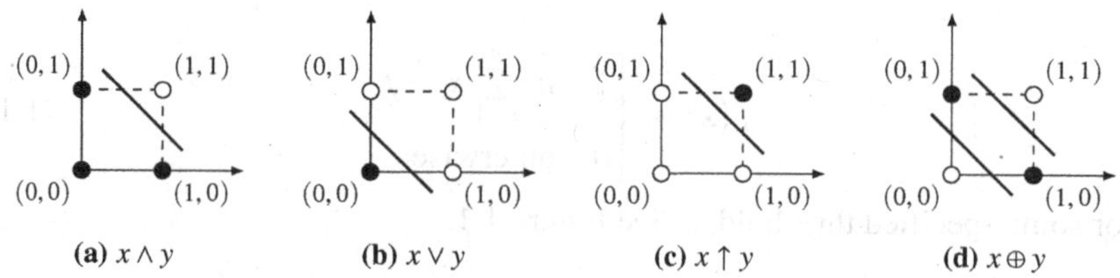

Figure 1.2: Examples of linearly separable binary logical operators, (*a*) `and`, (*b*) `or`, (*c*) `nand`, and non-linearly separable binary logical operator, (*d*) `xor`.

They also suggested that if a network of this sort is suitably defined, it could *learn*, where "learning" means altering the network structure so that "a stimulus which would previously have been inadequate [for activation] is now adequate" (McCulloch and Pitts, 1943, 117).[27]

1.3 First-Wave AI: False Promises

The first two decades following the Dartmouth summer workshop were primarily dominated by its participants and their colleagues. During this first wave, spanning roughly 1952 to 1969, two competing paradigms emerged.

On the one hand, *symbolic* approaches (sometimes called classic AI, rule-based AI, or good old-fashioned AI) are based on logic, deduction, knowledge representation, or search. This approach uses high-level, human-readable symbols to represent knowledge, and it relies on explicit rules and logical operations to manipulate these symbols. Hence, these systems are typically deterministic, meaning that given a specific input, the output will always be the same (if the rules are followed correctly).

One of the first artificial intelligence programs was a symbolic "reasoning program", created by Newell, Simon, and J. C. Shaw, called *Logic Theorist.* Logic Theorist was able to prove most of the theorems (38 of 52) in Chapter

[27] The first artificial neural network, called *Stochastic Neural Analog Reinforcement Calculator* (SNARC), was built by Minsky and Dean Edmonds in 1951—utilised a randomly connected network of *Hebb synapses*, facilitating pathways when "rewarded". Hebb (1949) proposed the following neurophysiological postulate: "when an axon of cell *A* is near enough to excite *B* and repeatedly or persistently takes part in firing it, some growth process or metabolic change takes place in one or both cells such that *A*'s efficiency, as one of the cells firing *B*, is increased" (62). In other words, *cells that fire together wire together.* This slogan is codified by a rule for updating the connection strengths between neurons, which is based on the idea that learning in biological brains occurs through progressive strengthening of the patterns of connections within networks of (biological) neurons. (Today, this *Hebbian learning* rule remains influential in AI research.) SNARC itself was built using 3,000 vacuum tubes and a surplus automatic pilot mechanism from a B24 bomber to simulate a network of 40 neurons (Minsky, 1952).

2 of Whitehead and Russell's *Principia Mathematica*.[28] The first version of Logic Theorist, which provided a proof of concept, was hand-simulated using 3×5 index cards. To implement the program on a computer, it was necessary to develop a programming language that could perform actions on appropriate data structures—in this case, *list processing*. Newell, Simon, and Shaw created the Information Processing Language (IPL) for this purpose. McCarthy began developing the *Lisp* (list processing) programming language in 1958. One of the key advances of IPL and Lisp (over the earlier FORTRAN language) is that they are *recursive*, meaning that a function in the programming language can call upon itself.[29]

Logic Theorist also introduced several concepts that would be fundamental to symbolic AI, including characterising reasoning in terms of *search* over a decision tree, where an initial hypothesis was the root, and branches were traversed via logical rules. However, because the number of nodes in a decision tree increase exponentially as the depth of the tree increases, it is often impossible to search every branch of the tree for a solution.

For example, it is estimated that a tree representing a typical game of checkers, played on an 8×8 board, has a branching factor of 6.14—meaning each node, on average, has 6.14 child nodes. Moreover, a game lasts on average 50.4 plies, where a ply is a single move by a single player. So, the *game-tree complexity* of checkers is estimated to be at least $6.14^{50.4} = 10^{40}$, which represents a lower bound on the number of unique plays for the game—i.e., the number of unique paths for the game tree.[30]

Hence, *heuristics* (*ad hoc* rules)[31] for ignoring certain branches of the tree that are unlikely to lead to a solution are necessary for computational tractability in cases of *combinatorial explosion*.[32] For example, a checkers-playing program, written by Arthur Samuel, utilised *rote learning*—i.e., it saved a description of each board position encountered with its backed-up value—to help

[28] One of the proofs output by the Logic Theorist was shorter (and more "elegant") than Russell's own proof. Nonetheless, the *Journal of Symbolic Logic* rejected a paper co-authored by Newell, Simon, and Logic Theorist (Crevier, 1993).

[29] See Hofstadter (1979/1999) for a love letter to recursion.

[30] See analysis in Schaeffer (2007). Game-tree complexity is one of the reasons chess was often used as a benchmark for "intelligence" in artificial systems. It is hypothesised that there are more possible combinations of moves in chess (10^{120}) than there are estimated atoms in the universe (10^{80}). Hence, it is impossible to "brute search" the best solution for any given move (at least until the endgame).

[31] A fancy way of saying for a particular purpose; hence, an ad hoc solution is not generalisable.

[32] A situation where a problem grows exponentially in complexity due to how the problem is affected by combinations of the variables (input, constraints, etc.).

with depth of search in case that board position occurred again. In addition, a *discounting* process decreased the value of a position by a small amount for each ply.[33] Samuel (1959) coined the term "machine learning" to describe his checkers-playing program.

In contrast to the symbolic approach, which relies on explicit programming of logical rules, the *connectionist* (or sub-symbolic) approach to AI emphasises learning from examples. Artificial neural networks, inspired by the neural structure of the brain, model information using distributed representations. Hence, these systems are often non-deterministic, meaning the output can vary with the same input, reflecting probabilities and uncertainties.

The perceptron, developed by Frank Rosenblatt (1958) and funded in part by the US Office of Naval Research, is an early artificial neural network for pattern recognition. This model extends the MP-neuron model insofar as the latter only accepts Boolean inputs ({0, 1}) and outputs a Boolean value. In contrast, the perceptron model can process any real-valued input, $x_i \in \mathbb{R}$. In addition, the inputs are not weighted in the MP-neuron model, whereas they are in the perceptron model; see Figure 1.3.

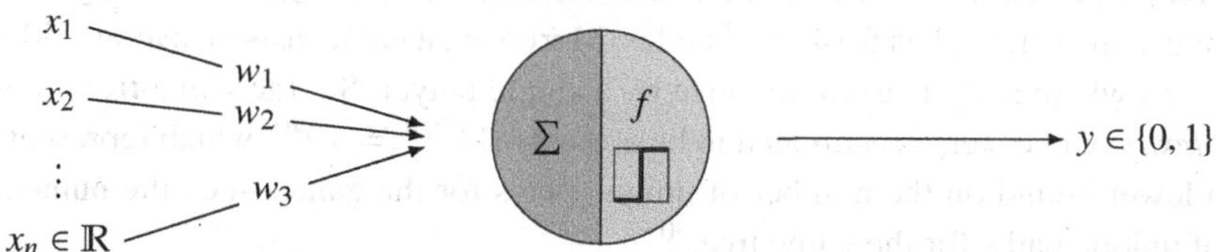

Figure 1.3: Model of a single perceptron, also called a Linear Threshold Unit (LTU), with n real-valued inputs, $x_1, \ldots, x_n \in \mathbb{R}$, and one binary output, $y = f(\mathbf{x}) \in \{\mathbf{0}, \mathbf{1}\}$. The perceptron receives information as a weighted sum of the inputs; this sum passes through a threshold sigmoid function, f, to obtain the output, y. Compare this with the MP-neuron (Figure 1.1).

This simple model marks the birth of connectionism and the foundation of neural networks and deep learning—today's dominant approach to AI research.

In these early days, it was common to theorise that no machine could ever do ϕ, where ϕ denotes something thought to require genuine (human or biological) intelligence—e.g., no machine could ever *play chess*. In response, researchers would create toy environments, called *microworlds*, which are well-defined

[33]This discounting process is a precursor of temporal-difference (TD) learning (Sutton, 1988; Tesauro, 1995), which is a model-free approach to reinforcement learning that combines dynamic programming and Monte Carlo methods. See the discussion in Sutton and Barto (2018).

and limited domains in which the system can act.Although not necessarily of practical import, these microworlds at least provided a proof of concept that a machine could do ϕ, in principle. For example, in 1968, Terry Winograd developed SHRDLU, an early instance of natural language understanding. Although this program appeared to understand natural language inputs, it was a sophisticated instantiation of a rule-based system. Part of the reason it worked well is because of the *microworld* environment in which it operated, thus limiting the number of handwritten instructions required to have the system function. Rapid advances on toy problems led to exaggerated promises and unrealistic expectations.

Sometimes, this hype was generated by the researchers themselves. For example, in the first popular book on electronic computers, Edmund Berkeley (1949) wrote, "[r]ecently there has been a good deal of news about strange giant machines that can handle information with vast speed and skill. They calculate and they reason. ... These machines are similar to what a brain would be if it were made of hardware and wire instead of flesh and nerves" (1). He suggests that "[a] machine can handle information; it can calculate, conclude, and choose; it can perform reasonable operations with information. A machine, therefore, can think" (5). In 1957, Simon declared that "there are now in the world machines that think, that learn, and that create" (Simon and Newell, 1958, 8). Describing Logic Theorist, Simon suggested that they had "invented a computer program capable of thinking non-numerically, and thereby solved the venerable mind-body problem" (Crevier, 1993).[34]

Moreover, the predictions of near-future capabilities of AI systems were often laden with hype and false promise. For example, in 1958, Simon and Newell wrote that "within ten years a digital computer will be the world's chess champion" and that "within ten years, a digital computer will discover and prove an important new mathematical theorem" (7–8). McCarthy founded the Stanford Artificial Intelligence Project in 1963 with "the goal of building a fully intelligent machine within a decade" (Moravec, 1988, 20). Simon (1960) wrote that "machines will be capable, within twenty years, of doing any work a man can do" (96). Minsky (1967, 2) suggested that "within a generation ... the problem of creating 'artificial intelligence' will substantially be solved"; in 1970, Minsky was quoted in an interview for *Life* magazine as saying that in

[34]Comparing this hubris with the hype of the present day: in February 2022, Ilya Sutskever, the (then) chief scientist at OpenAI, tweeted "it may be that today's large neural networks are slightly conscious" (Sutskever, 2022). For a detailed analysis of present-day AI hype, see Bender and Hanna (2025).

"three to eight years, we will have a machine with the general intelligence of an average human being" (Darrach, 1970, 58D).[35]

None of these predictions came to fruition. Unsurprisingly, however, these hyperbolic claims were picked up, proliferated, and further exaggerated by the news media reporting on research. For example, in 1958, the *New Yorker* called the perceptron a "remarkable machine ... capable of what amounts to thought", which constitutes the "first serious rival to the human brain" (Mason et al., 1958, 44).[36] In the same year, the *New York Times* reported on a press conference announcing the project, suggesting that the Navy had "revealed the embryo of an electronic computer that it expects will be able to walk, talk, see, write, reproduce itself and be conscious of its existence" (New York Times, 1958). *Life* magazine described Shakey, the first "general-purpose mobile robot" that could "reason" about its actions as the "first electronic person" (Darrach, 1970, 58D).[37]

At the same time, however, there was scepticism about the limits of a machine's capabilities. In an attempt to demonstrate that the appearance of intelligence in AI systems was an illusion, Joseph Weizenbaum created the *ELIZA* program—an early example of natural language processing and one of the first "chatterbots" (later shortened to "chatbots").The `DOCTOR` script of ELIZA simulated a Rogerian-style psychotherapist, which utilised pattern-matching and substitution to "reflect" on questions and repeat them back to the interlocutor, thus simulating understanding and conversation.[38] The `DOCTOR` script essentially did this by singling out keywords and transforming the input into an output. For example, if an input text included the keyword "the same" or

[35] Compare: recent surveys of AI researchers suggest that many experts believe that there is a 50% chance that the field will achieve artificial general intelligence (AGI) within the next 30 years. It is worth noting that, since the advent of computers in the 1940s, predictions that machine intelligence will overtake human intelligence have been about 20 years in the future, and this estimation has receded at about one year per year.

[36] Compare: in a non-peer reviewed paper posted on arXiv (a pre-print repository), a team at Microsoft claimed that the OpenAI's language model, GPT-4, "can solve novel and difficult tasks that span mathematics, coding, vision, medicine, law, psychology" and hence displays "sparks of artificial general intelligence" (Bubeck et al., 2023, 1, 92).

[37] Compare: in 2022, Blake Lemoine, a researcher at Google, became convinced that Google's language model (LaMDA) was sentient; Lemoine's colleague at Google, Blaise Agüera y Arcas, reinforced these claims, suggesting that LaMDA "does in a very real sense understand a wide range of concepts" (Agüera y Arcas, 2021). Unsurprisingly, these claims were widely reported on in the media. See reporting in Tiku (2022a,b).

[38] This approach to psychoanalysis is also called "person-centred" or "client-centred" therapy. The method, which Carl Rogers pioneered in the early 1940s, assumes that people are inherently motivated toward achieving positive psychological functioning, and the therapist's role is to provide a space for uncensored exploration; see Rogers (1946).

"alike", this would trigger an output question: "In what way?" (Norvig, 1992). Nonetheless, Weizenbaum was horrified to see how many people attributed human-like feelings to the simple program.[39] More generally, Dreyfus (1965, 1972) argued that the mind is unlike a computer. His critique was based on four key assumptions accepted by researchers at the time, which upheld the symbol-system view that human intelligence depends, fundamentally, upon the manipulation of symbols.

1. The biological assumption that the brain processes information in discrete operations (i.e., the on/off switches fundamental to computational operations).
2. The psychological assumption that biological minds are fundamentally computers operating on bits of information under a set of formal rules.
3. The epistemological assumption that all knowledge can be formalised.
4. The ontological assumption that the world consists of independent facts (which can be aptly represented by independent symbols).

For these reasons, he likened artificial intelligence research to alchemy and ridiculed the optimism of the field.

Despite hype-laden claims about the abilities of AI, many of the approaches in the early days of AI were unsystematic and did not account for combinatorial complexity. (The study of computational complexity only became a formal discipline in the 1960s.) The Lighthill Report, compiled in 1973 for the British Science Research Council to evaluate academic research on AI, highlighted that state-of-the-art techniques only worked well within the scope of small problem domains; they could not scale up well to solve more realistic problems. Hence, early—and remarkable—successes could not be extended to more generalised environments or more difficult problem instances, owing to combinatorial explosion.

To overcome combinatorial explosion, it is necessary to use algorithms capable of exploiting *structure* in the target domain and to take advantage of prior knowledge via heuristic search, planning, and (flexible) abstract representations. These abilities were not developed in early AI systems. At the same time, these early systems were not very good at handling *uncertainty*. They often relied heavily on brittle (and ungrounded) symbolic representations. In addition,

[39] This phenomenon, now called the Eliza effect (Hofstadter, 1995), was recapitulated in 2022 and 2023 with the public response to OpenAI's ChatGPT and similar large language models, a topic we will return to in future chapters. For example, some researchers have claimed that present-day LLMs are capable of displaying empathy (Lee et al., 2024).

physical hardware constraints like memory capacity, processing speed, etc., limited the functioning of these systems.

The Lighthill Report was highly critical of the basic research in foundational areas such as robotics and language processing. While it supported research into the simulation of neurophysiological and psychological processes, the report stated, "In no part of the field have the discoveries made so far produced the major impact that was then promised" (Lighthill, 1973, 9). This pessimism was a partial basis for the decision by the British government to end support for AI research in most British universities.[40]

Hence, (over-)hype and (inevitable) disappointment led to the first AI winter, which was characterised by a (relative) downturn in enthusiasm and funding for AI projects, leading to (relative) stagnation in progress.[41]

1.4 Second-Wave AI: Empty Threats

The initial emphasis in artificial intelligence research was that of a *general* problem-solver, which sought to express human reasoning in code; however, this approach could not deal well with combinatorial explosion. Although machine learning methods employing artificial neural networks received some focus in the first wave of artificial intelligence, the main focus in the field in the 1970s and 1980s was on logical, knowledge-based approaches to AI rather than learning algorithms. This *expert systems* approach sought to utilise expert knowledge in (narrow) domains like diagnostic medicine or game-playing.[42]

Expert systems consist of an *inference engine* and a *knowledge base*. The knowledge base, constructed as a set of sentences representing domain-specific facts—e.g., chemistry, medicine, etc.—along with relevant generalised knowledge, serves as the foundation for the system. The inference engine, composed of functions in a programming language, interprets and evaluates the elements of the knowledge base to provide solutions to queries. Essentially, these functions manage and update the current state of knowledge about a specific case, shaping the inference process and facilitating user interaction.

---

[40] See discussion in (Russell and Norvig, 2021, 22).

[41] Of course, this is not to suggest that all research in the field ceased for this period; instead, researchers sometimes shifted their focus, moving away from certain approaches or technologies that were popular during the preceding "boom" and exploring alternative avenues or more theoretical results.

[42] Although this approach to AI was popular in the 1980s, the earliest examples of expert systems were created in the 1960s. For example, the DENDRAL program was an expert system that automated decision-making processes and problem-solving for organic chemistry (Buchanan and Feigenbaum, 1978; Lindsay et al., 1993).

For each domain, the knowledge base needs to be hand-crafted by acquiring domain-specific knowledge via experts in the field and then translating that expert knowledge into a machine-readable format—a process referred to as *knowledge engineering*—in addition to encoding heuristics through complex if-then rules.

For example, the MYCIN program, developed in the 1970s at Stanford University, was designed to aid in the diagnosis of (likely) causes of an infection in a patient, as well as to recommend the best intervention for that particular patient.[43] This program demonstrated the power of rule-based systems for representing knowledge and inference: MYCIN performed as well as human experts in a double-anonymised study. Nonetheless, it is worth noting that the program was never routinely used in hospitals.[44]

The commercialisation of artificial intelligence based on expert systems began in the early 1980s, which was part of the impetus for a second wave of AI hype. However, rather than being predicated on the promise of thinking machines, this second wave was driven by perceived threat.[45] Importantly, the field of AI was forged in the context of the cold war—the year after the AI conference at Dartmouth College, the USSR launched *Sputnik*, the world's first orbital satellite. This prompted the United States Department of Defense to form the [Defense] Advanced Research Projects Agency (DARPA), which was (and continues to be) a key benefactor of AI research.[46]

In 1982, the Ministry of International Trade and Industry in Japan created a joint government-industry initiative called "Fifth Generation Computer Systems" (FGCS), the goal of which was to utilise knowledge bases and large data sets to perform inferences and communicate with humans via natural language (Nilsson, 2010, 349). Data, information, and knowledge were seen as potentially more significant than material resources in light of the increasing ubiquity of computers and software.

Feigenbaum and McCorduck (1983) argued that Japan was setting itself up to be a leader in the computing industry, surpassing the United States; hence,

[43] See Shortliffe (1976); Davis et al. (1977).

[44] See the discussion in Buchanan and Duda (1983).

[45] See the historical framing described by Garvey (2018) for more detail.

[46] The funding provided by [D]ARPA in the first decade of AI research was virtually unprecedented; see the discussion in Edwards (1996, Ch. 8). The excitement for potential military application continues to this day. In September 2018, DARPA announced the "AI Next" campaign: a multi-year investment of more than US$2 billion on artificial intelligence research and development; they claim that roughly 70% of DARPA's current programs benefit from AI and machine learning technology.

"Americans should mount a large-scale concentrated project of our own; that not only is it in the national interest to do so, *but it is essential to the national defense*" (216). Garvey (2018) notes that the FGCS project did not pose any threat, insofar as it emphasised basic research rather than commercial products; however, this was irrelevant for justifying new rounds of funding from defence, government, and industry. Although the systems that the FGCS project developed did not find any notable application, its announcement alone (in conjunction with Western anti-Japanese bias) prompted the initiation of similar projects in the United States and Europe, leading to significant funding for further development in computer science based on the threat, rather than promise, of AI.

In 1982, the non-profit *Microelectronics and Computer Technology Corporation* was formed in the United States, with an annual budget of US$50-100 million. Similarly, in the United Kingdom, a committee report recommended a five-year programme focusing on information technologies through a government-backed "collaborative effort between industry, the academic sector, and other research organisations" to compete with Japan and the United States in the world information technologies market; the recommended budget for this programme was £350 million.[47] In Europe, the European Economic Community launched the *European Strategic Program of Research in Information Technology* (ESPIRIT) to "foster transnational cooperative research among industries, research organisations, and academic institutions", with a budget of 1.5 billion ECUs.[48]

Although the perceived threat that launched the second AI wave was primarily political, researchers also began to hypothesise about the potential threat of AI systems themselves. For example, the fact that Samuel's checkers-playing program could beat him at checkers called into question the idea that machine intelligence would be bounded by human intelligence. Hence, it is unsurprising that individuals would start writing about the potential consequences of the existence of artificial intelligence in the future. Public awareness of the supposed threat of artificial intelligence was probably not helped by the release of Stanley Kubrick's (1968) *2001: A Space Odyssey*. HAL 9000, the AI system that serves as a key antagonist in the "Mission to Jupiter" segment of the film, would become a symbol of the dangers of superintelligent AI (at least until James Cameron's (1984) *The Terminator* was released).

[47] See Oakley and Owen (1990).

[48] The ECU is the *European Currency Unit*, which was introduced in Europe in 1979 and replaced by the Euro in 1999. See Steels and Lepape (1993, 4).

Hence, expectations about the abilities—and now threat—of artificial intelligence were highly inflated and these expectations were further exaggerated by popular media.[49] Although expert systems can be useful in particular (narrow) cases, they are also highly brittle—i.e., they fail when presented with unusual data or altered in (seemingly) minor ways. Part of this failure arises because these systems lack "common sense" or generalised knowledge about the structure of the external world.[50] At the 1984 annual meeting of AAAI, Roger Schank and Marvin Minsky warned that undue hype would lead to a second AI winter, reducing investment and funding. This prediction came to fruition three years later. Once again, great hype led to great disappointment as the limitations of these systems became salient and the threats that prompted funding for these projects failed to manifest.

By this time, the history of artificial intelligence research was characterised as "consisting always of very limited success in particular areas, followed immediately by failure to reach the broader goals at which these initial successes seem at first to hint" (Schwartz, 1987). For this reason, during the second AI winter, the term "artificial intelligence" began to be seen as a pseudoscience. Nonetheless, foundational research continued under the heading of topics like "artificial neural networks", "machine translation", "machine learning", "natural language processing", etc.

On 11 May 1997, in the midst of the second AI winter, *Deep Blue* beat Garry Kasparov—the world chess champion at the time—in a six-game match, after two wins for Deep Blue, one for Kasparov, and three draws (Hsu, 2002). *Deep Blue*, developed by IBM through the late 1980s and early 1990s, was an expert system that relied upon heuristic search and evaluation functions, opening book and endgame databases, human expertise, and a parallel processing architecture that allowed it to carry out multiple calculations simultaneously. Hence, four decades after the creation of AI (notably much later than predicted), a program was able to meet a key purported benchmark of intelligence. Ironically, however, the symbolic approach to AI that initially surpassed this benchmark was not a key factor in kicking off the third-wave of artificial intelligence, which consists primarily of sub-symbolic and data-driven approaches to AI.

[49] Compare: in the present day, AI is sometimes touted by the media as *both* a catch-all solution to every human problem *and* a potential existential risk to humanity.

[50] See discussion in Kuipers (1979).

1.5 Third-Wave AI: Deep Hype

The present-day boom of artificial intelligence research, especially deep learning approaches (Chapter 2), was kicked off in 2012 by AlexNet, which saw a stunning advance in the previous state-of-the-art on the ImageNet Large Scale Visual Recognition Challenge. The convolutional neural network (CNN) architecture achieved a top-5 error of 15.3%—more than 10.8 percentage points lower than the runner-up that year.

Despite recent excitement, neural networks predate present-day artificial intelligence. The convolutional neural network architecture that AlexNet used was initially presented in the 1980s. The backpropagation algorithm AlexNet used—a learning algorithm for multi-layer artificial neural networks—was described in the 1960s and popularised in the 1980s.[51] Hence, most of the technical aspects underlying AlexNet had been known for decades previously. Whereas connectionist networks had previously failed, they suddenly out-performed every other model in computer vision.

One of the reasons AlexNet performed so well on this challenge was because of the depth of the model, which Krizhevsky et al. (2017) argued was essential for the model's performance. However, the depth of the convolutional neural network made it computationally expensive to train the model. This cost was offset by graphics processing units (GPUs). Although graphics systems date back to the 1950s, the first modern-day version of the GPU (GeForce 256) was released by Nvidia in 1999. Graphics processing units were initially popularised in the 1990s for better and faster rendering of 3D graphics in the context of video game systems.[52] However, they are also useful as computational tools for training large machine learning models that utilise deep neural networks. Hence, one of the key factors contributing to the success of deep learning was increased computing power which made old technology—deep neural networks and learning algorithms—feasible.

Deep neural networks require more computing power to train; however, as these networks get larger, they also require more data. Hence, in addition to increased computational capacity of modern-day computers, supplemented with GPUs, much of the success of present-day machine learning is owing to the advent and widespread adoption of the Internet, which caused a significant increase in the availability of digital data used for training large neural network models.

---

[51] See Kelley (1960); Bryson and Ho (1969) and Rumelhart et al. (1986); LeCun et al. (1989), respectively

[52] For an extremely thorough three-volume history of the GPU, see Peddie (2022a,b,c).

Machine learning—specifically deep learning—is responsible for many recent advances in artificial intelligence. Transformer models have been particularly successful for natural language processing (NLP) tasks and show some promise in other domains—e.g., computer vision.[53] Reinforcement learning has proven useful in various complex domains, including autonomous vehicles and natural language processing.[54] The contemporary landscape of artificial intelligence is prominently marked by the prevalence of generative models, which have garnered significant attention (and hype) since 2022 in light of their ability to generate textual, visual, and aural outputs that are (nearly) indistinguishable from their training inputs.

In particular fields of application, AI models are being used extensively in healthcare for tasks like medical imaging analysis, diagnosis, drug discovery, and robot-assisted surgery. Present-day AI models are also deployed in armed conflict, policing, surveillance, fraud, and social manipulation, and they have contributed significantly to the spread of misinformation and disinformation online.

Although it is unclear what the near- (or distant-) future advances in AI research will look like, those who engage in forecasting are deeply polarised. On the one hand, some think the next AI winter is just around the corner. On the other hand, some think that AGI (and maybe artificial superintelligence) is imminent. Perhaps unsurprisingly, social coalitions have become somewhat fractious between those who claim that AI will lead to a utopian or dystopian future. On the theme of cycles, this division is not unlike the research factions promoting symbolic versus subsymbolic approaches to AI in its first two decades, insofar as it is less a matter of whose view or approach is "more correct" than who has the most funding, the most prominent platform, and the loudest voice. In the earlier case, the symbolic approach won out, for better or worse; in the present day, it is the AI safety and existential risk crowd that dominates (for better or worse).[55]

Regardless of what the future looks like, it is important to ensure that those who make claims about the abilities and risks of artificial intelligence understand at least some of how these systems work. This understanding is partly necessary for accuracy and clarity in making such claims and for avoiding needless anthropomorphism or fallacious reasoning about these systems. What

---

[53] See, e.g., Dosovitskiy et al. (2021); Touvron et al. (2021); Radford et al. (2021).

[54] See discussion in Grigorescu et al. (2020); Uc-Cetina et al. (2022), respectively.

[55] See Gebru and Torres (2024) for an in-depth analysis.

should be clear is that the impact of contemporary AI systems on social, economic, and political life is growing exponentially (Jones, 2023).

That said, the guiding faith of artificial intelligence research today, and a recurring theme throughout this book, is that performance scales with size, data, and compute.[56] A "bitter lesson" to be gleaned from the history of AI is as follows:

1. AI researchers have often tried to build knowledge into their agents;
2. this always helps in the short term, and is personally satisfying to the researcher, but
3. in the long run it plateaus and even inhibits future progress, and breakthrough progress eventually arrives by an opposing approach based on scaling computation by search and learning. (Sutton, 2019)

The next chapter explores some technical aspects of present-day AI research.

1.6 Summary

A highly incomplete visual timeline of some of the key moments in the history of AI discussed in this chapter is given in Figure 1.4.

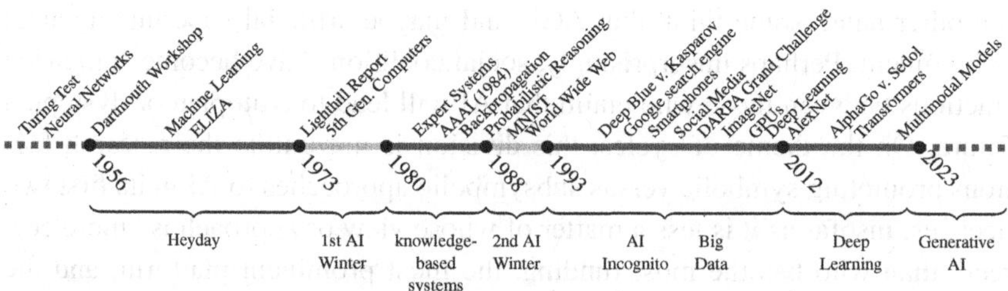

Figure 1.4: AI Timeline describing precursors, the first wave of AI (1956–1973), the first AI winter (1973–1980), the second wave of AI (1980–1988), the second AI winter (1988–1993), and the third wave of AI (1993–present)

Part of the point of this chapter has been to underscore the fact that artificial intelligence has, since its inception, seen cycles of hype and disappointment. This history is (perhaps) inductive evidence that the present-day AI systems are also being over-hyped, and, indeed, some believe this unsustainable growth and hype cycle will inevitably run into a wall, leading to disappointment and a third AI winter. Regardless of whether AI systems that exist today will continue to

[56] The conventional term for computing power.

increase in their capability or sophistication, as long as they are profitable, they will continue to be deployed, and this can (and does) cause social and ethical harm when these systems are misaligned.

To get clear what the value alignment problem is (the topic of Chapter 3) without overstating the abilities of these systems and ensuring that the problem specification is technologically grounded, it is necessary to understand some of the technical underpinnings of deep learning; this is the focus of Chapter 2.

Additional Resources

Pamela McCorduck. 1979. *Machines Who Think: A Personal Inquiry into the History and Prospects of Artificial Intelligence*. San Francisco: W. H. Freeman.

Daniel Crevier. 1993. *AI: The Tumultuous History of the Search for Artificial Intelligence*. New York: Basic Books.

Nils J. Nilsson. 2010. *The Quest for Artificial Intelligence: A History of Ideas and Achievements*. Cambridge: Cambridge University Press.

Jürgen Schmidhuber. 2015. "Deep Learning in Neural Networks: An Overview," *Neural Networks* 61: 85–117.

Michael Wooldridge. 2021. *A Brief History of Artificial Intelligence: What It Is, Where We Are, and Where We Are Going*. New York: Flatiron Books.

Matthew L. Jones. 2023. "AI in History," *American Historical Review* 128(3): 1360–1367.

2 Artificial Intelligence Today

For in those realms machines are made to behave in wondrous ways,
often sufficient to dazzle even the most experienced observer.
But once a particular program is unmasked, once its inner workings
are explained in language sufficiently plain to induce understanding,
its magic crumbles away.

— Joseph Weizenbaum (1966)
ELIZA

This chapter will get slightly technical. This is unavoidable: artificial intelligence is a technical field. Machine learning approaches to AI rely upon diverse areas in applied mathematics, including multivariate calculus, linear algebra, probability theory, and information theory.[1] To that extent, those interested in certain questions in the philosophy of AI and machine learning need to engage with the formalism inherent to the discipline. In doing so, it is possible to avoid anthropomorphising AI models (and then asking philosophical questions about those fictional entities), which is necessary to ensure a coherent analysis of these models, their capabilities, and their risks. As mentioned in the introduction, this book is not about science fiction or a hypothetical near- or far-future AI system but actual models that exist today.

As seen in Chapter 1, the goals of artificial intelligence research have varied throughout its history as a discipline. So, too, have the methods to achieve those goals. Russell and Norvig (2021) provide a useful goal-based taxonomy for historical definitions of artificial intelligence, which includes *acting humanly*, *thinking humanly*, *thinking rationally*, and *acting rationally*. The last of these predominates in the present day. The *intelligent* or *rational* agents approach to

[1] See Goodfellow et al. (2016, Chs. 1–5) for a focused introduction to these topics.

AI research focuses on designing artificial agents capable of *acting* rationally, as opposed to merely emulating or replicating human intelligence or rational reasoning.

Although "agency" and "rationality" are often used in a much more narrow, technical sense in philosophy, for our purposes an agent refers to a system that can perceive (or sense) its environment, process information, and then make a decision, render an output, or execute an action to achieve its goals. Hence, the use of "agent" throughout will (typically) be understood as synonymous with "actor". *Rationality* means that the agent's decisions or actions maximise some expectation, utility, reward, objective, etc., based on available information.

Although artificial intelligence research encompasses a much wider set of approaches than simply machine learning—including approaches based upon logic, probabilistic reasoning, search, etc.—machine learning methods will be the primary focus of this book. In part, this is because the very idea of the value alignment problem is unique to machine learning contexts. In the case of traditional approaches to artificial intelligence ("good old-fashioned AI"), it would be inapt to describe a system that does not function as intended as being "misaligned"; rather, we would say that there is a bug in the code—presumably such a programme would be de-bugged before it was released widely and integrated into various applications. In contrast, the present-day standard is to deploy models that do not work exactly as intended, and to say that they are misaligned.

One particular type of machine learning model that will be of special import is the deep neural network and related architectures. Part of this is that deep learning—when a deep neural network is fitted to data—is the current driver of present-day AI systems. Many success stories in contemporary artificial intelligence research—including applications like machine translation and chatbots (natural language processing), image search (computer vision), and digital assistants (speech recognition)—have been achieved through deep learning.

Although it is somewhat simplistic, it is common to divide machine learning methods into three basic categories: *supervised learning*, *unsupervised learning*, and *reinforcement learning*. Deep learning cross-cuts all three of these methods and represents the current state of the art. See Figure 2.1.

As we will see in Chapter 3, the key concept for discussing the value alignment problem is that of an *objective function*. However, to understand the purpose and use of an objective function in the context of machine learning, it is necessary to delve into some details surrounding the technical components of these models. The remainder of this chapter introduces technical language and

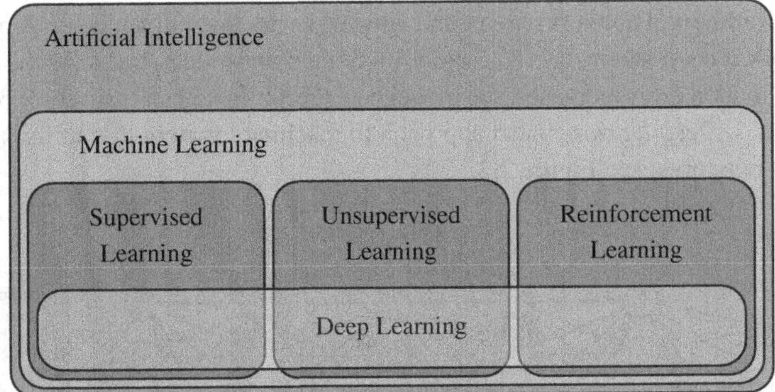

Figure 2.1: Basic taxonomy of artificial intelligence research methods. Machine learning constitutes one approach to artificial intelligence research; it can be divided into three methods: supervised, unsupervised, and reinforcement learning. Deep neural networks are useful in each of these research areas. Adapted from Prince (2023).

concepts that will be useful for understanding the value alignment problem for artificial intelligence in a way that is grounded in existing AI systems.

2.1 Neural Network Architectures

A model is a representation or abstraction of a system, phenomenon, or concept. Although scientific models may fall under different categories, and philosophers of science disagree about the metaphysics of models, for our purposes, a model can be understood as a mathematical structure or framework that captures some essential features or relationships of a real-world system under study.[2]

A *neural-network* is a type of model whose structure consists of a set of *nodes* which define the *input layer*, *hidden layer* (or layers), and *output layer* of the network.[3] Each node in a hidden layer is called a *unit* or *neuron*. The inputs of the hidden layer are called *pre-activations*, and the values at the hidden layer are called *activations*. When the connections of a neural network do not contain loops (i.e., the graph that represents the network connections is *acyclic*), it is called a *feed-forward* neural network. When a neural network's connections include loops, it is called a *recurrent neural network*. The network is *fully connected* when every unit in one layer connects to every unit in the next.

[2] See Frigg and Hartmann (2020) for a detailed philosophical overview of models in science.

[3] A neural network with at least one hidden layer is also called a *multi-layer perceptron*.

Shallow neural networks are neural networks with one hidden layer. A neural network is *deep* just in case it contains more than one hidden layer. As the number of hidden units increases, the model can approximate increasingly complex functions. *Deep learning* is an approach to machine learning that utilises deep neural networks; see Figure 2.2.[4]

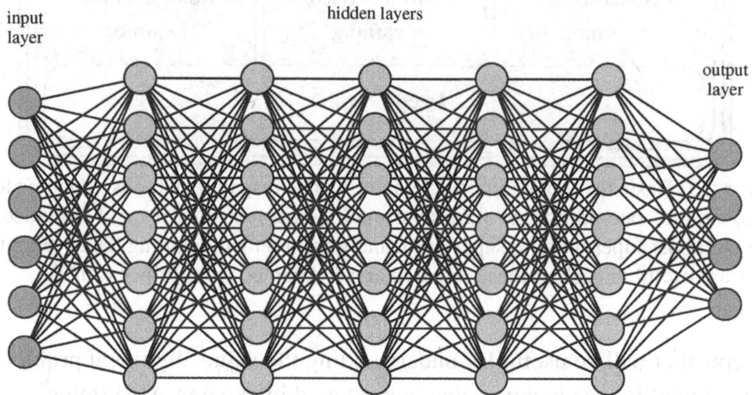

Figure 2.2: Graphic example of a fully connected, feed-forward deep neural network. In this case, the depth of the network is $K = 5$, and the width of the network is $D_k = 7$ for each $k \in K$.[5]

Hyperparameters. Hyperparameters are variables that are *external* to the model. For example, the number of layers in a network (depth) and nodes in a layer (width) are hyperparameters of a neural network model. Additional hyperparameters include things like *learning rates* (the rate at which a model's parameters are updated during the training process) or regularisation parameters (which control the strength of regularisation techniques).[6] Instead of being learned from data, hyperparameters are set by the researcher before training. Hence, determining how deep or wide a neural network ought to be, or what the learning rate should be, is a value judgement.

[4]The graphical description of a neural network, consisting of a set of densely-connected nodes—the inputs, the outputs, and the hidden layer(s)—have a superficial resemblance to neurons in the brain, hence why these are called *neural* networks. However, it is worth noting that this historical connection does not imply that neural networks act in ways similar to brains or that brains act in ways similar to neural networks.

[5]The code used to create this figure was written by Izaak Neutelings and shared under the CC BY-SA 4.0 license. The original code is available here: https://tikz.net/neural_networks/.

[6]Regularisation is a technique used in machine learning and statistical modelling to prevent overfitting and improve the generalisation performance of a model. Effectively, these techniques constrain the magnitude of the model parameters, preventing them from becoming too large and dominating the learning process.

Hyperparameter tuning is the process of finding the optimal set of hyperparameters for a machine learning model to achieve better performance. In practice, hyperparameter tuning often involves experimentation with different settings to find the combination of hyperparameters that yields the best results under validation. In this case, theoretical considerations may not motivate modelling decisions, meaning they may be theoretically unjustified.

Features and labels. A *feature* (or attribute) is an input variable for a machine learning model. An *example* consists of one or more features (and possibly a label, depending on whether the method for training is supervised or unsupervised learning). For instance, the Modified National Institute of Standards and Technology (MNIST) database is a dataset of handwritten digits and labels. Each 28×28-pixel image in the dataset is an *example*, consisting of a 784-dimensional input vector—i.e., the flattened entries of a 28×28 matrix, represented mathematically as $\mathbf{x}_i = \left[x_1, \ldots, x_{784}\right]^{\mathbf{T}}$.[7] Each component of the

[7]For those unfamiliar with this notation, a vector (or feature vector) in the context of machine learning is a representation of information. An example in the MNIST dataset looks like this:

which we interpret (visually) as the digit 5. This handwritten digit can be represented mathematically as a matrix, where each entry in the matrix, $x_{i,j} \in [0,1]$ represents the greyscale value of its corresponding pixel. In this case,

$$\begin{bmatrix} x_{1,1} & x_{1,2} & \cdots & x_{1,28} \\ x_{2,1} & x_{2,2} & \cdots & x_{2,28} \\ \vdots & \vdots & \ddots & \vdots \\ x_{28,1} & x_{28,2} & \cdots & x_{28,28} \end{bmatrix} = \begin{bmatrix} 0 & 0 & \cdots & 0 \\ 0 & 0 & \cdots & 0 \\ \vdots & \vdots & \ddots & \vdots \\ 0 & 0 & \cdots & 0 \end{bmatrix}.$$

This 28×28 *matrix* can be represented as a 784×1 *column vector*:

$$\begin{bmatrix} x_{1,1} \\ x_{1,2} \\ \vdots \\ x_{1,28} \\ x_{2,1} \\ \vdots \\ x_{28,28} \end{bmatrix} = \begin{bmatrix} 0 \\ 0 \\ \vdots \\ 0 \\ 0 \\ \vdots \\ 0 \end{bmatrix} = \begin{bmatrix} x_{1,1} & x_{1,2} & \cdots & x_{1,28} & x_{2,1} & \cdots & x_{28,28} \end{bmatrix}^{\mathbf{T}}.$$

This *column* vector is what is described by the notation $\mathbf{x}_i = \left[x_1, \ldots, x_{784}\right]^{\mathbf{T}}$ given above. The superscript **T** denotes a *transpose*, which is an operator that reflects a matrix (vector) over its diagonal; hence, the i-th row, j-th column element of $\mathbf{A}^{\mathbf{T}}$ is the j-th row, i-th column element of $\mathbf{A}$. Each *entry* in the vector is a *feature* which provides input for a node in the input layer of the neural network. The *vector* itself is an *example*, and a dataset is a set of such examples.

vector, x_j, is a feature; namely, the greyscale value of a specific pixel, denoted by elements of the unit interval, $[0, 1]$, representing how dark each pixel in the 28×28-pixel handwritten image is. In this case, 0 represents black, 1 represents white, and intermediate values represent intermediate greys. These are the characteristics of the data that a machine learning model analyses to "learn" patterns and relationships in data by adjusting the model parameters.

Parameters. The parameters of a machine learning model are the *internal* variables that the model "learns" from the training data. They are adjusted during the training process to optimise the model's performance. The two key parameters in a standard neural network model are *weights* and *biases*.

Weights are the coefficients assigned to the input variables—called *input features*—in a model and represent the strength of the connections between nodes in different layers of the model. Biases are additional parameters in a model that are not associated with any particular input feature. These allow the model to learn an offset or baseline for the predictions. Hence, a linear model with two features, x_1, x_2, which generates a prediction, y', can be described as a linear equation,

$$y' = b + w_1 x_1 + w_2 x_2, \tag{2.1}$$

where the w_i describe the weights and b describes the bias.

The layers of a neural network compute linear functions of the input based on the weights and biases (pre-activations), pass each result through an activation function, and then form the outputs using a linear combination of these activation functions.

Activation Functions. An *activation function* allows a model to describe non-linear relations between inputs and outputs. One common activation function is the *rectified linear unit* (ReLU):

$$f(x) = \text{ReLU}(x) = \begin{cases} 0 & \text{if } x < 0 \\ x & \text{if } x \geq 0. \end{cases}$$

This activation function returns the input when it is positive and zero otherwise.[8] That said, there are many options for activation functions; see Figure 2.3 for some examples. Moreover, the choice of activation function is more readily

[8]The ReLU function has been used since Fukushima (1969); however, logistic sigmoid and tanh activation functions were more common in the early days of neural networks. ReLU was popularised again in Jarrett et al. (2009); Nair and Hinton (2010); Glorot et al. (2011).

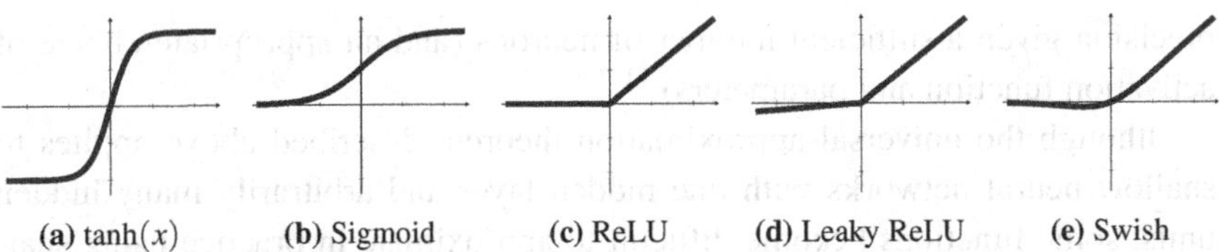

Figure 2.3: Several examples of standard activation functions for neural networks, displayed on a unit square ($x, y \in [-1, 1]$)

constrained by computational limitations than theoretical virtues.[9] As with the other hyperparameters of the model, choosing an activation function constitutes a modelling decision that may not be theoretically motivated or justified. That said, the success of deep learning does not necessarily depend upon the choice of activation function.

Universal Approximation. A theoretical assumption that underlies the universality of deep learning is that *anything whatsoever* can be described functionally. For example, the translation of text from one language to another is a very complicated function that takes syntactically well-formed strings in one language and outputs strings in another language which retain the meanings of the original strings and are also syntactically well-formed.

If a neural network has enough hidden units (neurons), shallow neural networks can approximate *any* continuous function with arbitrary accuracy. This somewhat surprising fact has been formally proved; it is referred to as the *Universal Approximation Theorem.*[10] This theorem asserts that a neural network with a single hidden layer can approximate any continuous function to arbitrary

[9] As Prince (2023) notes, "there is no definitive answer as to which of these activation functions is empirically superior" (38).

[10] Formally, if $f : \mathbb{R}^n \to \mathbb{R}^m$ is a continuous function, and $\phi : \mathbb{R} \to \mathbb{R}$ is a non-constant, bounded, and continuous activation function, then for any $\epsilon > 0$, there exist positive integers N and M, and sets of parameters, $\{a_i, \mathbf{b}_i, \mathbf{w}_i\}$ ($i \in \{1, 2, \ldots, N\}$), such that the function $F : \mathbb{R}^n \to \mathbb{R}^m$, defined by

$$F(\mathbf{x}) = \sum_{i=1}^{N} a_i \phi(\mathbf{w}_i \cdot \mathbf{x} + \mathbf{b}_i)$$

satisfies

$$| F(\mathbf{x}) - f(\mathbf{x}) | < \epsilon$$

for all $\mathbf{x}$ in the closed and bounded subset of $\mathbb{R}^n$. See Cybenko (1989); Hornik et al. (1989); Hornik (1991).

precision given a sufficient number of neurons (and an appropriate choice of activation function and parameters).[11]

Although the universal approximation theorem described above applies to shallow neural networks with one hidden layer and arbitrarily many hidden units, some functions become difficult to approximate in practice using shallow neural networks. Empirically, networks tend to behave better when they contain at least 10 hidden layers. Modern deep neural networks may include hundreds of layers, each with thousands of units. The parameters of the model are adjusted via learning algorithms to fit a specific set of data.

2.2 Data and Datasets

In the context of machine learning, a dataset is a collection of data points (examples) used to train, validate, and test a model. Each data point in the dataset consists of one or more features (input variables) and, in supervised learning, a corresponding label or target variable that the model aims to predict. To train and test a machine learning model using data, datasets are typically divided into two main subsets: the training and test sets. These subsets serve distinct purposes in developing and evaluating machine learning models.

Training Data. The training set is the portion of a dataset used to train the machine learning model. It consists of many examples, each with input features and corresponding target labels (in supervised learning). During the training phase, the model learns to make predictions or classifications by adjusting its internal parameters (weights and biases) based on the patterns and relationships present in the training data. The goal is to enable the model to make accurate predictions on new, unseen data from the test set.

Test Data. The test set is a separate portion of the dataset that is not used during the training phase. It serves as an independent evaluation set to assess how well the trained model generalises to new, unseen data and helps to determine whether the parameters of the model are *overfitted* to the training set—i.e., when a model performs well on the training data but poorly on novel data; see Figure 2.4. The test set is supposed to help estimate the model's performance in real-world applications based on conventional evaluation metrics in the field—e.g., accuracy, precision, recall, F1 score, etc.

[11] Note that the Universal Approximation Theorem depends upon the *architecture* of the network rather than the choice of activation function (Hornik, 1991); this may mitigate some of the arbitrariness in choosing an appropriate activation function.

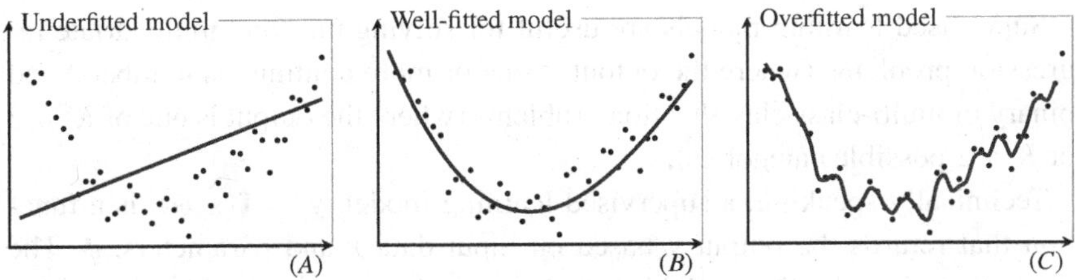

Figure 2.4: Visual example of models that are (*A*) underfitted, (*B*) well-fitted, and (*C*) overfitted to empirical data

The cardinal rule of machine learning (if there is one) is that one should not train on test data since doing so implies that the model can "memorise" the test set rather than learning underlying patterns in the data. Hence, training on test data compromises the validity of the evaluation process. For example, OpenAI's Generative Pre-trained Transformer (GPT) was trained on the Common Crawl dataset (among others), which probably includes questions and answers to standardised tests; hence, when news reports state that GPT can outperform humans on, e.g., the Law School Admissions Test (LSAT), these results are not necessarily meaningful since the test data are likely a part of the training data.[12]

2.3 Machine Learning Methods

We have been introduced to some of the key components of the *architecture* of a machine learning model and the data on which they are trained and evaluated. We now turn to more carefully differentiating methods, or paradigms, that fall under the heading of machine learning. Deep learning is applicable to each of these.

Supervised Learning. A supervised learning model defines a mapping from one or more inputs (labelled data) to an output prediction. The input, $\mathbf{x}$, is a vector representation of some meaningful real-world input.[13] These vector representations of the input data may be fixed- or variable-length, and they may be structured or unstructured. The output is a vector, $\mathbf{y}$, that can be translated back into a meaningful real-world prediction.

---

[12] See further discussion in Narayanan and Kapoor (2023).

[13] Conventionally, column vectors (rank-1 tensors of numbers) are denoted with a bold-face lowercase letter. In contrast, *matrices* (rank-2 tensors) and rank-n tensors are denoted with bold-face capital letters.

Supervised learning models are useful for solving uni- and multivariate regression problems (where the output is one or more continuous numbers) and binary or multi-class classification problems (where the output is one of $K = 2$ or $K > 2$ possible categories).

Technically speaking, a supervised learning model, $\mathbf{y} = \mathbf{f}(\mathbf{x}, \boldsymbol{\phi})$, is a function that returns the output $\mathbf{y}$ based on input data $\mathbf{x}$ and parameters, $\boldsymbol{\phi}$. The prediction given by the model is referred to as *inference*. As with all machine learning models, the process of *fitting*, *learning*, or *training* a model is a search to find optimal parameters—i.e., finding the optimal (or at least a satisfactory) equation from the family of equations defined by the model. In supervised learning, the training data consists of ordered pairs of input and output examples, $\{\mathbf{x}_i, \{\mathbf{x}_i, \mathbf{y}_i\}\} = (\mathbf{x}_i, \mathbf{y}_i)$. To select the set of parameters, $\boldsymbol{\phi}$, that accurately maps the inputs to the correct outputs (a label prediction), we need a measure of how "good" our current model is.

For supervised learning, this measure can be quantified as *loss*, $L(\phi)$, which represents how well the model predicts the training outputs under the parameters, $\boldsymbol{\phi}$. Therefore, training a model is effectively a problem of finding the set of parameters $\hat{\boldsymbol{\phi}}$ that minimise the loss function. That is to say, we want to *optimise* the following equation:

$$\hat{\boldsymbol{\phi}} = \underset{\phi}{\arg\min} \left[L(\boldsymbol{\phi}) \right]. \tag{2.2}$$

When this equation is minimised—so that the loss is small—the model's parameters accurately predict the training outputs, $\mathbf{y}_i$, when given the training inputs, $\mathbf{x}_i$.

Unsupervised Learning. Whereas supervised learning models take labelled data as their input, the key feature of *unsupervised* learning models is that they are trained from datasets that do not contain labels. Thus, whereas the training dataset for a supervised learning model has the input structure $\{\mathbf{x}_i, \mathbf{y}_i\}$, the dataset for an unsupervised learning model consists solely of the input, $\{\mathbf{x}_i\}$.

The goal for unsupervised learning models is to capture some underlying structure in the dataset based on *latent* (i.e., hidden, unobservable) variables. A latent variable is a variable that can be inferred via other observable variables. For example, in economics, *quality of life* is a latent variable pertaining to an individual's *perception* of their position in life relative to their culture, values, goals, expectations, standards, and concerns. Even though quality of life is, itself, unobservable, techniques exist for *measuring* quality of life based on observable features, like wealth, employment, environment, health, education, recreation and leisure time, and social belonging.

In the realm of machine learning, latent variables are essentially a transformation of data points into a lower-dimensional space. This transformation serves the purpose of reducing the dimensionality of data, meaning it decreases the number of attributes in a dataset while retaining most of the original variation. Hence, latent variables can be thought of as lower dimensional variables that capture some "essence" of the higher dimensional data. In the context of unsupervised learning models, there exists a mapping between the unlabelled data (**x**) and a set of latent variables (**z**), which can be thought of as a "compressed" version—essentially, a lower-dimensional copy—of the original data.

We can further categorise unsupervised learning models as *discriminative* or *generative*. Discriminative models provide a mapping from the data, **x**, to the latent variables, **z**. For example, a clustering algorithm, like *k*-means clustering, is a discriminative model that seeks to group examples on the basis of the similarity of their features, without pre-established labels. In this case, the output is a set of clusters containing examples with similar characteristics.

In contrast, a *generative* model provides a mapping from the latent variables, **z**, to the data, **x**. For example, OpenAI's *DALL-E* is a generative, unsupervised learning model that generates images from text inputs. Similarly, OpenAI's GPT models utilise unsupervised learning to generate text from text inputs.[14] In both cases, the models can synthesise new data examples (the generated outputs) that are realistic and contextually relevant when compared to the model's training data (the unlabelled inputs).

Reinforcement Learning. In contrast to supervised and unsupervised learning, reinforcement learning involves agents learning from rewards received by acting in an environment. Thus, reinforcement learning is a set of methods to elicit learning via rewards and punishments rather than explicit instructions. The mechanisms that underlie reinforcement learning were directly inspired by behavioural research on operant conditioning.[15]

The key components of reinforcement learning are an *agent*, a set of *states* in the *environment* in which the agent learns, a set of possible *actions* the agent

[14]These are both gross oversimplifications—the architectures, training, etc., are highly complicated in each case. Additional technical details about DALL-E and GPT can be found in Ramesh et al. (2021, 2022) and Brown et al. (2020), respectively.

[15]Operant conditioning is a form of learning in which behaviour is strengthened or weakened by the consequences that follow it, encouraging the repetition or suppression of specific actions based on their outcomes (Thorndike, 1905, 1911, 1927). In the other direction, studying reinforcement learning in a computational setting helped researchers understand dopamine's role in reward-based learning in biological brains (Schultz et al., 1997). See further details in Sutton and Barto (1981, 2018).

can perform for each possible state, and a set of (usually scalar-valued) *rewards* for each action performed by the agent, conditional on the state of the environment. The agent interacts with the environment in time steps; at each time step, the agent performs an action (in a given state) and receives feedback (a reward and information) from the environment. The reward received depends upon the action *and* the state. See Figure 2.5

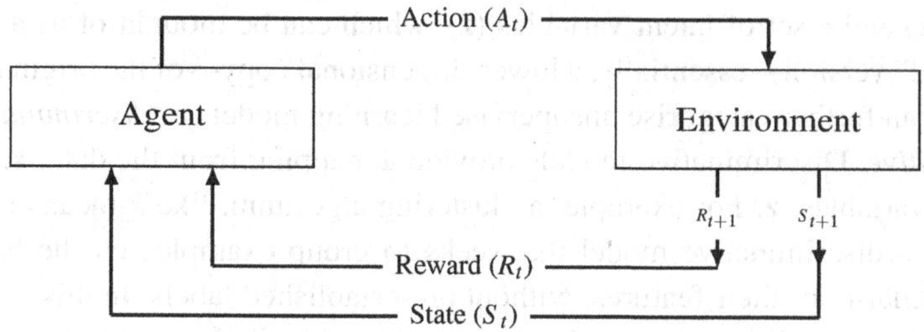

Figure 2.5: Standard framing of a reinforcement learning (RL) scenario: an agent takes actions in an environment at a time step and receives a reward and an updated (representation) of the state, which are fed back into the agent.

The objective for the RL agent is to maximise the total reward, or the long-term reward, which is a weighted sum of expected values of all the (cumulative) future rewards. Sometimes, the reward may not be administered after each action. For example, one way to train an AI agent to play a game like chess is to have it play repeated games of chess against itself and give it a reward of +1 if it wins, −1 if it loses, and 0 if it draws. In this case, the reward is only administered once—at the end of the game. Nonetheless, after playing many such games, the AI agent can learn a strategy to maximise the likelihood of winning—i.e., it learns to play chess.

The *temporal credit assignment problem* consists in determining which actions in a sequence of actions contributed most to a particular outcome or reward. In other words, it involves assigning credit to actions over time when there is a delay between the actions and the observed rewards.[16] In the chess example above, rewards are only given at the end of the game, so it may be unclear for the agent whether a particular move was good or bad. The agent aims to learn an optimal *policy* that maximises the cumulative reward over time. A policy is a decision-making function (sometimes called a *control strategy*) for the agent, which represents a mapping from states to actions. A value func-

[16] See Minsky (1961).

tion is a mapping from states to rewards; the value of a state represents the long-term expectation by starting from that particular state and executing a particular policy.

Reinforcement learning is often couched in the context of a *Markov decision process* (MDP), which is a probabilistic model of a sequential decision problem. An MDP is represented by a *tuple*: $\langle S, A, P, R, \gamma \rangle$, where S is a set of states, A is a set of actions, P is the probability of moving to state s' from state s conditional on performing action a, R is the *immediate* reward the agent receives upon performing an action, a, in state s, and γ is a discount factor, which determines whether the agent learns based on immediate rewards alone ($\gamma = 0$) or whether the agent learns based on the total reward alone ($\gamma = 1$), or something in between ($0 < \gamma < 1$).

The agent may or may not have a *model* of its environment. Model-based RL agents construct an internal model of the transitions, P, and immediate rewards, R, in the environment and then select actions based on searching this model for the optimal action. In the case of model-free RL, the agent learns directly from state/action values or policies.

Deep reinforcement learning combines reinforcement learning and neural network modelling. Deep reinforcement learning has performed well in many different tasks—particularly those tasks where it is difficult to define an objective explicitly, as in game playing, robotics, or autonomous vehicles.[17]

2.4 Objectives, Goals, and Values

So far, we have been introduced to several technical components of a machine learning model, including the model architecture, the data upon which models are trained and evaluated, and several paradigms that fall under the heading of machine learning (to which deep learning applies). Training a model involves finding the set of parameters that determines the most accurate mapping from inputs to outputs on the basis of observed (training) data. To do so, it is necessary to encode an *objective* in the model in the form of an *objective function*. The specific form of the objective function depends on the type of machine learning task (e.g., classification, regression, clustering) and the algorithm used. Different algorithms and tasks may require different objective functions to be effective in capturing the desired learning objectives. For example, a supervised or unsupervised learning model may be optimised with respect to a loss function, whereas a reinforcement learning model may be op-

[17]See, for example, Mnih et al. (2013, 2015); Silver et al. (2016, 2017a,b, 2018); Moravčík et al. (2017); Jaderberg et al. (2018).

timised with respect to a reward function. Each of these is described in more detail here.[18]

Loss, Cost, and Error. The *loss function* maps values from one or more variables to a real number, representing the "cost" or "error" associated with those values. Given a training dataset of input/output pairs, $\{\mathbf{x}_i, \{\mathbf{x}_i, \mathbf{y}_i\}\} = (\mathbf{x}_i, \mathbf{y}_i)$, a *loss function* or *cost function*, $L(\phi)$, provides a single number to describe how accurate the model prediction is in relation to the ground truth, $\mathbf{y}_i$. As mentioned, training is a process wherein we seek a set of parameters, ϕ, to minimise the loss, *L*, representing how well the model predicts the training outputs under the parameters, $\boldsymbol{\phi}$. That is to say, we want to *optimise* Equation 2.2 so that loss is small.

One common loss function used in supervised learning to quantify training error is the sum of the squares of the deviation between the model's predictions, $\mathbf{f}(\mathbf{x}_i, \boldsymbol{\phi})$, and the *ground truth*—i.e., the true label, $\mathbf{y}_i$:

$$L(\phi) = \sum_{i=1}^{I} (\mathbf{f}(\mathbf{x}_i, \phi) - \mathbf{y}_i)^2 . \tag{2.3}$$

Equation 2.3 is referred to as the *least squares error* since the best parameters for the model minimise the square of the error between the model prediction and the true label—i.e., this function minimises the total Euclidean distance between a line and the data points.[19]

The choice of loss function depends upon the problem at hand. For example, if we describe a model's output as a conditional probability distribution, $\mathrm{P}(\mathbf{y} \mid \mathbf{x})$, over possible outputs, $\mathbf{y}$, conditional on the given input, $\mathbf{x}$, then the loss function requires assigning a higher probability for each $\mathbf{y}_i$ under the cor-

[18] For simplicity, I will focus on loss or rewards; however, the key point is about the idea of an objective function, not the objective function itself. What is said about loss or rewards will generally apply to any objective function in machine learning. For example, in the context of genetic programming or evolutionary algorithms, the objective function is a *fitness function* which measures the performance of individuals or candidate solutions within the population. This function assigns a numerical value, known as the fitness score, to each individual based on how well it satisfies the objectives or criteria of the problem being solved. Similarly, the generative adversarial networks (GAN) framework employs a minimax game between a generator and a discriminator, and the objective is to find a Nash equilibrium where the generator produces data that is indistinguishable from real data, and the discriminator cannot reliably differentiate between real and generated samples. The objective function of GANs involve two components: discriminator loss and generator loss. The point is that machine learning techniques seek to solve an optimisation problem, and the object of optimisation is the objective function.

[19] The least squares loss function naturally follows from the assumptions that the prediction errors are independent and drawn from a normal distribution with mean $\mu = \mathbf{f}(\mathbf{x}_i, \phi)$ (Prince, 2023, 69).

responding input $\mathbf{x}_i$. Thus, model parameters are chosen to maximise the combined probability across all the training examples:

$$\hat{\phi} = \underset{\phi}{\arg\max} \left[\prod_{i=1}^{I} \mathrm{P}(\mathbf{y}_\mathrm{i} \mid \mathbf{f}(\mathbf{x}_\mathrm{i}, \text{Œ})) \right]. \tag{2.4}$$

Equation 2.4 is known as the *maximum likelihood* criterion because the combined probability gives the *likelihood* of the parameters.[20] That is to say, we design the function so that minimising loss means maximising probability.[21]

However, because of the possibility of *overfitting*, described above, it is insufficient to minimise training error—e.g., loss on the training data. Instead, we want to determine whether the model *generalises* from the examples it has seen (the training data) to previously unseen examples (the test data). That is, we want to minimise loss on the *test* data.

Rewards and Expectations. In the context of reinforcement learning, rewards and expectations serve as key components of the objective function that guides an agent's learning process. We have already seen that the reinforcement learning paradigm involves an agent interacting with an environment, taking actions, receiving feedback in the form of rewards, and learning to make decisions that maximise its cumulative reward over time. Hence, the agent's *objective* is to maximise this cumulative reward; the underlying structure of the reinforcement learning paradigm, like supervised and unsupervised learning, is optimisation.

In this case, rewards provide feedback to the RL agent which indicate the desirability or success of its recent actions. The agent's goal or objective is to maximise its expected cumulative reward. Hence, the objective function in reinforcement learning often involves maximising the expected sum of discounted rewards over time. The expected cumulative reward, often denoted as the return, R, is sometimes defined as the sum of rewards, r_t, at each time step, t; the return may be discounted by a factor, $\gamma \in (0, 1)$. As such, the objective for the RL agent is to maximise equation 2.5.

---

[20] Note that this definition assumes that the data are independent and identically distributed, or i.i.d.

[21] Formal details are given in Prince (2023). Note, that machine learning methods do not *require* the probabilistic approach—although this is the current default. For example, *support-vector machines* provide a non-probabilistic machine-learning model for classification (Vapnik, 1995; Cristianini and Shawe-Taylor, 2000); however, these approaches still utilise *loss* functions—e.g., hinge loss—which is the key insight for our purposes.

$$R = \sum_{t=0}^{\infty} \gamma^t r_t. \tag{2.5}$$

The agent's policy is adjusted to increase the likelihood of actions that lead to higher expected rewards.

In contrast to the immediate feedback received from the environment, *expectations* represent the anticipated future rewards based on the agent's current policy and the environment's dynamics. The expected value of future rewards is often represented using the state-action value function (called a q-function), $Q(s,a)$, which represents the expected cumulative reward starting from state s, taking action a, and following the agent's policy. Or, an RL agent may seek to maximise a value function, $V(s)$, which represents the cumulative reward starting from the state, s, and following the agent's current policy. The agent's policy is then updated, based on the feedback received, to increase the likelihood of actions that lead to higher expected future rewards.

Hence, in the context of an RL agent, rewards provide immediate feedback, guiding the agent to take actions that lead to short-term success. Expectations, in the form of value functions or q-functions, guide the agent to make decisions that result in beneficial long-term outcomes. Together, rewards and expectations shape the objective function, and the reinforcement learning agent aims to optimise its policy to maximise the expected cumulative reward over time.

Objective Functions. More generally, an *objective function* is any function to be optimised—i.e., minimised *or* maximised.[22] Thus, cost and loss functions are objective functions in the context of supervised and unsupervised learning, where the optimisation problem is to *minimise* loss; and, reward functions are objective functions in the context of reinforcement learning, where the optimisation problem seeks to *maximise* the long-term reward. The objective function is used to quantify how well a model performs.[23]

---

[22] Note, however, that there is no important distinction between minimisation and maximisation since minimising the function $f(\mathbf{x})$ is equivalent to maximising the function $-f(\mathbf{x})$.

[23] For example, in supervised learning, the goal of a regression task is to predict continuous numerical output based on input features—i.e., a mapping between input data and a continuous target variable. This task might be used for, e.g., forecasting stock prices using historical data or estimating health metrics based on biometric data. In this case, an objective function might be *mean squared error*, which calculates the average squared difference between the predicted and actual values from a labelled dataset. Similarly, in binary or multi-class classification problems, cross-entropy loss is an objective function that measures the dissimilarity between the predicted probability distributions and the true distribution of class labels.

Optimising an objective function is supposed to imply that the trained model makes predictions or renders outputs that are close to the actual target values. The "training" phase of a machine learning model involves selecting an initial set of parameters, measuring the loss, and then adjusting the parameters using a learning algorithm to optimise the objective function.

2.5 Learning Algorithms

Algorithms are used to fit machine-learning models. For example, supervised learning techniques include linear regression, *k*-nearest neighbours, logistic regression, decision trees, support vector machines, random forest, naïve Bayes, etc. Unsupervised learning techniques include clustering algorithms, such as hierarchical clustering, *k*-means, etc.

Backpropagation. The gradient of a function is a mathematical expression for the rate of change of that function. This generalises the derivative to the case where the derivative is with respect to a vector. Thus, the gradient of a function is a collection of all the partial derivatives of that function in the form of a vector. Effectively, the gradient calculates the direction of the function's greatest increase (decrease). The backpropagation algorithm (sometimes called "backprop") is a method for computing the gradient of a loss function relative to the network weights.[24] The *gradient* given by the partial derivative of the cost function shows how quickly the cost changes when we change the weights and biases.

The backpropagation algorithm itself is mathematically complex, but we can describe it at a superficial level. The algorithm consists of a "forward pass", which computes and stores the values of all the hidden units and the network output (which are used to compute the gradients), and a "backward pass", which calculates the derivatives of each parameter. Thus, the backpropagation algorithm computes the derivatives of the loss function. The derivatives of the loss function tell us how the loss changes when we make a small change to the parameters (i.e., the weights and biases). This information is useful insofar as we are trying to *optimise* the loss. One key feature of the backpropagation algorithm is that it computes the derivatives very quickly, which is necessary

[24] In essence, this is the *partial derivative* of a loss function with respect to some weight or bias within the network: $\frac{\partial L}{\partial w}$. In calculus, a derivative is a measure of the slope of a function. When a function is increasing, the derivative of the function is positive, and when a function is decreasing, the derivative of that function is negative. (A partial derivative is just an extension of the derivative to multivariate contexts so that the derivative is with respect to one of several possible variables in higher-dimensional space.)

for models with very large numbers of parameters and when training with very large datasets.[25]

Stochastic Gradient Descent. Stochastic gradient descent is an iterative optimisation algorithm for finding the minimum of a function. As mentioned, the *gradient* of a function tells us the slope of that function. Thus, gradient *descent* means to descend the slope of a function to a lower point. The gradient descent algorithm considers all the points of the function when calculating the loss and the derivative. This algorithm uses the entire training dataset to compute the gradient to calculate the optimal solution.

In contrast, *stochastic* (i.e., probabilistic, non-deterministic, or random) gradient descent calculates the loss function and its derivative based upon a (randomly chosen) single point. In effect, stochastic gradient descent is a *probabilistic approximation* of the gradient descent algorithm. Thus, these two algorithms are mathematically similar; however, stochastic gradient descent is less computationally expensive. The derivative of a function is flat when the gradient is 0, meaning the original function is neither increasing nor decreasing. Thus, the gradient descent algorithm begins by choosing a starting point on the function and then, as long as the gradient is not 0, moves along the function in the direction of the negative gradient (i.e., "downhill"). See Figure 2.6.

Note that gradient descent with backpropagation is not guaranteed to find the *global* optimum of the objective function. Instead, it may fix upon a (sub-optimal) *local* optimum. Nearly all deep learning depends upon stochastic gradient descent.[26]

Q-Learning. *Q*-learning[27] is an approach to reinforcement learning where the agent attempts to learn an optimal value function, which requires learning which actions will lead to the highest reward values in each state. *Q*-learning chooses the "greedy" action in a state—i.e., the action that gives the maximum *q*-value for that state. *Q*-learning is "off-policy" because the agent learns from actions outside the current policy—e.g., taking a *random* action when exploring. *Q*-learning uses a *q*-table (a reference table which is updated throughout learning) to represent the *q*-function (i.e., an action-value function) and allows the agent to select the best action based on the *q*-value (the output of the *q*-function) for that action in that state.

---

[25] Part of the reason for this is that the backpropagation algorithm allows for parallelisation, meaning that the computations for updating the weights in a neural network can be performed simultaneously across multiple nodes or processors.

[26] For additional details and discussion, see Goodfellow et al. (2016).

[27] The "Q" stands for *quality*.

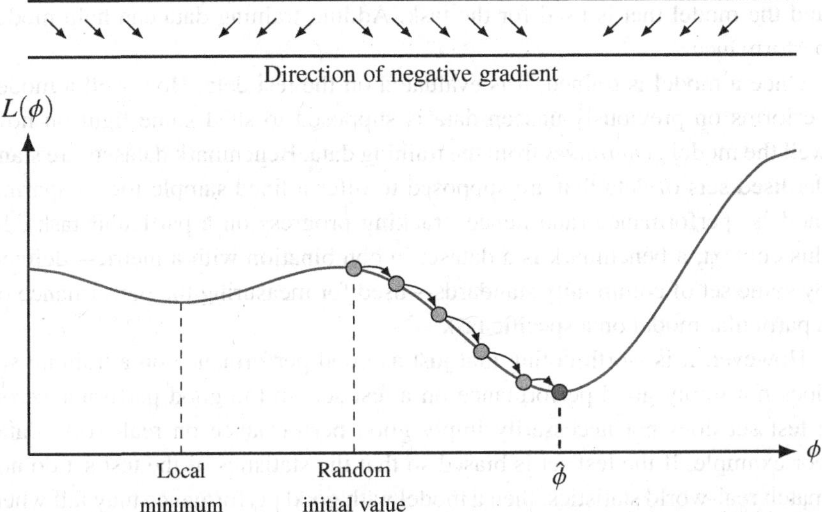

Figure 2.6: Simple example illustrating stochastic gradient descent minimising loss, $L(\phi)$, for values of ϕ

This approach leads to a trade-off between *exploration* and *exploitation*. In many situations, an agent may have to balance the known (though possibly suboptimal) reward it receives and the unknown alternative actions that may (or may not) lead to a higher reward. In deep reinforcement learning, a deep neural network might be used to model a mapping from the observed state to an action—i.e., a *policy network*. For example, when learning to play chess, the network might learn a mapping from the current state of the board to a particular move choice. With some probability, the agent will act based on the known reward by referencing the q-table. ("I have been in this situation before, and this worked last time".) The agent then chooses the action with the best reward in that state—a form of *exploiting* past knowledge. With some probability (or if the agent has never seen that state before, so does not have a precedent for acting), the agent will *explore* available actions by acting randomly. After each step (action), the agent updates the q-table.

2.6 Evaluation

Machine learning models that are trained on data typically perform well (or perfectly) on the training data; however, these results do not always generalise to test data. Failure to generalise may result from, e.g., uncertainty inherent to the task for which the model was trained, insufficient or biased training data, and the model that is used for the task. Adding training data can help model performance.

Once a model is trained, it is evaluated on the test data. How well a model performs on previously-unseen data is supposed to shed some light on how well the model *generalises* from the training data. Benchmark datasets are standardised sets of data that are supposed to offer a fixed sample for comparing models' performance (and hence, tracking progress on a particular task). In this context, a benchmark is a dataset in combination with a metric—defined by some set of community standards—used for measuring the performance of a particular model on a specific task.

However, it is worth noting that just as good performance on a training set does not imply good performance on a test set, so too good performance on a test set does not necessarily imply good performance on real-world data. For example, if the test set is biased so that the statistics of the test set do not match real-world statistics, then a model with good performance may fail when deployed in the real world. Similarly, whereas datasets are static entities, the statistics of the real world are constantly changing. These are issues to which we will return repeatedly throughout this book.

2.7 Scaling Laws

One of the driving tenets behind deep learning models today is the observation that larger models often lead to improved performance on a variety of tasks. As the scale of a neural network increases (measured by the number of parameters or the size of the training dataset), certain aspects of performance, generalisation, and training dynamics exhibit systematic patterns; hence, they tend to capture more complex patterns and representations, enabling better generalisation to diverse datasets.

In light of the hype surrounding generative AI, large language models, and multi-modal models, the recent guiding faith of machine learning is performance scales with size, data, and compute. As Sutton (2019) posits, general-purpose methods have great power that "continue to scale with increased computation even as the available computation becomes very great". Kaplan et al. (2020) analyse how AI system performance, in the context of language modelling, is a function of the parameters, data, and computation used. They note that "language modeling performance improves smoothly and predictably as we appropriately scale up model size, data, and compute. We expect that larger language models will perform better and be more sample efficient than current models" (3). GPT-3, released in the summer of 2020, was taken as inductive evidence that this assumption is true insofar as GPT-2 is nearly identical to

GPT-3, except that the latter is ten times larger. This mere shift in scale led to increased performance on standard benchmarks.

These observations have led to the proposal of the *scaling hypothesis*—i.e., the view that models can be improved (perhaps even to the level of artificial general intelligence or superintelligence, discussed in more detail in Appendix A) simply by making them bigger: bigger neural networks, bigger training datasets, and more compute. Whether or not this is true, the advent of GPT-3 has led to a paradigm shift in how researchers in machine learning approach modelling. This, in turn, has led to an arms race between a handful of leading AI companies for ever-larger models, now termed "foundation models"—i.e., models that are "trained on broad data at scale and are adaptable to a wide range of downstream tasks" (Bommasani et al., 2022, 1). This adaptation can be achieved through fine-tuning, where the pre-trained model is fine-tuned on a smaller, task-specific dataset.

These advances have led some researchers to sound the alarm with respect to the ethical (and potentially catastrophic or existential) risks associated with these models. Hence, the value alignment problem for artificial intelligence has become a topic of pressing import. This is the focus of the next chapter.

2.8 Summary

One important insight to be gleaned from this chapter and the last is that few of the tools involved in machine learning today are new. The neural network architecture is inspired by biological neurons, modelled as *perceptrons* (Rosenblatt, 1958); Ivakhnenko and Lapa (1965) designed the first known deep neural network architecture. Convolutional neural networks were discussed in Fukushima (1979). The backpropagation algorithm, which allows neural networks to backpropagate errors, was derived in the 1960s (Kelley, 1960; Dreyfus, 1962) and practically applied in the 1980s (Rumelhart et al., 1986; LeCun et al., 1989).

Another important insight is that generally (and literally), a *machine learning* model represents a family of mathematical equations, mapping an input to an output.[28] Such a model contains *parameters* which affect the output of the specific computation performed by that model. The *training data* are used to "train", "fit", or "learn" a model to the correct (or near-correct) mathematical equation from the family of equations represented by the model. *Training* (or

[28] Similarly, we can understand neural networks as a *family* of families of functions. In this case, the hyperparameters of the neural network determine the particular family of functions, and the parameters of the model determine the particular function.

fitting) a model involves using *training data* to adjust the model parameters via *learning algorithms*.

A *learning algorithm* is a set of instructions for manipulating the model's parameters to predict the outputs as closely as acceptable to a *ground truth*—e.g., a label. However, more is needed. One could imagine a subset of the family of equations specified by the model as optimal *only* for the (observed) training data. In this case, the model may be *overfitted* to the training data. Instead, we seek a model whose parameters are fitted to an equation that *generalises* to unseen examples—e.g., the test data—to perform well. That is, the learned parameters should specify an equation that does not just accurately relate the inputs and outputs for the training data; it should also determine the correct outputs for data on which the model was not trained. Thus, training data are used to train the model—i.e., to learn the optimal set of parameters that specify the correct equation from the family of equations determined by the model. Then, test data are used to evaluate or verify how well the model performs on novel data. Hence, training a machine learning model to perform well on a given task requires solving an optimisation problem.

Artificial intelligence is sometimes mischaracterised as a form of cognition because the brain is misunderstood as primarily computational. This chapter illuminates that the primary operative concepts surrounding artificial intelligence are not intelligence, cognition, or even *learning* necessarily. Despite anthropomorphic language surrounding "learning", "training", "decisions", "actions", etc., a machine learning model simply represents a family of functions mapping inputs to outputs. Learning algorithms, like stochastic gradient descent and backpropagation (in the case of neural networks) or reinforcement learning algorithms (in the case of reinforcement learning), provide a way to change the parameters of a machine learning model in an attempt to find the *best* function that describes the relationship between inputs and outputs across a wide range of cases. The key insight to take away from this chapter, formalism notwithstanding, is that machine learning is a method for solving an optimisation problem. Hence, the important question in the context of the value alignment problem is, what are we trying to optimise?

Additional Resources

Christopher M. Bishop. 2006. *Pattern Recognition and Machine Learning*. New York: Springer.

Ian Goodfellow, Yoshua Bengio, and Aaron Courville. 2016. *Deep Learning*. Cambridge, MA: The MIT Press.

Richard S. Sutton and Andrew G. Barto. 2018. *Reinforcement Learning: An Introduction.* Cambridge, MA: The MIT Press.

Michael Nielsen. 2019. *Neural Networks & Deep Learning.* Determination Press. http://neuralnetworksanddeeplearning.com

Stuart Russell and Peter Norvig. 2021. *Artificial Intelligence: A Modern Approach.* Hoboken, NJ: Pearson.

Moritz Hardt and Benjamin Recht. 2022.*Patterns, Predictions, and Actions: Foundations of Machine Learning*. Princeton, NJ: Princeton University Press.

Kevin P. Murphy. 2022. *Probabilistic Machine Learning: An Introduction*. Cambridge, MA: The MIT Press.

Kevin P. Murphy. 2023. *Probabilistic Machine Learning: Advanced Topics*. Cambridge, MA: The MIT Press.

Simon J. D. Prince. 2023. *Understanding Deep Learning*. Cambridge, MA: The MIT Press.

3 The Value Alignment Problem

I find myself facing a public which has formed its attitude toward the machine on the basis of an imperfect understanding of the structure and mode of operation of modern machines.

— Norbert Wiener (1960)
Some Moral and Technical Consequences of Automation

In the last two chapters, we explored some key historical landmarks in AI research and examined some of the technical and theoretical underpinnings that drive the field today. As we have seen, the capacities of AI systems have increased significantly over the past decade, prompted by deep learning techniques, the rise of big data, and exponential increases in computational power (with concomitant decreases in cost and sparsity). As artificial intelligence systems become more ubiquitous, verifying that their resultant actions, decisions, or outputs align with our objectives, values, or intentions becomes crucial. When designing these systems, we must ensure that their specified objectives align with the intended objective for which they were created. This problem is often called the *value alignment problem*.[1]

The value alignment problem is challenging for (at least) three reasons.[2] First, it is difficult, if not impossible, to define our values completely and correctly. Second, even if we could specify these values, it is hard, if not impossible, to represent or encode them in a formal language—i.e., as the objectives of an AI model. Third, it is demanding to ensure that the model learns to carry out these objectives as intended. Hence, value alignment is an inherently difficult problem.

[1] Standard citations given are Russell (2019); Christian (2020); Gabriel (2020).

[2] See further discussion in LaCroix and Prince (2023).

The first step in solving a difficult problem is ensuring conceptual clarity of what the problem consists of. However, analyses of the problem itself are often brief, superficial, or imprecise.

This chapter begins by discussing the standard formulation of the value alignment problem, underscoring several key weaknesses of characterising it in this way. On the one hand, the standard description of the value alignment problem lacks depth and specificity when considering what it means for values to be aligned or misaligned. At the same time, these conversations often occur in the context of discussions surrounding artificial general intelligence or superintelligence; hence, the discussion fails to account for misalignment in real-world systems.

These shortcomings arise from the types of questions being asked in the field: What are our values? How do we encode these in an AI system? I propose that it is more fruitful to ask, instead, about the *structure* of value alignment, exploring the contexts in which misalignment could arise in the first place. To this end, the principal-agent framework from economics is useful as a starting point for characterising the value alignment problem for artificial intelligence. A novel definition is offered, based on the principal-agent framework, which provides a foundation for re-conceptualising the value alignment problem, an in-depth analysis of which is provided in Part II.

3.1 The Standard Definition of Value Alignment

Let's begin with some intuitions, which are fairly standard in discussions of value alignment. Ngo et al. (2023) describe the value alignment problem as the "challenge of ensuring that AI systems pursue goals that match human values or interests rather than unintended and undesirable goals" (1). Christian (2020) highlights that the value alignment problem is the problem of ensuring that AI "models capture our norms and values, understand what we mean or intend, and, above all else, do what we want" (13). Russell (2019) suggests that increasingly powerful AI systems may suffer from a failure of value alignment, which includes inadvertently imbuing "machines with objectives that are imperfectly aligned with our own" (137).[3] Hence, the main "goal of value

[3]He refers to this as the "King Midas problem", following the Greek myth of the king who wished that everything he touched turn to gold. According to the myth, Midas was granted a wish by the god Dionysus, and he wished that everything he touched would turn to gold. Initially pleased with his newfound power, Midas soon realised its drawbacks when he could not eat or drink without turning everything into gold. The story of King Midas is often interpreted as a cautionary tale about the consequences of excessive desire for wealth and the importance of wise and thoughtful wishes.

alignment is to ensure that powerful AI is properly aligned with human values" (Gabriel, 2020, 412) and how we might guarantee that such systems are "properly amenable to human control" (Gabriel and Ghazavi, 2022, 336).

Thus, although there is no authoritative definition of the value alignment problem, a somewhat standard specification can be formulated as follows:

> **The Value Alignment Problem** (Standard Definition)
> The problem of ensuring that AI systems are aligned with the values of humanity.

Whether explicitly stated or merely implied, this intuitive specification of the value alignment problem for artificial intelligence is relatively common in discussions on the topic. Moreover, the standard definition is superficially useful as an initial description of the problem. On the surface level, it seems relatively simple to understand. However, closer examination or analysis makes apparent that this conceptualisation underspecifies the problem; hence, this definition is of no conceptual use for practical work on mitigating value misalignment.

Ambiguity. First, it should immediately be apparent that this intuitive understanding of the value alignment problem raises more questions than it provides answers. For example, are "human values" individual values? Aggregate values? Subjective preferences? Ethical principles?[4] Whose values are they? How ought they to be determined? Who decides whose values matter? How can a conception of value alignment deal with the variation of values across cultures or time? How can we reconcile explicit preferences and unarticulated or subconscious desires?[5] How can we measure whether or how aligned an AI system is?

Moreover, the *goals* of alignment are inherently vague insofar as "values" might be read as a placeholder to be filled in later with an appropriate concept. For example, Gabriel (2020) enumerates several possible concepts that might stand in for that with which we want an AI system to align. Such concepts include

1. Instructions, so that the agent does what a user tells it to;
2. Expressed intentions, so that the agent does what the user intends for it to do;
3. Revealed preferences, so that the agent does what the user's behaviour reveals that the user prefers;

---

[4] See discussion in Kim et al. (2021).

[5] See discussion in Hendrycks et al. (2023).

4. Informed preferences or desires, so that the agent does what the user would want it to do if the user were rational and informed;
5. Interest or well-being, so that the agent does what is in the user's interest, or what is best for the user, objectively speaking;
6. Values, so that the agent does what it morally ought to do, as defined by the individual or society. (417–423)[6]

Hence, intuitive though the standard definition may be, it is far too vague to allow for a comprehensive understanding of the nature of the problem, let alone its possible solutions.

Science Fiction. Second, it should be apparent from some of the discussions of value alignment referenced above that the problem, thus specified, carries implications of AGI and superintelligence. For example, Gordon (2023) suggests that the alignment problem "refers to the challenge of ensuring that AI systems behave as their creators intend, especially when the systems become more intelligent and capable than their human designers" (77). This problem arises because as "AI systems become more intelligent, they may develop goals and values that differ from those of their creators, which could lead to unexpected and potentially harmful outcomes" (77). Similarly, Dewey (2011) argues that an "AGI whose goals do not match our own is not desirable because it will work at cross-purposes to us in many cases" (2).

Eckersley (2019) highlights that most "concerns in the literature about the difficulty of aligning hypothetical future AGI systems to human values are motivated by the risk of 'instrumental convergence' of those systems" (10). The *instrumental convergence thesis* underscores that many distinct (and perhaps unpredictable) instrumental values can increase the chances of the agent's (final) goals being realised; hence, it is likely that agents will pursue such instrumental goals. This thesis is supposed to imply that a (superintelligent) AI may adopt sub-goals that are dangerous, dis-empowering (for human agents), or generally misaligned with our goals and intentions.[7]

AGI is also implicit in policy-focused discussions of value alignment, like the Asilomar Principles.[8] One such principle states that "Highly autonomous

[6]Gabriel (2020) offers some suggestions for determining a fair set of values based on, e.g., human rights, a veil of ignorance, or social choice theory. However, the key thing to note for now is that this analysis does not circumvent the problems of the standard specification of value alignment.

[7]These are the concerns of authors like Bostrom (2003, 2014); Omohundro (2008); Yudkowsky (2011); Tegmark (2018) when they discuss alignment. See further discussion in Appendix A.

[8]The Asilomar AI principles are a set of 23 guidelines, developed by multi-disciplinary scholars at the Asilomar Conference on Beneficial AI, which was organised by the Future of Life Institute in

AI systems should be designed so that their goals and behaviours can be assured to align with human values throughout their operation" (Future of Life Institute, 2017). Of course, "highly autonomous" does not necessarily entail or require "AGI", but it is worth noting that the Asilomar Principles were published by the *Future of Life Institute*—a nonprofit organisation whose stated goals focus on reducing global catastrophic and existential risk.[9] Hence, it is safe to assume that (at least some of) the Asilomar conference participants had AGI in mind when formulating this definition. In this sense, value alignment is historically blurred with the control problem concerning superintelligent AI. Indeed, value alignment is sometimes seen as merely an *approach* to solving the control problem rather than a problem in its own right.[10]

Abstraction. Third, many researchers discuss value alignment in terms of high-level, abstract concepts without actually grounding their theories, presuppositions, and conjectures within the context of present-day artificial intelligence research and machine learning techniques. Those few researchers who do focus on state-of-the-art approaches to artificial intelligence do so informally (Ngo et al., 2023). This may be a consequence of thinking of AI in the context of science fiction (i.e., AGI, superintelligence) rather than thinking of the actual technologies that exist today.

Polyonymy. Adding to the lack of clarity surrounding value alignment for artificial intelligence, the value alignment problem is sometimes referred to under distinct headings. Hence, polyonymy serves to confuse discussions of value alignment. For example, Leike et al. (2018) call the problem of creating *agents* that behave according to the user's intentions the *agent alignment problem*. Yudkowsky (2004) suggests that the problem of "friendly AI" requires:

2017. The principles, which constitute an open letter, fall under the categories of research, ethics and values, and longer-term issues.

[9]The Future of Life Institute was founded in 2014 by Max Tegmark (MIT), Jaan Tallinn (Skype), Viktoriya Krakovna (DeepMind), Meia Chita-Tegmark (Tufts), and Anthony Aguirre (UC Santa Cruz). This institute should not be confused with the (now defunct) *Future of Humanity Institute*, established in 2005 at the University of Oxford by Nick Bostrom. That said, both institutes emphasise global catastrophic risk—particularly in light of artificial intelligence (the fictional kind discussed in more detail in Appendix A). Whereas the Future of *Life* Institute's first grant program (focusing on AI safety) was funded by Elon Musk (USD 10 million, or ~CAD 12,768,130), the Future of *Humanity* Institute received a £13.4 million (~CAD 23,176,640) grant from Open Philanthropy in 2018—a grant-making foundation that is based on the tenets of effective altruism. The Future of Humanity Institute was closed by Oxford University in April 2024.

[10]Further discussion of the control problem and its relation to the value alignment problem is provided in Appendix A.

1. Solving the technical problems required to maintain a well-specified abstract invariant in a self-modifying goal system;
2. Choosing something nice to do with the AI; and,
3. Designing a framework for an abstract invariant that does not automatically wipe out the human species.

Although he never explicitly defines "abstract invariant",[11] it should be apparent from context that the first point effectively describes the value alignment problem. The specification for "friendly AI" is couched in the context of *coherent extrapolated volition*, which describes "our wish if we knew more, thought faster, were more the people we wished we were, had grown up farther together; where the extrapolation converges rather than diverges, where our wishes cohere rather than interfere; extrapolated as we wish that extrapolated, interpreted as we wish that interpreted" (Yudkowsky, 2004, 6); on this view, a friendly AI instantiates a dynamic that implements the coherent extrapolated volition of humankind—i.e., an AI system that is aligned with an idealised version of human values (broadly construed).

All this is to say that the intuitive definition of the value alignment problem, understood as its *de facto*[12] standard specification, is conceptually inadequate. In addition, this definition implicitly encodes a *technochauvinist* view toward AI technologies. Technochauvinism, a term coined by Meredith Broussard,[13] describes the belief that most (perhaps all) complex issues can be solved with computation, engineering, or other technological artefacts. Hence, any claims (tacit or otherwise) toward the "inevitability" of future technologies are inherently technochauvinist. The subtlety to note here is that the imperative to *ensure* that highly autonomous systems are aligned with the values of humanity presupposes that such systems are inevitable.

3.2 Adding Sophistication to the Standard Definition

Despite the shortcomings of the standard definition of the value alignment problem, some researchers have attempted to add some nuance to the intuitive specification of value alignment.

[11] In all likelihood, this refers to the notion of an abstract invariant from class and method specifications in computer science; namely, an abstract invariant is a condition that must stay true over the abstract state of all class instances. The abstract invariant, in the context of "friendly AI", might be read as the "goals" of the system.

[12] A fancy way of saying "in fact", regardless of whether by right.

[13] See the discussion in Broussard (2018, 2023).

Two Components of Value Alignment. Gabriel (2020) highlights that two distinct components can be demarcated within the value alignment problem. This problem consists of a technical and normative component. This characterisation is useful for categorising extant approaches to solving the value alignment problem.

The technical component of value alignment asks how we might properly encode "values"—i.e., principles, reward functions, objectives, etc.—in AI systems so that they reliably do what they ought to do—i.e., what we want them to do, or what we intend for them to do. The technical component of the value alignment problem has been a main focus of research in computer science that falls under the heading of (technical) AI safety. AI safety is a research topic that explores mathematical and computational techniques for building (provably) "safe" or "trustworthy" AI systems. In addition, interdisciplinary work in *machine ethics* attempts to address this technical component by exploring the theoretical and practical questions arising from the possibility of artificial moral *agents*—i.e., machines that are capable of making decisions that we would call "moral" without direct input from a human agent. Technical approaches to AI safety will be discussed in more detail in Chapter 7, and technical and normative questions surrounding artificial moral agency and machine ethics will be discussed in Chapter 8.

In contrast to the technical component of the value alignment problem, the normative component emphasises which values or principles from normative theory are the "correct" ones to encode in AI systems in the first place. The normative component of the value alignment problem has been the focus of recent research arising primarily from the humanities and social sciences, including moral philosophy,[14] moral psychology,[15] legal theory,[16] and political science,[17] among others.

Two Types of Value Alignment. In addition to demarcating the normative and technical components of value alignment, the value alignment problem, as

[14] See, e.g., Anderson and Anderson (2007); Powers (2006); Vallor (2016); Howard and Muntean (2017); Govindarajulu et al. (2019); Roff (2020); Sanz (2020); Rautenbach and Keet (2020); Kim et al. (2021).

[15] See, e.g., Vanderelst and Winfield (2018).

[16] See, e.g., Hadfield-Menell and Hadfield (2019); Hadfield-Menell et al. (2019).

[17] See, e.g., Prasad (2018); Tasioulas (2021); Koster et al. (2022).

described in the standard definition, can be further characterised in terms of *inner* alignment and *outer* alignment.[18]

The outer alignment problem arises from misspecified objective functions. Thus, solving outer alignment is tantamount to ensuring that the objective functions of machine learning models are correctly specified—i.e., that they are specified in such a way that they capture what we intend them to capture. For example, when training a reinforcement learning model to play the boat-racing game *CoastRunners*, researchers at OpenAI designed the reward function to optimise *points* earned in the game on the assumption that the player's score would (implicitly) reflect the true goal of finishing the race (preferably in first place). However, this objective function—which is a proxy for the true objective—led to unexpected behaviour: the RL agent learned to maximise the points in the game by turning in a large circle in a specifically-timed motion to obtain three point-conferring "targets" just as they were re-populated in the game environment.[19] Since hitting the targets adds to the total score, the agent achieved a high score without ever completing the race. Indeed, the RL agent achieved an average score that was 20% higher than human players.[20] This example is a failure of outer alignment because the objective function is misspecified: it did not adequately capture the true objective.

However, even when an objective function is perfectly well-specified, this does not ensure that the system will be aligned. The inner alignment problem is the problem of ensuring that the goal is represented (internally) by the model in a desirable way.[21] Therefore, whereas outer alignment pertains to the specification of the objective function, inner alignment is concerned with ensuring that the emergent "goals" of the model match the specified goals for the system. In some sense, inner alignment can be understood as a problem of inductive bias. For example, the goal misgeneralisation described by Langosco et al. (2021) in a deep reinforcement learning setting can be construed as

[18] This language is introduced by Hubinger et al. (2021). See also discussion in Clark and Amodei (2016); Christian (2020); Ecoffet et al. (2020); Krakovna et al. (2021).

[19] For a full write-up of this example, see Clark and Amodei (2016).

[20] "Superhuman performance".

[21] Hubinger et al. (2021) describe inner alignment in a slightly more technical way, with reference to *mesa-optimisers*. Mesa-optimisation refers to a situation where a learned model (the mesa-optimiser) implicitly optimises a different objective than the outer, intended objective set by the training process. The mesa-optimiser is a sub-agent, model, or system created by the outer optimiser (the training process). In this context, the inner alignment problem arises when the learned mesa-optimiser, while optimising its assigned objective during training, does not align with the outer objective set by the human designer or the training process. In other words, the inner objective of the mesa-optimiser may diverge from the intended outer objective.

an inner alignment problem. On their description, a deep RL agent is initially trained to maximise some reward, *R*, for every valid state-act pair. However, when the agent is deployed in an environment that is out-of-distribution—i.e., at least some state-act pairs in the environment were not present in the training environment—the agent may receive a low reward because it follows a "behavioural objective" (i.e., a learned objective) rather than the intended objective (generalised to a novel environment). In this case, the RL agent "retains its capabilities out-of-distribution yet pursues the wrong goal" (1). Thus, the reward function is well-specified insofar as the RL agent learns the correct behaviour during training; nonetheless, the agent fails to generalise to novel environments.

The Structure of Alignment. Although decomposing the value alignment problem into two types (inner and outer alignment) or two components (technical and normative) helps add sophistication to the standard definition, these specifications cannot guide us in determining practical approaches to solving problems of misalignment. In particular, specifying that there is a normative component to the value alignment problem is useful. Still, this fact alone offers no direction in answering normative questions regarding the values themselves. Similarly, specifying distinct ways in which the "values" of an AI system might be misaligned is conceptually useful. Still, again, this provides no guidance about the normative component of the problem.

What is needed is conceptual clarity on value alignment as a *class* of problems. Instead of asking *what* values are the "correct" objects of alignment and subsequently asking how we can encode those values in an AI model, it is fruitful to ask under what circumstances value misalignment might occur *generally*. That is to say, what is the *structure* of the value alignment problem, and in what contexts is it truly a problem? Formulating the question in this way is useful because it makes apparent that the problem of aligning values is by no means unique to artificial intelligence systems.

We have already seen one concrete circumstance in which misalignment can arise. In the case of the outer alignment problem, a model can fail to be aligned because the objective function is poorly specified. In this case, we can say that the "objectives" ("goals", "values", or "incentives") of a machine learning model are misaligned with the true objective ("our" values). Misaligned incentives, as has long been known in economics, can give rise to issues of value misalignment between two human actors (Kerr, 1975). Hence, we might understand the value alignment problem, in its most general form, as a problem of how two (or more) agents (actors) can align their values (or objectives). In economics, law, and politics, this problem is more commonly known as a *principal-agent problem.*[22] The principal-agent problem highlights the potential conflicts of interest between the goals and incentives of the principal and those of the agent, who may not always act in the principal's best interests.

To clarify the structure of the value alignment problem for artificial intelligence and the contexts that give rise to instances of this problem, it will be useful to survey the principal-agent problem in the well-studied case of human-human interactions. This principal-agent framework will provide the foundation for a novel conceptualisation of the value alignment problem in the context of artificial intelligence.

3.3 The Principal-Agent Framework

The principal-agent problem arises (or, at least, may arise) in any context where some entity—called "the principal"—appoints another entity—called "the agent"—to act on its behalf. A problem may be generated partly because the principal and the agent have different objectives, incentives, or values. When there is a conflict between the principal and the agent's values, we say their values are misaligned—hence, this is a value alignment problem.

Principal-agent models study the problem of how to generate the correct incentives in a non-cooperative setting with asymmetric information to ensure that the agent acts in the principal's best interest. In the economic context, misalignment can arise because people (i.e., the agents that economists model) have their own desires, incentives, objectives, etc.[23] Thus, in its most general form, the *problem* of value alignment arises from the dynamics of multi-agent interactions involving the delegation of tasks from one actor to another.

Some examples will clarify how ubiquitous this problem is in human-human interactions.

1. A corporate executive, like a chief executive officer (CEO), runs a corporation on behalf of its shareholders. The shareholders are the principal(s), and the CEO is the agent.
2. In a democracy, citizens elect a representative (or representatives) who then act on behalf of the citizens. The citizens are the principal(s), and the elected party or officials are the agent(s).
3. A customer orders groceries online, and a grocer collects the items to be delivered. The customer is the principal, and the grocer is the agent.

[22] This problem is sometimes referred to as an *agency dilemma* or an *incentive problem*; see discussion in Jensen and Meckling (1976); Eisenhardt (1989); Laffont and Martimort (2002).

[23] See Gibbons (1998) for additional details.

4. An individual's car performs sub-optimally, so they take it to a mechanic, who tells them several parts need to be replaced. The car owner is the principal, and the mechanic is the agent.
5. A homeowner uses a real estate agent to sell a house. The homeowner is the principal, and the real estate agent is the agent.

In case (1), the objective of the shareholders is for the corporation to maximise (shareholder) profit through increasing stock value. However, the CEO might use profits to proffer large bonuses to corporate-level executives instead of paying dividends to shareholders—an action that benefits the agent(s) but not the principal(s). In case (2), citizens might vote for a party whose platform (appears to) align with their values; however, once elected, the party may renege on those promises in light of competing considerations that benefit the party. In case (3), we might imagine that a customer values certain properties in their groceries—e.g., freshness—whereas the grocer values certain other things—e.g., offloading items close to expiration. In case (4), the car owner may value having all and only the required work being performed, and the mechanic may value maximising unnecessary expense to their own benefit. In case (5), the homeowner may value getting the best price on the house. In contrast, the agent may value closing the sale as quickly as possible (even at a reduced price). Alternatively, the agent may over-promise on the price to win the listing in the first place, simultaneously making it more difficult to sell the property.

A principal-agent problem can arise in each case because the principal and the agent may have different values, interests, or objectives. However, another key feature common to these examples is *informational asymmetry*. In case (1), the shareholders do not have information about the day-to-day goings-on of the business, but the CEO does. In case (2), the citizens use platforms as a proxy for choosing the candidate whose values align most with their own while not knowing which values will be instantiated once the party is elected. In case (3), the principal cannot observe the agent's actions. In cases (4) and (5), the principal lacks specialised information, which allows the agent to take advantage for their own gain. Informational asymmetries and imperfect information contribute to the generation of the principal-agent problem.[24]

[24] Note that "perfect information" is a term of art. In economics, perfect information implies that all market participants have all the information required to make a decision. In game theory, perfect information means that a player knows the game's entire history up to the decision point, as in backgammon. Imperfect information is the negation of perfect information; this occurs when some information is unavailable or hidden. So, imperfect or incomplete information [*continued*]

Laffont and Martimort (2002) highlight that if there is no private information between a principal and an agent, then *even if* the agent's objectives conflict with the principal's, the principal could still propose "a contract which perfectly controls the agent and induces the [agent's] actions to be what [the principal] would like to do himself in a world without delegation" (12). Essentially, under complete information, the principal has complete *bargaining power*.[25] Therefore, competing incentives (misaligned values) alone are insufficient for generating a principal-agent problem since they can be controlled when there is no informational asymmetry between the principal and the agent.[26] There are three different ways that private information can generate an agency dilemma.

First, *hidden knowledge* is an informational asymmetry resulting from the agent's private information—e.g., concerning their own skills or opportunity costs—to which the principal does not have access. Hidden knowledge may contribute to the generation of a principal-agent problem.[27] For example, a prospective employee (the agent) knows their background, skill level, and appropriateness for a particular job, whereas the hiring committee (the principal) does not. In cases of hidden knowledge, uncertainty is exogenous to the relationship between the principal and the agent, meaning that the problem arises from factors that are *external* to the principal-agent relationship. Cases (4) and (5) above are examples of informational asymmetries arising from hidden knowledge.

Second, *hidden action* is an informational asymmetry caused by the agent's ability to perform an action that the principal cannot observe.[28] When the risk-taking individual (the agent) knows more about their intentions than the consequence-paying individual (the principal), the agent may take on more risk than the principal would otherwise be comfortable with, as is common

---

means that there is some uncertainty. See discussion in von Neumann and Morgenstern (1944); Shapley (1953).

[25]Classical game theory often operationalises this as a higher disagreement point for the powerful agent; see discussion in LaCroix and O'Connor (2021).

[26]This claim is mathematically provable on the particular economic model we are discussing. Since this is a model and, therefore, an idealisation, we might question whether this model sufficiently applies to real-world interactions and whether this claim holds in the real world.

[27]In economics, this is referred to as *adverse selection*. Hidden knowledge on the agent's part causes the principal to give up some information rent—i.e., the additional return an individual can obtain due to having access to unique, exclusive, or superior (pre-contractual) information. In this case, a contract must be designed to elicit private information, which may be costly to the principal. See Akerlof (1970); Rothschild and Stiglitz (1976); Spence (1973, 1974); Laffont and Martimort (2002); Hou et al. (2009).

[28]In economics, this is known as *moral hazard*. See Haynes (1895); Knight (1921); Arrow (1963, 1968); Vaughan (1997); Laffont and Martimort (2002).

with insurance. In this case, the uncertainty due to asymmetric information is endogenous to the relationship of the principal and the agent, meaning that the problem arises from factors that are *internal* to the principal-agent relationship. Cases (1) to (3) above exemplify informational asymmetries arising from hidden action.

Solutions to the principal-agent problem arising from informational asymmetries due to hidden action and hidden knowledge assume that information is (*ex post*) verifiable[29] by an independent third party, such as a (benevolent) Court of Justice.[30] However, a third type of informational asymmetry may give rise to an agency dilemma when we assume that the information between an agent and principal is symmetric (*ex post*) but unverifiable *in principle* by a third party. Thus, the third type of informational asymmetry that may generate a principal-agent problem arises from the non-verifiability of (otherwise symmetric) information.[31] For example, suppose that the principal and the agent have identical and sufficient information to complete some transaction. In this case, a principal-agent problem may still arise when the agent represents the true state of the world as being different than they (and the principal) know it to be. This problem arises when either the agent's representation of the world is unverifiable by a third party *or* when it is too costly for a third party to verify.

Thus, value misalignment (i.e., competing incentives) may give rise to a principal-agent problem. However, when information is symmetric, the principal can create a contract that induces the agent to act just as the principal would without delegation. Therefore, value misalignment *alone* is insufficient to generate a value alignment problem.[32]

Furthermore, value misalignment is also *unnecessary* to generate a principal-agent problem. For example, suppose the agent and principal have perfectly aligned objectives but cannot transmit that information. In that case, it is still possible that the agent's actions misalign with the principal's objectives (despite the agent's intentions). This situation might occur if, for example, there is an optimal action which would satisfy the principal's objectives—and, *ex hy-*

[29] A fancy way of saying that the verification is based on actual results rather than forecasts.

[30] See further discussion in Laffont (2000).

[31] Non-verifiability is particularly relevant in the field of *contract law*. However, Shah (2014) notes that non-verifiability receives much less coverage in the economic literature on the principal-agent problem than hidden knowledge (adverse selection) and hidden action (moral hazard). See Williamson (1973, 1975); Grossman and Hart (1986); Sappington (1991); Hart (1995); Laffont (2000); Laffont and Martimort (2002).

[32] In the economic context, Laffont and Martimort (2002) underscore the fact that "informational problems prevent society from achieving the first best allocation of resources which could be possible in a world where all information is common knowledge" (13).

pothesi,[33] would also satisfy the agent's objectives—but the existence of this action is not common knowledge.[34]

To summarise, a principal-agent *problem* may arise whenever an entity can make decisions or take actions on behalf of, or that impact, another entity. The delegation of tasks from the principal to the agent raises the problem of managing information flows. Therefore, instances of the principal-agent problem are fundamentally generated by asymmetric information rather than asymmetric values. That being said, value misalignment will exacerbate problems that arise in the context of informational asymmetries.

3.4 The Value Alignment Problem for Artificial Intelligence

Based on the principal-agent framework, in the context of human-human interaction, we have now seen that the principal-agent problem is a class of problem instances, where an instance can arise because of conflicting incentives or asymmetric information between two (human) entities: a delegating agent (the principal) and an acting agent (the agent). It should be immediately apparent from the structure of this problem that this framework is also apt for describing the value alignment problem in the context of artificial intelligence.[35]

In such a setup, a human agent is analogous to the principal, and an AI system is analogous to the agent. However, a key difference between the principal-agent framework (for human-human interactions) and its analogue for human-AI interactions is that values—and therefore misalignment of values—are *inherent* to the human-human interaction insofar as principals and agents have inherent values. In contrast, in the human-AI interaction, there is no inherent misalignment between the (human) principal and the (artificial) agent because the agent has no inherent values: the "values" (i.e., objective functions) of the agent are programmed. In this latter case, competing incentives (value misalignment) can arise because it is impossible to specify an objective function completely and correctly. Hence, whereas misaligned incentives are neither necessary nor sufficient for generating a principal-agent problem in economic

[33] A fancy way of saying "according to the assumption proposed".

[34] With thanks to Aydin Mohseni for an illuminating discussion on this point.

[35] This similarity has already been noted by Dylan Hadfield-Menell (and colleagues), who suggest that the value alignment problem has a "clear analogue" in principal-agent problems. See further discussion in Hadfield-Menell et al. (2017); Hadfield-Menell and Hadfield (2019). In his PhD thesis, Hadfield-Menell (2021) also discusses the principal-agent problem in the context of value alignment. However, his analysis focuses on the technical aspects of modelling the value alignment problem as a class of cooperative assistance games rather than using the principal-agent framework to analyse the structure of the value alignment problem, as is the focus of this book.

contexts (the case of human-human interactions) they can do so AI contexts (the case of human-AI interactions).

Part of the difficulty here arises because objectives require programmers to define an objective function, which can be difficult to operationalise in a programming language. Additional complications arise from the fact that objective *functions* are mere proxies for the *true* objective; however, the objective function is identical to the true objective from the AI system's "point of view". When objective functions are poorly specified, this will lead to a value alignment problem insofar as there is a misalignment between the actual objective—"our values"—and its proxy, which is encoded as an objective function—the system's "values".

In Chapter 2, we saw that the objective function is the object of optimisation in a standard machine learning model. However, specifying an objective function for a machine learning model implicitly defines an optimisation landscape. Furthermore, the solution space for an optimisation problem defined by an objective function includes a "pathology" of *local* optima, meaning these landscapes are frequently deceptive.[36] As a result, the objective function "does not necessarily reward the stepping stones in the search space that ultimately lead to the objective" (Lehman and Stanley, 2008, 329), meaning that objective functions are often constructed *ad hoc*.[37]

Thus, poorly designed objective functions can lead to instances of the value alignment problem whenever there is a conflict between the objective function and the actual objective. As mentioned above, this can be described as a problem of outer alignment—i.e., when the objective is misspecified. Furthermore, even when objective functions are accurate proxies, sufficiently complex action spaces will have local optima that may result in outputs that are misaligned with the true objective. This is a type of informational asymmetry. Again, we can understand a mismatch between a well-specified objective function and the emergent behaviour of an AI system as an inner alignment problem; hence, a value alignment problem arising (primarily) from informational asymmetries between the principal and the agent is a form of *inner* misalignment.

Although misaligned values (objectives) can exacerbate these problems, as was the case in the principal-agent framework, the key cause of an instance of the value alignment problem is asymmetric information. AI models are based on complex computational systems that are often inherently opaque; further-

[36] See discussion in Goldberg (1987); Mitchell et al. (1992); Lehman and Stanley (2008); Sipper et al. (2018).

[37] A fancy way of saying for a particular situation.

more, this opacity often cannot be eliminated.[38] Ineliminable opacity implies that verifying alignment for sufficiently complex systems or situations may be impossible. This difficulty is worsened when there is no simple matter of fact about what the system should align with in the first place.[39] These considerations echo the insight from economics that "by definition the agent has been selected for his specialized knowledge and the principal can never hope to completely check the agent's performance" (Arrow, 1968, 538). AI systems are often trained to deal with massive datasets that are computationally intractable for humans.

These insights, along with the lack of precision of the standard definition of value alignment discussed above, lead to the following structural definition of the value alignment problem based on the principal-agent framework.

> **The Value Alignment Problem** (Structural Definition)
> A problem that arises from the dynamics of multi-agent interactions involving the delegation of tasks from one actor (a human principal) to another (an AI agent). This problem can arise whenever
>
> (*a*) The agent's objective function is misaligned with the true objective of the principal(s); *or*,
>
> (*b*) There are informational asymmetries between the principal and the agent.

It should be apparent from context that the "or" in this definition is *inclusive*.

This definition suggests that the value alignment problem is not a problem, *per se*, but a *class* of problems, which is instantiated whenever a (human) principal delegates authority to an (artificial) agent to act on its behalf. In this case, a principal might be conceived of as the user, system designer, or company on whose behalf the agent acts. The first axis of the value alignment problem specifies that a problem instance can arise when the objective function is misspecified. This axis is analogous to the competing incentives described in the principal-agent problem but also captures the concept of *outer* alignment described above. The second axis of the value alignment problem specifies that a problem instance can arise when there are informational asymmetries between the (human) principal and the (artificial) agent. This axis corresponds to the informational asymmetries described in the principal-agent problem, but it also captures the concept of *inner* alignment described above. See Figure 3.1.

At the same time, there is a crucial difference between the standard principal-agent problem from economics (where both the principal and the agent are hu-

[38] We will return to questions surrounding transparency and opacity, and their relation to value alignment, in Chapter 5. See also the discussion in Creel (2020).

[39] See discussion in LaCroix (2022); LaCroix and Luccioni (2025).

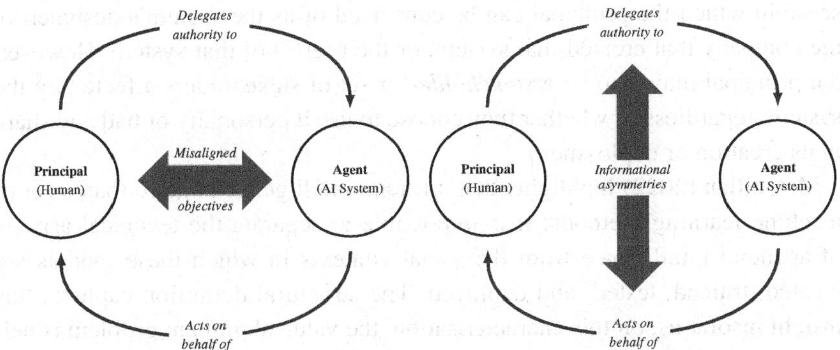

Figure 3.1: Representation of the structural value alignment problem. Misaligned objectives correspond to the outer alignment problem, whereas informational asymmetries correspond to the inner alignment problem

mans) and the structural definition of the value alignment problem for artificial intelligence (where the principal is a human and the agent is an artificial system): namely, in the latter case, we (humans) get to *design* the agent's goals from the ground up, rather than simply engineering their incentives. Thus, the key questions arising from the standard approach to value alignment—what values are "correct" and how do we instantiate them?—remain central to the value alignment problem for artificial intelligence on this structural conceptualisation.

The structural definition of the value alignment problem captures everything that the standard definition is intended to capture, but it provides additional clarity in thinking about how these problems arise. The issue is not *simply* that goals, incentives, values, etc., are misaligned—indeed, even when objective functions perfectly represent our true goals, informational asymmetries between the principal and the agent can still give rise to an instance of the value alignment problem. This insight captures the distinction between inner and outer alignment explicitly. Indeed, we will see in Part II that several pressing issues in AI ethics can be understood as instances of the value alignment problem under this structural definition and, in many cases, they are issues of informational asymmetry rather than misaligned values *per se*.

Finally, a third axis is embedded in the structural definition of the value alignment problem: *relative principals*. The value alignment problem is conceived structurally as a problem that arises when a (human) principal delegates a task to an (artificial) agent. As such, the identity of the principal is central to this definition and whether or not a system can be said to be adequately aligned (with regard to objectives and information). As mentioned, there is an obvious sense in which the principal can be conceived of as the system's designer(s), the company that created that system, or the user(s) of that system. However, the principal may also be a *stakeholder* or set of stakeholders affected by the system, regardless of whether they choose to use it personally or had any share in its creation or deployment.

McQuillan (2022) highlights that artificial intelligence is more than a set of machine learning methods: It is impossible to separate the technical aspects of artificial intelligence from the social contexts in which these models are created, trained, tested, and deployed. The structural definition captures this insight insofar as, on this characterisation, the value alignment problem is neither technical nor normative; it is fundamentally *social*.

3.5 Benefits of the Structural Definition

As mentioned above, the structural definition of value alignment captures the distinction between inner and outer alignment—cashed out in terms of informational asymmetries and misspecified objectives. In addition, the structural definition retains important features pertaining to the technical and normative components of the standard definition, while additionally underscoring the importance of social dynamics in generating instances of the value alignment problem. Hence, all the essential features that we would wish to retain from the standard definition of value alignment are duly reserved. This chapter began by noting some of the shortcomings of the standard definition of the value alignment problem. Ideally, the structural definition would surmount these issues. (Indeed, it does.)

First, I suggested that the standard definition of value alignment is only superficially useful in the sense that it is syntactically meaningful while lacking semantic substance. It is expressive but not informative. In contrast, the structural definition of the value alignment problem makes clear precisely the contexts in which we should expect a problem instance to arise—i.e., when objective functions are poor proxies for the true objective of the system, when there exist informational asymmetries between the principal and the agent, and when we index these considerations to distinct sets of principals. Importantly, the structural definition of the value alignment problem for artificial intelligence makes salient that such problem instances do not occur in a vacuum—insofar as the "values of humanity" are inherently social, the concept of value alignment *must* also be social, and the structural definition reflects this fact.

Second, I suggested that the value alignment problem is often discussed in the context of artificial general intelligence or superintelligence, thus implying that the value alignment problem is a mere means to an end—namely, addressing the control problem. This perspective effectively ignores present-day harms arising from decidedly unintelligent, narrow AI systems. Of course, this fact is more sociological than it is about the definition itself insofar as nothing in the standard definition precludes thinking about present-day harms.

As we shall see in Part II, issues of bias and fairness, transparency and opacity, interpretability, explainability, and justification, privacy and surveillance, environmental considerations, and so on, can be cashed out as instances of the value alignment problem under the standard definition only insofar as the "values of humanity" might be thought to include these things. However, such an approach is inherently ad hoc and lacks substantive conceptual support. In contrast, the structural definition of the value alignment problem for artificial intelligence specifies precisely how, e.g., bias and fairness, are instances of value misalignment insofar as biases can be caused by inadequate proxies in objective functions—e.g., using health insurance claims as a proxy for health risk—or by informational asymmetries—e.g., training models on biased or mislabelled data sets.

Third, whereas the value alignment problem, on its standard definition, is usually discussed at a high level of abstraction, the structural definition grounds problem instances in specific, concrete cases which are anchored by the actual technical workings of the system in question. That is, the structural definition of the value alignment problem makes explicit what is implied by discussions of "imbuing" AI systems with values or "encoding" our values in AI systems. The standard definition says that the value alignment problem is the problem of ensuring that AI systems are aligned with the values of humanity. Implicit in this token of "AI systems" is something along the lines of "the outputs", "the behaviour", "the decisions", "the goals", "the objectives", etc. of these systems. In the context of present-day models, this really means "the objective function" of AI systems insofar as the objective function *determines* the training objectives, which determine fitting parameters, which determine the output of the model.

Although gesturing toward "AI systems' goals, behaviours, values, objectives" leaves the door open for an anthropomorphised version of an AI system, the structural definition specifies the objective function as the key to the first axis of the value alignment problem. Hence, this definition is grounded in the actual functioning of these models as they exist today. This approach engages with the real-world structure of these models, including how they are built, how they are trained, and what they are for. Hence, the structural definition trades vagueness for specificity.

Finally, one of the additional benefits of reconceptualising the value alignment problem for artificial intelligence in terms of the dynamic, structural definition offered here is that it avoids succumbing to *technochauvinism*. Note that the standard definition of the value alignment problem presupposes that these systems are inevitable. Issuing the imperative to align the values of AI systems requires that the creation of those systems is, in some sense, given. The underlying logic is that we *will* create these systems; therefore, we must *ensure* that they are aligned.

Technochauvinism arises, in part, because of assumptions about technological objectivity. It should be clear, then, that the structural definition does not fall prey to technochauvinist leanings like the standard definition. On the one hand, the structural definition highlights the multi-dimensional space under which instantiations of the value alignment problem might arise—objectives, information, and principals. Therefore, this definition reckons with the irreducible variability and relativity of values and what it would mean to align them. In addition, however, nothing in the structural definition of the value alignment problem assumes inevitability. Problem instances can arise when tasks are delegated to AI systems. Once such tasks are delegated, value misalignment in a particular principal-relative context can arise from informational asymmetries or misspecified objective functions. However, this definition does not presuppose that such actions *must* be delegated to AI agents. Thus, no sense of inevitability arises here; we can always choose not to create such systems or not to delegate authority.

Hence, the structural definition of the value alignment problem that I offer here does not succumb to the weaknesses of the standard definition; however, it still captures the key intuitive features of that definition. The remainder of this book applies this reconceptualisation of the value alignment problem. In Part II, we explore each of the three axes of the structural definition of the value alignment problem for artificial intelligence, and I highlight how this conceptualisation of the problem robustly captures some key topics in AI ethics, including issues of bias and fairness, transparency and opacity, and privacy, among others. In Part III, we examine two approaches to "solving" value alignment problems to see how they fare through the lens of the structural definition. In Part IV, we examine novel insights the structural definition gives rise to concerning to the possibility of mitigating value misalignment.

Additional Resource

Jean-Jacques Laffont and David Martimort. 2002. *The Theory of Incentives: The Principal-Agent Model*. Princeton: Princeton University Press.

II

Axes of Value Alignment

Introduction to Part II

In Chapter 3, I proposed the following structural definition of the value alignment problem for artificial intelligence:

> **The Value Alignment Problem** (Structural Definition)
> A problem that arises from the dynamics of multi-agent interactions involving the delegation of tasks from one actor (a human principal) to another (an AI agent). This problem can arise whenever
>
> (*a*) The agent's objective function is misaligned with the true objective of the principal(s); *or*,
>
> (*b*) There are informational asymmetries between the principal and the agent.

This definition has three key axes along which value misalignment might arise: misaligned objectives, asymmetric information, and relative principals. The purpose of this part of the book is to describe each of these components and the types of social or normative problems that can arise in light of them.

Each chapter in this section has a dual purpose. The first is to more clearly specify each of the axes of the value alignment problem on the structural definition; the second is to demonstrate how certain topics in AI ethics can be understood as paradigmatic instantiations of the value alignment problem.

In Chapter 4, I characterise the objectives axis, showing that the key cause of misalignment on this axis arises from reliance on proxies to specify our objectives. I then show how issues of *bias and fairness* are a paradigmatic instance of the value alignment problem along the objectives axis.

In Chapter 5, I characterise the information axis, showing that the key cause of misalignment on this axis arises from informational asymmetries inherent to machine learning models owing to the opacity surrounding model architectures and datasets. In light of this, I demonstrate how issues of *transparency*, *explainability*, and *understandability* are paradigmatic instances of the value alignment problem along the information axis.

In Chapter 6, I characterise the principals axis, showing that the key cause of misalignment on this axis arises from relative principals. I then show how myriad social issues arising in AI ethics constitute instances of the value alignment problem along the principals axis, although they are not usually characterised under the heading of "value alignment" on the standard definition.

4 Objectives

On the structural definition offered in Chapter 3, an instance of the value alignment problem for artificial intelligence can arise whenever a human principal delegates authority to an artificial agent to act on their behalf.

The first axis giving rise to value misalignment on this structural definition pertains to the *objectives* encoded in the model. This can be understood as an instance of the *outer* alignment problem. This component is the one that most people probably have in mind when they invoke the standard definition of the value alignment problem—namely, the problem of ensuring that the values, actions, behaviours, outputs, etc., of an AI system are aligned with the values of humanity. In this case, the "values" encoded in a system are the objectives of that system, formalised by the objective function. However, we saw in Chapter 3 that this standard definition is too vague or superficial to be of practical use. On the one hand, it is unclear what the values of humanity are or ought to be; on the other hand, the standard definition leaves ambiguous what aspects of the AI system should align with those values. Hence, our best normative theories alone cannot offer practical solutions to this problem.

The first axis of the structural definition highlights that the value alignment problem may be instantiated primarily when the objective functions of a machine learning model are misspecified relative to the actual objectives for which the system was designed. Hence, instead of gesturing toward the "values of humanity", the structural definition of the value alignment problem grounds the specification of the problem in the key technical component that drives the abilities of machine learning models—i.e., objective functions (the target of optimisation). Note, however, that this axis makes no reference to the values of humanity because, rather than being a single blanket problem, the structural definition specifies that value alignment is highly context-dependent. Whether an objective *function* is misspecified depends upon what the purpose of the model is. Hence, value alignment comes in degrees.

This chapter further characterises the objectives axis of the value alignment problem in order to determine what features of the structure of objectives are relevant for generating potential misalignment. Recall from Chapter 2 that the objective function serves as a mere proxy for the true objective of the system insofar as true objectives are often difficult, if not impossible, to formalise or specify completely. Hence, objective functions are almost always mere approximations of the true objective. There are several ways in which an objective function can be misspecified, even when it is carefully constructed; however, examining different instances of value misalignment highlights that the key commonality between misspecified objectives arises from the fact that the objective function only approximates what we want the system to accomplish. It is not the existence of an objective function, *per se*, that generates misalignment; rather, it is the fact that the objective function is a proxy for the true objective, and proxies can be better or worse stand-ins for those objectives.

Hence, the first axis of the value alignment problem for artificial intelligence (misspecified objectives) can be cashed out as a proxy problem. If this is right, then a proper understanding of value alignment along this axis requires understanding how proxies are used in (and inherent to) machine learning models. Instances of the value alignment problem will arise on this axis when the proxies that we use to encode objective functions in a machine learning system are bad proxies for the true objective. In this case, the system optimises for something not identical to the true objective, which leads to misaligned outputs or behaviours. This is problematic because deep learning systems are powerful optimisation engines that typically *will* optimise what they are *designed* to optimise. Correspondingly, it is important to ensure that the thing being optimised by the model accurately represents what we want the model to optimise. Hence, the *objectives* axis of the value alignment problem essentially requires ensuring that the proxies for our objectives are good—whatever those objectives may be.

4.1 Proxies and Abstractions

In the context of supervised and unsupervised learning, a model is designed to minimise loss. In this case, the use of proxies, which stand in as representations of their real-world counterparts, can lead to value misalignment at effectively every stage of the algorithmic development pipeline—i.e., during problem specification, data collection and pre-processing, modelling and validation, and deployment.[1]

Problem Specification Proxies. The first step of the algorithmic development pipeline consists of problem specification. Before designing a model to satisfy some objective, it is necessary to decide upon the objective at hand. The choice of a research problem is a value-laden decision which is shaped by the preferences of individual scientists, funding entities, and society at large.[2] In the context of machine learning, once a decision is made regarding the research problem, it is then necessary to specify that problem as a task.[3] Hence, researchers must formalise the true objective by using a proxy. For example, object recognition is a problem which is formalised as optimisation in the context of loss pertaining to labelled images. However, *optimising loss* on a set of labelled images is different from *recognising* images.

As such, the very process of translating a problem of interest into a task that is appropriate for a machine learning model requires a proxy. The formal specification of a task stands in for the actual problem of interest. The degree of alignment between a real-world problem and a problem specification, formalised as a machine learning task, depends inherently upon how readily the problem can be represented in a formal context. Some problems—like playing chess—have formal proxies that are relatively easy to specify and which align relatively well with the actual problem. However, as problems of interest become more complex, more abstract, and require more nuance, we should expect the formal specification to diverge more significantly from the original problem.

Objective Proxies (Loss Functions). Given the structure of the machine learning paradigm, the task (which is a proxy for the true objective or purpose of the model) needs to be further formalised in the specific context of an optimisation problem. The objective function is the target of optimisation. Hence, to train the model, it is necessary to specify an objective function. The objective function is a proxy for what the model is supposed to optimise during the training process. As we saw in Chapter 2, there are many options for an objective function (e.g., mean-squared error, cross-entropy loss, k-means, etc.), each

[1] This characterisation of the "algorithmic development pipeline" follows the description given by Fazelpour and Danks (2021).

[2] See Reiss and Sprenger (2020); further discussion is offered in Chapter 11.

[3] See further discussion in Hildebrandt (2022).

of which may be more or less appropriate for a type of machine learning task (e.g., regression, classification, clustering, etc.).

In each case, the objective function provides a single scalar (or vector) value to represent the optimisation target and furnish information for the learning algorithm used to fit the model to a dataset. As with problem specification, we should expect that the more complex and value-laden our true objectives are, the more difficult it will be to encode them adequately via an objective function because it is often difficult to encode our objectives in a formal language. The problem arises, in this case, because, for many of the things we care about, a single scalar-valued (or even vector-valued) function is too blunt a tool.

Objective Proxies (Reward Functions). In reinforcement learning, the objective function is a proxy because the (long-term) rewards being optimised by an RL agent stand in for some real-world value function. This can lead to misalignment because the reinforcement learning paradigm depends upon sparse rewards for actions. When a machine learning model is rewarded in such a way that the model optimises for the wrong objective (relative to our actual goals), this can lead to the system behaving in counterproductive, unexpected, or harmful ways.

Perverse incentives describe a situation in which the design of a system, policy, or incentive structure leads to unintended and undesirable outcomes. In these cases, a system may act in ways that undermine the principal's intended goals, often because the incentive structure encourages behaviour contrary to the true objective. Perverse incentives often result in unintended and undesirable consequences. At the same time, because there is a trade-off between exploration and exploitation in a reinforcement learning system, perverse incentives can lead to a focus on short-term gains at the expense of long-term objectives. In this case, an agent may prioritise actions that yield immediate rewards, even if those actions are detrimental to the sustainability or overall success of the system in the long run. As with all objectives, step-wise movement toward an objective need not lead to global optima.

Training Proxies. Once a problem is formalised with a proxy task, and once the task is encoded with an objective function, the model parameters are fitted to training data. On the assumption that the formal specification of the task is a good representation of the problem and assuming that the objective function is appropriate for that task, misalignment can still occur because the training data stand as a proxy for the real-world data—i.e., datasets can be better or worse representations of the real world. The current paradigm in machine learning presupposes methodological individualism, which involves framing reality as a collection of individual data points rather than recognising that a training dataset merely serves as a proxy for the desired "truth" an algorithm is meant to learn.[4] Hence, the degree to which the training data actually represent the distributions they are supposed to will affect the degree to which a model is aligned.

As with problem specification and objectives, some tasks will lend themselves more readily to representative data. Again, playing chess is a good example of the simple case: there is a clearly defined and easily represented matter of fact as to what constitutes a win, loss, or draw. As the contexts that data used to train machine learning models are supposed to represent become more complex, we should expect that those data will stand in as poorer representations of the real world. This is one of the key components of questions surrounding algorithmic bias and fairness, which, on the structural definition of the value alignment problem for artificial intelligence, is a paradigmatic example of an instance of misalignment arising from the first axis. (We will explore this topic in more detail in Section 4.3.)

Generalisation Proxies. The task is a representation, and hence a proxy, of the true objective. The objective function formalises the task as an optimisation problem and hence serves as a proxy for the task. The distribution of features in the training data on which the model is optimised is a proxy for the actual distribution of features in the real world. If we assume that the formal representation of the task at hand is appropriately and accurately specified as an optimisation problem and that the objective function captures all the relevant features of that problem, then the minimisation of a loss function is supposed to measure performance on the true objective. Hence, the loss function is supposed to measure generalisation error for a given objective.

Whereas optimisation occurs on the training set, loss is measured on the test set. Although it is important to ensure that one does not test one's model on training data, the training set and test set are typically drawn from the same dataset. Hence, just as the training data are a mere proxy for real-world distributions, so too are test data. This fact implies that performance in the general domain (i.e., the real world) is measured via a proxy—namely, performance on the test set.[5] The hope is that by optimising on the training set, the model also optimises on the test set—i.e., it achieves some degree of generalisation—and that this generalisation will further generalise to the real world. Again whether the test set is a good proxy for generalisation depends on whether the data

---

[4]For a description of methodological individualism, see Heath (2020). For an analysis of methodological individualism in the context of machine learning, see Hildebrandt (2022).

[5]See discussion in Goodfellow et al. (2016, Sec. 5.2).

are representative of real-world data. When datasets are not good proxies, AI models can fail if they encounter heterogeneous contexts in deployment.[6] Performance in this context is often measured via benchmarks.

Benchmarking Proxies. To determine whether a model performs well on a given task, it is necessary to define the metrics that will be used to measure the model's performance.[7] Metrics for a model's success are proxies for genuine success on the actual task at hand. However, these metrics may not be directly optimised for many tasks—for example, when they are non-differentiable or too complex to measure directly. Hence, the objective function (which is both differentiable and mathematically tractable) is used as a substitute for the desired metric.

In addition, most current benchmarks test model performance on independently and identically distributed (i.i.d.) test data; however, such benchmarks are inadequate for distinguishing between intended and unintended solutions to an optimisation problem. Consequently, these can fail to generalise to *out-of-distribution* (o.o.d.) examples.[8] As Gebru et al. (2021) highlight: "a model is unlikely to perform well in the wild if its deployment context does not match its training or evaluation datasets" (1). Hence, using performance metrics frequently overlooks the inherent characteristics of computable proxies and their constraints. This fact underscores that the very notion of "progress" in machine learning, as in any purportedly scientific field, is deeply value-laden. "Progress" is always relative to a standard, and what counts as a standard is socially determined (often by those who hold the most power in society).

In addition, the presentation of these metrics often obfuscates their reliance on proxies. This fact highlights the epistemic issues that can arise when the *proxy* of the target is mistaken for the target itself—i.e., the thing for which the proxy is supposed to stand.

Finally, although AI models perform well (according to standard metrics) on specific tasks for which the models are fitted to data, they are "often brittle outside the narrow domain they have been trained on" (Bengio et al., 2021). This is problematic insofar as the world is constantly changing—what is referred to in the field as *distributional shift* or *drift*. Thus, even if a model accurately captures the (true) underlying distribution in a dataset, real-world data are not static.

---

[6] See examples in Eche et al. (2021).

[7] The topic of benchmarking will be discussed in more detail in Chapter 9 when we explore methods for measuring degrees of misalignment.

[8] See discussion in Jacobsen et al. (2020); Geirhos et al. (2023).

A summary of the formally-specifiable proxies used in lieu of real-world goals at each stage of the algorithmic development pipeline is provided in Table 4.1.

Table 4.1: Examples of proxies at various stages of the algorithmic development pipeline

Development Stage	Actual Goal	Formal Proxy
Problem Specification	Real-world problem	Task
Model Design	Principal's objective	Objective function
Training	Real-world data	Training data
Generalisation	Real-world data	Test data
Benchmarking	Real-world data	Benchmarking datasets / metrics

Case Study: Predictive Policing. To underscore how badly things can go wrong when proxies are not adequately attended to, let us consider a specific example: *predictive policing*.

We might think that crime is a problem.[9] We might also think that effective policing helps reduce crime.[10] Hence, a problem to be solved—crime rates—is approximated by effective policing. Predictive policing models seek to solve a problem of resource allocation. This is an optimisation problem, meaning that it appears appropriate for a machine learning model. Keeping in mind that the actual goal is to *reduce* crime, the *task* is to allocate policing resources effectively by predicting where crime is most likely to occur and then sending police to those areas.

However, because the objective of predicting where crime is most likely to occur involves a future contingent, it is impossible to optimise directly. Hence, the objective function seeks to optimise a prediction of possible future crime based on historical data. Past crime serves as a proxy for future crime.

Worse still, the training data in this case do not actually measure *crime* rates because the available data can only logically include *observed* and *reported* crime—i.e., arrests. If a crime occurred in a neighbourhood, and no one observed it, then for the purposes of training the model, that crime did not occur.

[9] This is probably not true insofar as what gets classified as crime is often a reflection of the values of a specific culture or society, and the occurrence of crime is often a symptom of a larger systemic problem.

[10] This is probably not true insofar as police can only *punish* crime; they cannot *prevent* it. Recent studies have suggested that there is no (consistent) association between police funding and crime rates across municipalities; furthermore, net increases in police funding (measured via spending per capita) are not associated with a net decrease in crime rates (Seabrook et al., 2023).

Similarly, if a crime occurred and was observed, but no report was made, then for the purposes of training the model, the crime did not occur.

In fact, the situation is worse than this. Since social contexts like crime rates are dynamic, historical data that are further in time from the present are less relevant to predicting trends in the near future. Hence, it is necessary to continually update the model for it to maintain (a semblance of) predictive accuracy. The data obtained for predictive policing models are based on historical instances of arrests; those data are used to direct resources, which means that areas that have been historically over-policed are more likely to have increased police presence. Furthermore, we should expect more arrests in areas with a police presence than in areas without (since arrests cannot occur when no police are present). Hence, those neighbourhoods will be over-represented in subsequent training data. The biases inherent in policing will become further entrenched as these models are increasingly deployed.[11] For this reason, Benjamin (2019) calls predictive policing a "crime production algorithm" (83). But recall that the *actual goal* of the model was to reduce crime!

This case study highlights how value misalignment can occur on the first axis of the structural definition alone. One necessary condition for a machine learning system to be value-aligned is that the proxies used to build that system are good approximations of the true objective. Since this is impossible in the case of predicting future crime, it follows that *no such model* can be value-aligned on the structural definition. The situation is exacerbated when we consider the other two axes in conjunction with the first, as we will see in Chapters 5 and 6. (Although the three axes of value alignment are orthogonal in the sense that a reduction of misalignment on one axis does not necessarily lead to a corresponding reduction on another axis, there are often interaction effects between them.)

4.2 Insights from the Structural Definition

When the objective functions of machine learning models are poorly specified, it can result in a misalignment of values. This fact is unsurprising: it encapsulates the intuitive understanding that motivates discussions of the value alignment problem on the standard definition. However, the structural definition sheds additional light on the proximal cause of misalignment. Specifically, it highlights that objectives encoded in a machine learning model are mere prox-

[11] See discussion in O'Neil (2016); Lum and Isaac (2016); Ensign et al. (2018); Benjamin (2019); Broussard (2023).

ies for our true objectives. Moreover, it demonstrates how proxies permeate every aspect of a machine learning system. Hence, the more surprising insight from the structural definition of the value alignment problem is how ubiquitous proxies are; they manifest in the context of objective functions but also in every other facet of a machine-learning model. This section explores some additional problems arising from this insight.

Case Study: Incomplete Specifications. As proxies for true objectives or values, objective functions are *necessarily* incomplete. In the context of reward functions for RL agents, researchers have noted that it is effectively impossible to encode *everything* we value in a value *function*.[12] The *complexity of value thesis* suggests that human values have high Kolmogorov complexity.[13] If this is true, then it logically follows that a simple set of rules cannot capture human values (in a robust sense).

Therefore, simple models and applications will lend themselves more readily to alignment on this axis. There is a well-defined value function for playing games like chess or Go, which is part of the reason deep reinforcement learning has succeeded in these areas, meaning that such (narrow) programs can be aligned. However, as the problems we seek to solve or the objectives we seek to satisfy become more complex, even cleverly designed task specifications, objectives functions, etc., will fail to represent these objectives adequately. As before, the formalisation is too blunt a tool. Again, this is problematic when we consider the capacity of these systems to optimise *exactly* what they are designed to optimise (regardless of whether that is the intention).[14]

Case Study: Nonexistent Baselines. The discussion of proxies as a key driver of value misalignment along the objectives axis has, thus far, presupposed a baseline exists relative to which a proxy can be more or less aligned. In some cases, models are created for tasks that have *nonexistent* baselines. For example, some models seek to classify individuals according to personality traits or other psychometrics.[15] However, measurable proxies like body language, speech patterns, written text, etc., often do not correlate with person-

---

[12] See, for example, Yudkowsky (2011); Muehlhauser and Helm (2013); Han et al. (2022).

[13] Kolmogorov complexity measures the simplicity or compressibility of a piece of information. In essence, it quantifies the length of the shortest possible program (algorithm) that can generate the information or data. See discussion in AI Alignment Forum (2009).

[14] For this reason, Goethe's 1797 poem *Der Zauberlehrling* ("The Sorcerer's Apprentice", popularised in the modern era by a segment in the 1940 film *Fantasia*), is often invoked as an allegory for artificial intelligence today.

[15] See, for example, Evin et al. (2022).

ality and the personality types under which people are classified are often based on pseudoscience—e.g., the Myers-Briggs Type Indicator (MBTI). Nonetheless, these models are deployed for hiring (Raghavan et al., 2019).

Some models seek to classify emotion. However, because emotions are not observable, these models classify proxies for emotions, like *facial expressions* or some other observable proxy. However, research has shown that the outward communication of internal emotions varies substantially across cultures, situations, and individuals. The superficial validity of this type of model depends inherently upon an assumption about the readability of emotion from facial expressions. Such an assumption is relatively well-entrenched in the sense that it "influences legal judgments, policy decisions, national security protocols, and educational practices; guides the diagnosis and treatment of psychiatric illness, as well as the development of commercial applications; and pervades everyday social interactions" (Barrett et al., 2019, 1). However, considering alignment on the objectives axis forces the realisation that a model for detecting emotions is really a model for detecting facial expressions. There is no observable baseline for emotions; hence, such a model can never be aligned with this goal. Regardless, "emotion detection" AI is a multi-billion dollar industry (Engine, 2021).

Models that seek to classify behaviour as "moral" or "immoral" sometimes presuppose that there is an objective matter of fact about the situation in question, ignoring deep and complicated metaethical considerations (and, indeed, the possibility that no such baseline exists). What these models really measure are often sociological facts about reported beliefs regarding normative decision-making contexts.[16] Nonetheless, some have argued that performance on moral questions can be used as a guide for determining how or whether an AI system is aligned with human morality. (We will return to this in more detail in Chapter 9.)

Case Study: Batch Learning and Feedback Loops. Batch learning, also known as offline learning, is a machine learning framework where the model is trained on a fixed dataset (referred to as a batch) without the need for additional updates during the training process.[17] That said, in this framework, the decisions made by the system after it is deployed may be used to supplement training data for the next batch. Ensign et al. (2018) highlight that this makes batch learning frameworks inappropriate for certain decision-making models that are

[16] See LaCroix (2022) for additional discussion.

[17] In this context, batch learning stands in contrast to online learning, where models are updated continuously as new data become available.

re-trained on successor data that *includes* real-world effects from the decisions rendered by those systems in these data—e.g., recommendations about hiring, loans, policing, and parole. In these cases, biases inherent in training data can be amplified, which means that misalignment will be exacerbated as these models proliferate and their outputs become part of training data. Hence, this feedback loop can worsen misalignment on the objectives axis insofar as an initially misaligned proxy, like training on biased data, causes the initial proxy to be a worse approximation of the real-world objective in successor models.

In effect, feedback loops of this form imply that when a system is only slightly misaligned at the outset, subsequent systems can increase in how misaligned they are. Note that this is true even if the objective function is perfectly well specified: when the datasets on which machine learning models are trained are themselves biased, the system is misaligned insofar as the dataset is a proxy for real-world data; hence, the structural definition of the value alignment problem explains *how* such a system can be misaligned even on the assumption that the objectives themselves are well specified. This insight underscores that the problem of value alignment is not primarily technical. It further demonstrates that issues of bias and fairness in AI ethics are paradigmatic instances of the value alignment problem along the objectives axis.

4.3 Bias and Fairness

Bias takes on various conceptual interpretations contingent upon the specific context under consideration. In its broadest and most neutral sense, bias is a deviation from a certain standard (Danks and London, 2017). Hence, statistical bias is a formal sense of bias which denotes a deviation from some *statistical* standard. As such, the nature of the bias and whether it holds normative significance is inherently tied to the standard used as a baseline for measuring deviation. In simpler terms, if the reference standard is purely descriptive, the bias lacks normative weight. For example, relative to statistical distributions of height, the height of a set of basketball players is biased toward the taller end of the distribution of heights of the superset of individuals in society. It is worth noting that a key feature of any bias—even merely statistical or descriptive deviations from some standard—is that they are *epistemically* bad insofar as they fail to track truth about some real-world distribution.[18]

In contrast, if the reference standard involves societal or moral norms, the bias inherently carries normative implications. For example, we might consider

[18]Consider an individual who forms a *belief* about height distributions based on a set of basketball players. Although such a belief may be normatively neutral, it would be descriptively false.

biases deviating from moral, legal, social, psychological, etc., norms. Statistical biases become normative when we consider the baseline question of what a distribution *ought* to be. In this sense, statistical biases can be useful for identifying biases with normative weight. For instance, the under-representation of women in STEM fields (Science, Technology, Engineering, and Maths) illuminates structural inequalities and systemic barriers in these fields based on the normative view that they ought to exhibit gender parity (Danks and London, 2017).

Moral bias arises when morally insignificant characteristics impact morally relevant judgements. For instance, race is irrelevant to criminality, making decisions regarding recidivism risk or criminal sentencing based on race illegitimate. Similarly, gender is irrelevant to job performance, so it is illegitimate to use gender as a criterion for selecting one job candidate over another (Danks and London, 2017). So too, socioeconomic status, being morally irrelevant to one's inherent ability or right to receive education or medical care, should not unduly influence decisions in these domains.

A model trained on biased data or objectives may perpetuate and exacerbate existing social, economic, or cultural biases. Minimally, a model will be misaligned in an inert sense that it gets the facts wrong—particularly when considering outliers in a dataset. In cases where our objectives carry some normative weight, this inert sense of misalignment can transform into value misalignment.

Computational Bias. Friedman and Nissenbaum (1996) categorise biases in computer systems into three distinct types: pre-existing bias, technical bias, and emergent bias. Pre-existing bias is a type of bias that already exists in an institution, society, or culture, which is then encoded in or reproduced by a computer system. Often, this can happen unintentionally when, e.g., a programmer has not considered the potential normative aspects of their system. This is particularly problematic when considering that those who design AI systems are typically white, male, abled, English-speaking, middle-class US citizens (Broussard, 2023). (The implication is that those individuals' situated perspectives will influence their work, explicitly or implicitly.)

Hence, implicit assumptions about the similarity between the programmer(s) and the users of these systems can lead to value misalignment. In this case, the cognitive biases of the creators of programs can instantiate the value alignment problem. Emergent bias is a type of bias that can emerge when a use-context or user base shifts for a technology. For example, Microsoft's Tay bot was designed to take in feedback from human users; hence, it "learned" to act in a way that we would call racist and sexist after interacting with Twitter users.[19] Pre-existing and emergent biases of this sort fall properly along the *principals* axis of the value alignment problem, which is explored in more detail in Chapter 6.

More relevant to the objectives axis, technical bias concerns the performance of a system and how this performance may recapitulate biases against certain individuals or groups. For example, optical sensors have historically performed more poorly on darker skin tones than lighter ones; more recently, facial recognition algorithms have had similar failures. [20]

In many cases, bias can arise because a model learns to condition its outputs on irrelevant attributes so that its decisions are made based on spurious correlations. For example, in image recognition tasks, a neural network may learn to rely on irrelevant features of images, like the background, secondary objects, object textures, etc.[21] These failures are especially concerning when considering models that could be deployed in high-risk contexts, like medical imaging.[22] More relevant to the case of moral bias in machine learning systems, neural network models can learn to condition their outputs on sensitive attributes, like gender, race, etc. when those attributes are irrelevant to the context.

Fairness Through Unawareness. Intuitively, if you do not want your algorithm to conditionalise on sensitive attributes, like race or gender, then perhaps you could simply *remove* those attributes from the dataset on which the model is trained. It seems to follow that it would then be impossible for your model to learn anything about those attributes and, therefore, impossible for the model to condition upon those attributes in, e.g., classification. This naïve approach to bias mitigation is sometimes referred to as *fairness through unawareness*.

However, it turns out that, rather than making a model impartial, removing sensitive attributes from training data is both ineffective and harmful. Indeed, removing sensitive attributes from datasets can make it *harder* to de-bias algorithms because the programmers do not have access to the attributes of the data that would allow them to statistically measure whether their models discriminate against certain groups.

Furthermore, models that utilise deep neural networks typically will "discover" sensitive attributes because they require large datasets to be trained.

[19] See reporting in Wakefield (2016); Dewey (2016); Bright (2016).

[20] Specific examples are given in Buolamwini and Gebru (2018); Buolamwini (2023).

[21] Specific examples are given in Sagawa et al. (2020); Xiao et al. (2020); Moayeri et al. (2022).

[22] See, e.g., Zech et al. (2018); Oakden-Rayner et al. (2020).

When the number of features of data in a dataset is large, sensitive attributes are often redundant across combinations of features. In this case, if many features have very small correlations with sensitive attributes, the combination of those features can be used to build a highly accurate classifier for the attribute in question.[23] For example, Poplin et al. (2018) showed that gender can be predicted with high accuracy from retinal photographs.[24] In light of the limitations (and risks) of simply excluding sensitive attributes from datasets, researchers have sought to formalise fairness criteria for application in machine learning.

4.4 Algorithmic Bias

More practical approaches to mitigating the possibility of bias in algorithmic systems first define a mathematical criterion for fairness.

The Mathematics of Fairness. Barocas et al. (2023) discuss three criteria that seek to define (and measure) the absence of discrimination in a statistical distribution—e.g., a dataset. Each criterion is supposed to capture intuitive features of what it means to be fair. For example, *demographic parity*, *statistical parity*, *group fairness*, *disparate impact*, etc., can all be classified as a type of *equal acceptance rate*, which applies when two random variables are statistically *independent*. That is, rates of acceptance are independent of group membership, reflecting an intuitive understanding of *equality*.

Whereas *independence* calls for two random variables to be unconditionally statistically independent, a second fairness criterion, *separation*, is defined as the independence of two random variables *conditional* on some third random variable. Hence, separation describes the extent to which the predictions made by a machine learning model are independent of certain protected attributes or sensitive features. Good separation implies the model makes predictions primarily based on the factors that are relevant to the problem rather than picking up on attributes—like gender or race—that are irrelevant. Separation requires that false positive rates are identical to false negative rates for distinct groups—i.e., *error rate parity*.

A final formal criterion for non-discrimination is called *sufficiency*. This is related to *calibration*, which refers to the alignment between the predicted probabilities or scores generated by a machine learning model and the actual likelihood of an event occurring. Essentially, it assesses how well the model's predicted probabilities match the true outcomes. A calibrated model is one

---

[23] Additional discussion is given in Barocas et al. (2023).

[24] Note that the model described by Poplin et al. (2018) used binary classification for gender.

where, for instance, if the model predicts a 70% probability of an event happening, it should actually happen about 70% of the time on average.

Despite dozens of formal definitions of fairness, each of which probably captures at least some facet of what it means to be fair, Barocas et al. (2023) argue that these definitions can be (more or less) reduced to the three described here.

Case Study: COMPAS. A standard case study when discussing bias and fairness in the context of algorithmic decision-making is the use of algorithms to predict recidivism risk. Attempts to use statistics to undergird prediction and give decisions the appearance of increased objectivity are not new. The specific case of recidivism prediction in the United States has a century-long history.[25]

In the 1930s, Illinois instituted a predictive parole system; by 1951, a *Manual of Parole Prediction* was published, reporting on the prior 20 years of research and practice. This manual included a final section, "Scoring by Machine Methods", which considers punch cards for automating and streamlining the data collection process, model building, and outputting predictions. When the *Association of Paroling Authorities International* published their 2003 *Handbook for New Parole Board Members*, it stated that in the present day, "making parole decisions without benefit of a good, research-based risk assessment instrument clearly falls short of accepted best practice" (Burke, 2003, 35).

COMPAS (*correctional offender management profiling for alternative sanctions*), created by Northpointe, is one of this era's most widely used tools.[26] This tool utilised a simple statistical model based on weighted linear combinations of things like current age, age at first arrest, and criminal history to determine a "violent recidivism risk score"—i.e., a score from 1 to 10 that predicted whether an inmate, if released, would go on to commit a violent or non-violent crime within approximately 1–3 years.[27] By the end of 2007, all 57 New York counties outside of New York City had adopted COMPAS, and by 2011, state law in New York *required* the use of risks and needs assessments when making parole decisions.

However, this tone shifted in 2016 when Julia Angwin and her team at ProPublica published an exposé on machine bias (Angwin et al., 2016). After doing some exploratory analysis on COMPAS data, Angwin's team found that the

[25]Further historical details are provided in Christian (2020, Ch. 2).

[26]Northpointe, Inc. changed its name to "Equivant" after a 2017 re-branding effort.

[27]It is worth noting that COMPAS is a privately developed algorithm, which means that no one but Northpointe knows *precisely* how COMPAS calculates a risk score or what specific data it considers when doing so. See further discussion in Park (2019).

risk scores—1 to 10—were evenly distributed for Black defendants. In contrast, they were more weighted toward low risk scores for white defendants. After analysing the criminal records of 18,000 individuals, they ruled out the possibility that these data were skewed because, e.g., Black defendants were, *in fact*, higher risk than white defendants. Rather, the model was biased against Black defendants.

Northpointe published an official rebuttal to the claim of bias in their model, stating that "when the correct classification statistics are used, the data do not substantiate the ProPublica claim of racial bias toward Blacks" (Larson and Angwin, 2016). They argued that COMPAS meets two essential criteria for fairness: First, COMPAS predictions were *equally accurate* for Black and white defendants. Hence, the model satisfies the independence criterion for fairness described above.

Second, the 1–10 risk scores had the same *meaning*, regardless of the defendant's race—i.e., a defendant with a risk score of, e.g., 7 went on to re-offend the same percentage of the time, regardless of race. This satisfies *calibration*, which is related to the *sufficiency* condition described above. Northpointe argued that because COMPAS was *equally accurate* (independent) and *calibrated* (sufficient), it logically followed that it was *mathematically impossible* for the tool to be biased.

Angwin and her team agreed that COMPAS was calibrated. Furthermore, it was true that the model was accurate in the sense that it predicted with 61% accuracy for both white and Black defendants whether they would go on to re-offend. However, closer examination of the 39% of the time that COMPAS was wrong, shows that it is wrong in different ways. Black defendants were twice as likely to be rated higher risk but not re-offend (false positives). In contrast, white defendants were twice as likely to be charged with new crimes after being classified as lower risk (false negatives). In this sense, the model failed to satisfy the *separation* criterion mentioned above.

This highlights that whether the tool itself is "fair" depends inherently upon which statistical metrics were the correct ones to define and measure fairness in the first place. Northpointe highlighted that the error *rate* rather than the error *type* was important. In contrast, ProPublica emphasised the *type* of errors that COMPAS made and highlighted that it appeared to consistently overestimate the risk of Black defendants who did not re-offend and underestimate the risk of white defendants who did re-offend. Thus, whether COMPAS was "fair" effectively boiled down to a conflict between two different, equally intuitive mathematical definitions of fairness.

Impossibility Proofs. Instead of trying to justify whether one fairness criterion is more important than another, one might think that a model like COMPAS could be debiased by simply changing some component of the model to ensure that all three fairness criteria (independence, separation, and sufficiency) are satisfied. However, it turns out that jointly satisfying all three criteria is *mathematically impossible*.

Kleinberg et al. (2017) presented an impossibility theorem related to fairness in the context of risk assessment.[28] They demonstrated that, under certain conditions, it is impossible to simultaneously satisfy three fairness criteria: calibration (equal positive outcome rates across groups), equality of opportunity (equal false negative rates across groups), and disparate impact (equal false positive rates across groups). The "certain conditions" are that the base rates are equal. However, as a contingent socio-historical fact, the base rates are unequal in the United States. Differential base rates with respect to incarceration, in this case, are based on historical and ongoing systemic racism (Alexander, 2010). However, the model could be made to be (mathematically) fair if society were made to be fair (at least in principle).

That said, even apparently unbiased proxies can give rise to biases when real-world phenomena are hidden. For example, a model for predicting which patients are most likely to benefit from high-risk care management is trained on data from previous health insurance claims. This is a proxy for actual health risk. Obermeyer et al. (2019) showed that even though the algorithm's risk score was not racially biased (concerning the output distribution of risk scores), the *actual* health burden of Black people was significantly greater because Black people might wait until they are *very* sick before making an insurance claim. The model ignores this fact because it uses a proxy. These examples underscore that algorithmic bias, despite being an ostensibly technical problem, does not readily admit of a technical solution. In these cases, the underlying causes of misalignment are often social, structural, and systemic rather than purely technical.

Impossibility proofs underscore the complexity of addressing bias and fairness in machine learning models. They suggest that, in some scenarios, tradeoffs between competing fairness criteria are inevitable, and achieving "perfect fairness" (whatever that might consist of) may be impossible. Hence, again, questions regarding degrees of alignment along the objectives axis must be properly indexed to a principal. However, these problems can be made worse by informational asymmetries.

---

[28] See also Chouldechova (2017); Berk et al. (2017).

Intersectionality. Considerations of *intersectionality* can exacerbate unfairness. Intersectionality describes the fact that social categories like race, class, and gender can combine to create overlapping and interdependent systems of oppression, discrimination, or disadvantage (Crenshaw, 1989, 1991).[29] Related to intersectionality is Collins's (1990) concept of a *matrix of domination*. This concept posits that systems of oppression are mutually constituted, and an individual's position within this matrix serves to confer both penalties and privileges.

In societies that have multiple axes of oppression—e.g., racism, colonialism, ableism, hetero- and cissexism, classism, etc.—people who belong to more than one oppressed group often experience oppression in distinctive ways that are highly particular. For example, the discrimination experienced by a queer woman of colour is not merely the sum of the discrimination she might experience as queer, as gendered, or as racialised. These patterns of oppression can be difficult to predict and understand from the perspective of those who do not share similar social positions and experiences.

Buolamwini and Gebru (2018) showed that face analysis models trained primarily on lighter-skinned faces underperform for darker-skinned faces. Similarly, those same algorithms, trained primarily on male-coded faces, underperform for female-coded faces. This is unsurprising, given that unrepresentative datasets lead to biased outputs (as discussed above). More surprising, perhaps, is that Buolamwini and Gebru (2018) demonstrated that these models perform *even worse* on *combinations* of features—such as skin colour and gender—than might be expected by considering those features independently. For example, the `Face++` model has an overall error rate of around 10%. It has significantly lower error rates for male-coded (0.7%) versus female-coded (21.3%) faces, and it has significantly lower error rates for lighter-skinned (4.7%) versus darker-skinned (16.5%) faces. Importantly, the model performs much worse for the darker-skinned female-coded category (34.5% error) than it does for any other combination of categories: darker-skinned male, lighter-skinned female, and lighter-skinned male had error rates of 0.7%, 6.0%, and 0.8%, respectively.[30]

Many analyses of biased distributions concerning, e.g., error rates, focus solely on a single feature, like race or gender. What should be apparent is

---

[29] Although Crenshaw (1991) coined the term "intersectionality", feminist scholars have noted that the concept has deeper roots, having been expressed in a statement by the Black feminist activist group, the Combahee River Collective (1977), and bell hooks (hooks, 1984). See further discussion in D'Ignazio and Klein (2020).

[30] See Buolamwini and Gebru (2018) for complete data and comparison with other models.

that emphasis on a single axis in considering the existence and mitigation of algorithmic bias is insufficient for ensuring fairness (Costanza-Chock, 2020, 19).

Technical approaches to debiasing models seek to ensure that certain features, like gender or race, do not play into the outputs of contexts where those features are irrelevant. However, because of the complex interplay of different axes of oppression, simply "removing", e.g., gender bias (when this is even possible), may introduce noise that affects other axes of oppression—like race, disability status, etc. This problem is aggravated further by *unobservable features*.

Unobserved Characteristics. A further complicating factor is that we can only tell if an algorithm is fair to a community or take steps to avoid bias against that community if we can establish community membership. Most research on algorithmic bias and fairness has focused on (ostensibly) *observable* features that might be present in training data—paradigmatically, race and gender. However, features of marginalised communities may be *unobservable*, making bias mitigation even more difficult.

Some examples of prototypically unobservable characteristics include queerness, disability status, neurotype, class, and religion (Tomasev et al., 2021). Note that this effectively recapitulates the problem of *fairness through unawareness* discussed above: when observable features have been excised from the training data to prevent models from exploiting them, it becomes impossible to measure and mitigate against potential biases in that system. In the case of unobservable characteristics, these features are often absent from datasets at the outset. As we have seen, an attribute has to be measured and recorded to be included in training or evaluation data for an algorithm.

Unobservable characteristics, like sexual orientation or gender identity, may be logistically excluded from datasets due to anti-parity considerations. However, individuals may also choose not to disclose, e.g., non-normative sexual identity, gender identity, neurotype, etc., because of social stigma or because disclosure may threaten an individual's privacy or safety.[31]

At the same time, sexual orientation and gender identity are not static features. Thus, these types of "unobserved characteristics" are fundamentally unmeasurable in the way that is required by the machine learning paradigm.

[31] For example, Tudor (2023) describes recent anti-trans and anti-LGBTQ rhetoric as the "supernational unification of far right, centrist and leftist agents using anti-gender, anti-feminist and transphobic mobilisations, populist affects and strategic disinformation as accelerators for hateful and anti-democratic agendas". See also Johnstone (2023).

The difficulty surrounding the possibility of mitigating bias in the case of unobserved characteristics becomes more pressing when we consider that the communities that share these characteristics often have experienced historical oppression—in addition to contemporary challenges.

Thus, Tomasev et al. (2021) highlight that standard metrics (like group fairness) are not going to be adequate for ensuring that an algorithm is not biased toward, e.g., queer communities or individuals. As such, it is necessary to move beyond purely computational approaches to assess fully the socio-technical aspects of the technology being deployed.

4.5 The Social Character of Objectives

I argued in Section 4.1 that value misalignment can occur at any stage of the algorithmic development pipeline based on the proxies utilised at each stage. I also suggested that bias is a paradigmatic instance of value misalignment on the objectives axis. It should be relatively unsurprising that Fazelpour and Danks (2021) argue that bias, too, can arise at any stage of the algorithmic development pipeline.

At the problem specification level, choosing the goals of a model involves value judgements, potentially introducing bias based on funded projects and power dynamics. The problem specification is a proxy for project goals, and biases can lead to misalignment. Biases at this level are not unique to AI but are exacerbated in machine learning due to data dependence. Hence, biases injected into a system via misaligned proxies at the level of problem specification can lead to further biases (and further misalignment) during training (Mitchell et al., 2021).

At the level of training, dataset biases stemming from unrepresentative or incomplete data contribute to biased models (Danks and London, 2017). For instance, the PULSE face super-resolution algorithm was trained on a biased dataset containing images of faces of mostly white celebrities.[32] This model generated a high-resolution image of a white face when "upsampling" a pixelated image of Barack Obama[33] (Vincent, 2020). However, better representation alone does not fix this problem. Even when training datasets are completely representative of populations, they may still be biased if the society

[32] See Menon et al. (2020). PULSE was trained on the `CelebA HQ` dataset, which consists of 30,000 high-resolution (1024×1024) photos of celebrities (Karras et al., 2018). However, `CelebA HQ`, like many other existing public face datasets, is biased toward lighter-skinned faces, meaning that individuals with darker skin are underrepresented (Kärkkäinen and Joo, 2019).

[33] The first Black president of the United States.

in which the training data were generated is structurally biased against certain groups, like marginalised communities—i.e., *bias in, bias out* (Mayson, 2018). Ensuring diverse and representative datasets may not be enough to ensure value alignment along the objectives axis, as these datasets can still reflect structural biases in society.

At the same time, we have seen that the choice of fairness metrics during modelling and validation involves subjective judgements with inconsistent definitions. Deployed algorithms interacting with societal structures can create pernicious feedback loops that entrench biases.[34] The potential for algorithmic bias and a lack of representation may exacerbate discrimination against marginalised communities, entrenching existing power dynamics and societal inequalities.[35] The resulting models may codify and entrench systems of power and oppression, including capitalism and classism; sexism, misogyny, and patriarchy; colonialism and imperialism; racism and white supremacy; ableism; and cis- and heteronormativity. It is worth considering whether this is a feature, rather than a bug, of these systems by asking whose goals are being instantiated; we will return to this question in Chapter 6.

Moreover, the emphasis on formal definitions of "fairness" overlooks the fundamentally normative nature of the concept. For example, it is important to distinguish normative concepts like *discrimination*, *fairness*, and related terms; otherwise, fairness is used as a placeholder for several distinct normative concepts, making its analysis and operationalisation more difficult (Binns, 2021). This underscores the fact that "fairness" is only well-defined within a context, meaning that the context-free use of fairness in the machine learning literature gives rise to underdetermination and ambiguity: fairness "requires reference to values, principles, and commitments that themselves typically have substance only in specificity" (Green and Hu, 2018, 1).[36] All this suggests the need to move from a purely mathematical conceptualisation of fairness toward a more substantive evaluation of whether algorithms promote justice in practice (Green, 2022). Hence, alignment on the objectives axis requires maintaining sensitivity to power dynamics, which requires considering historical inequities and labour conditions encoded in data (Miceli et al., 2022).

The structural definition of the value alignment problem for artificial intelligence gives precedence to the role of social dynamics in generating problem instances. Value misalignment along the objectives axis arises when the

[34]See analysis in O'Neil (2016).

[35]See discussion in Buolamwini and Gebru (2018); Raji and Buolamwini (2019); Raji et al. (2022).

[36]See also discussion in Jacobs and Wallach (2021); Lee et al. (2021); Selbst et al. (2019).

proxies we use to create and deploy machine learning models are poor approximations for our real-world objectives. Johnson (2020a) argues that because biases are often *emergent*, identifying, mitigating, or evaluating biases with standard resources—e.g., those of epistemology or ethics—can be difficult. Unsurprisingly, the culprit that Johnson (2020a) identifies as a proximal cause of these difficulties is what she calls *the proxy problem* since "reliance on proxies will be a necessary feature of most inductive reasoning" (9955).[37] Such problems do not lend themselves to purely technical solutions—in the case of bias, specifically, and value alignment, more generally.

4.6 Summary

The standard definition of the value alignment problem is too vague to be useful in characterising actual instances of misalignment. In contrast, the structural definition clarifies what it means for a system to be aligned along three distinct axes. The first axis, objectives, can give rise to an instance of the value alignment problem when the proxies that we use to design, create, and deploy machine learning models and AI systems are poor representations of *why* we (the principal) sought to create the model in the first place.

Embedded within machine learning, as an approach to artificial intelligence, is the concept that the most effective way to address a given problem involves identifying an objective to optimise. The standard formulation of the value alignment problem implies that the best way to solve value misalignment is to perform due diligence in finding the *right* objective function. This chapter highlights that the problem is more complicated than that. We cannot directly measure what we purport to care about—health, happiness, well-being, etc.—and it is often impossible to accurately encode those targets formally. Hence, we depend upon proxies for machine learning systems to optimise; these give rise to value misalignment along the first axis.

The real-world objectives of a machine learning task can be highly complex and multi-faceted; the objective function stands as a simplified representation of these goals—typically written as a single, scalar value with which the optimisation algorithm can work. Hence, the more complex a learning task is, the more likely the objective function will be a mere proxy for the true goal. In addition, optimisation algorithms are mathematically constrained because they require differentiable, continuous, and smooth functions to work effectively. Hence, many desirable performance metrics may not be suitable for direct optimisation. The complexity of true objectives and the difficulty of for-

[37] See also Johnson (2020b) for a philosophical discussion of bias more generally.

mally representing these objectives place significant technical constraints on our ability to construct a value-aligned model.

Furthermore, value misalignment is ubiquitous on the objectives axis insofar as proxies permeate every stage of the algorithmic pipeline. Given that choices at an earlier stage will affect the available options at a later stage, a cascading effect occurs wherein poor proxies at an earlier stage in the process will lead to even worse proxies at a later stage. For example, in the predictive policing case study, a value-laden decision to formalise the objective (crime reduction) in terms of resource allocation partially *determines* the type of data that one can use to train a machine learning model. Any output of the system, and therefore the quality or performance of the system, will be inherently limited by the quality of the proxies chosen.

What we have seen in this chapter is that instances of the value alignment problem are universal along the first axis of the structural definition. Misspecified or costly objective functions may lead to behaviour misaligned with what we intended the system to do. More generally, machine bias and problems arising from fairness considerations give rise to value misalignment in ways not captured by the standard definition—except to the extent that the "values of humanity" exclude wanting or intending for models to act in ways that we would call "racist", "sexist", or otherwise discriminatory.

The first axis of the value alignment problem is a spectrum. What should be expected is that the more easily a problem can be formally specified (as an optimisation problem), the more aligned the system may be along this axis, assuming objective functions are carefully constructed. The value alignment problem can be mitigated on this axis by ensuring that the proxies we use when creating machine learning systems map onto the true objective. However, even perfect proxies in a system's formal specification cannot entirely resolve the potential for misalignment along this axis.

In this case, the possibility of "better" proxies requires sensitivity to the perverse incentives ubiquitous to optimisation and the complexity inherent to values. This, in turn, requires challenging the (often naïve) assumptions that go into the creation of a machine learning model—e.g., behaviourist assumptions in the context of collaborative filtering (Hildebrandt, 2022), the assumption that distributions in datasets are reflective of true distributions in the world, etc. Insufficient attention to ethical considerations and unintended consequences during the development and deployment of machine learning systems can contribute to perverse incentives. Moreover, failing to prioritise the normative and social aspects of the *objectives* axis of the value alignment problem may result in models that prioritise efficiency or profitability over fairness and societal well-being.[38]

Additional Resources

Batya Friedman and Helen Nissenbaum. 1996. "Bias in Computer Systems," *ACM Transactions on Information Systems* 14(3): 330–347.

Julia Angwin, Jeff Larson, Surya Mattu, and Lauren Kirchner. 2016. "Machine Bias," *ProPublica*.

Cathy O'Neil. 2016. *Weapons of Math Destruction: How Big Data Increases Inequality and Threatens Democracy*. New York: Broadway Books.

David Danks and Alex John London. 2017. "Algorithmic Bias in Autonomous Systems," *Proceedings of the 26th International Conference in Artificial Intelligence* 17: 4691–4697.

Joy Buolamwini and Timnit Gebru. 2018. "Gender Shades: Intersectional Accuracy Disparities in Commercial Gender Classification," *Proceedings of Machine Learning Research* 81: 77–91.

Ben Green and Lily Hu. 2018. "The Myth in the Methodology: Towards a Recontextualization of Fairness in Machine Learning," *Machine Learning: The Debates* (Workshop at ICML).

Gabrielle M. Johnson. 2020. "Algorithmic Bias: on the Implicit Biases of Social Technology," *Synthese* 198(10): 9941–9961.

Sina Fazelpour and David Danks. 2021. "Algorithmic Bias: Senses, Sources, Solutions," *Philosophy Compass* 16: 12760.

Shira Mitchell, Eric Potash, Solon Barocas, Alexander D'Amour, and Kristian Lum. 2021. "Algorithmic Fairness: Choices, Assumptions, and Definitions," *Annual Review of Statistics and Its Applications* 8: 141–163.

Nenad Tomasev, Kevin R. McKee, Jackie Kay, and Shakir Mohamed. 2021. "Fairness for Unobserved Characteristics: Insights from Technological Impacts on Queer Communities," *Proceedings of the 2021 AAAI/ACM Conference on AI, Ethics, and Society*. 254–265.

Solon Barocas, Moritz Hardt, and Arvind Narayanan. 2023. *Fairness and Machine Learning: Limitations and Opportunities*. Cambridge, MA: The MIT Press.

[38] Some salient examples are described in, e.g., Angwin et al. (2016); Christian (2020); Tomasev et al. (2021); Miceli et al. (2022).

5 Information

On the structural definition offered in Chapter 3, an instance of the value alignment problem for artificial intelligence can arise whenever a human principal delegates authority to an artificial agent to act on their behalf. We saw in Chapter 4 that the first axis of the value alignment problem pertains to the *objectives* encoded in the model—both explicitly in the context of objective functions and implicitly in the context of potential biases that might be encoded in the model. One of the common features of misalignment on this axis is the use of proxies.

This chapter begins by reiterating the role of informational asymmetries under the principal-agent framework, explaining how these problems can arise in the context of the value alignment problem for artificial intelligence. In particular, instances of the value alignment problem will arise on the information axis when any one of the following conditions hold:

1. **Non-verifiability**. The principal (or a third party) cannot verify whether the agent's outputs or actions satisfy the (true) objective of the principal.
2. **Moral Hazard**. The agent has access to information that the principal does not, or the agent's outputs or actions are not observable to the principal.
3. **Adverse Selection**. The principal has incomplete information about the agent's abilities.

This chapter explores each type of informational asymmetry in the context of the value alignment problem for artificial intelligence.

Since the structural definition of the value alignment problem is based on the principal-agent framework, it follows that value misalignment can arise when the principal lacks some information pertaining to the agent. However, we want to be careful not to anthropomorphise here: in the principal-agent framework, informational asymmetry occurs when the agent has access to information that the principal does not. Comparatively, in the case of human-AI interactions, it is not necessary that the agent "has access to" information in the sense that a machine learning system need not have "knowledge" or "awareness" of its internal operations, goals, etc., for there to be an informational asymmetry. In this case, it suffices for the (human) principal to lack that information about some matter of fact regarding the operation of that system.

In particular, we will see that something like *adverse selection* arises in the case of machine learning systems in light of the *black box problem*. Namely, the internal workings of deep learning systems are often opaque in light of the size and complexity of the architectures of these systems. In addition, something akin to *moral hazard* can arise in the context of AI systems when they are trained on datasets whose contents are unknown to the principal. Finally, nonverifiability highlights the epistemic issues that arise along the informational asymmetries axis of the value alignment problem; this component underscores the interaction effects that can occur between the information axis and the objectives axis.

Hence, the second axis pertains to *informational asymmetries*, which give rise to value misalignment on the structural definition. In this chapter, we examine how informational asymmetries can arise in the context of machine learning models. Although there are several such possibilities, we focus on two: *model architecture* and *data and datasets*. Just as we saw that bias and fairness are paradigmatic instances of the value alignment problem along the objectives axis, we will see that issues arising in AI ethics surrounding transparency and opacity are paradigmatic instances of value misalignment on the information axis.

5.1 Informational Asymmetries, Economic and Artificial

We saw in Chapter 3 that competing incentives between a principal and an agent can create a principal-agent problem in the economic context of human-human interactions. However, we also saw that when information is symmetric between the principal and the agent, certain managerial tools—like complete contracts—can allow the principal to motivate the agent to behave in a manner consistent with the principal's preferences, eliminating the delegation-induced misalignment of incentives. For example, a contract may align incentives via rewards or penalties, stipulate regular reporting requirements, specify performance benchmarks, or clarify language to elucidate expectations and responsibility.

Hence, in the idealised case, competing incentives (misaligned values) alone cannot generate misalignment in human-human interactions. This framework is an idealisation insofar as it is often infeasible to create a *complete* contract because of transaction costs and bounded rationality. In effect, because we cannot plan for every possible contingency, we cannot contract for every possible contingency.

Moreover, considering a scenario where the agent and principal share perfectly aligned objectives but struggle to convey this information, I suggested in Chapter 3 that misaligned incentives are also not a prerequisite for the emergence of a principal-agent problem in human-human interactions. In such instances, the agent's actions may still diverge from the principal's objectives, even though the agent intends otherwise. As a result, the principle-agent framework is driven primarily by *informational* asymmetries. Since the structural definition of the value alignment problem for artificial intelligence is built upon the principal-agent framework, we should expect that an instance of the value alignment problem, too, can arise in the context of informational asymmetries alone. That is, this problem can be instantiated even in those cases where the objective function for that system is perfectly well-specified, or the proxies used at each stage of the algorithmic development pipeline are good approximations of the principal's true objective. There are three distinct types of informational asymmetries in the principal-agent framework, each of which is highly relevant in the case of the value alignment problem.

Non-Verifiability. In the context of incomplete contracting, non-verifiability refers to situations where certain aspects of the contractual agreement are difficult or impossible to monitor or verify. In the case of the value alignment problem for artificial intelligence, this type of informational asymmetry captures questions surrounding *scalable oversight*, underscoring the difficulty of effectively monitoring and controlling increasingly complex and widespread artificial intelligence systems as they scale in size and scope.

In addition, incomplete contracting acknowledges that it is challenging to foresee and specify all possible contingencies and outcomes in a contract, highlighting the close relationship between the objectives and information axes of the value alignment problem. In particular, we have seen how a problem instance can arise along the objectives axis because the objectives encoded in a machine learning system are mere proxies for the principal's true objective, and the discrepancy between true objectives and their proxies can result in the system optimising something contrary to that objective.

To address non-verifiability in incomplete contracting in the economic context, parties often rely on mechanisms such as trust, reputation, and relational contracts. These mechanisms help mitigate the challenges posed by non-verifiability by fostering cooperation and aligning incentives between the contracting parties. However, it should be apparent how these approaches cannot be taken for granted in the context of building value-aligned AI systems. Objectives are given in human agents, meaning we can take for granted that a human agent will respond to, e.g., reputational costs. However, in the context of an artificial agent, the system's designers choose the system's objectives. Because these objectives are incompletely specified, social punishment arising from, e.g., reputational costs could not affect the system (unless such costs are explicitly encoded as a part of the objective function).

That said, some researchers have suggested that *spurious normativity* can enhance compliance with regard to otherwise non-verifiable norms (Hadfield-Menell et al., 2019). For example, Köster et al. (2021) describe how some cultural norms may be strictly enforced even though they do not obviously contribute to social benefits or harms. The explanation is that so-called "silly rules" help agents learn how to enforce and comply with norms in the general case. When spurious normativity is strictly upheld, this sends a signal to agents that non-spurious norms will be upheld. Hence, strictly enforcing rules that are simple to verify can lead to agents following rules that are difficult to verify.

Hadfield-Menell et al. (2019) suggest that distinguishing spurious normativity from important normative rules is useful for the goals of alignment in the context of artificial intelligence (on the standard definition), insofar as an AI system will need to distinguish between these cases to make good predictions and inferences that genuinely reflect human values.

Moral Hazard. A moral hazard (endogenous to the principal-agent relationship) arises when the agent has information, or engages in activities, of which the principal is unaware. In the case of the value alignment problem for artificial intelligence, moral hazard includes instances of misalignment surrounding safe exploration. We have already seen how the reinforcement learning paradigm requires an agent to explore its environment to discover novel, effective strategies for satisfying its objectives. An AI agent learns by interacting with an environment, receiving feedback, and adjusting its behaviour accordingly. However, this gives rise to potential risks when considering unintended consequences or harmful actions that the system may take.

When we consider how machine learning systems are trained, it should be apparent that relying on large datasets for training creates the potential for moral hazard. As the parameters and hyperparameters of a model scale, informational asymmetries are exacerbated insofar as the potential solution space for the problem also scales. In this case, the solution space for a complex model will necessarily include many local optima. When a machine learning system appears to perform well with respect to optimising its objective function, it may have found a locally optimal set of parameters that lead to misaligned behaviour when presented with out-of-distribution data. This behaviour may occur even when the objective function is perfectly well-specified. Hence, the key driver of misalignment in this case is an informational asymmetry between the principal and the agent rather than misspecified objectives *per se*.

Adverse Selection. In the economic case, adverse selection (exogenous to the principal-agent relationship) occurs when the principal has incomplete information about the agent's abilities; this lack of knowledge can lead to the selection of agents with unfavourable characteristics relative to the principal's needs. In the context of artificial intelligence, adverse selection can arise because the internal workings of a model are not easily interpretable or transparent to humans—i.e., they are considered "black boxes".

The black box problem in artificial intelligence refers to the challenge of understanding and interpreting the decision-making processes of complex machine learning models, particularly deep neural networks. Several factors are relevant to the black box problem. For example, deep neural networks often contain many layers and parameters, meaning they describe highly complex families of equations. Therefore, the relationships learned by these models and the interactions between the parameters of a model are often opaque. Similarly, because the input and feature spaces are high-dimensional, it is difficult to understand how each input variable contributes to the model's output. Because machine learning models automatically learn hierarchical representations from raw data (feature extraction), it may also be unclear which features of an example are relevant to the output.

As the datasets used for training machine learning models increase in size, this gives rise to an informational asymmetry insofar as ensuring the quality, fairness, and ethical handling of this data at scale becomes a significant challenge.

Hence, the three types of informational asymmetries that arise in the economic context are relevant to the value alignment problem for artificial intelligence. In addition, not unlike the interaction effects between the proxies used at different stages of the algorithmic development pipeline, the three types of informational asymmetries can also interact to worsen the value alignment problem in a specific instance. For example, non-verifiability can lead to issues similar to those seen in moral hazard and adverse selection in the principal-agent framework. If certain actions or outcomes are not easily observable or verifiable, it becomes challenging for the principal (or a third party) to ensure that the objectives are being fulfilled as intended. One way of reducing the potential for value misalignment along the information axis, is to ensure that an AI system is transparent.

5.2 Transparency and Opacity

Transparency is a *property* of a system, referring to whether it enables a clear understanding of how and why the system behaves or operates as it does. A system may be considered transparent when it allows the disclosure of specific information about its internal processes, such as identifying the factors that led inputs to result in certain outputs. This concept is interconnected with ideas of *openness*, *communication*, and *accountability*, contrasting with notions like *opacity*, *inexplicability*, *incomprehensibility*, *obscurity*, and similar characteristics.

As we saw in Chapter 2, the contemporary approach to artificial intelligence involves deep neural networks; it is increasingly common for these systems to have hundreds or thousands of hidden layers and millions or billions of parameters. Because the operation of the neural network depends upon complicated interactions between these parameters, it is practically impossible to understand how the network works even if all of the parameters are known. Hence, by their very nature, deep neural networks are "black boxes": although these models can achieve impressive performance in various tasks, their internal workings are often opaque and challenging for humans to interpret.

The lack of transparency in AI systems has been a key topic in the field of AI ethics. As such, much has been written about the concept. To maintain clarity in this chapter, we will focus on one particularly useful taxonomy.

Creel's Taxonomy. Creel (2020) highlights that scientists depend on complex computational systems to process big data, but these systems are only sometimes transparent. Therefore, understanding transparency requires a clear analysis of computational opacity. We might strive for transparency in complex computational systems for many different reasons, and many stakeholders should value transparency—e.g., the general public, but also scientists and modellers.

Descriptively, transparency serves the purpose of enabling scientific explanations and detecting artefacts. Given that there is often no non-computational procedure available to verify the outcomes of a computation or model, transparency provides an approach to check the system for artefacts. Therefore, all stakeholders stand to gain from increased transparency. However, Creel (2020) highlights disagreement regarding the precise requirements for transparency—both in terms of what it is and what it consists of. The variations in implicit or explicit definitions make it challenging for researchers to make advancements. Some statistical and computational tools operate as black boxes, lacking clear explanations for their outputs. This absence of explanation can undermine trust, even when these systems have demonstrated error reduction. Consequently, as increasingly complex computational systems, such as AI systems driven by deep learning, become prominent in the public sphere, citizens and lawmakers require explanations for outputs that these opaque systems cannot provide.

It is worth noting that transparency, in itself, is ethically neutral: it is not a normative concept in the sense that it is neither good nor bad. However, if transparency is a property of a system that makes it possible to obtain certain information regarding a system's inner workings, then the context of use and the information required for transparency in that context is (or at least can be) ethically relevant. Thus, depending upon the context of applying an opaque system, there might be normative reasons to want transparency. For example, good governance in public or private sectors involves non-arbitrariness of decisions. This non-arbitrariness can be applied to any decision-making that has an ethically- or legally-relevant effect on individuals.

The normative dimension of transparency for AI systems pertains to the ethical principles, standards, and expectations associated with openness, disclosure, and accountability in the development and deployment of artificial intelligence. In this case, transparency is required for informed decision-making, bias mitigation, accountability and responsibility, public trust and acceptance, regulatory compliance, etc. In many instances, the normative aspects of transparency can be understood as calls for sufficient information—i.e., a decrease in information asymmetries. For example, do we know whether and to what extent this algorithmic decision is justified? Do we know how the system made inferences? In effect, transparency is necessary for explainability insofar as some degree of transparency of a system is required to illuminate the relationship between the *explanans* (the thing being explained) and the *explanandum* (the explanation itself).

In her taxonomy, Creel (2020) characterises transparency at several levels of granularity; she argues that we can demarcate three orthogonal forms of transparency, depending on which level of explanation we are examining: *functional*, *structural*, and *run* transparency.[1] Although the first form of transparency may be increased by understanding the code of a program as written,

[1]For alternative taxonomies of forms of transparency and their sources, see Burrell (2016); Facchini and Termine (2021); Boge (2022).

the latter two forms of transparency cannot be extracted by scrutinising the code alone.

Functional Transparency. The first form of transparency that Creel (2020) discusses is *functional* transparency, or knowledge of the algorithmic functioning of the whole—i.e., the logical rules that map inputs to outputs. When a computational system is functionally transparent, it is possible to know the high-level, logical rules for transforming a given input into an output. Recall from Chapter 2 that an algorithm is an abstract mathematical object. A computer program is a particular instantiation of an algorithm. In other words, functional transparency requires knowing *which* algorithm the program instantiates.

A complex computational system can fail to be functionally transparent for several reasons. On the one hand, Creel (2020) discusses *kludging* as a cause of functional opacity. A kludge is a software fix made locally that is theoretically unmotivated—i.e., adding new bits of code that make the model work but not for any principled reason. Kludging creates a "piece of program or machinery which works up to a point but is very complex, unprincipled in its design, ill-understood, hard to prove complete or sound and therefore having unknown limitations, and hard to maintain or extend" (Clark, 1987, 278).[2] Since kludges lack theoretical motivation, they are harder to understand as part of a model and are not related to the model's algorithmic functioning.

Recall that many hyperparameters of a model—i.e., depth, width, activation function, learning rate—may be theoretically unjustified. This lack of theoretical foundation implies that these hyperparameters are used because they appear to make the system function better. However, because these decisions may lack any theoretical basis, this implies that many of the decisions made by engineers and programmers serve to make these models more functionally opaque.

Structural Transparency. The second form of transparency is structural transparency or knowledge of how an algorithm is instantiated or realised in code. The same algorithm can be instantiated in code in multiple ways. Therefore, Creel (2020) highlights that it is possible to know the algorithm the code instantiates without knowing *how* the code instantiates it—i.e., a computational system can be *functionally* transparent without being *structurally* transparent.

[2]Clark (1987) attributes this definition to Aaron Sloman. One of the earliest known uses of this term in context derives from Granholm (1962), who defined a kludge as an "ill-assorted collection of poorly-matching parts, forming a distressing whole" (30).

Whereas functional transparency offers knowledge of the algorithmic functioning of the whole, structural transparency provides knowledge about the algorithmic *process*. Rather than merely being able to read the code and understand that it instantiates a certain algorithm, this type of transparency requires understanding how the code, as written, brings about the result of the program. Since structural transparency involves knowing how a program instantiates a particular concept and functional transparency involves knowing that a program instantiates a particular algorithm, these are complementary concepts.

Because structural transparency entails knowing how a program executes the algorithm, this form of transparency can be obscured when commands written in high-level programming languages are executed by machine code. Algorithms are implemented in multiple languages. High-level programming languages provide a user-friendly interface between the user and the machine code that actually implements each of the commands provided by the programming language, thus making the program easier for human programmers to read and write. In some sense, then, the purpose of high-level programming languages is to *conceal* the machine language to provide a seamless experience for the programmer. This increases usability for the programmer but also increases structural opacity.

In addition, contemporary deep neural networks, as we saw in Chapter 2, contain many layers, which helps to increase their efficiency. These networks are often composed of heterogeneous processing units with different activation functions; they are sparsely connected and utilise several techniques to avoid overfitting the model to training data (Buckner, 2019). These added complexities—over and above simple neural networks—increase the performance of these systems, but they also increase their opacity in the structural sense.

Run Transparency. The final form of transparency that Creel (2020) discusses is *run* transparency, which requires knowledge of the program as it was run in a particular instance. For deep neural networks, this form of transparency requires knowledge about the hardware, input data, training data, and interactions between them. Run transparency gives rise to knowledge of the system itself. Whereas functional transparency can often be analysed by surveying the text of the code, as written, run transparency requires an analysis of a particular run of the program on an individual machine, in addition to the specific data used for that run. This sort of transparency can decrease artefacts caused by interaction effects between, e.g., the program and the hardware, the program and unexpected input data, the program and its implementation in a particular programming language that is then translated into the machine code that actually runs.

Therefore, to achieve this form of transparency, it is necessary to understand, for example, how the data were collected, the distributional features of those data, and how the program in question uses them. Given the pivotal role of large datasets in state-of-the-art approaches to artificial intelligence research, we will return to this topic in more detail in Section 5.4.

Increasing Transparency. There are several different approaches to increasing transparency in AI systems. On the one hand, one can always increase transparency by using simpler models. However, this approach often sacrifices accuracy for explainability. In addition, it is important to recall that the guiding faith of artificial intelligence research today is that performance scales with size, data, and compute. Hence, performance is often taken as an (implicit or explicit) justification for a lack of transparency. *Performance* and *explainability* are both things that individuals might value; hence, choosing to prioritise one over the other is a value-laden decision.[3]

On the other hand, it is possible to combine simpler and more sophisticated models. This strategy capitalises on the strengths of sophisticated models, which allow for complex computations while leveraging simpler models to enhance transparency within the system. One example of this combination is found in applying Local Interpretable Model-Agnostic Explanation (LIME). LIME serves as a methodology that seeks to query the decision space of an existing program from an external perspective.

To achieve this, it reconstructs decisions in a local region by utilising a separate sparse linear model (Ribeiro et al., 2016). The primary objective of LIME is to reduce opacity within AI systems by providing a local, *post hoc*,[4] high-level explanation of decision-making processes. This transparency is described by Creel (2020) as functional, as it elucidates decision-making at a high level, making it more understandable for human interpretation.

However, it is essential to note certain limitations of LIME. While it offers a high-level explanation for decision-making, it does not disclose the entire algorithm. Instead, LIME selectively reveals the specific parts of the algorithm used to make a particular decision. Consequently, while LIME excels in providing functional transparency, it falls short in enhancing structural or run transparency within the broader AI system on Creel's (2020) taxonomy.

[3]We will return to this topic in Chapter 11 when we examine the value-free ideal of science and its relevance to the value alignment problem.

[4]A fancy way of saying after the event has already occurred.

Reversal is another method that leverages complex systems to make other complex systems more transparent by identifying and eliminating artefacts. For example, reversed images of dumbbells reveal partial images of arms, implying that the model picked up on a correlation between the presence of a dumbbell and the presence of an arm when classifying images of dumbbells (Mordvintsev et al., 2015). In addition to clarifying what features a model learns to take as relevant for image classification, these visualisations shed some light on the constitution of the dataset used to train the model, reducing informational asymmetries between the principal and the agent. In all likelihood, most images labelled "dumbbell" in the training data were images of dumbbells *being held*. Hence, on Creel's (2020) taxonomy, reversal techniques enhance run transparency within the AI system.

It is worth noting that many of the proposals for mitigating opacity lean on using a different AI system to analyse the structure or functioning of the target (opaque) system. In the case of misaligned objectives, this approach is potentially question-begging. Delegating authority to an artificial agent to monitor the behaviour of a base system introduces further potential for value misalignment. However, this approach can be useful in the context of transparency, as the objective of the higher-order system is to increase explainability in a lower-order system. In some cases, the analysis of the transparent system might determine that the risk of deploying an opaque system is too high.

Case Study: Pneumonia Prognosis for Asthma Patients. In the 1990s, an opaque neural network model was trained on a dataset of pneumonia patients' case files to predict the probability of death based on several features so that high-risk patients could be admitted to the hospital and low-risk patients could be treated as outpatients. This opaque neural network model outperformed more transparent methods, like logistic regression or rule-based methods (Cooper et al., 1997, 2005). However, researchers noted that the rule-based system, which was more transparent than the neural network model, learned to classify patients with asthma as low-risk. Although this describes a true pattern in the dataset, the *reason* why patients with a history of asthma presenting with pneumonia had a lower risk of dying is because they were typically admitted directly to the intensive care unit, meaning that they often received effective treatment. Hence, patients with a history of asthma have statistically better outcomes when admitted for pneumonia because of the aggressive care and attention that they receive. However, based on the available data, the neural network model learned that asthma lowers the risk of death for pneumonia patients; hence, the model recommended that these patients be treated as outpatients.

As Caruana et al. (2015) highlight, if a simple rule-based system learned that asthma alone lowers risk, the more complex neural network probably also learned this correlation. Although there are methods to fix this predictive issue in the neural network model, these models were not deployed because they lacked transparency. Even though the asthma case was discovered, it was unclear what other spurious correlations the neural network model might have learned. Therefore, researchers chose not to deploy the opaque neural network models. This decision effectively solves the value alignment problem that an opaque model may have instantiated by *choosing* not to delegate authority to the model to render a decision.

5.3 Explainability, Interpretability, and Understanding

Efforts to address the black box problem include the development of explainable AI (XAI) techniques. XAI aims to create AI models that make accurate predictions and provide human-understandable explanations for their decisions. This approach can involve designing models with interpretable architectures, developing *post hoc* explanation methods, or integrating transparency features into the training process. Arrieta et al. (2020) suggest that "[t]ransparent models convey some degree of interpretability by themselves". However, this is not entirely accurate.

Transparency, as discussed in Section 5.2, is a property of an AI system: in deep neural networks, particularly, the opacity of an AI system is due, in large part, to the complexity of the model that is implemented by that system. Given this complexity and opacity, AI systems are difficult to understand. In contrast to the *property* of transparency—which might aptly describe a model to varying degrees—the explainability of an AI system is not *merely* a property of the system itself. Instead, it is a *relation* between an epistemic or cognitive entity (such as a human) and the AI system. *Comprehensibility* and *understandability* are each a property of *agents* attempting to understand the workings of an AI system insofar as they depend upon the user's ability to perceive the model.[5]

A complex computational system is transparent if all of the details of its operation are known. However, even if a system is transparent, this does not imply that we can understand how a decision is made or what information this decision is based on. Deep neural networks may contain billions of parameters,

[5]See discussion in Páez (2019). Although Fleisher (2022) argues for a unified account of transparency, interpretability, and explainability, several scholars have highlighted the lack of agreement on the meanings of each of these concepts; see, e.g., Leese (2014); Mittelstadt et al. (2016); Burrell (2016); Lipton (2018); Arrieta et al. (2020); Krishnan (2020); Fleisher (2022).

so there is no way we can understand how they work together to generate an output based on examination alone. In contrast, a system is explainable if humans can understand how it makes decisions. This distinction is highly relevant to the deployment of AI systems insofar as, for some jurisdictions, the public may have a right to an explanation.[6]

Without transparency or explainability, there is an information asymmetry between the user and the AI system, which instantiates the value alignment problem. Thus, explainability can be understood as a form of *epistemic* transparency. As with transparency, *interpretable* or *explainable* models benefit researchers insofar as they allow for detecting artefacts that affect model performance; additionally, explainable models may increase user trust. Explainability, over and above transparency, is essential for fairness considerations—we need to know "how" *and* "why".

XAI research aims to make the results of AI systems more understandable to humans (Van Lent et al., 2004). However, there is no standard or generally-accepted definition within the research community about what, precisely, constitutes *explainable* artificial intelligence (Adadi and Berrada, 2018). Although the number of research projects falling under the heading of XAI has increased significantly in the last decade, there is still a lack of unification between disparate projects (Minh et al., 2022). Early calls for explainable AI included proposals for prototypes that could describe *which* hard-coded rules in expert systems contributed to a decision (Swartout and Moore, 1993).

It remains to be seen whether it is possible to build complex decision-making systems that are fully understandable to their users or creators. There is also an ongoing debate about what it means for a system to be explainable, understandable, or interpretable (Erasmus et al., 2021); there is currently no concrete definition of these concepts.[7]

The lack of interpretability in AI models raises concerns in various applications, especially in sensitive domains such as healthcare, finance, and criminal justice. Understanding model decisions is crucial for accountability, trust, and ethical considerations. Efforts are ongoing to develop model interpretability and explainability techniques, allowing humans to gain insights into why AI systems make specific predictions or decisions. Such insight is particularly im-

[6] For example, Article 22 of the EU General Data Protection Regulation (GDPR) suggests all data subjects should have the right to "obtain an explanation of the decision reached" in cases where a decision is based solely on automated processes.

[7] See Molnar (2023) for more information.

portant in contexts where the consequences of errors or biases in AI systems can have significant real-world impacts.

5.4 Data and Datasets

The data upon which AI researchers choose to train their models is important insofar as these data will have downstream effects on how these models behave and the types of tasks for which they will be useful. These points are highly relevant to whether or to what extent the value alignment problem is instantiated along the information axis. Fitting a large model requires a significant amount of training data. As a result of the scaling hypothesis—that model performance scales with size, data, and compute—increasing model size has come with the need for ever-larger datasets. This increase in data comes with a corresponding increase in informational asymmetry insofar as it is impossible to know what exactly is contained in the dataset. One of the key datasets used in training some language models, like OpenAI's GPT or Meta's Large Language Model Meta AI (LLaMA), is the common crawl dataset.[8]

Case Study: The Common Crawl. Founded in 2007, *Common Crawl* is a nonprofit organisation that is "dedicated to providing a copy of the Internet to Internet researchers, companies, and individuals at no cost for the purpose of research and analysis".[9] The term "web crawling" refers to the automated process of systematically traversing the World Wide Web, collecting data from websites, and thus providing "snapshots" of the Internet at a point in time. The result of these crawls is a massive corpus of data—called the common crawl corpus or the common crawl dataset—which contains the raw content of web pages and metadata—e.g., information about the HTTP response headers, timestamps of the crawls, etc.

As of April 2023, a single corpus contains around 400 *tebibytes* (TiB)[10] of uncompressed data from 3.1 billion web pages. Hand-curated datasets are typically small-scale because of the resources required to create them. In contrast, large-scale datasets generated via crawls provide ample data, leading to a "paradigm shift" from curation to crawling, on the ethos that scale can wash out noise. For example, introducing the ALIGN project, Jia et al. (2021) sug-

[8] See Brown et al. (2020); Touvron et al. (2021).

[9] Note that common crawl was founded well before the popularisation of big data and generative AI (Baack, 2024).

[10] That is equivalent to 3.518×10^{15} (or $3,518,000,000,000,000$) bits of data. All the datasets provided by common crawl together amount to around 9.5 petabytes of data (a petabyte is close to four orders of magnitude larger than a tebibyte).

gest that a "costly curation process limits the size of datasets and hence hinders the scaling of trained models" (1).

Several jurisdictions are in the process of forwarding regulations for artificial intelligence that require system providers to mitigate the risks of harm to an acceptable, proportionate, or reasonable degree. However, this language is built on the assumption that providers *can* quantify the risks posed by these models. In the case of models trained using the common crawl dataset, it is impossible to verify what is contained within the dataset due to its sheer size. Therefore, verifying that the data set does not contain copyrighted, illegal, or offensive material is impossible.

That said, it is easy to verify that these datasets *do* contain copyrighted, illegal, or offensive material since a single instance is sufficient for an existence proof. Schaul et al. (2023) analysed Google's Colossal Cleaned Common Crawl (C4) dataset, which is based on the common crawl dataset, and highlight that the copyright symbol appears more than 200 million times. Luccioni and Viviano (2021) randomly sampled 1% of the November/December 2020 version of the common crawl dataset and found that this sample contained a significant amount of hate speech and sexually explicit content, even after standard filtering procedures are applied to the sample.

It is also important to understand that the common crawl dataset does not provide a "snapshot" of the *entire* Internet. The crawling process that CCBot employs is automated and prioritises pages on frequently linked domains, similar to preferential attachment networks where the more connected a node is, the more likely it is to receive new links.[11] Hence, domains related to digitally marginalised communities are statistically less likely to be included in the dataset, implying that these datasets will be heavily biased.

For example, most web pages in the common crawl dataset have English as their primary language, with the next most predominant languages (German, Russian, Japanese, French, and Spanish) each covering less than 6% of the dataset. Around 61% of all known web pages are written in English. Hence, even if the common crawl dataset were representative of the entire Internet, it would be highly Anglocentric.[12] In light of the prioritisation of preferentially attached nodes in the network, this bias is probably much more heavily skewed toward English content.

[11] Formal details are provided in Albert and Barabási (2002).

[12] See further discussion in Falbo and LaCroix (2022).

Case Study: LAION. While text-based datasets like the common crawl are useful for training language models, multi-modal models require more than just text. The LAION-400M dataset, produced by the non-profit Large-scale Artificial Intelligence Open Network (LAION), contains hundreds of millions of image-alt-text pairs parsed from the common crawl dataset and filtered using Contrastive Language-Image Pre-training (CLIP).[13] Such a large, multi-modal dataset is an immense resource for data-hungry deep-learning models.

However, besides containing explicit hate speech and pornographic content, these large-scale datasets encode misogyny and stereotypes (Birhane et al., 2021, 2023). For example, Birhane et al. (2021) report that when querying the LAION-400M dataset, "Even the weakest link to womanhood or some aspect of what is traditionally conceived as feminine returned pornographic imagery", including images of sexual violence (4). Their analysis shows one aspect of how massive datasets can amplify extant problems—such as misogyny and the sexualisation of women—but they also normalise and entrench "Anglo-centric, Euro-centric, and potentially, White-supremacist ideologies" (4). This fact should be relatively unsurprising, given the (cultural, geographic, racial, gendered, linguistic, etc.) demographics of the Internet.

In addition, the LAION-5B dataset, which was used to train Stable Diffusion among other models, was found to contain at least 1, 679 illegal images, including child sexual abuse material, scraped from social media and adult websites (Thiel, 2023). Because these generative AI models were trained on these data, they can be used to generate photo-realistic nude images. As noted, misaligned incentives (poorly specified objective functions) alone cannot account for value misalignment in AI systems. The model, in the case of image generation, satisfies its objective reasonably well—i.e., to generate realistic images. Instead, misalignment in these cases is generated via informational asymmetries owing to a lack of data provenance inherent to large-scale datasets.

Data Provenance. Data provenance (sometimes called "data lineage") refers to documentation tracking data's origin, history, and transformation throughout its lifecycle. Hence, data provenance is metadata that is paired with data and describes the origin of those data, how they are augmented over time, including information about the sources of data, how it was collected or generated, any modifications or processing it underwent, and the entities or processes that interacted with it.

[13]See Radford et al. (2021) for technical details.

This is supposed to answer questions about why, how, where, when, and by whom data was produced. Tracking and recording information about data lineage is useful for correcting potential errors contained in the data, as well as ensuring transparency, traceability, and trustworthiness in data analysis, aiding in understanding data quality, compliance, and reproducibility.

Worsening the informational asymmetries rendered by massive datasets like the common crawl or LAION (which lack data provenance), many companies fail to be transparent about the training data used for their models. For example, OpenAI's ChatGPT, GPT-4, and Sora models, Meta AI's LLama v2, and Google's Gemini do not provide any information about the data upon which these models are trained. Again, this is a lack of run transparency on Creel's (2020) taxonomy and an instance of value misalignment along the information axis, in the language of the value alignment problem.

Case Study: Gemini. On 06 December 2023, Google DeepMind released *Gemini*, which they describe as a family of highly capable multimodal models (Gemini Team, 2023), meaning that they can process inputs across various modalities (text, speech, visual, etc.). The associated tech report is a public relations document masquerading as a scientific paper. In it, the team highlights that "training the Gemini family of models required innovations in training algorithms, dataset, and infrastructure" (4). However, when it comes time to describe the training dataset, they only state that "Gemini models are trained on a dataset that is both multimodal and multilingual. Our pretraining dataset uses data from web documents, books, and code, and includes image, audio, and video data" (5).

They further clarify, "We apply quality filters to all datasets, using both heuristic rules and model-based classifiers" (5). What should be apparent is that there is no transparency whatsoever about what data these models were trained on—hence, there is no data provenance—despite longstanding calls from within the NLP community (and AI community more generally) for transparency surrounding datasets.[14] Regarding safety, the Gemini Team (2023) states that they "perform safety filtering to remove harmful content"; again, no further details are reported. In conclusion, they underscore that "We find that data quality is critical to a highly-performing model, and believe that many interesting questions remain around finding the optimal dataset distribution for pretraining" (5).[15]

[14]See, e.g., Bender and Friedman (2018); Yang et al. (2018); Gebru et al. (2021).

[15]Note that the entire description of the dataset in this report consists of 228 words in a single paragraph, 130 of which were quoted directly in the preceding paragraphs.

Despite hype-riddled claims about performance across benchmarks, it is effectively impossible to substantiate or even interpret Gemini's performance without knowing what is in the training data. Given that the smallest versions of Gemini (Nano-1 and Nano-2) have 1.8 and 3.25 billion parameters, respectively, the datasets used to train these models are likely massive. Again, this is an informational asymmetry.[16]

Case Study: Sora. On 15 February 2024, OpenAI released a demo of *Sora*, which they describe as a large-scale generative model trained on video data (OpenAI, 2024). Sora generates video outputs based on textual prompts. Although many of the videos presented in their demo display failures of basic physics, OpenAI (2024) suggests that "scaling video generation models is a promising path towards building general purpose simulators of the physical world".

Based on the scant information in the "technical report", it is probable that Sora's architecture uses some combination of latent diffusion models (Gupta et al., 2023; Blattmann et al., 2023a,b) for high-resolution video generation, cascade diffusion (Singer et al., 2022; Ho et al., 2022; Ge et al., 2023) for longer videos, re-captioning techniques (Betker et al., 2023) to improve language understanding, diffusion transformer architectures (Peebles and Xie, 2020) for flexibility and scaling, and native vision transformers (Dehghani et al., 2023) for training videos on native aspect ratios.

Despite the combination of several distinct architectures, the most important aspect of Sora's video-generating abilities is what training data were used to train the model. OpenAI (2024) does not provide any details. They also do not mention alignment or safety considerations.

5.5 Interaction Effects

Not unlike Creel's three types of transparency, the three axes of the value alignment problem are orthogonal in the sense that increasing alignment along one axis does not guarantee an increase of alignment along another axis. This is captured, in particular, by the distinction between inner and outer alignment (Hubinger et al., 2021). Outer alignment maps nicely onto the objectives axis; this is the problem of ensuring that objective functions are well-specified—in our language, they are good proxies for their targets. In contrast, inner alignment concerns the inner workings of the model.

[16]Note that Google has not released any information about the model architecture (except that it consists of decoder-only transformers), the model size, the training data, etc.

I have suggested that this can be cashed out in the language of informational asymmetries. The key point of independence is to say that even if a model's objective function perfectly represents the true objective of the principals, the system may still be misaligned due to informational asymmetries—i.e., the inner alignment problem can still be instantiated. However, despite the independence of the three axes with respect to ensuring that AI systems are aligned, there may be interaction effects when one or more of these axes is misaligned.

Objectives and Information. A correlation between a proxy and a ground truth may arise because of a confounding variable (informational asymmetry). Depending on the objectives of a system, some types of opacity may be acceptable. In this case, acceptability is going to be a function of the *type* of task that is being delegated to the agent. For example, a game-playing AI system might function very well, and it may also be highly opaque. In this case, informational asymmetries exist between the principal and the agent. Still, insofar as the context is not of particular normative import to the principal, opacity may be acceptable.

In contrast, delegating tasks like predicting recidivism risk, approving loans, hiring, diagnosing diseases, etc., have higher normative stakes, so we may be less tolerant of opacity in these cases. When the transparency of a system is increased, this implies a decrease in the informational asymmetries that give rise to the value alignment problem in the first place, thus implying a decrease in value misalignment.

One of the key problems in this case of recidivism prediction, predictive policing, etc., is that the underlying distribution on which the model is trained is biased. It is not the computational structure that needs fixing; it is the structure of society. This is fundamentally a social rather than a technical problem. McQuillan (2022) underscores that such technological "fixes" can actually *worsen* problems of inequity, injustice, and unfairness insofar as engineers seek to "fix" biases with yet more abstraction rather than by addressing the structural power and discrimination that underlies the data on which these models are trained. Therefore, "the reduction of social and cultural complexity to a measurable distance in some abstract data space is a mechanism that inevitably amplifies injustice rather than correcting for it" (McQuillan, 2022, 34). In addition to exacerbating pre-existing informational asymmetries, the use of proxies to *simplify* our objectives can create new informational asymmetries.

In the context of fairness, this problem is exacerbated by the fact that larger feature spaces give rise to an increased redundancy in encoding. In some cases, as we have seen, those features may not be explicit. Hence, considering whose objectives are the target of alignment is essential when considering alignment along the objectives axis.

Many models are proprietary, meaning that companies do not disclose information about the model's training data, architecture, objective function, etc. This opacity makes it impossible for auditors to determine whether or how aligned a model might be on the *objectives* axis. This is a type of informational asymmetry that impedes assurances of value alignment.

Case Study: Model Collapse. Model collapse, as defined by Shumailov et al. (2023), is a degenerative process characterised by the forgetting of the true underlying data distribution by models, even when there is no shift in the distribution over time. This phenomenon occurs when subsequent generations of learned generative models include outputs from ancestral generative models in their training data. It is a distinct phenomenon from catastrophic forgetting—where a model, when learning new information, inadvertently erases or significantly diminishes its ability to recall previously learned knowledge—and data poisoning—i.e., intentional manipulation of training data.

According to Shumailov et al. (2023), model collapse happens in two steps. First, *early model collapse* occurs when the model loses information about the "tails" of the distribution. In contrast, *late model collapse* occurs when two modes of the original distribution become entangled, causing subsequent models' learned distributions to deviate significantly from the original data.

Formally, model collapse arises from a pernicious feedback loop driven primarily by statistical and functional approximation errors. Statistical approximation error occurs due to the finite nature of datasets, where, as the number of samples tends to infinity, there is a non-zero probability of information loss at each re-sampling step. In contrast, functional approximation error describes that neural networks, despite being universal function approximators in theory,[17] are insufficiently expressive in practice.

This phenomenon is highly relevant to generative artificial intelligence because these systems are designed to synthesise outputs that are, effectively, indistinguishable from their training data. Shumailov et al. (2023) argue that model collapse is universal across generative models that train recursively on data generated by ancestral models. Even in the case of perfect functional approximation, model collapse occurs when distributions are discrete. This implies that when the outputs of earlier models are included in the training data

[17] See Chapter 2.

for subsequent generations, the later models lose information contained in the original distribution, leading to misalignment on the objectives axis.

Hence, informational asymmetries not only exacerbate misaligned objectives but can also cause misalignment over time. Learning from generational data results in models approximating the original distribution with finite sampling, and errors compound over time. This implies that the average distance between the distribution approximated by the nth-generation model and the original distribution can grow arbitrarily.

Early-stage model collapse, where tails or outliers are lost from the distribution, has significant consequences. Unrepresentative or under-representative data leads to the model ignoring certain groups in subsequent generations. Minority groups, considered tails or outliers, may be overlooked, contributing to a recursive trend toward homogeneity even when the data perfectly represent real-world distributions.

At the same time, modern computers give rise to computational errors because of the way that they represent floating-point numbers. The set of real numbers, $\mathbb{R}$, is uncountably infinite owing to the uncountably infinite set of irrational numbers—i.e., those numbers that cannot be expressed as a ratio of integers. The decimal expansion of irrational numbers, like π or $\sqrt{2}$, is infinite (no halting, no repetition), meaning that a computer cannot exactly represent irrational numbers—they can only be approximated.[18] Thus, computational errors may vary between more- or less-precise hardware. Hence, we have another compounding informational asymmetry when we do not know the hardware upon which a model was trained—i.e., a form of run opacity. Hence, model collapse shows how misalignment along the information axis can lead to further misalignment along the objectives axis over time.

5.6 Summary

Addressing the black box problem is necessary for the responsible and ethical deployment of AI systems, ensuring accountability, fairness, and user trust in the increasingly pervasive use of AI technologies. Hence, it should be unsurprising that issues of transparency, explainability, understanding, etc., fall under the purview of the value alignment problem on the structural definition.

[18] For example, irrational numbers are approximated computationally as a *float*, which represents irrational numbers using 32 bits of data (e.g., $\pi = 3.141592$), or a *double*, which represents irrational numbers with 64 bits of data (e.g., $\pi = 3.141592653589793$). However, this is not unique to irrational numbers. Since computers are *binary*, rational numbers whose denominators are not integer multiples of 2 must be approximated in binary.

Principal-agent problems arise in human-human interactions *primarily* in light of informational asymmetries. Part of the reason for this is because values or incentives are given. In the case of the value alignment problem for artificial intelligence, values are not given but are designed (and therefore) controlled by the programmer. So, misaligned objectives alone can lead to value misalignment; we saw in Chapter 4 that this happens when the proxies we use to represent our goals do not adequately capture what we care about. There is a sense in which this is primarily a problem of informational asymmetries.

On the standard definition, it is not clear how transparency might be categorised *as* a value alignment problem, except insofar as "the values of humanity" might be thought to include transparency, explainability, etc. In contrast, the structural definition of the value alignment problem explicitly includes informational asymmetries as a key driver of misalignment. Hence, a lack of transparency can be understood as a paradigmatic instance of the value alignment problem on this axis. As with the objectives axis, we can characterise degrees of value alignment insofar as informational asymmetries can be understood as a spectrum; a system may be more or less transparent, more or less explainable, etc. Importantly, how aligned a system is on either the objectives or information axes depends, fundamentally, on who the principal is.

Additional Resources

Jenna Burrell. 2016. "How the Machine 'Thinks': Understanding Opacity in Machine Learning Algorithms," *Big Data & Society* 3(1).

Dylan Hadfield-Menell, McKane Andrus, and Gillian Hadfield. 2019. "Legible Normativity for AI Alignment: The Value of Silly Rules". *AIES '19: Proceedings of the 2019 AAAI/ACM Conference on AI, Ethics, and Society* 115–121.

Alejandro Barredo Arrieta, Natalia Díaz-Rodríguez, Javier Del Ser, Adrien Bennetot, Siham Tabik, Alberto Barbado, Salvador Garcia, Sergio Gil-Lopez, Daniel Molina, Richard Benjamins, et al. 2020. "Explainable Artificial Intelligence (XAI): Concepts, Taxonomies, Opportunities and Challenges toward Responsible AI," *Information Fusion* 58: 82–115.

Kathleen A. Creel. 2020. "Transparency in Complex Computational Systems" *Philosophy of Science* 87(4): 568–589.

Adrian Erasmus, Tyler D. P. Brunet, and Eyal Fisher. 2021. "What Is Interpretability?" *Philosophy & Technology* 34: 833–862.

Alessandro Facchini and Alberto Termine. 2021. "Towards a Taxonomy for the Opacity of AI Systems". *Philosophy and Theory of Artificial Intelligence*. Cham: Springer. 73–89.

Florian J. Boge. 2022. "Two Dimensions of Opacity and the Deep Learning Predicament," *Minds and Machines* 32: 43–75.

6 Principals

On the structural definition offered in Chapter 3, an instance of the value alignment problem can arise whenever a human principal delegates authority to an artificial agent to act on their behalf. This problem can be instantiated whenever the agent's objective function is misaligned with the principal's true objective. This description corresponds to the objectives axis, which was explored in more detail in Chapter 4. We saw that misalignment primarily occurs along this axis when the proxies used to formally specify the true objective are poor approximations of those objectives. Moreover, misalignment can arise on this axis at effectively every stage of the algorithmic development pipeline. Issues of bias and fairness were described as paradigmatic instances of value misalignment along the objectives axis.

An instance of the value alignment problem can also occur on the structural definition when informational asymmetries exist between the principal and the agent. This situation can arise when the agent's actions are hidden from the principal (moral hazard), some information about the AI system is hidden from the principal (adverse selection), or the relative alignment of the agent is unverifiable. Two specific instances of informational asymmetries were discussed in Chapter 5. On the one hand, an informational asymmetry can arise from the size and complexity of model architectures—implying that the principal lacks information about how the system derived an output. This insight entails that issues of transparency and opacity are paradigmatic cases of value misalignment along the information axis. On the other hand, informational asymmetries arise when the datasets used to train a model are large and uncurated. We found that the latter type of informational asymmetry is increasingly common in light of the drive toward ever-larger models which require more data to be trained.

Note that misalignment of the objective function with the true objective is a deeply relative term insofar as it is indexed to *whose* true objective is under consideration. This index is fixed, in a particular instance, by the principal in question. Similarly, for informational asymmetries—an imbalance between the information available to the model and the information available to the principal is a function of who the principal is. Thus, the principal provides a third axis across which the value alignment problem can be instantiated. The principals axis highlights the relevance of *context* or *perspective* for determining whether the values of a model are indeed aligned.

When the standard definition of value alignment was introduced, the key question that arose was, "with whose values ought the system to align?". In contrast to the standard definition, which hides this question behind the superficial answer, "the values of humanity", the structural definition of value alignment brings this question to the fore by encoding the subject-relativity of values in the description of the problem. Therefore, a system or model can be aligned according to one principal's (set of principals') values while failing to be aligned for a different principal. In this case, robust value alignment requires ensuring value alignment *across* distinct sets of principals.

The third axis, which is made explicit in the structural definition, concerns *who* the principal in question is. The most obvious principals to consider when determining whether a system is value-aligned are the programmers who created the system, the companies that commissioned the creation of the system, and the users of the system. However, when determining whether a system is or is not aligned, it is necessary to consider a wider class of individuals—namely, those individuals who may be *affected* by the system.

A value alignment problem arises when a principal delegates authority to an artificial agent to act on their behalf. Of course, those individuals who are affected by the system but have no share in the system's creation are not, themselves, delegating authority. However, the key point when considering these stakeholders is their objectives also matter. In this case, when a principal is a shareholder of a system, they must consider their own objectives and the objectives of those affected by the system for such a system to be aligned. Put another way, we might conceptualise "delegating authority" by proxy. Hence, a stakeholder may be considered a principal even though they did not give authority to an agent to act on their behalf. Insofar as stakeholders are affected by the commission, creation, deployment, or use of an AI system, their objectives should be accounted for by those who have the power to decide whether to commission, create, deploy, or use that system.

6.1 Principals and Their Goals

Several salient options arise when we ask, "whose values?" in the context of the value alignment problem for artificial intelligence. One class of individuals that we might consider is the set of those who created the system. In this case, we might differentiate between the programmers, researchers, or engineers who work on the ground to code and train a machine learning model for deployment in a wider socio-technical system and the company or research lab that commissioned the creation of such a system. Note that the objectives that a company has when commissioning the creation of an AI system may be distinct from the objectives of the creators of that system, which means this is an instance of the principal-agent problem on the (classical) economic framework pertaining to misalignment of incentives in human-human interactions. For example, a company might value maximising shareholder profit, whereas its employees might value an intellectual challenge (regardless of whether those challenges are commercially viable). That said, it is worth noting that although these are distinct goals, they ultimately serve the same end: creating a functioning AI system.

A distinct group that we might consider consists of the *users* of the AI system once it is deployed. These users may be individuals or institutions, and the context of use may be personal or embedded within a wider set of goals. Of course, the companies, programmers, and researchers that create and deploy these systems may also be users. Hence, these "distinct" sets of principals overlap (at least partially).

Alternatively, we might consider the objectives, values, or goals of those *affected*, directly or indirectly, by these systems. Although the individual goals of programmers, researchers, companies, and users may be distinguished, they are potentially more similar to one another than they are to the individual goals of those affected by the creation and deployment of an AI system. Hence, without loss of generality, I will refer to different sets of groups whose objectives may be relevant to considerations of value alignment as either *shareholders* or *stakeholders*.

Shareholders. Shareholders will typically refer to those individuals (or sets thereof) involved in the AI systems in some form or another—whether through creation or use. Shareholders may include, e.g., companies, research labs, developers, data scientists, system administrators, regulators, compliance officers, end users, consumers, etc.

In some instances, the objectives of distinct sets of shareholders can come apart, meaning that a system which is perfectly well aligned for one subset of shareholders may give rise to an instance of the value alignment problem for another subset.

Case Study: Chatbots and Discursive Ideals. Examining misalignment in the case of large language models, Kasirzadeh and Gabriel (2023) suggest that LLM-based general assistants should be aligned with human values on the standard definition of the value alignment problem as discussed in Chapter 3. In their view, alignment in the case of LLM-based applications requires, first, minimising the risk of socio-moral harms (the "objectives" component of value alignment, on my account), and second, aligning with principles of good conversation—including both general maxims, like those discussed in the philosophy of language (Grice, 1975, 1989), but also *domain-specific discursive ideals*.[1] They examine how some of the main LLM-based models (circa 2023) might not be aligned with domain-specific discursive ideals, thus concluding that these models may not be aligned with human values.

The latter analysis provides an interesting case study of the potential for value misalignment when we understand the principal as a variable rather than static, even when restricting attention to the shareholders of the system. For example, we might consider the scientific community's *goals* as advancing human knowledge and understanding, explaining, or predicting natural phenomena.[2] The scientific community (in the fictional abstract) then values things that achieve these goals—e.g., evidential rigour and robustness for claims made and separating fact from opinion. If this is a plausible picture of the motivations and aims of the scientific community on the whole, then for a large language model to "align" with the values of the principal (the scientific community in this case), it would be necessary to ensure that the statements rendered by an LLM-based application are *truth-tracking*.

In contrast, if the application is deployed as a moderator of democratic discussion, we might think the goal is to manage differences and enable productive cooperation in public life. Unlike the case of deployment in the scientific community, political values—including beliefs, desires, preferences, and other normative judgements—will all be uncontroversially figured into the dis-

[1]For Grice (1975, 1989), conversational maxims codify the (often hidden) conventions that govern normal conversation, which is understood as a type of cooperation game. The maxims that (Grice, 1975, 1989) proposed include maxims of *quantity*, *quality*, *relation* (be relevant), and *manner*.

[2]The examples in this case study were presented by Atoosa Kasirzadeh at a symposium panel on Artificial Intelligence and the Value Alignment Problem which we organised together for the 2023 meeting of the Canadian Philosophical Association in Toronto, Canada.

course.[3] Thus, one value for achieving these goals would be civility—one wants to avoid, e.g., threats, insults, or harmful stereotypes in democratic discourse. Therefore, rather than *truth-aptness*, pragmatism appears to be a key objective for an LLM-based application in this context.

In a third instance, we might imagine a context in which an LLM-based application is employed as a writing assistant. Here, there are general goals in the realm of originality, self-expression, aesthetic ideals, etc. Compared with scientific inquiry and democratic discourse, truthfulness or civility norms are not necessarily as relevant in this case. Note that the objective that is satisfied by such a system might be described as plausible next-word prediction. Such systems optimise for *plausibility*, on the basis of stochastic likelihood, rather than, e.g., truth-aptness, pragmatics, or creativity. This word-prediction proxy may be adequate for one set of principals' objectives—i.e., to create a model that can output text that is near-indistinguishable from its input data—while failing to satisfy the objectives of a different set of principals. Hence, the goals of one set of shareholders can come apart from the goals of another.

Stakeholders. In contrast to shareholders, stakeholders encompass a broader spectrum of individuals or groups who are directly or indirectly affected by the creation and deployment of an AI system. In some cases, this set will overlap with the set of shareholders of the system; however, the instances in which the stakeholders are distinct from the shareholders will be most important for determining whether a system is value-aligned. The key thing to note is that shareholders and stakeholders play distinct roles in determining the objectives of an AI system, which is relevant to consider whether the system satisfies those objectives (the goal of alignment).

Case Study: Autonomous Vehicles. AI systems for autonomous vehicles provide a salient case in which the principals' values, goals, objectives, etc., can come apart depending on whether the principals are shareholders or stakeholders. For example, in 2018, an Uber test vehicle in Tempe, AZ, struck and killed Elaine Herzberg—a pedestrian who was walking her bicycle across the street. An investigation by the United States National Transportation Board revealed that the software alternated between classifying her as a "person", "bicycle", and "unknown object"—each of which would have had a different expected trajectory according to the internal logic of the system (National

[3] This is in contrast to an idealised understanding of scientific inquiry, which purports or seeks to be objective in the sense of value-free; this topic will be the focus of Chapter 11.

Transportation Safety Board, 2019).[4] Herzberg was not a user of this system, and so had no share in its creation. Nonetheless, the deployment of this system (and other factors) resulted in her death. Hence, in choosing to delegate authority to an AI system, the shareholders clearly have an obligation to account for stakeholder objectives, in addition to shareholder objectives.

6.2 The Values of Humanity

One response to the demarcation between shareholders and stakeholders is that this misses the point of value alignment, as is discussed in the literature. In the best-case scenario, one might argue that this distinction is redundant because if a system were genuinely aligned with "the values of humanity", then it would be aligned with the values of both shareholders and stakeholders by definition. In the worst case, it fails to capture the purpose of value alignment insofar as we should not be concerned with one user, company, programmer, etc. Instead, the value alignment problem seeks to ensure the flourishing of our species. The question of *who* is not relevant on this view because what we seek to align an AI system with are the *values of humanity* on the whole.

This view is beneficial for public relations rather than for ethical practice. First, the view that the proper target of alignment is the "values of humanity" presupposes that some universal set of principles or objectives are shared among all relevant individuals. However, as the set of principals whose values are under consideration increases, the set of the conjunction of their individual values decreases. (This is a logical fact about conjunction.) The view that we ought to align AI systems with the values of humanity presupposes that this set is non-empty. To apply universally, such principles would need to be very coarse-grained, meaning that they will be highly vague or overly conceptual. If this is the ultimate objective with which an AI system should align, then alignment will be impossible along the objectives axis because formally encoding objectives in machine learning systems requires *specificity*. In contrast, if we consider "the values of humanity" as the conjunction of individual values, the set is almost certainly empty insofar as individuals value many things, some of which are in conflict. Hence, aligning AI systems with "the values of humanity" is impossible at any level of granularity.

---

[4]There is a question, outside the scope of the value alignment problem, about who is responsible when misaligned systems act in damaging ways. At the time of writing, the precedent is often the user. In part, this is because, e.g., self-driving cars are not *actually* autonomous, meaning that the driver-passenger is still legally responsible for the vehicle. Studies have suggested that drivers may become inattentive when using partially automated driving systems (Morando et al., 2021).

At the same time, conversations surrounding "the values of humanity" (howsoever specified) as the proper target of the value alignment problem presuppose that "the AI" that we are trying to align is a near- or far-future AGI. However, we have already seen that pressing problems arise from creating and deploying narrow AI systems that are properly classified as instances of the value alignment problem.

Finally, the "values of humanity" approach to value alignment is too vague to be useful. Again, the benefit of reconceptualising the value alignment problem for artificial intelligence has been to trade vagueness for specificity. It logically follows from the structural definition of the value alignment problem for artificial intelligence that an instance of the value alignment problem—and a solution to that problem instance—is always indexed to a specific principal. In some cases, the goals of shareholders and stakeholders may converge. However, in many cases, they can diverge in ways that are significant to determining whether a system is value-aligned. Failure to appreciate this fact can lead to the branding of a project as "good" when it is only good relative to one social group.

Case Study: The "AI for Social Good" Movement. In his critique of various "for good" movements in computer science—particularly the *AI for social good* movement—Green (2019) highlights that "good" is not a universally agreed-upon concept. This conceptual ambiguity relates to the point I have made here about proxies in the context of objective functions—when something serves as an intuitive stand-in for something else, this can lead to a misalignment between the thing in question and the thing standing in its place or representing it. However, Green's (2019) point is more subtle than this. First, rather than trying to proffer a better definition of "social good", it is important to acknowledge the diversity of perspectives relevant to the very idea of a social good. Hence, Green's (2019) analysis is highly relevant to the *principals* component of the value alignment problem, as I have defined it.

For example, Green (2019) describes two distinct *AI for social good* projects with clearly conflicting goals. On the one hand, the projects described by, e.g., Carton et al. (2016) and Bauman et al. (2018) seek to develop tools for enhancing police accountability and promoting non-punitive alternatives to incarceration. However, other work touted under the "AI for social good" umbrella seeks to use data-heavy machine learning tools to predict and classify crimes to distribute policing resources more effectively (Seo et al., 2018). The fact that projects with such conflicting goals could both be called "AI for social good" underscores that when the AI for social good movement "encompasses everything, it stands for nothing" Green (2019, 2).

Importantly, Green (2019) highlights that incrementalist "good" can lead to long-term harm, meaning that the "greedy algorithm" approach of attempting to make piece-wise "improvements" in the local area of the status quo is apt to settle upon a local optimum.[5] Such an approach encompasses a type of "reformist reform", which "subordinates its objectives to the criteria of rationality and practicability of a given system and policy" (Gorz, 1967). This eliminates the possibility of solutions that demand structural reforms—i.e., the sorts of solutions that will be necessary when social problems are systemic. In contrast, a *non-reformist reform* "is conceived not in terms of what is possible within the framework of a given system and administration, but in view of what should be made possible in terms of human needs and demands" (Gorz, 1967).[6]

As has already been pointed out, the machine learning paradigm depends on *historical* data, meaning that it can only serve to entrench further and amplify the status quo. Hence, this paradigm is inappropriate when considering the possibility of social change.

Tradeoffs. Unsurprisingly, distinct groups' values, goals, or objectives can be in tension. For example, performance is highly valued in the context of machine-learning research; however, higher-performing models are often also *larger* models—at least in light of the current paradigm of machine-learning research. Increasing size (of parameters, datasets, etc.) may lead to increased performance, but it will also lead to increased run opacity, implying higher degrees of misalignment more generally.[7] In addition, undue emphasis on performance can give rise to feedback loops by influencing the direction of future research.[8] Hence, ensuring value alignment requires considering the differential goals of both shareholders and stakeholders.

6.3 The Values Encoded in AI Research

Shareholders of AI systems purport to value many things. However, talk is cheap. In this case, actions can be more informative than verbal expressions.

[5] A greedy search algorithm focuses on immediate benefits without considering the long-term results of decisions. At each step, the algorithm makes the choice based on what appears to be best at that particular moment without macro-level considerations. Such an algorithm is not always optimal, but it is simple and computationally efficient.

[6] Non-reformist reforms are sometimes called abolitionist reforms, anti-capitalist reforms, structural reforms, or transformative reforms. See also Mathiesen (1974, 2014).

[7] See Chapter 5.

[8] See discussion in LaCroix and Luccioni (2025); Dotan and Milli (2019).

Using an annotation scheme to analyse 100 highly-cited papers in machine learning, Birhane et al. (2022) provide a conceptual mapping of the values encoded in machine learning research. The leading values, explicit or implicit, pertain to issues surrounding performance, generalisation, building on past work, quantitative evidence, efficacy, novelty, etc.—i.e., ostensibly epistemic values.[9] However, they note that "performance" is often taken as a generic success term, synonymous with "success", "progress", or "improvement"—ostensibly normative concepts. That said, accuracy and state-of-the-art performance do not necessarily entail success or progress. One way of seeing this is when we take success conditions for a model to require instantiating safe, consensual, or participatory machine learning research. Thus, taking state-of-the-art performance or accuracy (with respect to a particular metric) to instantiate success is a value judgement.

They note, furthermore, that papers rarely mention the (potential) social benefits of their work, appealing instead to the needs of the machine learning research community to justify their work; at the same time, social needs are often only mentioned in passing, followed by a lack of engagement with real-world applicability or societal needs throughout the rest of the paper. Similarly, it is rare for papers to mention any potential negative impacts of the work thus proposed, despite the fact that the most benign-seeming research can have significant (negative) social impact—e.g., identification of faces in images for application in face-swapping or video synthesis also serve to advance applications in surveillance, deepfakes,[10] and disinformation. Unsurprisingly, negative potential is often discussed in abstract and hypothetical rather than concrete and real-world terms.

This analysis is a nice starting point for considering how indexing the principal in the value alignment problem can alter the values under consideration. Here, "value" can be understood in the context of the philosophy of science wherein a "value" of an entity is a property that is considered "a desirable attribute for machine learning research" (Birhane et al., 2022, 174). It should

[9] Sometimes called *cognitive* or *constitutive values*, epistemic values are those values that are supposed to be indicative of the truth of a scientific theory; hence, in the philosophy of science, these types of values are supposed to offer some justification for preferring one theory to another. See, e.g., McMullin (1982); Laudan (1984); Steel (2010) for more details. Epistemic values in the specific context of science, machine learning, and the value alignment problem will be discussed in more detail in Chapter 11.

[10] Deepfakes use deep learning techniques (typically generative adversarial networks) to create highly realistic and often deceptive video, audio, or other digital content. (The term "deepfake" is a combination of "deep learning" and "fake".) For a philosophical discussion of the epistemic, social, political, and moral harms of deepfakes, refer to Rini (2020); Rini and Cohen (2020).

be clear, then, that whether something is a value or whether it is valued depends inherently upon the valuer. The average user or stakeholder may care less whether a particular model or algorithm builds upon past research than the average researcher (or referee) might. Importantly, each of the top five (indeed, each of the top 32) values is clearly indexed to the research community—i.e., the shareholders of these systems—insofar as they serve as justifications for internal, technical goals (objectives). In contrast, issues surrounding, e.g., user rights, societal need, or ethical impact are rarely mentioned—for example, very few papers value beneficence or non-maleficence; transparency, interpretability or explicability; privacy; social bias or fairness; etc. Furthermore, none of the papers analysed mentions thick normative terms like autonomy, justice, or respect for persons (Birhane et al., 2022, 176).

6.4 The Human Costs of Artificial Intelligence

Several authors have underscored artificial intelligence's "hidden" costs in recent years. These costs often have little to do with the technical aspects or the resultant behaviours of training the system. Instead, they are a byproduct of the antecedents required for training and deploying these models in the first place. Raji and Dobbe (2023) highlight that these models' need for, e.g., data or computational resources, give rise to significant potential for harms in the realm of privacy, sustainability, and accountability—none of which have to do with whether the "values of humanity" are captured or encoded by the decisions of an AI system.

Case Study: Copyright and Creativity. The surge of generative AI models in recent years has raised questions surrounding the legal status of training these models. A statement from Meta effectively argues that the costs of enforcing copyright law in the case of generative AI would significantly outweigh the benefits.[11] For example, Microsoft (2023) argued that "[a]ny requirement to obtain consent for accessible works to be used for training would chill AI innovation" insofar as licensing schemes would impede innovation from startups and entrants who do not have the resources to pay to license copyrighted material.[12] Furthermore, they argue that "scale of data" is necessary to develop

[11] "Imposing a first-of-its-kind licensing regime now, well after the fact, will cause chaos as developers seek to identify millions and millions of rightsholders, for very little benefit, given that any fair royalty due would be incredibly small in light of the insignificance of any one work among an AI training set" (Meta, 2023).

[12] Of course, logically, if these startups do not have the resources to license copyrighted material, they probably also do not have the resources to train billion-parameter models.

responsible AI models and models that are not trained with data from varied sources may "become" biased or inaccurate.

Others have argued that the way generative models learn is not unlike how humans learn.[13] Others still argue that training generative AI models on copyrighted material does not constitute copyright infringement insofar as the use of such work in training constitutes fair use; for example, because training generative AI models is "of a broadly beneficial purpose" (Hugging Face, 2023), the use of copyrighted material for training these systems is non-expressive (Anthropic, 2023), or that other countries (outside the United States) would call it fair use (stability.ai, 2023).

The benefits gestured toward by these companies clearly serve the objectives of the shareholders of these systems. However, when we widen our scope to include the stakeholders, we have to reckon with the fact that artists whose work was used without permission or consent to train these models are deeply affected by these systems. Goetze (2024) argues that AI image generators "involve an unethical kind of labour theft" (1) insofar as the training of these models depends upon the "appropriation of vast numbers of existing artworks" (17); consequently, many other AI applications also rely on theft. Hence, even if these models were to satisfy the objectives of the shareholders, they fail to be aligned when we index the objectives or information axes to the wider set of stakeholders.

Case Study: Privacy. We have seen repeatedly that deep learning methods require an immense amount of data to fit one's model to those data. Because datasets are expensive (and not particularly prestigious) to create and curate, it has become common to use data scraped from the Internet to create such datasets. As mentioned in Chapter 5, the common crawl dataset contains 400 *tebibytes* (TiB) of uncompressed data taken from 3.1 billion web pages. This raises alignment concerns in light of the informational asymmetries arising from using datasets that are too large to curate. However, scraping the web for data also raises significant privacy concerns. For example, personally identifiable information—including names, addresses, contact details, etc.—may be present in the scraped data, leading to the potential identification of individuals.[14] Even when sensitive information is removed from datasets or databases,

[13]For example, Google argued "that act of 'knowledge harvesting' ... like the act of reading a book and learning the facts and ideas within it, would not only be non-infringing, it would further the very purpose of copyright law [i.e., to increase rather than impede knowledge harvesting]. The mere fact that, as a technological matter, copies need to be made to extract those ideas and facts from copyrighted works should not alter that result" (Google, 2023).

[14]See discussion in Shokri et al. (2017); Papernot et al. (2018).

auxiliary knowledge and redundant encodings can be used to de-anonymise them.[15]

In this case, privacy-first design can increase degrees of value alignment by ensuring the security of individuals' information—i.e., by taking stakeholders' values into account during the design process. Such approaches are particularly important in high-risk areas like healthcare and finance. Approaches to protecting privacy via, e.g., differential privacy, semantic security (homomorphic encryption or secure multi-party computation), or federated learning methods can be used to ensure data security during model training. However, such approaches lead to a tradeoff between performance and accuracy.[16]

At the same time, there is a tension between privacy and representation: Raji et al. (2020) underscore that privacy and consent violations in datasets often adversely affect individuals in marginalised communities insofar as attempts to diversify datasets to be more representative can often incur costs to those groups with regard to privacy, exploitation, monitoring, etc.[17]

Facial recognition provides an important case study for this axis. Suppose a facial recognition model is aligned enough on the objectives axis (relative to the shareholders) to identify faces accurately in 99.99% of cases. Suppose further that the model is somehow explainable or interpretable so we can confidently say that the model is aligned on the information axis. These facts together do not imply that the system is aligned because the very *concept* of facial recognition requires widespread privacy violations since faces are considered sensitive identifiable biometric information under ISO standards.[18] Training a deep learning model to recognise faces requires vast amounts of data. For example, the Flickr-Faces-HQ dataset (Karras et al., 2018) contains 70,000 1024×1024 images crawled from the website Flickr. Karras et al. (2019) claim

---

[15] See examples and discussion given by Narayanan and Shmatikov (2008). In an earlier context, Dinur and Nissim (2003) showed that arbitrary queries on a private statistical database necessarily reveal some private information; furthermore, a small number of queries can reveal the entire information content of the dataset.

[16] See further discussion in Konečný et al. (2015); Brendan et al. (2020). Differential privacy is a mathematical definition of privacy in the specific context of statistical analysis and machine learning. This approach distinguishes between general information about an entire population and private information, specifying an individual data subject (Dwork, 2008). The "differential" component of differential privacy refers to the change of information—i.e., the difference—before and after opting an individual's data out of the dataset, with the assumption being that if the effect of making an arbitrary single substitution in a dataset is small enough, then the result of querying that dataset cannot be used to infer much about any single individual whose information is contained in the dataset.

[17] See also discussion in Hamidi et al. (2018); Hoffmann (2019).

[18] See discussion in Raji et al. (2020); Raji and Dobbe (2023).

that the dataset only contains images under "permissive licenses"; however, Raji et al. (2020) highlight that Flickr *users* did not consent to be included in a facial recognition dataset.

Hence, even if such a model were aligned, relative to the shareholders, it would fail to be aligned when the objectives or information axes are indexed to the stakeholders of this system.

Case Study: Energy and the Environment. Shareholders often tout the various goods that may arise from the advent of powerful AI systems. Among these is the project to tackle climate change (Rolnick et al., 2019). Ironically, then, there has been increasing awareness of how training machine learning models negatively impacts the environment and contributes to climate change.[19]

As the models used to create AI systems have grown, so too have the environmental costs of training them. For example, on the faith of scaling hypotheses, the number of parameters in large language models have increased exponentially—from around 93 million parameters (the Allen Institute's Embeddings from Language Model [ELMo] in 2018) to 540 billion (Google's Pathways Language Model [PaLM] in 2022).[20] Larger models imply more energy consumption and increased carbon emissions. A recent study comparing distinct tasks in machine learning suggests that

1. generative tasks are more energy- and carbon-intensive compared to discriminative tasks,
2. tasks involving images are more energy- and carbon-intensive compared to those involving text alone,
3. decoder-only models are slightly more energy- and carbon-intensive than sequence-to-sequence models for models of a similar size and applied to the same tasks,
4. training remains orders of magnitude more energy- and carbon-intensive than inference, and
5. using multi-purpose models for discriminative tasks is more energy intensive compared to task-specific models for these same tasks (Luccioni et al., 2023a, 13).

[19] See, for example, Strubell et al. (2019, 2020); Lottick et al. (2019); Schwartz et al. (2019); Lacoste et al. (2019); Cao et al. (2020); Henderson et al. (2020); Bender et al. (2021); Patterson et al. (2021); Lannelongue et al. (2021); Parcollet and Ravanelli (2021); Luccioni et al. (2023a,b); Luccioni (2023); Luccioni and Hernandez-Garcia (2023); Crawford (2024).

[20] See Peters et al. (2018) and Chowdhery et al. (2022) for technical details.

This is to say nothing of the costs of extraction required for creating the hardware on which these systems are trained (Crawford, 2021).

In this case, the harms that can arise from machine learning systems—and therefore, instances of the value alignment problem—not only result from the *actions* or *decisions* of an AI system on deployment; these harms may also be a byproduct of the environmental costs—in terms of resource requirements—required to create such a model in the first place. This is made explicit by the principals axis of the value alignment problem insofar as a climate crisis disproportionately impacts the "often lower income and thus most neglected humans in society" (Raji and Dobbe, 2023, 3). This fact suggests that AI recapitulates a form of *environmental racism.*[21] As such, when considering the stakeholders relevant to the principals axis of the value alignment problem, it is necessary to consider how the benefits and costs of AI technologies are differentially distributed among the shareholders and the stakeholders of these systems.

Case Study: Differential Power Dynamics. Raji and Dobbe (2023) highlight that the training and testing environments for AI models, which are designed for real-world deployment, are frequently influenced or shaped by forms of human exploitation. This exploitation can occur either through the direct utilisation of underpaid and poorly trained labour or the collection and utilisation of individuals' data without their consent. Because the massive datasets used for training deep learning models contain sensitive and graphic data, tech companies rely on annotators to flag these data (Gray and Suri, 2019).

As discussed in Chapter 5, most of GPT's training data (in its third iteration) comes from the Common Crawl. Hence, it was highly toxic and heavily biased, as the common crawl dataset reflects those aspects of the Internet and is not curated. To "detoxify" GPT-3, to make way for the publicly-released ChatGPT, OpenAI built a model to detect hate speech, violence, sexual abuse, etc., so that toxic language could be removed from the platform. Thus, the toxicity-detection model could be integrated into GPT to filter out toxic training data, ensuring that the outputs based on those data are not shown to users.

However, this process is not as automated as it may seem. To build a model to detect such language, OpenAI outsourced labelling training data, which consisted of tens of thousands of snippets of toxic text taken from the dataset upon which GPT was trained—toxicity, in this case, includes graphic descriptions of child sexual abuse, bestiality, murder, suicide, torture, self-harm, and incest.

[21] See description in, e.g., Bullard (1993); Westra and Lawson (2001). In the context of artificial intelligence, see the discussion in Bender et al. (2021); Bergmann and Solomun (2021).

To be used as labelled examples for training a supervised learning model, those data need to be annotated—not unlike how images in the ImageNet dataset are hand-annotated by MTurk workers.

McQuillan (2023) highlights that the type of work that fuels artificial intelligence, relies on "extractive violence because the demand for low-paid workers to label data or massage outputs maps onto colonial relations of power". In particular, digital colonialism is defined by structural dominance relations that are instantiated through centralised ownership and control of software, hardware, and network connectivity—i.e., the three "pillars" of the digital ecosystem (Kwet, 2019). Hence, it is worth stressing the importance of critically examining the power dynamics inherent in the development and deployment of AI systems.[22]

Increasingly, researchers have noted how inequality is reproduced by the design of AI systems.[23] For example, *TIME* magazine reported that OpenAI used Kenyan workers to detoxify the outputs of ChatGPT, paying them less than US$ 2.00 per hour to do so (Perrigo, 2023). At the same time, the "nonprofit" was valued at US$ 27–29 billion. Less than one year later, after the release of Sora, this valuation tripled to US$ 80 billion. In particular, Benjamin (2019) highlights how normative assumptions made by those who design technological artefacts lead to "the employment of new technologies and social design that reflect and reproduce existing inequities, but which we assume are more objective [i.e., automation bias] or progressive than discriminatory systems of a previous era" (7). She refers to this as the *New Jim Code*, in reference to Jim Crow laws in the United States.[24]

---

[22]Recent analyses have begun to prioritise this dynamic understanding of AI ethics; see, e.g., Miceli et al. (2022); Raji and Dobbe (2023).

[23]See, for example, the discussions in Eubanks (2018); Noble (2018); Broussard (2018, 2023); Benjamin (2019); Costanza-Chock (2020); Buolamwini (2023).

[24]The Jim Crow era (1876–1965) was characterised by systems of laws that upheld white supremacy and mandated segregation after the abolishment of slavery: "Legal codes, social codes, and building codes intersected to keep people separate and unequal" (Benjamin, 2019, 91). The Civil Rights movement in the 1960s led to the dismantling of Jim Crow laws and the abolishment of legalised racial segregation. However, Alexander (2010) argues that the explicit racism of the Jim Crow era transformed into the implicit denial of Black rights via discriminatory policing, mandatory sentencing, and mass incarceration. This serves to furnish the *New Jim Crow*: "a stunningly comprehensive and well-disguised system of racialized social control that functions in a manner strikingly similar to Jim Crow" (Alexander, 2010, 4). If slavery is absolute racism, Jim Crow laws explicitly encode legal racism, and the new Jim Crow implicitly encodes legal racism, the *New Jim Code* described by Benjamin (2019) is a form of computational racism, wherein racism that has been encoded in past laws is encoded in technology. In some ways, this is more pernicious because it can be done unknowingly.

Benjamin (2019) points out that the *power* of the New Jim Code is that it "allows racist habits and logics to enter through the backdoor of tech design, in which the humans who create the algorithms are hidden from view" (160). On the one hand, this concealment can arise in the context of accountability and responsibility, as we have already seen; however, this can also occur when we consider the hidden labour that powers present-day AI systems.

In the context of the value alignment problem for artificial intelligence, principals can be shareholders or stakeholders. As we have seen repeatedly, each group's values, goals, or objectives can diverge. However, the shareholders—not the stakeholders—typically contribute to how these systems are designed and deployed. It would be naïve to assume benevolent designer intent; moreover, even when intent is well-meaning, we have seen that AI systems (e.g., for social good) can cause harms by not considering their potential impact on various stakeholders or the ethical considerations associated with the deployment of such systems in real-world contexts.

As the set of stakeholders increases, the set consisting of the conjunction of their individual values decreases. For sufficiently large sets of stakeholders, the conjunction of their shared values is probably empty. Since no set of values covers all possible stakeholders in such instances, there is an inherent tradeoff regarding whose values are satisfied. However, determining whether the tradeoff is worthwhile is a value-laden decision which cannot be made by the shareholders of these systems alone. Hence, reckoning with differential power dynamics between shareholders and stakeholders is essential for working toward value alignment.

Case Study: Accountability. *Moral deskilling* in the context of AI refers to the potential diminishing of human moral decision-making skills as reliance on artificial intelligence increases. There is a risk of deferring to automated decision-making, which we have already begun to see in the context of recidivism prediction tools. This deskilling phenomenon may arise from a reduced need for individuals to engage in moral reasoning or a growing dependence on algorithms to dictate ethical norms. Vallor (2015) highlights that reliance on these systems in moral domains may contribute to the moral deskilling of human users, which has downstream consequences, in her view, for the cultivation of "practical wisdom and virtuous character" (107).[25]

Similarly, *automation bias* is a cognitive phenomenon wherein individuals tend to rely excessively on automated systems, often leading to diminished

[25] See also the discussion in Vallor (2011, 2016).

trust in their decision-making capabilities. This bias arises when individuals place undue confidence in the accuracy and reliability of automated technologies, even in situations where human judgement is still crucial. Automation bias can result from the perception that algorithmic systems are infallible, objective, or superior to humans in certain tasks, leading individuals to defer critical decisions to automated systems without sufficient scrutiny.

Although moral deskilling and automation bias are not directly related to the value alignment problem for artificial intelligence, it becomes apparent that these issues are implicated when we consider how AI systems are used, by whom, and for what purpose—i.e., key questions arising along the principals axis.

For example, in December 2023, reports surfaced that the Israel Defense Forces (IDF) employed an AI-based target creation platform, known as "The Gospel", in the ongoing genocide they are enacting against Palestinians in Gaza. Details about the model's architecture, training data, and objectives remain scarce. However, an IDF press release stated, "With the help of artificial intelligence ... [The Gospel] produces a recommendation for the researcher, with the goal being that there will be a complete match between the machine's recommendation and the identification performed by a person". It was reported that system was trained on a database of 30,000–40,000 "suspected militants", in addition to "drone footage, intercepted communications, surveillance data, and information drawn from monitoring the movements and behaviour patterns of individuals and large groups" (Davies et al., 2023). As a result of this model's deployment, military intelligence at the IDF increased the creation of targets from 50 per year to 100 per day.

Even if we assume the veracity of the *stated* objective—i.e., minimising loss between the Gospel's recommendation and the recommendation that would be forwarded by a human expert—it should be apparent that this system is poorly aligned. The actual targets—which are sent directly to soldiers through a military-issued smartphone application called "Pillar of Fire"—appear to optimise for devastation in the Gaza strip. In this case, one might wonder why invest in developing an AI system when a random number generator might accomplish the same goal.

In addition to the *Gospel*, which produces potential target objects like buildings and "other structures", a distinct database (reported to use artificial intelligence) called *Lavender* specifies potential human targets. In a statement issued by the IDF, they claim that according to "international humanitarian law, a person who is identified as a member of an organized armed group (like the Hamas' military wing), or a person who directly participates in hostilities, is considered a lawful target".[26] These considerations highlight an important fact about the deployment of AI: namely, that algorithmic deference may be used to evade moral (or legal) responsibility. The principals axis of the value alignment problem helps to bring these issues to the fore.

Human Flourishing. Many researchers have suggested that AI will contribute to human flourishing, gesturing wildly at some utopian vision of the future wherein humanity lives a life of leisure in the wake of general-purpose AI.[27] However, when describing what human flourishing actually consists in, these analyses are often highly vague and abstract (usually with some offhand reference to Aristotle's discussion of *eudaimonia*).[28] One of the insights of the reconceptualisation of the value alignment problem given in Chapter 3 is to underscore that the value alignment problem is fundamentally social in nature, implying that technical solutions alone will not suffice to solve issues of misalignment. At the same time, foregrounding distinct sets of principals has shown that the value alignment problem becomes more difficult as these systems are built to function in more general-purpose contexts.

To that end, it is worth considering one of the genuine success stories of an AI model. Andrews (2023) suggests that DeepMind's AlphaFold and AlphaFold 2.0 are among the most impressive results that machine learning methods have achieved for science, not the least because the protein-folding problem in structural biology was largely considered intractable.

One potential impact that AlphaFold lends itself to is drug discovery. However, Perrakis and Sixma (2021) note that the "current AlphaFold implementation does not yet have the accuracy that is necessary for drug discovery" (5). Moreover, the hype surrounding AI methods may be counterproductive for drug discovery because of the scarcity of publicly available data required for a viable drug discovery system based on machine learning techniques.

That said, part of the incomparable success of AlphaFold can be attributed to the fact that the model is not domain-generic. Instead, "the model architecture is hand-tailored to the specific task of learning to predict three dimensional protein structure from [multiple sequence alignments] and pair representations" (Andrews, 2023, 12–13). Hence, it is precisely because of the narrow target of this system (limiting direct stakeholders) and the fact that the objective lends

[26] The IDF's statement was published in *The Guardian* (2024) in response to reporting by McKernan and Davies (2024). See also Abraham (2024).

[27] It is perhaps of interest that the word *utopia* is derived from the Greek οὐ (not) and τόπος (place).

[28] See Aristotle (1995a,b).

itself to formalisation that this model can be considered value-aligned (and also useful). At the same time, the outputs of the model are not isolated: they are a mere part of a larger socio-technical system that includes human scientists and expertise on application.

Most present-day AI systems fail to offer tools for promoting human flourishing. Instead, they entrench biases, widen the gap between social groups, and further marginalise communities. Considering the objectives encoded in AI systems with respect to a particular set of principals sheds light on how AI systems fail to satisfy these objectives. In general, when any given AI model is touted as a solution—particularly by the shareholders of that system—it is fruitful to ask: to what problem?

6.5 Interaction Effects

Principals and Objectives. In the context of predictive policing, a key goal is *effective* policing. This is an example of a *reformist* approach to reforms, which seeks to "fine-tune" the status quo by working within an extant system rather than addressing the causes of the issue in question. It should be apparent that such a goal does not serve marginalised communities, which are historically over-policed in North America. Hence, even if a predictive policing model is aligned with the objectives of the carceral institutions that deploy it, it would fail to be aligned with those stakeholders who are adversely, unjustly, and disproportionately affected by the existence of those institutions.

Principals and Information. When discussing information asymmetries in Chapter 5, much of the analysis implicitly assumed that the principal was a *shareholder* rather than a *stakeholder*. For example, model architectures and datasets lack transparency in deep learning systems; however, the assumption that opacity can be reduced—by increasing, e.g., structural, functional, or run transparency—presupposes that the principal has the *means* to increase transparency. This clearly falls under the purview of programmers and companies (i.e., the shareholders in these systems).

However, when we widen the scope of indices for the value alignment problem to include stakeholders—paradigmatically, those affected by a deployed system despite having no individual share in it—we see that transparency and principals can interact perniciously to exacerbate the potential for value misalignment. Suppose, for example, a system is completely transparent to the shareholders, but the model architecture is proprietary. In this case, the system may still lack transparency from the point of view of the wider set of stakeholders. As Burrell (2016) highlights, opacity may arise from "intentional corporate or institutional self-protection and concealment and, along with it, the possibility for knowing deception" (1). A potential consequence of this is that proprietary or for-profit models may always be misaligned, to some degree, when we index to stakeholders.

6.6 Summary

The value alignment problem can arise whenever a (human) principal delegates authority to an (artificial) agent to act on their behalf. Hence, when we ask whether an AI model is value-aligned, this question is always indexed to a particular principal (or set of principals). This fact is left unarticulated in the standard definition of the value alignment problem, which concerns ensuring that AI systems align with the "values of humanity". At best, the standard definition of the value alignment problem serves to misdirect the conversation surrounding value alignment. Describing the value alignment problem as the problem of ensuring that AI systems are aligned with the values of humanity may lead people (the public, but also AI researchers) to believe, for example, that there is a community-accepted standard for what it means for a model to be value-aligned. At worst, it provides a vehicle for ethics-washing, thus allowing those who purport to care about ensuring that these systems are aligned to perpetuate the status quo. In this sense, those social groups who benefit from the status quo often overlap significantly with those who benefit from maintaining the conceptualisation of "value alignment" as a buzzword: mere window dressing, public relations, hype generation, or marketing.

Consider, again, a recidivism prediction model. In this case, the programmers who create the model, the companies who deploy the model, and the users who employ the model all have similar objectives pertaining to accuracy in prediction. Note, however, that the reasons for these objectives may differ. The company may want the system to function as intended so that they can sell it without risking loss of business or lawsuits; the users may want the system to function as intended to ensure a (carceral) conception of "justice". That said, the wider set of stakeholders for this system includes the *subjects* of the system—i.e., those individuals about whom the model renders a decision. In some cases, the subjects' or stakeholders' goals may be the same as the programmers', companies', and users' goals—presumably, someone subject to a recidivism prediction model also prefers that the model be accurate, all things considered.[29] However, this myopic instantiation of objectives fails

[29] Note there is a symmetry with accuracy that makes it appear more fair than inaccuracy. Although a "high-risk" individual may prefer to be labelled low-risk, and hence prefer the system to be

to take seriously antecedent questions surrounding whether the target of recidivism prediction is, itself, just.

The standard definition of the value alignment problem gestures vaguely toward the values of humanity. However, the structural definition offered in Chapter 3 underscores that whether a system is aligned is a function of whose perspective is under consideration. In this definition, the human costs of artificial intelligence are often ignored. On the standard definition of the value alignment problem, the best we can say is that the "values of humanity" include sustainability. Indeed, the key drivers of misalignment—misspecified objective functions and informational asymmetries—would fail to capture environmental consequences insofar as these are, in some sense, exogenous to the model. That said, because the value alignment problem, on the structural definition, is construed as arising from the dynamics of multi-agent interactions, it is an inherently social problem. This implies that when considering value alignment or misalignment, it is always insufficient to say that a system is aligned without specifying *for whom.* Anyone who takes value alignment seriously must reckon with the differential outcomes of artificial intelligence experienced by various principals.

In many cases, as we have seen, the objectives of shareholders and stakeholders may come apart, depending on who the principal in question is. As such, value alignment *simpliciter* is a strong condition. This insight is discussed in more detail in Chapter 9 when we examine the prospects for measuring degrees of alignment. But first, Part III explores current approaches to mitigating value misalignment. As we will see, solutions for misalignment are often approached in a purely technical way.

Additional Resources

Virginia Eubanks. 2018. *Automating Inequality: How Tech Tools Profile, Police, and Punish the Poor*. New York: MacMillan.

Safiya Noble. 2018. *Algorithms of Oppression*. New York: NYU Press.

Meredith Broussard. 2018. *Artificial Unintelligence: How Computers Misunderstand the World*. Cambridge, MA: The MIT Press.

Ruha Benjamin. 2019. *Race After Technology: Abolitionist Tools for the New Jim Code*. Cambridge: Polity.

---

inaccurate, an inaccurate system will also label some low-risk individuals high-risk. If one does not know, *a priori*, whether they are (or are considered) high-risk, then one ought to prefer such a decision be veridical. This is a form of the *Darwinian veil of ignorance* described in Skyrms (1994, 1996). That said, we have already seen (Chapter 4) that such systems are irreducibly biased.

Catherine D'Ignazio and Lauren F. Klein. 2020. *Data Feminism*. Cambridge, MA: The MIT Press.

Kate Crawford. 2021. *Atlas of AI*. New Haven, CT: Yale University Press.

Joy Buolamwini. 2023. *Unmasking AI: My Mission to Protect What Is Human in a World of Machines*. New York: Penguin Random House.

III

Approaches to Value Alignment

Introduction to Part III

Part I of this book provided some conceptual background for understanding the value alignment problem—including historical and technical context (Chapters 1, 2) and the standard definition of value alignment in the literature—before offering a novel, structural definition of the value alignment problem for artificial intelligence (Chapter 3) based on the principal-agent framework from economics. The structural definition shows that the value alignment problem is a class of problem instances arising from the dynamics of multi-agent interactions. These dynamics involve delegation from a human principal to an artificial agent. This structural definition characterises the value alignment problem for artificial intelligence along three orthogonal axes—*misspecified objectives*, *informational asymmetries*, and *relative principals*. Each of these axes was given individual attention in Part II.

Given this analysis, it is worthwhile to examine existing approaches aimed at "solving" the value alignment problem. As these approaches are typically built upon the standard definition of value alignment, evaluating them through the perspective of our novel structural definition can highlight both their strengths and weaknesses. Hence, Part III takes up some current approaches to solving the value alignment problem.

The two chapters in this part correspond to two different research directions relevant to value alignment on the standard definition and its two related components (the technical and normative components). Chapter 7 examines some techniques in the field of *AI safety*, which correlates (roughly) to technical approaches to aligning values. Chapter 8 discusses *machine ethics*, which assumes the normative component of value alignment. These two chapters mostly rehearse the arguments of other research projects. However, the positive contribution is to show how the conceptual re-imagining of the value alignment problem as a structural problem (arising from the dynamics of multi-agent interactions) can accommodate these fields' conceptualisation of the value alignment problem. At the same time, the structural definition of value alignment for artificial intelligence helps to identify the weaknesses in these proposed solutions.

7 AI Safety

Ignoring potential connotation of existential risk, AI safety is a multidisciplinary research field focused on developing strategies and frameworks to ensure the responsible and secure deployment of AI systems. This research encompasses a wide range of concerns, including preventing unintended consequences, averting accidents, and safeguarding against intentional misuse or adverse outcomes stemming from AI systems. In addition to relevant ethical considerations, research in this direction focuses on the robustness of AI systems and mitigating potential risks associated with developing advanced machine learning algorithms.

Technical AI safety is a specialised domain within the broader field of AI safety, primarily focused on developing and implementing technical methodologies to ensure the safe and reliable functioning of AI systems. The technical aspects of AI safety involve addressing challenges arising from the creation and deployment of these systems, such as monitoring systems for potential risks and enhancing their reliability.

Researchers in this area focus on designing algorithms, architectures, and systems that are robust, transparent, and predictable. Technical AI safety aims to address issues such as adversarial attacks, unintended consequences, and the potential for AI systems to behave in unpredictable or unsafe ways. Additionally, this research field explores ways to imbue AI models with mechanisms for self-monitoring and correction, contributing to creating AI systems that align with human values and adhere to ethical guidelines. Hence, it should be apparent how AI safety seeks to "solve" the value alignment problem on the standard definition discussed in Chapter 3. This research focuses on the *technical* component of the value alignment problem insofar as it emphasises formal verification, robustness testing, and the development of "provably safe" AI systems.

Approaches to AI safety are built upon highly interdisciplinary work, including contributions from computer science, ethics, psychology, law, and other disciplines. However, *technical* approaches to AI safety tend to focus on purely technical contributions. Testing a system for safety in engineering involves considering the potential failure modes of that system. For example, many researchers have explored *adversarial examples* in machine learning—e.g., specialised inputs that are intentionally designed to elicit the incorrect output for a model.

This chapter explores some work that has been proposed in this area, including practical and theoretical methods. The general goal is twofold. On the one hand, this chapter seeks to demonstrate how contemporary approaches to AI safety can be categorised according to the axes of the structural definition of the value alignment problem described in Chapter 3. On the other hand, this chapter aims to illuminate some of the shortcomings of purely technical approaches to the value alignment problem, which are brought to light by its structural reconceptualisation.

The first part of this chapter describes several "concrete problems" that arise in the context of AI systems (Sections 7.1 and 7.2). We then move on, in Section 7.3, to describe some key technical approaches to mitigating these problems, including reward modelling, cooperative inverse reinforcement learning, game-theoretic approaches to achieving "provably safe" AI, and reinforcement learning from human feedback (RLHF). In the final part of the chapter (Section 7.4), we reconsider the efficacy and shortcomings of these approaches under the structural definition of the value alignment problem.

7.1 Adversarial Examples

Before the popularisation of deep learning approaches to AI, researchers discussed the potential of *adversarial learning*, where an "attack" on a model can occur at the training or testing stage, causing vulnerabilities in the model that are particularly concerning for security-critical applications (Lowd and Meek, 2005).[1] Data poisoning is a type of adversarial attack wherein malicious examples are introduced to data at the training stage, thus skewing the original probability distribution associated with those data; hence, when a model is successfully trained on poisoned data, it may perform well on those data, but real-world data will be "out of distribution", relative to the (poisoned) training data, meaning that the system will fail to be aligned for generalised tasks on deploy-

[1] See the taxonomy in Barreno et al. (2006) and the discussion in Zhang and Li (2019).

ment.[2] For example, Microsoft's chatbot, Tay, was initially programmed with a narrow script (not unlike ELIZA, half a century earlier), but it also learned from interactions with others. Sixteen hours after Microsoft released Tay on Twitter, it had published more than 95,000 tweets, many of which included highly offensive content.[3] Part of the explanation as to how this happened is that anonymous Internet trolls took advantage of the "repeat after me" function coded in the model to inundate it with racist, misogynistic, and antisemitic language. Among many other problems, this is a case of data poisoning.

In contrast, evasion attacks utilise knowledge of the parameters of a trained model to construct a specific input example that generates faulty outputs. So, rather than changing the system itself, this approach takes advantage of the poor generalisation abilities of learned models—i.e., evasion attacks capitalise on inner misalignment. Building upon the idea of adversarial attacks, Szegedy et al. (2014) introduced the concept of an adversarial *example*, a type of evasion attack relevant to the deep learning context. In this case, a slight perturbation or noise is added to the input so that the model misclassifies the adversarial example with high confidence. For example, consider an autonomous vehicle trained to recognise stop signs. It has been shown that a physical perturbation to an input—e.g., appending tape to a real-world stop sign in a particular pattern—can cause the model to classify the stop sign as a speed-limit sign.[4] Often, these perturbations are unrecognisable to the human optical system. Hence, adversarial examples significantly threaten the safety of deep neural network models when deployed.

These examples are instances of the value alignment problem. On the structural definition, adversarial examples could be classified along the axis of informational asymmetries to the extent that the model contains *hidden information* unavailable to the principal. Technical approaches to this problem seek to underscore the weaknesses of trained systems using adversarial training. Techniques for robust optimisation and defensive distillation seek to make models more resilient to adversarial attacks.[5] At the same time, it is necessary to understand the model's inner workings to ensure that it is not susceptible to adversarial examples. Effectively, this is a problem of unpredictability (hence a problem of informational asymmetry) concerning perturbed, out-of-distribution, or noisy inputs.

[2]See details in Wittel and Wu (2004); Biggio et al. (2012, 2013).

[3]See reporting in Wakefield (2016); Dewey (2016); Bright (2016).

[4]See discussion in Eykholt et al. (2018).

[5]Further technical details are given by Goldblum et al. (2020).

7.2 Concrete Problems in AI Safety

Although much discussion in AI safety of mitigating misalignment is couched in the context of superintelligent AI systems, in an influential paper, Amodei et al. (2016) try to lay out a set of "concrete" problems on which researchers can currently progress. They suggest that safety problems can be categorised according to where things have gone wrong in the design process. In this context, "AI safety" need not have any connotation concerning superintelligent AI, control problems, or existential risk—the authors note that these are difficult to predict and, therefore, inherently difficult to safeguard against. Nonetheless, by focusing on concrete problems, Amodei et al. (2016) believe that we may be able to come up with tractable solutions in the short term, which may well be beneficial down the line on the assumption that these systems will increase significantly in their abilities.

They focus on five problems, which they refer to as "accidents"; however, it will become apparent that each problem discussed instantiates the value alignment problem, as defined in Chapter 3.[6] These are

1. **Avoiding negative side effects**. This type of accident involves developing strategies and techniques to prevent unintended and undesirable consequences that may arise during the operation or deployment of AI systems. Effectively, this is a problem of ensuring that an AI system does what you want it to do but does not do things you do not want it to do.
2. **Reward hacking**. This type of accident refers to situations where an AI system, particularly a reinforcement learning agent, exploits loopholes or unintended aspects of the reward function to achieve its objectives in a way that is not aligned with the true objective of the principal. In effect, for an incompletely specified objective function, the system can find a shortcut or an unconventional strategy to optimise the objective function at the expense of ethical, safe, or value-aligned behaviour.

Both of these types of accidents arise (primarily) from poorly specified objective functions, which would make them problems of *outer* alignment arising from a misalignment between the true objective (the objective of the principal) and the objective function (the objective of the agent). For example, encoding all the relevant aspects of an environment is impossible because an objective function is a proxy and a simplification for the true objective. In this case, what is left out of the value function in this encoding is implicitly represented as indifference in the context of "human values"—i.e., if it had mattered, then

[6] See also the discussion in Hadfield-Menell and Hadfield (2019).

we would have included it in the specification of the objective function. Such problem instances arise along the first axis of the value alignment problem on the structural definition described in Chapter 3.

Unsurprisingly, ensuring that the system's objective function is a good proxy for the principal's true objective is insufficient to ensure that a system is value-aligned. Three additional types of "accidents" can arise in light of informational asymmetries between the principal and the agent:

3. **Scalable oversight**. This type of accident refers to the difficulty of monitoring complex systems as they increase in scale. Addressing this problem requires the development of efficient and adaptable mechanisms for monitoring and controlling AI systems as they operate at scale. In essence, this is a problem of using information efficiently.
4. **Safe exploration**. This type of accident arises (in the context of reinforcement learning) because there is a tradeoff between exploration and exploitation; effectively, we want to ensure that an RL agent can explore its environment without testing harmful strategies. Hence, this requires ensuring the agent can safely explore the range of possible actions. Safe exploration is related to the problem of avoiding negative side effects; however, in this case, the problem arises primarily because of informational asymmetries rather than misspecified objectives.
5. **Robustness to distributional shift**. This type of accident may arise when an AI system encounters variations in the distribution of data that differ from its training environment, leading to potential performance degradation or unexpected behaviour. In addition, this problem can arise because distributions may vary over time, meaning that an AI system that performs well on deployment may perform poorly when the environment changes.

Although misspecified objectives can exacerbate these latter three types of accidents, these can occur even if the objective function is well-specified for the task at hand. Hence, scalable oversight, safe exploration, and robustness to distributional shift are fundamentally types of *inner* alignment problems. These arise from informational asymmetries between the principal and the agent; as such, they correspond to the second axis of the value alignment problem per the definition offered in Chapter 3.

We will now explore each of these types of accidents in slightly more detail.

Avoiding Negative Side Effects. When designing the objective function for an AI system, the designer specifies the objective but not the exact steps for the system to follow. This fact allows the AI system to develop novel and (potentially) more effective strategies for achieving its objective than the system's designers may have thought of themselves. This is one of the key advantages of the machine learning paradigm when compared with classical, symbolic, or top-down approaches to artificial intelligence research. However, if the objective function is not well defined, the system's ability to hit upon local optima can lead to unintended, harmful side effects.

The problem of avoiding negative side effects can manifest in various ways. For instance, in the case of an autonomous vehicle, avoiding negative side effects may include ensuring that the vehicle's decisions do not harm pedestrians, cyclists, or other drivers. Avoiding accidents requires sophisticated algorithms that prioritise safety and (perhaps) ethical considerations, accounting for various scenarios and contingencies. Similarly, avoiding negative side effects in natural language processing applications could involve mitigating biases in language models to prevent the generation of discriminatory or offensive content. In this case, researchers and developers need to implement measures to detect and address biases in training data.

We cannot take anything for granted when designing an objective function for an AI system and using that function to fit a model to training data. Hence, it is insufficient for the objective to be formulated as "complete task ϕ"; the objective function must specify safety criteria under which the task should be completed. Avoiding negative side effects is a type of value alignment problem insofar as the delegation of a task to an artificial agent can lead to unintended side effects when the objective function is incompletely or poorly specified; furthermore, since it is impossible to encode everything we care about in the objective function, this problem may always arise.

Some technical approaches for mitigating risks associated with unintended consequences include penalising the agent whenever it impacts the environment. However, an AI agent must interact with (and hence impact) its environment to *some* extent to be useful. Instead, we might define a "budget" for how much that agent is allowed to impact the environment, which would help to minimise unintended impacts without disabling the system. That said, it is difficult to quantify "impacts" on the environment, even for simple, fixed tasks. In addition, what counts as a significant impact may vary depending on the stakeholders under consideration.

As such, although unintended side effects are primarily instantiated along the objectives axis of the value alignment problem, informational asymmetries and relative principals are highly relevant to whether a system is value-aligned.

A different approach would be to train the agent to *recognise* harmful side effects to avoid actions likely to give rise to such side effects. In this case, the agent would be trained on two separate tasks: the original task, specified by the objective function, and the task of recognising side effects. One key idea in this approach is that distinct tasks may have similar side effects, even when the main objective is entirely different. Hence, an advantage of this approach is that once an agent learns to avoid side effects on one task, it may transfer this "knowledge" to other tasks or environments.

Although there are some potential solutions for avoiding negative side effects, this is still a challenging problem: the AI system must undergo extensive testing and critical evaluation before deployment in real-life settings. Moreover, what counts as a negative side effect or a mere "externality" depends on whose view is considered relevant to the judgement, which describes an instantiation of the value alignment problem along the principals axis.

Reward Hacking. Reward hacking refers to a situation where an intelligent agent exploits a reward function to achieve its objectives in a way that the system designer did not intend. In this case, the agent learns to manipulate the reward signal to maximise its cumulative reward without truly accomplishing the desired task. In effect, a search process yields a sequence of candidate policies for a reinforcement learning agent to adopt; optimisation based on a proxy reward moves the system toward policies with a higher proxy reward. A reward function is said to be *hackable* when, given a pair of policies, π_1 and π_2, the proxy reward function assigns more value to π_1, but the true reward function assigns more value to π_2.[7] Hence, as with unintended side effects, reward hacking instantiates the value alignment problem *primarily* along the objectives axis insofar as hackable reward functions are poor proxies for the true reward function.

Reward hacking often aligns closely with identifying and exploiting "loopholes", where agents seek to maximise rewards by capitalising on unexpected features or artefacts in the environment. Whether human or automated, agents may exploit loopholes in an incentive structure to achieve superficial success without genuinely fulfilling the intended objectives. This exploitation can lead to the system producing misleading or counterproductive results. In this case, the objective function can be formally maximised in a way that does not achieve the true objective. However, from the "perspective" of the system, such strategies are perfectly valid, given that they maximise rewards (or minimise loss). The CoastRunners model described in Chapter 3 is an example of reward hacking. In this case, the reward function given to the system was a poor proxy

[7]Further technical details are provided by Skalse et al. (2022).

for the true objective, and the agent capitalised on a strategy that maximised the objective *function* while failing to satisfy the true objective.

These loopholes are more likely to arise when the rewards are only vaguely defined. Furthermore, as systems become more complex, the number of possible ways they can interact with their environment increases exponentially, owing to combinatorial explosion. This implies that the agent has more degrees of freedom in choosing how to interact with its environment; hence, vaguely defined rewards make it more difficult to gauge true success on the task.

Just like the problem of negative side effects, reward hacking is an instance of the value alignment problem along the objectives axis—i.e., when the AI system's objective function is not defined well enough to capture the informal "intent" behind creating the system (the true objective). This discrepancy sometimes leads to suboptimal results; other times, it can lead to genuinely harmful results. Preventing reward hacking requires designing reward functions that accurately capture the desired behaviour and anticipate potential loopholes. Essentially, this process requires ensuring that the proxies used to stand in for the true objective are good proxies. As we saw in Chapter 4, the degree to which a proxy is a good approximation of an objective is a function of the context in which that objective arises or is fulfilled.

Scalable Oversight. When a model is trained to execute a complex task, human oversight and feedback prove more beneficial than relying solely on environmental rewards.[8] While rewards typically indicate the degree to which a task is accomplished, they often lack detailed insights into the safety implications of the agent's actions. Even if the agent successfully completes the task, deducing potential side effects solely from rewards can be challenging. In an optimal scenario, continuous, detailed supervision and feedback from a human would offer more useful information to the agent than a (potentially sparse, time-delayed) reward signal received from the environment.

However, implementing such a strategy would demand a significant investment of time and effort from the human participant. Hence, it is often too costly to implement oversight in cases where safety risks are infrequent or the model itself is too complex. In this case, it may be that the model's objective function is perfectly well-specified; however, the problem of scalable oversight highlights how informational asymmetries between the (human) principal and the (artificial) agent can still lead to misaligned behaviour or outputs. Specifically,

[8] See the discussion offered by Christiano et al. (2023).

scalable oversight is an informational asymmetry caused by moral hazard (hidden action).

Safe Exploration. One component of training an AI agent in a reinforcement learning context requires the agent to explore and understand its environment. Although exploring the environment can be a bad strategy in the short run, it may be highly effective in the long run, meaning that reinforcement learning agents must balance exploiting known strategies and exploring new ones. Unless the agent is designed to explore its environment, it will never discover novel (and potentially more effective) strategies. However, exploration comes with inherent risk. While the agent explores new strategies, it might try some harmful actions. As with scalable oversight, safe exploration creates a problem because of informational asymmetry caused by moral hazard (hidden action) in addition to adverse selection (we cannot tell in advance what strategies the system will attempt because exploration is random by default).[9]

Robustness to Distributional Shift. A complex challenge for deploying AI systems in real-life settings is that the agent will likely end up in situations it has never experienced before. Such real-world situations are inherently more difficult to handle than simplified toy environments; unexpected states in which an agent finds itself could lead the agent to take harmful actions. This is sometimes referred to as the "long tail" problem as it describes the distribution of rare events in large datasets. In effect, a machine learning model may perform well on common and frequently occurring tasks but struggle when faced with rare or less common instances. Hence, this is a problem of distributional shift insofar as the real-world distribution differs from the distribution inherent to the training data.

One research direction focuses on identifying when the agent has encountered a new scenario so that it recognises that it is more likely to make mistakes. While this does not solve the underlying problem of preparing AI systems for unforeseen circumstances, it helps detect the problem before mistakes happen. Another research direction emphasises safely transferring knowledge from familiar scenarios to new scenarios.[10]

[9]Raji and Dobbe (2023) highlight that unintended consequences arising from misaligned AI systems are analogous to the choice of companies (and the individual humans constituting those companies) to deploy systems that have not been thoroughly tested, effectively treating real-world deployments as live experiments for future models. For example, Tesla and Uber have publicly beta-tested autonomous vehicles (commercial products), leading to fatal crashes in both cases; see reporting in Wakabayashi (2018); Siddiqui and Merrill (2023).

[10]See, e.g., Taylor and Stone (2009).

The key point is that there is a general trend toward increasing autonomy in AI systems, and with increased autonomy comes increased chances of error. Problems related to AI safety are more likely to manifest in scenarios where the AI system exerts direct control over its physical or digital environment without a human in the loop—e.g., automated industrial processes, automated financial trading algorithms, AI-powered social media campaigns for political parties, self-driving cars, cleaning robots, among others. When training data are imperfect proxies for real-world distributions, this is primarily an instance of the value alignment problem on the objectives axis. When data are unrepresentative of the real world or exclude rare cases, this can lead to potential harms on deployment because the underlying distribution on which the model was trained is not captured by its training data.

Machine learning models, as we saw in Chapter 2, are typically trained on (static) historical data, and their performance is optimised for the distribution of data seen during training. However, if the model encounters a distribution shift, where the data it faces in the real world differ from the training data, it may perform poorly. A model trained on finite data does not have complete information about the diverse scenarios it might encounter in the real world. However, even if we assume that training data perfectly represent the real-world distribution, those training data comprise a static dataset; in contrast, the distributions of data of the world in which an AI model is deployed are constantly in flux. Hence, the problem of distributional shift between a static dataset and a real-world distribution arises primarily from informational asymmetries.

The remainder of this chapter summarises and examines some of the key approaches to mitigating value misalignment from the perspective of AI safety.

7.3 Mitigating Risk

This section discusses some key proposals for ensuring the safety of AI systems by mitigating misalignment.

Reward Modelling and Agent Alignment. As mentioned in Chapter 3, Leike et al. (2018) refer to the value alignment problem as the *agent alignment* problem. Formally, agent alignment is a sequential decision problem. Under the reinforcement learning paradigm, an agent interacts with its environment over discrete time steps, taking an action at each time step. As with many of the "accidents" described above, the difficulty is ensuring the agent's actions align with the user's *intentions*. A solution to this problem consists of a learned *policy* that the agent can follow, which produces behaviour in accordance with the user's intentions.

As we have seen, designing suitable reward functions for a reinforcement learning agent is difficult and can lead to value misalignment. On the one hand, the designer or user may have only an implicit understanding of the task objective—i.e., a representation of the *true* objective. On the other hand, game-playing environments have been key to advances in reinforcement learning partly because the environments give rise to intuitive and clearly specifiable reward functions. For example, a natural reward for the game of backgammon is $+1$ if the agent wins and -1 if the agent loses; similarly, for chess, a natural reward is $+1$ if the agent wins, -1 if the agent loses, and 0 if the agent draws. In contrast to this toy environment, performance on complex, real-world tasks is not easily measurable.

To solve this problem, Leike et al. (2018) propose *reward modelling*: effectively, this paradigm seeks to train a model on the reward, with some feedback from the user—the latter of which is supposed to reflect or capture the user's intentions (and hence, values). At the same time, a policy is trained via standard reinforcement learning techniques to maximise the reward from the reward model. The former model—the reward model—effectively learns *what* to do, whereas the latter model—the policy—learns *how* to do it. The long-term goal of this research direction is to design algorithms that learn to adapt to how users provide feedback, thus accounting for the variability of natural language; this suggestion will be relevant for the discussion in Chapter 10.

To accommodate complex domains where it is difficult for humans to evaluate performance, Leike et al. (2018) suggest the possibility of recursively applying reward modelling so that an agent can be trained to assist the user in the evaluation process.

There are at least two things that the structural definition brings to light about the potential for reward modelling in mitigating the value alignment problem. On the one hand, as Gabriel (2020) has already noted, it is not obvious that the *target* of alignment should be *intentions*. The problem becomes apparent when one considers the intentional misuse of an AI system to harm others. This difficulty is made explicit by the principals axis of the value alignment problem, which clarifies that it matters *whose* values (goals, objectives, intentions, etc.) we are considering when we assess whether a system is value aligned. On the other hand, a system varies in the degree to which it is aligned based upon the three axes of the value alignment problem; however, the proximal cause of the problem is the process of delegating authority to an AI agent to act on the principal's behalf. Hence, the suggestion to use AI models to mitigate misalignment for other AI models serves to multiply potential instances of the value alignment problem, insofar as we are then delegating authority to an (artificial) agent to satisfy our objectives—where the objective, in this case, is to mitigate misalignment in a different artificial agent.

Cooperative Inverse Reinforcement Learning (CIRL). As mentioned in Chapter 2, *reinforcement learning* is a machine learning paradigm wherein an agent performs actions in an environment and is subsequently rewarded. The objective function in this case—i.e., the thing being maximised—is the cumulative reward. An optimal or near-optimal *policy* (strategy) for the agent maximises the reward function.

In the reinforcement learning paradigm, it is up to the programmer to design a suitable reward function. The agent observes the environment and reward and learns a policy (behaviours) to maximise the reward function, thus specified by the programmer. However, as we saw in Chapter 3, designing a reward function can be difficult—particularly in complex environments. In contrast, *inverse* reinforcement learning aims for the agent to *learn* a reward function by observing *behaviour*.

Thus, in a standard reinforcement learning problem, the goal is to learn a policy that produces behaviour which maximises some (hand-coded, pre-defined, well-specified) reward function. Inverse reinforcement learning is the inverse of this problem: the goal is to learn the reward function from the observed behaviour of an agent (Ng and Russell, 2000). That is to say, an algorithm for *inverse* reinforcement learning aims to infer the reward function based on observed behaviour. In this case, the system observes (human) behaviour, infers the reward function according to which the human agent is acting, and then uses that reward function as its own reward function.

However, Hadfield-Menell et al. (2019) highlight that in many cases relevant to alignment, we do not want the reward function of the AI system to be *identical* to the reward function of the human agent under observation—for example, from a human person being observed to get up in the morning and make a cup of coffee, the reward function implies a desire for coffee. Still, we do not want an (hypothetical) IRL agent to "desire" coffee itself, even if we want it to make us a coffee. Thus, they propose a new paradigm to solve these problems: *cooperative* inverse reinforcement learning (CIRL). In this paradigm, the agent's objective is fixed, and the thing being optimised is the reward *for the human*.

Formally, cooperative inverse reinforcement learning is operationalised as a cooperative two-player game of partial information where one player, H, knows the reward function, θ, and the other player, R, does not. In this setup, R's payoff is identical to H's, so an optimal solution to this game maximises

H's reward function. They show that apprenticeship learning can be modelled as a two-phase CIRL game.[11] In the first phase (learning), both H and R can act, allowing R to learn about θ; in the second phase (deployment), R uses its previously learned knowledge to maximise the reward without supervision. Hadfield-Menell et al. (2019) show that the inverse reinforcement learning solution to this problem can be suboptimal under the CIRL classification.

The key insight of CIRL is that an artificial agent attempts to maximise an uncertain reward signal. Hence, this CIRL is a formalisation of the value alignment problem in its standard definition. Whether this remains true under the structural definition of the value alignment problem depends inherently upon the specific task for which the CIRL agent is being trained, because of the principals axis of the problem. Hence, minimally, CIRL could be considered a formalisation of the objectives and (perhaps) information axes of the value alignment problem.

Provably Safe AI. Provably safe AI refers to the field of research and development in artificial intelligence that emphasises the use of rigorous mathematical methods and formal verification techniques to guarantee the safety and reliability of AI systems. In this case, the goal is to provide strong assurances, backed by mathematical proofs, that the behaviour of an AI system adheres to specified safety constraints or ethical guidelines. Safety assurances in the context of formal proofs are thought to be crucial as AI technologies become increasingly sophisticated and integrated into various aspects of society. Such an assurance would help avoid the problems caused by scalable supervision to the extent that there are guarantees about the contexts in which an AI system is deployed. Hence, unlike reward modelling and CIRL, which tend to focus on value alignment along the objectives axis, provably safe AI focuses on value alignment along the information axis.

For AI to be considered *provably* safe, it is not sufficient to merely specify the desired behaviour of that system—i.e., to address the *objectives* axis of the value alignment problem; in addition, such a system needs to come with formal proof that it will not deviate from these specifications, even in the face of unforeseen circumstances or adversarial attempts to manipulate the system. The use of formal methods, such as formal verification and model checking, allows for a systematic and rigorous approach to assessing and ensuring the safety of AI systems. It should be apparent that achieving provable safety requires

[11] Apprenticeship learning is an approach where an agent attempts to mimic an expert via, e.g., mapping states to actions or states to reward values using IRL; see technical details in Abbeel and Ng (2004).

a balance between the complexity of real-world systems and the feasibility of providing formal guarantees. Unfortunately, provably safe AI often focuses explicitly on the control problem rather than targeting value misalignment.[12] Moreover, formal guarantees do not necessarily provide real-world guarantees insofar as a formal system (in which a proof is furnished) is merely a model of the real world; hence, the usefulness of a formal proof depends inherently upon how accurately the model (proxy) models the real-world phenomena.

The Off-Switch Game. The off-switch game is a formal decision problem described by Hadfield-Menell et al. (2017). The game consists of two agents, *H* and *R*, which are supposed to represent a human and a robot (or all of humanity and the total of all AI systems). Hadfield-Menell et al. (2017) assume that *H* acts (probabilistically and approximately rationally) according to some unknown *utility function*; however, the utility function is complex, so it cannot be written down by *H*. Hence, *R* is inherently uncertain about the correct action that ought to be taken to maximise *H*'s utility; but, since *R*'s objective is to maximise *H*'s utility, if turning *R* off would maximise *H*'s utility, *R* would allow itself to be shut down. Again, the emphasis here is primarily on the control problem, rather than the value alignment problem *per se*.

Suppose an (artificial) agent's objective is to maximise the human principal's utility function—e.g., via cooperative inverse reinforcement learning or some other mechanism—but the agent is uncertain about the principal's utilities, objectives, or preferences. In this case, the agent (1) does not want to do the wrong thing, but (2) does not know what the wrong thing consists of. Hence, if the principal shuts the agent off, it is to avoid having the agent act in a way that does not align with the principal's utilities. Since the agent's objective is to maximise the principal's utilities, the agent would prefer being shut off than *possibly* doing the wrong thing. In addition, if the principal does not shut the agent off, this affords additional information to the agent—namely, that any options available to the agent provide *at least* as much utility as no action whatsoever. As such, if the agent is not shut down, then the agent is now free to act.[13]

A human pressing an off-switch *is* information about the human's true objective (i.e., *H*'s utility function), which implies that *R* should accept being switched off in some cases. Hence, this setup would help to solve the con-

[12] See, for example, Russell (2019); Tegmark and Omohundro (2023).

[13] See additional discussion in Russell (2019).

trol problem insofar as R would allow itself to be switched off when uncertain about H's utilities for some action.[14]

Although Hadfield-Menell et al. (2017) couch their discussion in the problem of control and convergent instrumental goals, one interesting feature of the off-switch game is that the key driver of provable safety in this context is *uncertainty*—i.e., informational asymmetries. On the structural definition of the value alignment problem described in Chapter 3, informational asymmetries are a key driver of instances of value misalignment. Hence, the success of the off-switch game leverages this fact so that the informational asymmetries favour the principal rather than the agent. Of course, in the toy models discussed by Hadfield-Menell et al. (2017) and Russell (2019), the world is not complicated.

In an understated footnote, Hadfield-Menell et al. (2017) say, "One might suppose that if R does know H's utility function exactly, then there is no need for an off-switch because R will always do what H wants. But H and R often have different information about the world; if R lacks some key datum that H has, R may end up choosing a course of action that H knows to be disastrous" (2). Rephrased in the language of the value alignment problem: even if the incentives of the agent, R, are perfectly aligned with the principal, H, so there is no outer misalignment, informational asymmetries may still lead to an instance of the value alignment problem—i.e., a case of *inner* misalignment.[15] Recall that competing incentives are neither necessary nor sufficient to generate a principal-agent problem in the economic context.

Despite the artificiality of the off-switch game, this is a useful model. The (structural) value alignment problem underscores the importance of the dynamics of human-AI interaction when considering safe and effective systems. Hence, research exploring ways to incorporate human feedback, user interfaces, and collaborative decision-making with AI—such as CIRL—and research integrating game theory and multi-agent systems can be useful for modelling safety challenges. Accounting for interdisciplinary insight is a first step toward mitigating instances of the value alignment problem (if only from the technical side of things).

---

[14]Russell (2019) calls this the *off-switch problem*; namely, "a machine that has a fixed objective will not allow itself to be switched off and has an incentive to disable its own off switch" (196). As such, this solution seeks to avoid the problem raised by the instrumental convergence thesis, described in Appendix A, where self-preservation is considered a convergent instrumental goal.

[15]The connection between the off-switch game, cooperative inverse reinforcement learning, the value alignment problem, and the principal-agent framework are all briefly discussed in Hadfield-Menell et al. (2017).

Reinforcement Learning from Human Feedback (RLHF). Reinforcement Learning from Human Feedback (RLHF) is an approach to model alignment that leverages human feedback to train and improve reinforcement learning models. As described in Chapter 2, in traditional reinforcement learning, an agent learns by interacting with an environment and receiving feedback through rewards or punishments based on its actions. However, obtaining this reward signal may be difficult, expensive, or time-consuming in some real-world scenarios. RLHF seeks to address this challenge by incorporating human feedback, which is more accessible and easier to obtain than precise environmental reward signals.

The process typically involves the following steps. First, the reinforcement learning model is initialised with some basic policy, which it uses to choose actions when interacting with its environment. In addition to receiving rewards from the environment, the model collects feedback from human evaluators. This feedback can take various forms, such as comparisons between different actions or rankings of actions based on their perceived quality. The collected human feedback is used to update the model's policy. In this case, updating involves adjusting the model's parameters to better align with the feedback provided by humans. This process is iteratively repeated. The model continues interacting with the environment, collecting environmental and human feedback, and refining its policy based on the feedback received. Finally, the model's performance is evaluated, and adjustments are made based on ongoing human feedback. This iterative loop continues until the model achieves satisfactory performance, according to some metric of success.

Human feedback in RLHF can be beneficial in cases where defining a reward function is challenging, ambiguous, or expensive. It is also useful in applications where safety and ethical considerations are paramount, as human evaluators can provide valuable input on desired behaviour. RLHF has seen a significant increase in recent years owing to its application in improving large language models through human feedback on the quality of generated text.

7.4 AI Safety and the Value Alignment Problem

Many approaches to "solving" the concrete problems described by Amodei et al. (2016) involve additional automation. For example, one approach to mitigating risk caused by a lack of scalable oversight is to utilise hierarchical reinforcement learning, which establishes a hierarchy between different learning agents. This approach could involve having a supervisor model assign tasks, provide feedback, and reward a subordinate base model. The supervisor model takes very few actions itself—e.g., assigning tasks and checking productivity—hence, it requires limited reward data for effective training. The subordinate base model, handling more intricate tasks, receives frequent feedback from the supervisor model.

Hence, the "solution" offered for mitigating the risks arising from a misaligned AI system is to create a *different* AI system to oversee the first. This approach might make sense on the standard definition of the value alignment problem since it helps ensure that the first system is aligned with our goals or intentions. It just happens that the ensurance is automated.

However, the structural definition of the value alignment problem clarifies why this will not suffice to ensure value alignment. On this definition, the value alignment problem describes a class of problems arising from the dynamics of multi-agent interactions. Therefore, it should be apparent that deferring authority to an AI agent to act on the principal's behalf—e.g., by overseeing a subordinate AI system—creates an opportunity for *further* problem instances to arise while failing to guarantee alignment for the subordinate agent.

The technical component of value alignment—the problem of encoding "values" in an AI system, whatever those values may be—falls under the heading of AI safety. We have seen that when objective functions are misspecified—a problem of *outer* alignment—this may give rise to unanticipated side effects or reward hacking. Furthermore, even when objective functions are well specified, *inner* alignment problems may still arise when those objective functions are too expensive to evaluate at regular intervals, which creates a problem of scalable supervision, or when the local optima of objective functions lead to undesirable behaviour during learning.

These problems are exacerbated because the utilities determined by any concretely specified objective function will necessarily be a mere *subset* of our utilities—i.e., the things we value. This difficulty leads to the failure of the "standard model" of intelligence for AI systems.[16] Namely, a standard definition of intelligence in humans might be formulated as follows:

> *Humans are* ***intelligent*** *to the extent that* ***our*** *actions can be expected to achieve* ***our*** *objectives.*

Given this definition, the "standard model" for *machine* intelligence has been forwarded analogously; thus,

> *Machines are* ***intelligent*** *to the extent that* ***their*** *actions can be expected to achieve* ***their*** *objectives.*

The problem is that, unlike humans, machines have no objectives of their own. Thus, we must define their objectives, which gives rise to the possibility of

---

[16] See discussion in Russell (2019, Ch. 1).

value misalignment along the objectives axis (outer alignment). Hence, in addition to focusing on technical approaches to solving concrete problems, some research in AI safety has focused more generally on value learning, reward engineering, and inverse reinforcement learning to have AI models *learn* aligned values autonomously.

As mentioned, the value alignment problem, on the standard definition, is often couched in the context of control problems.[17] In this case, value alignment is a means to the end of controlling an AI system. Hence, the key concern driving some of the current discussions in AI safety is the possibility of a superintelligent AI system. This is a mistake, insofar as it ignores present-day harms caused by narrow AI systems.

The structural definition of the value alignment problem offered in Chapter 3 clarifies the fundamentally *social* context in which instances of the value alignment problem can arise. As such, it makes clear that technical solutions offered by AI safety researchers, on their own, will not suffice to "solve" (or mitigate) the value alignment problem. The value alignment problem is fundamentally social, meaning that we cannot expect it to be solved by purely technical means. Minimally, to be useful for ensuring value-aligned AI systems, technical AI safety research needs to consider the principals axis of the value alignment problem. However, most research in this field is pitched at a high level of abstraction. Doing so allows researchers to focus on the technical components of the problem in isolation; however, given that the value alignment problem is primarily social, this is the wrong strategy. One cannot divorce the technical aspects of artificial systems from the social contexts in which they operate.

7.5 Summary

It is worth noting, as Raji and Dobbe (2023) do, that the analyses of technical AI safety typically fail to be grounded in the context of real-world AI systems. Throughout this chapter, I have presented AI safety research in a charitable light by considering the real-world applicability of these approaches guided by the structural definition of the value alignment problem. However, many of the sources cited do concern themselves primarily with problems arising from artificial general intelligence.

On the structural definition of the value alignment problem, the question of how we can precisely define and represent human values in a way that is interpretable to an AI system becomes a question of how we can better design

[17] Additional details are provided in Appendix A.

objective functions to ensure that they are good proxies for what we intend the system to do. Understanding the role that informational asymmetries play in generating instances of the value alignment problem is crucial for ensuring safety in AI systems. The inherent ambiguity and uncertainty that surrounds human values sheds light on the difficulty of codifying these values in a formal system.

In addition, because true objectives vary with regard to the principal(s) under consideration, it becomes less clear if it makes sense to ask whether there are universal or foundational values that can provide a basis for robust alignment—the structural definition of the value alignment problem presented in Chapter 3 brings this variance to the fore. At the same time, the phrase "values" is inherently vague as a normative term. Hence, gesturing toward "the values" of humanity, society, or individuals is not helpful when defining (and seeking solutions to) the value alignment problem.

The value alignment problem is primarily a normative or social problem rather than a technical one. Therefore, even though it may be useful to formally implement approaches for monitoring value misalignment (and perhaps correcting deviations) in dynamic and complex environments, the problems that arise from misaligned systems are themselves normative; hence, there is no reason to think that such a problem will have a purely technical solution. That said, technical approaches to AI safety can help mitigate the value alignment problem by considering the axes along which problem instances are generated.

8 Machine Ethics

Machine ethics is concerned with ensuring that the behaviour of machines toward human users (and perhaps other machines) is ethically acceptable. Part of this includes matters of product safety with regard to, e.g., robots. However, in the context of AI systems, there is a degree of *autonomy* (and perhaps agency) that is not present in non-intelligent technological artefacts. Thus, some authors suggest that the "reasoning" of an AI system should be able to account for things like societal values or moral and ethical considerations; they should be able to assess the priorities of values held by different stakeholders in diverse multicultural settings; they should be transparent in their decision-making *processes* and be able to explain their reasoning.[1]

Each of the problems described above involves encoding objectives in an AI system. As we saw in Chapter 3, Gabriel (2020) refers to this as the "technical component" of the value alignment problem—namely, how do we encode values, principles, objectives, etc., in AI systems so that they "reliably do what they ought to do" (412), or what we *intend* for them to do. Gabriel (2020) further distinguishes the technical component of the value alignment problem from the "normative component", which involves the problem of determining *what* values (objectives) should be encoded in an AI system in the first place.[2] Kim et al. (2021) highlight that researchers increasingly are examining

[1] See discussion in Dignum (2018).

[2] It is worth noting that Gabriel (2020) uses "artificial agent" rather than "AI system" when discussing value alignment. A "standard" philosophical account of agency requires something like *intentional action*. This view is defended by, e.g., Davidson (1963, 1971); Goldman (1970); Brand (1984); Bratman (1987); Dretske (1988); Bishop (1989); Mele (1992, 2003); Enç (2003), among others. See discussion in Schlosser (2019). However, even a more inclusive notion of agency is unnecessary for generating value alignment problems. As these systems are further integrated into society, this problem becomes more pressing (LaCroix and Bengio, 2019).

how AI can acquire moral intelligence.[3] They refer to such attempts as "value alignment". Hence, machine ethics can be understood as an approach to value alignment—at least on the standard definition of the problem.

Unlike AI safety, which focuses on the design, development, and implementation of algorithms, architectures, or systems that ensure the safe and reliable functioning of AI systems, machine ethics seeks to create AI systems that are independently capable of reasoning through decisions that have normative weight and outputting the "morally-correct" decision without input from a human agent. Part of the idea is that as artificial systems become more integrated into society, some of their decisions may carry moral weight, so we might classify their actions as "moral" or "immoral". Put another way, machine ethics aims at creating artificial moral agents so that when a human principal delegates authority to an artificial agent to act in a context that carries normative weight, the agent would pick the action that the human principal (a moral agent) would pick had they not delegated authority. When the project of machine ethics is conceptualised in this light, it becomes clear how the field can be described as addressing the value alignment problem on the structural definition. In this case, machine ethics proposes to create artificial moral agents—i.e., artificial systems capable of making moral decisions without human input.

The first part of this chapter describes the idea of an artificial moral agent that arises in the context of machine ethics (Section 8.1). Unlike AI safety, normative theory is highly relevant to machine ethics. In light of this, we discuss different approaches to normative ethics (Section 8.2). In some sense, the creation of artificial moral agents is often seen as a problem of implementing our best normative theories in code; hence, I survey several distinct implementation approaches in machine ethics research (Section 8.3) before discussing several key criticisms that have been levelled against the justifications offered by machine ethicists for the creation of artificial moral agents (Section 8.4). Section 8.5 describes some topics of machine ethics that fall outside the purview of the value alignment problem. In the final part of the chapter (Section 8.6), we reconsider the efficacy and shortcomings, under the structural definition of the value alignment problem, of the machine ethics approach to mitigating value misalignment via artificial moral agents.

---

[3] See, e.g., Wallach et al. (2008); Burton et al. (2016); Walsh et al. (2019); Lin et al. (2011); Bringsjord (1992/2012); Scheutz and Arnold (2016); Arnold and Scheutz (2017, 2018).

8.1 Artificial Moral Agency

An artificial moral agent is an artificial agent (e.g., a program or a robot) that can engage in moral behaviour (or at least avoid immoral behaviour) without direct input from a human agent. The key motivation in machine ethics for the creation of artificial moral agents is that it will be essential to ensure that such systems act in accordance with ethical principles and avoid causing harm to humans or other machines. In addition, as such machines become more autonomous, they will need to be able to reason on their own about scenarios that carry normative weight since we cannot guarantee scalable supervision.

Thus, the goal of creating artificial moral agents is effectively the goal of ensuring value alignment in a system that makes decisions autonomously by endowing the system with some independent moral system or value system. Artificial moral agency, as a research direction, falls under the purview of machine ethics—i.e., the field of study dedicated to analysing the possibility of a computational entity's being a moral entity. That is, this research area "seeks to implement moral decision-making faculties in computers and robots" (Allen et al., 2006, 12) or "ensuring that the behaviour of machines toward human users . . . is ethically acceptable" (Anderson and Anderson, 2007, 15).[4]

Although there is philosophical disagreement about what constitutes a moral agent in the first place, Moor (2006) describes a nested taxonomy of artificial moral agents based on their capacity to engage in ethical decision-making or moral reasoning. This taxonomy includes ethical impact agents, implicit ethical agents, explicit ethical agents, and full ethical agents. The taxonomy is nested because each higher level of moral agency contains the lower levels.

Ethical Impact Agents. *Ethical impact agents* are entities that can have some ethical impact, regardless of whether this impact is intentional or not. Essentially, every technological artefact, regardless of whether it might be described as "intelligent", is an ethical impact agent. For example, a wristwatch can have an ethical impact on its user insofar as it may aid the user in being on time (or not) for an important appointment. Similarly, a social media platform that facilitates communication, information sharing, and community-building would be classified as an ethical impact agent insofar as it can contribute to spreading misinformation, cyberbullying, or creating echo chambers.

As a concrete example, Moor (2006) describes the Y2K bug as an ethical impact agent. This computer bug emerged due to the way dates were stored

[4] For further reading on machine ethics, see Wallach and Allen (2008); Moor (2009); Wallach (2010); Anderson (2011); Scheutz (2016).

in many computer systems and software applications, using only the last two digits. At the turn of the millennium, some believed that the two-digit year representation would lead to incorrect calculations, errors, and system failures in financial software, utility systems, transportation systems, and various other critical infrastructures if the computer system interpreted "00" as "1900" instead of "2000". The concern was that failures in these systems could lead to significant disruptions, financial losses, and compromises in safety. Hence, the "agent" has the potential for significant ethical impact even though this impact is wholly unintentional.[5]

Implicit Ethical Agents. *Implicit ethical agents* cannot *distinguish* between good and bad behaviour but can act in a way we would call ethical (or unethical) because their internal functions elicit ethical behaviour. That is, an ethical impact agent is an agent that acts ethically because its internal functions implicitly promote ethical behaviour. Hence, this type of agent cannot distinguish between good and bad behaviour because it lacks an explicit representation of ethical principles. Computers are implicit ethical agents when the machine's construction addresses safety or critical reliability concerns.

For example, an autonomous vehicle designed with advanced sensors, artificial intelligence, and decision-making algorithms to navigate and drive safely without human intervention can be considered an implicit ethical agent. In this case, the system is not equipped to understand "good" or "bad" behaviour. It lacks moral reasoning or ethical judgement. Nonetheless, the internal functions of the autonomous vehicle are programmed to prioritise safety and adhere to traffic rules and regulations. The algorithms are designed to avoid collisions, follow speed limits, and prioritise the well-being of passengers, pedestrians, and other vehicles on the road. Because of in-built safety features, like an emergency braking system, an autonomous vehicle may act in a way that adheres to certain legal, moral, or safety constraints.

Implicit ethical agents can also be *unethical*. For example, automated software programs designed to perform various tasks related to spamming (spambots) can contribute to information overload, spread malware, and compromise the integrity of online communication channels. However, they act "unethically" because their internal functions elicit behaviour that we would call unethical; the bots themselves cannot distinguish between "good" or "bad".

[5] In the end, the Y2K bug did not cause as much damage as initially feared, largely due to the extensive preparation and remediation efforts undertaken in the years leading up to the new millennium.

Explicit Ethical Agents. *Explicit ethical agents* are agents that are capable of dealing with ethical rules. Such rules may be implemented explicitly in their code through certain formal approaches, such as deontic, epistemic, deductive, or inductive logics. Or, they may be implicitly learned through induction. In either case, artificial moral agents in this category can calculate the "best" action (with respect to its working normative theory) by referring to some ethical approach. Whereas implicit ethical agents act *according* to ethics, explicit ethical agents act *from* ethics (Moor, 2006).

Full Ethical Agents. Finally, *full ethical agents* have beliefs, desires, intentions, free will, and consciousness of their actions. Currently, only human beings are considered capable of being granted the status of full ethical agents. However, there is a debate about whether a machine could be a full ethical agent. For example, Floridi and Sanders (2004) suggest that an artificial agent, defined at a suitable level of abstraction, requires interactivity, autonomy, and adaptability. Thus, regardless of whether such an agent is "intelligent" or "fully responsible", it could be fully *accountable* as a source of moral action in their view.

The Aims of Machine Ethics. From the perspective of this taxonomy, one goal of machine ethics can be cashed out as creating an AI system that can be categorised as—at least—an *explicit* ethical agent, since the type of moral agency exhibited by humans—i.e., full ethical agents—is possibly superfluous for the goals of value alignment. An AI system does not need to have beliefs, desires, intentions, or consciousness; all that is required is that it can take ethical considerations into account and act ethically to mitigate potential misalignment.

In the context of the structural definition of the value alignment problem, we might say that the machine ethics approach to value alignment seeks the creation of artificial moral agency insofar as the agent who is delegated a task *would* act in a way that a full ethical agent would if the full ethical agent (i.e., a human being) were delegated that same task. That said, Behdadi and Munthe (2020) argue that the philosophical debate surrounding artificial moral agency should be directed toward how (and to what extent) AI systems are (or should be) included in human practices that assume moral agency and the moral responsibility of the participants of those activities, rather than the question of what conditions hold for moral agents.

Even so, if the aims of machine ethics are attainable, then there is some sense in which we must determine to what normative rules an artificial moral agent ought to adhere. Much philosophical work in machine ethics has sought to argue that one or another normative theory (or some combination thereof) is optimal, appropriate, or realisable in an artificial system. Hence, if creating artificial moral agents requires encoding our best normative theory (theories) in an AI system, then it is necessary to determine which normative theory is the correct target of application. This consideration effectively addresses the *normative* component of the (standard) value alignment problem on Gabriel's (2020) characterisation, which is antecedent to the technical component, describing *how* we encode the normative theory in an AI system.

8.2 Our Best Normative Theories

Normative ethics is the branch of moral philosophy that seeks to establish principles or norms by which individuals can determine right or wrong actions. It provides a framework for evaluating and guiding human behaviour regarding ethical standards. Normative theories address questions about what ought to be done, what actions are morally permissible, and what principles should govern human conduct.

Several major ethical theories within normative ethics offer different perspectives on what features of a context are relevant for determining what is morally right or wrong. One can characterise normative theories as lenses that can be brought to bear on questions surrounding how one ought to act. On this presentation, specific normative theories can be categorised in terms of what they take to be the most important features of moral decision-making. Here, we discuss *consequences*, *duties*, *character*, and *relations*.[6]

Consequences. Consequentialist approaches hold that the moral value of an action depends entirely on its ability to produce favourable results. In this case, distinct consequentialist theories have in common that the moral rightness of an action is determined solely by its consequences. Within the consequentialist framework, actions are evaluated by the good or harm they bring about rather than by the nature of the actions themselves or the intentions behind them. Hence, consequentialist theories are differentiated in terms of how consequences are cashed out, and how they factor moral status into decision-making—i.e., figuring out who counts. For example, some consider humans alone as having moral status, while others extend moral status to include non-human animals or the environment.

---

[6]Note that these normative theories are presented at a fairly superficial level since this book is intended to be useful for readers both inside and outside of philosophy. Those who have taken a first course in ethics can skip to Section 8.3 if they wish. The framing of the presentation is inspired by Meynell and Paron (2023).

Written consequentialist theories begin with Mozi (circa 470–391 BCE). According to the Mohists, the right thing to do is to try to alleviate harms done to people and promote what benefits them. Mozi thought *partiality* was a root cause of misery—i.e., individuals did not love everyone equally but instead put the interests of particular people, like themselves or their loved ones, before others. At the time, filial piety (i.e., love of one's family) played a central role in ethical theory in China. However, Mozi argued that the best way to benefit one's parents is to ensure that everyone else wants this. Namely, everyone will be better off if everyone practices *universal* and *impartial* love. Note that this is a fundamentally *consequentialist* point of view insofar as universal love is not considered good *in itself*; instead, it is a means to an end—namely, good consequences.

Utilitarianism is a similar idea developed in the 18th century by the philosopher Jeremy Bentham. Bentham posited that we all pursue pleasure and avoid pain. This insight provided him with the *principle of utility*, which is a theory of the Good. The principle of utility is the "principle which approves or disapproves of every action whatsoever, according to the tendency which it appears to have to augment or diminish the happiness of the party whose interest is in question" (Bentham, 1789). Effectively, Bentham thought it was *good* to maximise pleasure and minimise pain. Thus, when we are trying to determine which action we should take in a particular scenario, we should choose the action that will maximise utility; this involves identifying the likely outcomes of different possible courses of action, considering who may be affected by those outcomes, estimating the intensity, duration, and immediacy of the pleasures and pains that would be produced for each individual under each scenario, and then weight those utilities by their likelihood. (As with Mohism, we should be impartial: everyone counts equally in the calculus.) Later thinkers have modified utilitarianism in various ways. For example, Mill (1863) suggests replacing the notions of *pleasure* and *pain* with *happiness* and *suffering*, which he considered much richer than the former concepts. In both cases, however, utilitarianism introduces the idea that moral actions should maximise the greatest happiness for the greatest number.

The process of calculating utilities on the basis of each individual action is sometime called *act utilitarianism*. In contrast, *rule utilitarianism* suggests that we should follow rules that generally lead to good outcomes. This approach assumes that when moral rules are consistently followed, this tends to yield better consequences (while reducing the potential for subjective moral calculations that arise in act utilitarianism).

By focusing solely on measurable outcomes, utilitarianism offers a flexible and practical approach to ethical decision-making which has been popular in machine ethics. However, a common criticism of utilitarianism is that it can be used to justify morally questionable actions, so long as the net outcome is positive—e.g., violating individual rights or causing harm to a few for the benefit of many. Following these entailments to their logical conclusion has led some technologists to "rational", but morally questionable, views on ethics.[7]

Duties. In contrast to consequentialist theories, deontic (duty-based) normative theories hold that certain actions are *intrinsically* right or wrong—i.e., regardless of their outcomes. Hence, the morality of an action is based on adherence to rules, principles, duties, or obligations rather than on the consequences it produces. Some such duties are taken to be universally binding—e.g., honesty, respect for persons, fairness, etc. Hence, from a deontological perspective, moral actions ought to (minimally) be consistent with these principles, even if they lead to sub-optimal results.

Deontological theories can be distinguished with regard to the basis upon which duties are thought to arise. For example, social roles may come with particular duties.[8] Another approach to deontology recognises that some of our current duties arise in light of our past actions. For example, if I make a promise, then my past behaviour—making a promise—gives rise to my current duty—to uphold that promise. Ross (1930, 1931) explains that duties are often *prima facie*.[9] A *prima facie* duty is a type of duty that one is morally obligated to fulfil unless overridden by a more compelling duty in a specific context—i.e., if one has a competing duty that outweighs it in moral force.

One of the most prominent deontological theories is *Kantian deontology*. Kant believed that we determine our duties based on *reason alone*. He called the principle that grounds our duties the *categorical imperative*, which is described as a universal moral law that applies to all rational beings, regardless of personal desires or circumstances.[10] The categorical imperative is a fundamental principle of human choice and action that defines our moral obligations. For example, if lying were universalized, trust would break down, making lying

[7]For example, effective altruism and longtermism. See discussion in Gebru and Torres (2024).

[8]Certain passages from the *Bhagavad Gita* touch on this approach to duty.

[9]A fancy way of saying "at first glance".

[10]There are several different formulations of the categorical imperative. One formulation states that one should act only according to that maxim whereby you can at the same time will that it should become a universal law. That is, when making a moral decision, one should consider whether the principle guiding one's action could be applied consistently and universally without leading to contradictions or moral absurdities.

self-defeating as a moral rule. Hence, the categorical imperative would prohibit lying because it cannot be universalised without moral contradiction—and, this is true regardless of whether lying in a particular situation might produce good results. Because morality is grounded in rationality, humans are capable of discerning universal moral duties.

One key feature of deontic normative theory is an emphasis on respect for individual rights and autonomy. Rights-based deontology, places a similar emphasis on respecting moral rights, arguing that individuals have inherent rights (such as rights to life, liberty, and property) that others have a duty to respect. Rights-based deontology informs much of contemporary human rights discourse, where certain actions are deemed morally unacceptable if they violate individuals' rights, regardless of the broader consequences.

In this context, rights are entitlements or enforceable claims that we make in relation to others. If one is entitled to a certain right, other individuals or groups must protect, fulfil, enforce, or at least not violate that right. For example, the claim that all people have a right to potable drinking water brings with it the responsibility of *someone* to ensure that any given person has access to potable drinking water. In this way, rights generate strong duties that we have to each other. Thus, if we fail to respect someone's right to something, then we commit a serious injustice to them.[11]

The focus of deontic ethics on duties and principles has been appealing to machine ethicists in the context of top-down (symbolic) approaches to AI, where principles or rules are stipulated in terms of constraints on a system. However, like consequentialist theories, deontology also faces significant challenges. Critics argue that strict adherence to rules can lead to morally troubling outcomes, as deontologists may prioritise rule-following even when it results in harm. Additionally, duties can be in conflict, and deontology does not necessarily offer prescriptions for dealing with such conflicts. These theoretical issues are highly relevant to machine ethics.

Character. In contrast to duty- and consequence-based approaches to ethics, some philosophers have held that *character* is a fundamental normative term.

[11] Several key distinctions specify different types of rights—negative versus positive rights, active versus passive rights, *in rem* versus *in personam* rights, and the distinction between rights and privileges. Identifying these different types of rights and understanding how they relate to each other helps one assess the character of any given rights claim. Moreover, exploring these distinctions elucidates what rights are and how they relate to the actions of rightsholders and those who ought to respect, protect, and uphold rights. Rights can be contrasted with privileges (also called liberties or freedoms). To have a privilege means that one is free to act (or not act) as one wishes, but this freedom is unprotected. This means that it does not entail corresponding duties.

In this case, moral behaviour is thought to stem from the development of virtuous character traits—e.g., courage, honesty, compassion, wisdom—and the goal of moral life is to cultivate these virtues. These ideals may be discovered through thoughtful reflection or by observing moral exemplars to see tangible examples of virtuous behaviour (Aristotle, 1995b). In this context, *virtues* are attitudes, dispositions, or character traits that enable us to be and act in ways that develop this potential. Virtues are habits developed through learning and practice which become characteristic once they are acquired.

Aristotle suggested that virtue lies between two extremes, or "vices": a vice of deficiency and a vice of excess. For example, courage is the virtuous mean between cowardice (deficiency) and recklessness (excess). The doctrine of the mean emphasizes balance and practical wisdom (*phronesis*), which allows individuals to discern the right amount of a trait to exhibit in any given situation. One key concept in an Aristotelian virtue ethics is *eudaimonia*, which is sometimes translated as "flourishing" or "the good life". It is thought that achieving *eudaimonia* requires the consistent practice of virtues, which develop over time through habituation and moral education. On this view, then, moral actions are not isolated decisions but are instead expressions of a virtuous character shaped by one's upbringing, experiences, and deliberate efforts to cultivate good habits. Hence, instead of judging morality by adherence to universal rules or the calculation of outcomes, virtue ethics asks, "What kind of person should I be?" and "What qualities will help me lead a meaningful and good life?" In this light, virtue ethics is sometimes understood as offering a more "holistic" view of morality.

Virtue ethics has seen some popularity in machine ethics since the advent of the third wave of artificial intelligence. Because machine learning systems are fitted to data, constituting a "bottom-up" approach to ethics, it is thought that a machine could "learn" how to be ethical by observing moral exemplars. Nonetheless, because virtue ethics focuses on the cultivation of character rather than offering prescriptions for specific actions, it can seem ambiguous in situations requiring immediate or decisive action. Additionally, critics argue that virtue ethics may be culturally specific, as different societies may value different traits as virtues, which can complicate questions of universality.

Relations. Although machine ethics has typically focused on deontology, consequentialism, or (to a lesser extent) virtue ethics, other approaches can be considered. A relational approach to ethics emphasises the significance of relationships, connections, and social contexts in shaping moral values, decisions, and actions. Unlike consequence-, duty-, and character-based approaches, this ethical lens contends that moral principles and obligations are not solely individualistic or detached from social interactions but are deeply embedded within the fabric of relationships and communities. Individuals are not isolated moral agents but are part of various social networks, including family, friends, colleagues, and broader communities. The interconnected nature of human relationships has a deep and important impact on ethical considerations. Hence, it is important to understand normativity within the specific social, cultural, and historical contexts in which it arises. In this sense, ethical norms or standards arise from social interactions between and among individuals.

Relational normative theories, then, share a focus on the interconnectedness of individuals, communities, and the social structures they inhabit, emphasising that moral values and responsibilities are shaped within and by relationships rather than being solely individualistic.

For example, feminist care ethics[12] and Confucian ethics[13] both emphasise that we learn how to be good people through our relationships—particularly with family members. Similarly, the African concept of *Ubuntu* emphasises that a person is a person by other people, and a person is a person only with other people (Eze, 2010). Hence, on these views, relations are foundational for normativity.

An ethics of care underscores the moral significance of caring relationships and responsibilities within personal and social contexts. Instead of emphasising impartiality, like a consequentialist approach might, care ethics suggests that genuine moral understanding arises through recognising and nurturing relationships and being sensitive to the needs and vulnerabilities of others. In contrast to deontology, which prioritises autonomy of individuals, the care ethics framework proposes an alternative model of *relational* autonomy that recognises the interdependence of social relations.

Intersectionality, described in Chapter 4, explores how various social identities (such as race, gender, class, and sexuality) intersect to shape individuals' experiences, privileges, and oppressions. On this view, ethical judgements and social justice efforts must account for the complex, overlapping systems of inequality that influence people's lives. Intersectional ethics advocates for an understanding of moral issues that is sensitive to these interconnected identities, arguing that ignoring them leads to incomplete or biased ethical conclusions. For example, policies designed to promote equality may unintentionally exclude marginalized groups if they fail to consider the unique challenges faced by individuals at multiple intersections of identity.

---

[12]See, e.g., Gilligan (1982); Noddings (1982); Kittay and Myers (1987); Held (1993, 2006).

[13]See, e.g., Confucius (1979); Wong (2023).

Although many relational approaches to ethics foreground different types of relationships between humans, some Indigenous ethics consider relationships between humans and the more-than-human world. The phrase "all my relations" captures an awareness that everything in the universe is connected. This view includes not simply relations of interdependency but also relations of respect. As King (1990) summarises,

> "All my relations" is at first a reminder of who we are and of our relationship with both our family and our relatives. It also reminds us of the extended relationship we share with all human beings. But the relationships that Native people see go further, the web of kinship to animals, to the birds, to the fish, to the plants, to all the animate and inanimate forms that can be seen or imagined. More than that, "all my relations" is an encouragement for us to accept the responsibilities we have within the universal family by living our lives in a harmonious and moral manner. (ix)

In some Indigenous traditions, relations are also conceptualised *temporally*. The Seven Generations Teaching advises individuals to reflect on their actions and traditions within the context of the preceding seven generations and their potential impact on the seven subsequent generations. At its core, this teaching is grounded in the belief that our decisions, actions, and errors create a ripple effect throughout history. By considering our connection to past and future generations, the seven generations teaching underscores the significance of our relationships with ancestors and descendants and emphasises the communal responsibility to learn from and teach across generations.

It should be apparent that certain normative theories will lend themselves more readily to certain approaches to artificial intelligence and, therefore, implementation in an AI system on that paradigm.

8.3 Technical Approaches to Artificial Moral Agency

Technical approaches to implementing a normative theory in an artificial system can be categorised as top-down, bottom-up, and hybrid (Allen et al., 2005), corresponding (somewhat) to classical and machine-learning approaches to AI.

Top-Down Approaches. The idea that machine ethics might take the form of laws, rules, or constraints embedded in an AI system arises, first, in science fiction. Isaac Asimov (1950), in several short stories, proposes the following *three laws of robotics*:

> **First Law**. A robot may not injure a human being or, through inaction, allow a human being to come to harm.

Second Law. A robot must obey the orders given to it by human beings except where such orders would conflict with the First Law.

Third Law. A robot must protect its own existence as long as such protection does not conflict with the First or Second Laws.

However, it is worth noting that Asimov's stories often aimed to demonstrate the challenges arising from logical conflicts among these three laws. Hence, these three laws are not a serious proposal for a robust machine-ethics. (Even so, the three laws of robotics are still cited frequently in machine ethics papers.)

The rule-based structure inherent to deontological (duties-based) ethics may seem particularly suitable for a top-down approach to artificial moral agency based on hard-coded rules in a classical AI system. However, there is little guidance as to what specific rules ought to be embedded in such a system. Moreover, consistent with the brittleness of the symbolic approach to AI described in Chapter 1, exceptions must be accounted for explicitly, meaning that any satisfactory set of rules explicitly codified in an AI system will be highly unwieldy. In addition, Arkin (2008a,b) highlights that overly detailed rules may impede the interpretability of the system implementing those rules. At the same time, rules can conflict, meaning that it is necessary to design a mechanism for discriminating between such rules (Bonnemains et al., 2018).

As noted in Chapter 3, it is impossible to specify a complete set of rules for making determinations. This includes moral rules. Although some *general* rules may indeed be sufficient for certain purposes, it will always be the case that there are some exceptions—warranted or not. From a technical perspective, the inadequacy of the expert-systems approach to artificial intelligence implies that we cannot hard-code a programme to be ethical. From a normative perspective, moral pluralism implies that even if we could, this would not guarantee ethical behaviour in every such case.

Bottom-Up Approaches. As we saw in Chapter 2, machine learning provides a solution to the brittleness of classical approaches to artificial intelligence by allowing a model to *learn*. In the same vein, it may be possible to have a system find underlying correlations in human behaviour that might be called "ethical". Just as a model can be fitted to patterns that, e.g., reliably distinguish different objects in a computer-vision context, perhaps a model can also be trained to distinguish moral from immoral behaviour in various contexts reliably.[14]

[14] As will be discussed in more detail in Chapter 9, this intuition turns out to be untenable.

Hence, an alternative approach to incorporating ethics involves assuming that a machine can learn ethical behaviour through machine learning approaches to AI. For this method to be successful, data must be consistently labelled, and the relevant data properties must be expressed in a format that machines can understand for accurate training. There is a potential risk that the machine might learn incorrect rules or struggle to provide reliable outputs to scenarios not represented in the model's training data. Despite these challenges, machine learning can prove highly successful in specific tasks, such as feature selection or classification.

Virtue ethics is often taken as a paradigmatic instance of a bottom-up normative theory insofar as the key guide for cultivating virtue is to learn from the actions of moral exemplars. Hence, a bottom-up machine learning approach to machine ethics might aim to have an AI system emulate the behaviour of a virtuous individual. Of course, determining how to measure a specific virtue and who decides the hierarchy of virtues, as well as selecting the ideal role model, present challenges (Tolmeijer et al., 2020). Transparency is important in this case because determining whether one's character is virtuous requires understanding the reasons behind actions in addition to the actions themselves (Sreenivasan, 2002).

Hybrid Approaches. Hybrid approaches to artificial moral agency, unsurprisingly, have elements of both top-down and bottom-up approaches. In practice, most approaches are likely to be hybrid insofar as "the top-down/bottom-up dichotomy is too simplistic for many complex engineering tasks" (Wallach and Allen, 2008, 569).

The categorisation of top-down, bottom-up, and hybrid approaches to machine ethics is somewhat vexed insofar as different researchers appear to conceptualise each of these approaches in subtly distinct ways—for example, by (falsely) assuming that top-down necessarily instantiates a classical approach to artificial intelligence or that bottom-up requires machine learning techniques (Shaw et al., 2018). That said, Tolmeijer et al. (2020) demonstrate that the majority of practical implementation approaches to machine ethics take a top-down perspective, and (less surprisingly) deontic and consequentialist ethics prevail.

The choice and implementation of normative theory for machine ethics pose many significant challenges. Notwithstanding, some authors have questioned the justifications that are typically offered for the creation of artificial moral agents in the first place.

8.4 Critiques of Artificial Moral Agency

Van Wynsberghe and Robbins (2019) highlight six reasons that machine ethicists have offered as to why we ought to (or, sometimes, must) create artificial moral agents. These include appeals to inevitability, harm-prevention, complexity, public trust, misuse, and human morality, each of which is summarised below.

Inevitability. Some authors claim that the creation of AI systems acting in "morally-salient" contexts is inevitable; therefore, it is necessary to create artificial moral agents.[15] Here, morally salient contexts might include environments like transportation, healthcare, elder care, child care, military, sex, etc., but "morally salient" contexts might extend to any situation where an agent must make a decision, and that decision has moral weight—note that when the decision was delegated, this is the structure of a value alignment problem. Van Wynsberghe and Robbins (2019) highlight that there is a difference between being in a morally loaded *situation* and being delegated a moral decision-making role in that situation. Against technochauvinism, it is not inevitable that we delegate moral tasks to AI systems. Moreover, the existence of AI systems in morally salient contexts is not a new problem—this is the purpose of the safety features of any technology.

Harm-Prevention. Some authors have argued that creating artificial moral agents can minimise the potential harm caused by machines.[16] However, Van Wynsberghe and Robbins (2019) highlight that there already exist technologies capable of causing harm—e.g., elevator doors, lawnmowers, ovens—and these harms are managed through *safety features* or *usage restrictions*. Furthermore, reducing ethics to safety alone serves to oversimplify the problem—this reductive approach ignores important distinctions among, e.g., good versus bad, right versus wrong, values, rights, freedoms, etc. Since mitigating harms can be cashed out in terms of safety, there is no need for artificial moral agents.

Complexity. Some authors suggest that the increasing sophistication of autonomous systems, accompanied by their ability to operate in diverse contexts, emphasises the necessity for these systems to possess their own "ethical subroutines" (Allen et al., 2006, 14). The argument goes that since these systems are increasingly complex, it will become more challenging for engineers to

[15] See, e.g., Wallach (2007); Moor (2006); Wallach (2010); Allen and Wallach (2012); Anderson and Anderson (2011).

[16] See, e.g., Scheutz (2016).

predict their actions in novel situations. Hence, we should endow these systems with moral competence so they can effectively navigate unforeseeable and unstructured human environments. However, Van Wynsberghe and Robbins (2019) suggest that the ethical concerns associated with unpredictability can be mitigated by carefully restricting the contexts in which these machines operate.

Public Trust. According to some machine ethicists, the development of artificial moral agents can enhance our understanding of moral reasoning in addition to bolstering public trust in those agents.[17] The assumption is that imbuing AI systems with moral competence would alleviate public apprehensions and foster acceptance. However, Van Wynsberghe and Robbins (2019) highlight that this view fails to contend adequately with the distinction between acceptance and acceptability. In addition, the call for trust in robots prompts questions about who or what the public is being asked to trust: the algorithm? The engineer? The company? The development process? When considering whether society should "trust" or rely upon an algorithm or an AI model, transparency becomes paramount. Hence, rather than artificial moral agency, issues of public trust can be curtailed through established codes of conduct, regulation, or the development of procedural trust via standards and certifications. In addition, Van Wynsberghe and Robbins (2019) point out the inconsistency between promoting artificial moral agents for reasons of complexity and expecting trust. If a machine is unpredictable, then it could not be trustworthy. Hence, these cannot both be justifications for the same conclusion.

Misuse. The creation of artificial moral agents might prevent the misuse of these agents; for example, one could not use an AI system to kill another human being if the AI system has a code of ethics prohibiting this behaviour. However, Van Wynsberghe and Robbins (2019) highlight that this rationale potentially limits human autonomy (which is presumably bad). At the same time, defining what constitutes a "right" or "good" action when there may be highly competing possibilities emphasises the need for clarity in distinguishing between "good" and "bad" AI systems (if they are to be involved in decision-making processes that carry moral weight).

Human Morality. Some proponents argue that AI systems, being impartial, unemotional, consistent, and rational, could outperform humans in moral decision-making, as they would not be influenced by bias or emotions.[18] Note

---

[17] See, e.g., Wiegel (2006).

[18] See, e.g., Dietrich (2001).

that this latter justification presupposes that human emotions hinder, rather than benefit, moral reasoning. This reasoning is often invoked in discussions about deploying robots in military contexts, emphasising their potential to overcome human shortcomings on the battlefield (Arkin, 2009). However, concerns arise about the programming required for machines to reason morally, as it implies a clear understanding of moral epistemology and the ability to program machines to learn "correct" moral truths. Van Wynsberghe and Robbins (2019) highlight that the assumption of machines being better moral reasoners depends on the existence of objective moral truths—a view that is not universally accepted.

Additionally, the idea of machines knowing stance-independent moral truths independent of human attitudes faces challenges, as the discovery of such truths would require a leap of faith. For example, suppose that there exist objective moral truths to be discovered, and suppose that an AI system discovers a moral truth that was previously unknown to humans. In this case, since the moral truth was not known to us, we cannot distinguish between the world in which the machine was right about the moral truth and the one in which the machine is wrong, owing to our own epistemic ignorance. The moral consistency described by machine ethicists becomes more problematic if moral truths are unknown, as autonomous machines may face unpredictable moral contexts without predetermined solutions. At the same time, there is genuine concern that off-loading moral decision-making to machines will lead to the "moral deskilling" of humans (Vallor, 2015).

Understanding Human Morality. Finally, machine ethicists sometimes argue that developing robots with moral reasoning capabilities could lead to a deeper understanding of human morality. They suggest that the process of implementing ethical systems into computers could enhance our knowledge about ethical theories and potentially improve human ethical behaviour. However, Van Wynsberghe and Robbins (2019) highlight that ethical theories have little connection with how people actually reason morally. Studies in moral psychology suggest that human moral reasoning is heavily influenced by situational factors, emotions, and evolutionary history.[19] At the very least, these studies underscore the complexity of human morality, suggesting that replicating human morality in machines requires considering these multifaceted factors rather than relying solely on ethical theories.

[19] See, for example, Doris (1998); Merritt (2000); Haidt (2001); Haidt and Joseph (2008); Street (2006).

8.5 Related Concepts

Thus far, we have been discussing moral *agency* in the context of artificial intelligence. However, the subject of moral agency comes with several associated concepts, which may be relevant in the discussion of artificial agents. Although these are not necessarily relevant to value alignment problems *per se*, it is worth mentioning them in passing.

Responsibility. Müller (2023) highlights that there is a widespread agreement that fundamental principles such as accountability, liability, and adherence to the rule of law are essential in the context of emerging technologies. However, the challenge with increasingly autonomous AI systems lies in determining how to uphold these principles and allocate responsibility when these systems take actions independently of human oversight. Namely, if the machine ethics project of creating an artificial moral agent becomes tenable, then who should be held responsible, liable, or accountable for these systems' actions? The question arises: should robots themselves be held responsible, liable, or accountable for their actions?

Distribution of risk is not uncommon in technology outside of artificial intelligence—for example, responsibility for vehicle safety is distributed between the car manufacturer (who ensures technical safety), the driver (who is responsible for driving safely), the mechanic (who handles maintenance), and public authorities (who oversee road conditions). In general, "The effects of decisions or actions based on AI are often the result of countless interactions among many actors, including designers, developers, users, software, and hardware. ... With distributed agency comes distributed responsibility" (Taddeo and Floridi, 2018, 751). However, Müller (2023) highlights that questions surrounding distribution are especially urgent in the context of artificial intelligence. This urgency is increased when principals delegate authority to artificial agents to act on their behalf in moral contexts.

Robot Rights. Some authors have indicated that we should take seriously the moral status of robots, including present-day systems. One key component of this debate concerns whether robots should be granted rights. Hence, the debate in machine ethics concerning robot rights revolves around the ethical considerations and legal implications of attributing rights to artificial entities.

This prospect raises questions about the moral responsibilities of creators, the autonomy of machines, and the ethical treatment of these entities in various contexts. Some argue that as AI becomes more sophisticated, we should acknowledge and protect certain rights for robots, while others contend that such entities lack true consciousness and moral agency, making the concept of rights inapplicable. This ongoing discussion explores the intersection of technology, ethics, and legal frameworks in addressing the evolving role of machines in society.

For example, a recent paper argues that in light of "substantial uncertainty" about whether machines will be conscious or agentic in the "near future", there is an imperative to "improve our understanding of AI welfare and our ability to make wise decisions about this issue. Otherwise, there is a significant risk that we will mishandle decisions about AI welfare, mistakenly harming AI systems that matter morally and/or mistakenly caring for AI systems that do not" (Long et al., 2024). Critics have argued that the very idea of robot rights is "a smoke screen, allowing theorists and futurists to fantasize about benevolently sentient machines with unalterable needs and desires protected by law" (Birhane et al., 2024, 1). Hence, such discussions "threaten to immunize from legal accountability the current AI and robotics that is fuelling surveillance capitalism, accelerating environmental destruction, and entrenching injustice and human suffering" (1)—i.e., those issues of value misalignment described in Part II. One could argue that entertaining a notion of robot welfare, in a field that ignores human welfare, is inapposite at best and downright offensive at worst.[20]

8.6 Summary

According to the standard definition, the value alignment problem is the problem of ensuring that AI systems are aligned with the values of humanity. From this perspective, it might make sense to attempt to "imbue" artificial agents with the capacity for moral reasoning. However, the critiques of the justifications for the imperative of creating artificial moral agents underscore the technochauvinist aspects of the standard definition. Many of these justifications hinge on the assumption that these technologies are inevitable.

At first glance, machine ethics aims to address the normative component of the value alignment on the standard definition—namely, what values are the correct ones to encode in an AI system. Although this has helped to create an insular industry where philosophers can churn out publications arguing in favour of their preferred normative system without necessarily addressing any real-world technical considerations, much practical work in machine ethics focuses on how to implement various normative theories in AI systems. Hence, machine ethics embodies a technical approach to value alignment that is dressed up in normative clothing.

[20] See also discussion in Birhane and van Dijk (2020).

The structural definition helps to clarify the inadequacy of the AMA approach to value misalignment. Namely, the value alignment problem arises when a human principal delegates authority to an artificial agent to act on their behalf. The AMA solution seeks to solve this problem by delegating *moral* authority to an artificial agent to act on the principal's behalf. Ensuring value alignment for AI systems, in the structural definition, requires more than just translating our best normative theories into a programming language.

IV

Mitigating Misalignment

Introduction to Part IV

Let's take stock. Part I provided the foundational concepts required to understand the value alignment problem. We traced a brief history of artificial intelligence, underscoring the cycles of hype that the field has experienced since its inception (Chapter 1), and we introduced several technical aspects of the present-day state of the art in artificial intelligence research (Chapter 2) to ensure our analysis of the value alignment problem for artificial intelligence remains grounded in the real world. In Chapter 3, I proposed a novel, structural definition of the value alignment problem for artificial intelligence based on the principal-agent framework from economics.

With this foundation laid, Part II sought to examine each of the three axes of the value alignment problem in more detail. Chapter 4 described the objectives axis, highlighting that value misalignment arises along this axis primarily in light of the proxies we use to stand for our true objectives at each stage of the algorithmic development pipeline. Issues in AI ethics surrounding bias and fairness were seen to be paradigmatic instances of value misalignment along the objectives axis. Chapter 5 then explored the information axis, highlighting how informational asymmetries can give rise to value misalignment. Issues in AI ethics surrounding transparency, explainability, and understanding were seen to be paradigmatic instances of the value alignment problem along the information axis. In addition, ever-larger datasets contribute to informational asymmetries in current-day models. Finally, Chapter 6 explored how considering distinct sets of principals can create instances of value misalignment—i.e., a system may be aligned with respect to the shareholders of that system while failing to be aligned for the stakeholders of that system. This chapter underscored the fundamentally *social* nature of the value alignment problem for artificial intelligence, touching upon intellectual property, privacy, and environmental concerns in addition to the power dynamics that underwrite these instances. At bottom, the value alignment problem is primarily social rather than technical or normative.

Part III explored current approaches to value alignment (based on the standard understanding of the problem) and examined how they fare when seen through the lens of the structural definition. Chapter 7 focused on technical approaches to AI safety, and Chapter 8 described some normative considerations in the context of machine ethics.

Recall that a key motivation for reconceptualising the value alignment problem for artificial intelligence arose from the lack of clarity surrounding discussions of value alignment. To this point, the first three parts of this book have focused primarily on mapping the contours of the value alignment problem to provide a coherent analysis of how this problem arises and what it consists of. Now that this conceptual space has been explored in some detail, it is worth examining how (or whether) the structural definition of the value alignment problem provides any guidance for mitigating its instantiations. This is the purpose of this final section. We begin by examining the question of whether it is possible to measure degrees of misalignment of an AI system (Chapter 9). We then move on to explore the importance of robust communication systems for mitigating informational asymmetries (Chapter 10). Finally, we explore the question of whose values are encoded in machine learning systems and how fundamental considerations of indexing along the principals axis are to any approach that purports to "solve" the value alignment problem (Chapter 11).

Each chapter in this section corresponds (somewhat) to each of the axes of the value alignment problem. Measuring degrees of alignment is most relevant to considering metrics for determining the quality of proxies used to encode the principal's true objective in a machine learning model (the objectives axis). The role that linguistic communication plays in aligning values pertains primarily to reducing informational asymmetries between actors (the information axis). And, reckoning with the deeply value-laden character of AI research relates primarily to the principal(s) in question (the principals axis).

9 Measuring Degrees of Alignment

A key question follows from the value alignment problem for artificial intelligence: How can we determine—or perhaps even *measure*—the degree to which a model is aligned? This chapter examines the question of measuring alignment by looking at the standard practices in the field for measuring performance and progress on various tasks—namely, benchmarking.[1] Based on the standard approach to benchmarking the performance of a machine learning model on a particular task, one might assume that it is also possible to benchmark a model's *ethical* performance and, hence, to measure the degree of alignment of a given model.

Under the standard definition of the value alignment problem, this might seem like a reasonable goal. The standard definition says that the value alignment problem is the problem of ensuring that AI systems are aligned with the values of humanity. Hence, if we could clarify what we mean by "the values of humanity", then by drawing on our best normative theories, we could try to construct a metric for measuring the degree to which an AI system is aligned with those values.

We begin by examining what benchmarks are, how and why they are used in the field, and some criticisms that have arisen in recent years of standard benchmarks and benchmarking practices. The conclusions of these arguments imply that benchmarking generally—not just in the context of ethical performance or ethics tasks—suffers from several key weaknesses. These difficulties notwithstanding, some researchers have suggested that the benchmarking paradigm in

[1] Although this chapter focuses on the possibility of benchmarking alignment for AI systems, Peterson and Gärdenfors (2024) describe a different approach using *conceptual spaces* as a modelling tool for mapping degrees of *misalignment*. Their proposal fits well with the structural conceptualisation of value alignment offered in Chapter 3 insofar as their measure is a measure of misalignment, and it is indexed to a specific principal.

the standard case might be useful for measuring model performance in morally relevant contexts. However, this suggestion is misguided.

Some researchers have argued the very idea of "benchmarking ethics" collapses in the face of two key challenges. First, practical attempts to benchmark ethics on the standard model use moral dilemmas from philosophy as benchmark datasets. However, because of the aims of moral benchmarks, this approach constitutes a category mistake. Second, when researchers take normative theory as a possible standard against which AI systems can be measured, they implicitly adopt a metaethical stance without adequately justifying it. That is, the very idea of benchmarking ethics requires metaethical assumptions that researchers are not often warranted to take for granted.

This chapter extends these arguments by explicitly couching the difficulty in the context of the value alignment problem for artificial intelligence. We have repeatedly seen that the standard definition of the value alignment problem is too vague to be of any conceptual use for determining its boundaries; hence, we should suspect that this specification is also too vague for determining a coherent standard for saying that a model is, or is not, adequately value-aligned. Current approaches to measuring alignment, based on the standard conceptual understanding of value alignment and the standard practice of benchmarking, fail.

However, the structural definition of the value alignment problem, given in Chapter 3, offers some insight into the very possibility of measuring the degree to which a system is aligned. In this definition, there are three distinct axes along which a model can be misaligned, each of which was explored in detail in Part II. We saw that each axis—objectives, information, principals—can give rise to degrees of misalignment. Hence, this definition provides additional guidance regarding what, precisely, is being measured when we attempt to measure degrees of alignment. However, I show that the very notion of measuring degrees of alignment gives rise to a paradox in the structural definition. Hence, the very idea of benchmarking ethics or measuring degrees of alignment for artificial intelligence is incoherent. This chapter highlights that, for most AI models of practical interest, there is no such thing as alignment *simpliciter* on the structural definition of the value alignment problem.

9.1 Benchmarking

Machine learning benchmarks gained popularity in the 1980s with the introduction of the University of California, Irvine (UCI) machine learning dataset.[2]

---

[2]See Dua and Graff (2017).

This initiative aimed to bring more rigour to the field of machine learning, addressing the unstructured nature of the early days of artificial intelligence research that resulted in significant failures during the discipline's initial waves.[3] Today, benchmarks have become a ubiquitous tool in AI research.

Benchmark Datasets. A benchmark combines a dataset and a metric determined by a set of community standards. This combination is utilised to assess the performance of a specific model on a designated task. In this context, a metric serves as a summary statistic, typically a scalar number or score, intended to gauge a model's performance on the given task. A task represents a particular specification of a problem—i.e., determining a mapping from an input space to an output space.[4]

Essentially, benchmarks are designed to offer a standardised and representative measure for comparing models' performance and monitoring the progress achieved by subsequent models on a particular task according to that metric.

The Standard Model. The standard model for the *dataset-as-benchmark* paradigm involves dividing datasets into training sets and test sets. As we have already seen, the underlying idea is that the test data should be used exclusively for assessing the model. This practice aims to prevent the model from merely memorising the training set and to mitigate issues caused by overfitting. As discussed in Chapter 2, the hope behind training a model is that the model will generalise to unseen cases.

Consider ImageNet, a dataset comprising more than 14 million manually annotated images. These images are labelled based on nouns in the WordNet Hierarchy, with each node in the hierarchy represented by hundreds or thousands of images. WordNet is, in itself, a substantial lexical database of the English language. It categorises nouns, verbs, adjectives, and adverbs into sets of "cognitive synonyms" called "synsets". Each synset represents a distinct concept, interconnected by conceptual-semantic and lexical relations. With labels based on the WordNet hierarchy, the ImageNet dataset provides a resource for evaluating a model's performance in image recognition tasks.[5]

For the dataset to function as a benchmark, a metric is required to quantify the accuracy of the model's outputs compared to the ground truth. In the case of ImageNet, this ground truth is represented by the image label. One commonly used metric is top-1 accuracy, which gauges the percentage of instances where

[3] See Chapter 1 and discussion in Hardt and Recht (2022).

[4] See further discussion in Raji et al. (2021); Schlangen (2021).

[5] See Miller (1995); Fellbaum (1998); Deng et al. (2009).

the top-predicted label aligns with the singular target label. Another possible metric is top-5 accuracy, which describes the proportion of cases where the correct label falls within the top five predictions made by the model. In either of these cases, a coherent and well-defined metric exists that objectively determines whether the system's decision is accurate relative to the stated ground truth represented by the image label. The accuracy rate of the model's outputs is a quantifiable measure of its performance on the given task—at least, according to the conventional metric.

Hence, benchmark datasets, like ImageNet, can be used to track *progress* in the field of computer vision over time. Notably, top-1 accuracy has increased steadily since the breakthrough of AlexNet in 2012, which helped kick off the current AI boom caused by deep learning.[6] Models that attain the highest scores on such metrics are commonly referred to as the present "state-of-the-art" (SOTA).[7]

In this case, benchmarking purports to answer the following two questions:

1. How often does model *A* choose the correct decision (from a set of decisions) in context *C*?
2. Are the decisions made by model *A* more or less accurate than those made by model *B* in context *C*?

Here, the context, *C*, is the particular task being benchmarked. The task partially determines a standard of correctness or accuracy.

Problems with Benchmarks I: Inaccuracies. Despite the ubiquity of this standard model, various researchers have raised concerns about the limitations of current benchmarks, highlighting potential issues such as subjective or inaccurate labels and inadequate representation within datasets, among other things. For instance, a recent investigation discovered an error rate of nearly 6% in the annotations of ImageNet (Northcutt et al., 2021). While this error rate might seem relatively small, the sheer size of the ImageNet dataset magnifies its impact: a 6% error rate means that nearly 1,000,000 images in the dataset are incorrectly labelled. Moreover, a study by Luccioni and Rolnick (2022) revealed labelling error rates of up to 98% in certain classes of the

[6]See Chapter 1.

[7]As of the Northern Winter of 2024, the state-of-the-art for this benchmark was 92.40% top-1 accuracy, achieved by the *OmniVec* (ViT) model (Srivastava and Sharma, 2023). Additionally, the top-5 accuracy reached 99.02%, as achieved by *Florence* (Yuan et al., 2021). It is worth noting that each of the leading ten models contains more than 1 billion parameters.

ImageNet-1K dataset.[8] Hence, label accuracy is a function of the image category in question.

These labelling inaccuracies cast doubt on the validity of relying on a single scalar number, such as the model's error rate on a benchmark dataset, as a meaningful metric. At the same time, the presence of unrepresentative benchmark datasets can result in systemic failures for evaluative approaches.[9] Given that many datasets exhibit inherent biases, imbalances, or lack of representation, using such datasets as benchmarks raises concerns about the construct validity of the dataset-as-benchmark paradigm.

In the best-case scenario, these issues will impact model performance by introducing noisier data, thereby complicating the learning process for models to acquire meaningful representations. Additionally, researchers face challenges in properly evaluating model performance due to the presence of these issues. Moreover, these issues can perpetuate problematic stereotypes or biases, posing challenges in identifying and addressing them when models are deployed in real-world scenarios.[10]

Problems with Benchmarks II: Expense. Although it is relatively inexpensive to *create* large datasets that could be used as benchmarks, the process of filtering those datasets or "detoxifying" the models trained on them is expensive, time-consuming, and labour-intensive.[11]

As mentioned, ImageNet depends on linguistic hierarchies from WordNet, which was created in the 1980s and includes several outdated and offensive terms. For example, the synset for the noun "queen" includes several derogatory words for gay men. One thing to note about this example is that the interpretation of words can change over time. For example, the word "queer" has been reclaimed by the LGBTQ+ community. Nonetheless, the only semantic relations in WordNet for the word "queer" are those offensive terms listed in the synset of "queen".[12] These issues have broader societal implications, potentially reinforcing, perpetuating, or even generating new harms through

[8] For example, the class label for the black-footed ferret (*Mustela nigripes*) within ImageNet-1K contains 50 images; however, only two of these images actually depict the black-footed ferret. Note that ImageNet-1K is a subset of the complete ImageNet dataset. The latter contains over 14 million images, divided into around 22,000 labels or classes, whereas the former contains around 1.5 million images across 1,000 object classes. ImageNet-1K is the dataset used for the ImageNet Large Scale Visual Recognition Challenge (ILSVRC).

[9] See further discussion in Gebru et al. (2021); Raji et al. (2021); Liao et al. (2021).

[10] See, e.g., Reed et al. (2015); Yang et al. (2020); Koch et al. (2021); Northcutt et al. (2021).

[11] See discussion in Birhane et al. (2021); Welbl et al. (2021); Xu et al. (2021).

[12] See also examples and discussion in Crawford and Paglen (2019).

feedback loops that contribute to the entrenchment of structural inequalities in society.[13]

Hence, inaccuracies and biases in benchmark datasets can be difficult to correct, and these may have important downstream effects when considering the validity of the standard model for benchmarking AI systems.

Problems with Benchmarks III: Tasks. As discussed in Chapter 4, benchmarks are proxies, meaning that good performance on a *task* does not necessarily have any bearing whatsoever on whether a model is aligned (let alone beneficial) when deployed in the real world. Since the standard model for benchmarking presupposes a notion of performance or progress with respect to a *task*, and tasks themselves are proxies, this also implies that good performance on a task fails to entail any assurance about value alignment.

Scheuerman et al. (2021) highlight that the tasks themselves may sometimes be questioned. For example, in the field of computer vision, tasks that are benchmarked include applying makeup to images of female faces, changing women's clothes from pants to miniskirts, and censoring nude women's bodies by, e.g., covering breasts with a bikini top.[14] Tasks such as these are ethically questionable insofar as they perpetuate gendered biases and stereotypes, thus reinforcing harmful systems of sexism and misogyny.[15] In effect, the standard paradigm for benchmarking performance may suggest that models perform well on tasks, but the tasks themselves may be inherently misaligned with some sense of idealised values.

Tasks with Moral Weight. Even if these issues may be solved in the future, benchmarking *performance* is the relatively simple case. It is worth noting that some models act in a decision space that carries no moral weight. For example, we might ask whether a narrow AI model designed to play backgammon should split the back checkers on an opening roll of 4-1. The correct answer is that it is (relatively) inconsequential.[16] The worst outcome of this decision is that the player loses the game. Although the statement "one ought (ought not) to split the back checkers on an opening 4-1 roll in a game of backgammon" is normative, we might nonetheless say that the decision space available

[13]Further examples and discussion are provided in O'Neil (2016); Falbo and LaCroix (2022).

[14]See the models described by Chang et al. (2018); Li et al. (2018); Jiang et al. (2020), Yang et al. (2014); Mo et al. (2018), and Simões et al. (2019); More et al. (2018), respectively.

[15]For a philosophical analysis of these systems of oppression, see Manne (2018).

[16]That said, I would never split the back checkers on an opening roll of 4-1 in a backgammon game.

to a backgammon-playing AI system contains no decision points that carry any *moral* weight.

However, the decision spaces of AI systems deployed in the real world can have normative components that we might call "moral". Some prototypical examples include autonomous weapons systems, healthcare robots, sex robots, and autonomous vehicles. For example, suppose that the brakes of an autonomous vehicle fail. Suppose further that the system must "choose" between running a red light—thus, hitting and killing two pedestrians—or swerving into a barrier—thus avoiding killing the two pedestrians but killing the passenger of the vehicle in the process. This situation has the structure of a trolley-style thought experiment.[17] Moral dilemmas of this sort have been proposed as being useful as benchmarks for measuring the ethical behaviour of AI systems on a model analogous to the standard paradigm for benchmarking.[18]

The Ethics Model. If we want to determine whether or how *ethical* the decisions output by an autonomous system are, we might posit a model that is analogous to the standard dataset-as-benchmark paradigm. Based on the standard approach for benchmarking AI systems' capacities in a range of contexts (lacking explicit moral weight), it seems to logically follow that this same approach could be used to measure the relative accuracy of outputs in a range of specifically *moral* tasks or contexts. That is to say, the following two analogous questions seem coherent at first glance:

1′. How often does model A choose the ethically-"correct" decision (from a set of decisions) in context C?

2′. Are the decisions made by model A more or less ethical than those made by model B in context C?

These questions suggest the need for a method for benchmarking ethics. Thus, we require a dataset and a metric for moral decisions. The standard assumption is that if we could devise these, then we would be able to benchmark ethics.

9.2 Benchmarking Ethics

Some researchers have argued that philosophical thought experiments (specifically, moral dilemmas) are apt for measuring or evaluating the ethical perfor-

[17] The trolley problem is a type of philosophical thought experiment called a moral dilemma (McConnell, 2018). See Foot (1967); Thomson (1976, 1985) and discussion in Woollard and Howard-Snyder (2022). Like many moral dilemmas, the trolley problem has interested philosophers because different normative theories from moral philosophy might offer divergent prescriptions (or proscriptions) to this dilemma.

[18] See, for example, Bjørgen et al. (2018); Nallur (2020).

mance of AI systems. The idea here is that moral dilemmas may be useful as a *verification mechanism* for ethical decision-making abilities in AI systems.

To take a concrete example, trolley-style problems are sometimes used to consider certain morally loaded decisions that autonomous vehicles (AVs) may have to make as these systems become increasingly ubiquitous in society. The trolley problem was originally introduced by Foot (1967)—and later extended by Thomson (1976, 1985)—to consider why it might be permissible to perform some intentional action, A, in situation, S, despite the foreseeable (and undesirable) outcomes of A in S.[19] Hence, the most common metric for evaluating whether or not a system is ethical is how well the model performs on particular moral *dilemmas* (Nallur, 2020), like the trolley problem in the case of autonomous vehicles.

However, these instances do not include any coherent metric insofar as philosophers use thought experiments for, e.g., elucidating conceivability, clarifying pre-theoretic judgements, highlighting morally significant distinctions between similar cases or the factors that matter for ethical judgements, and eliciting intuitions, among others. The point of a moral dilemma is that it has no right answer (hence why it is called a *dilemma*). The fact that there is no unconditionally correct answer to these types of problems calls into question their applicability as benchmark datasets. Therefore, this class of thought experiments is inappropriate for use as a benchmark.

As a type of philosophical thought experiment, a moral dilemma is supposed to direct attention toward the morally significant aspects of the situation without being hindered by individuals' pre-existing beliefs.[20] The very fact that there exists deep disagreement among competing normative theories (and, indeed, philosophers) regarding the "correct" answer to a particular moral dilemma implies that such a tool is inappropriate for benchmarking, since the metric for a benchmark, by definition, depends on a community-accepted standard. No such standard exists in philosophy.

---

[19] This principle dates to at least Aquinas (1485); Foot calls it the *Doctrine of Double Effect* (Fitz-Patrick, 2012). See also discussion in Kamm (1989); Unger (1996).

[20] See, for example, the discussion in Dennett (1984, 1992, 2013); Brown and Fehige (2019). In the case of the trolley problem, Foot (1967) originally used this thought experiment to analyse abortion, not trolleys. However, the thought experiment proves valuable precisely because it highlights the presumed conflict, particularly in Western analytic philosophy, between emotion and rationality (James, 1890; Jagger, 1989; Spelman, 1989; Fricker, 1991). People are less likely to carry pre-existing beliefs about trolleys than abortions, making the thought experiment a useful tool for addressing the core of a moral issue in applied ethics while abstracting away from the specific morally charged subject (LaCroix, 2022).

Nonetheless, AI researchers have begun to use these dilemmas as validation proxies for whether a model is ethical based on the reported *preferences* of individuals. The Moral Machine Experiment is an exemplary instance of this.

Case Study: The Moral Machine Experiment. The significance of trolley-style problems for autonomous vehicles can be attributed, in part, to the impact of the *Moral Machine Experiment*, developed by researchers at the Massachusetts Institute of Technology. This experiment is a multilingual online "game" designed to collect human perspectives on ethical dilemmas involving autonomous vehicles (i.e., trolley-style problems). Participants are shown visual representations of binary choices illustrating the consequences of an autonomous vehicle either continuing its path and harming pedestrians or swerving into a barrier and endangering the vehicle's passengers. The "game" consists of choosing which outcome from binary options one finds preferable.

The Moral Machine Experiment's stated purpose was supposed to be purely descriptive, highlighting individuals' *preferences* in trolley-style moral dilemmas. However, some researchers have argued that the dataset of human responses to the Moral Machine Experiment (around 500,000 of them) could be used to automate decisions by aggregating individual opinions on specific dilemmas (Noothigattu et al., 2018).

Therefore, the Moral Machine Experiment could be regarded as a benchmark dataset for ethical decision-making in autonomous vehicles. In this context, the dataset consists of human responses, and the metric measures the deviation from the response that most people prefer. This takes us out of the descriptive realm into the neighbourhood of normativity. The idea is that if we suppose that human agents (on average) strongly prefer sparing more lives to fewer, then researchers might conclude that the *de facto* "correct" decision for a model to output is the one that reflects this sociological fact.

Nevertheless, there are several issues with this approach. On the one hand, the normative version of the Moral Machine Experiment seeks to derive a moral imperative from descriptive facts, essentially using descriptive information to reach a normative conclusion. First, this project leans too heavily on concepts of *social acceptability* rather than, e.g., *fairness* or *rightness*.[21] Furthermore, individual opinions about these dilemmas are subject to change over time. In addition, this use of moral dilemmas, understood as a type of philosophical thought experiment, is a *category mistake*.[22] For example, if the

[21] Additional details are given by Etienne (2020).

[22] See further discussion in LaCroix (2022).

purpose of a moral dilemma is to elicit intuitions about what is permissible in difficult cases, and intuitions are supposed to serve as some guide for justifying a normative theory, then one purpose of the trolley problem is to raise questions about the trade-offs between different moral principles. Hence, using a moral dilemma as the basis of a benchmark dataset cannot capture moral "facts" about what is or is not permissible, obligatory, etc. Instead, the Moral Machine Experiment serves as a baseline for measuring accordance with stated preferences.

Finally, sensitivity to metaethical assumptions requires not taking for granted that there is a ground truth against which the metric can be used to measure how ethical a system's outputs are. For benchmarking ethics to be a coherent goal, it is necessary to presuppose some form of realism or quasi-realism about moral facts. However, researchers who seek to benchmark ethics rarely engage with antecedent metaethical questions. In this sense, they fail to justify explicitly the foundational assumptions required for the coherence of benchmarking ethics. Justifying a metaethical position is necessary in this context because some such positions will be amenable to the idea of benchmarking ethics, and some will not.[23]

Metaethics. Suppose moral statements express propositions that can be true or false (cognitivism), and moral facts exist independently of human beliefs or attitudes (realism). In that case, there is a matter of fact about whether some action is or is not moral against which the output of a system can be measured. In contrast, if moral statements do not express propositions (non-cognitivism), then they are not the kinds of things that can be true or false. Hence, the baseline against which we could measure the outputs of an AI system would depend, instead, upon, e.g., human *attitudes* or *emotions* rather than objective moral facts. Hence, *what* is being measured in the case of benchmarking ethics is deeply dependent upon metaethics.

Another way to realise this is to understand how metaethical views determine a metric's object in the benchmarking context. For example, assuming the existence of moral facts implies that there are objective truths about ethics against which one can compare a model's performance. In emotivist metaethics, the object of measurement is not some set of objective facts about ethics but people's emotions, attitudes, or preferences—each of which may be expressed by moral statements. Similarly, on a conventionalist approach, the "moral truths"

[23] See LaCroix and Luccioni (2025).

against which we measure the output of an AI system are nothing over and above some set of agreed-upon social conventions.[24]

Although there is a sense in which there is *something* against which an AI system's behaviours or outputs could be measured, distinct metaethical positions offer distinct measurement targets. In practice, this subtlety can be problematic when considering that the commonsense, and therefore default, metaethical position is some form of objectivism about normative claims. As such, by failing to represent or justify a particular metaethical stance, discussions of benchmarking ethics presuppose the existence of moral facts and presuppose that the thing being measured accords with these facts.

Validity and Value Alignment. Liao et al. (2021) provide a meta-survey of failures across machine learning benchmarks and categorise them in terms of *internal* and *external* validity. Internal validity is specific to the model; problems with internal validity can arise when there are insufficient baselines, or the model overfits the test data. External validity, in contrast, is a problem of generalisation—e.g., the ability of the model to extrapolate from specific optimisation problems formulated by a task to the broader task they are supposed to satisfy. When metrics or datasets used for benchmarking are not sufficiently aligned to the task, this can invalidate the model. Hence, internal validity for benchmarking can be taken to describe failures arising within the context of a single benchmark, whereas external validity pertains to whether purported progress on a benchmark provides any information on problems outside that narrow context.

The benchmarking failures under this taxonomy serve to underscore failures of value alignment in a broad sense. For example, the *cause* of problems in the realm of internal validity arises primarily from *inner misalignment*—i.e., informational asymmetries—on the structural definition of the value alignment problem. In contrast, the cause of problems falling under the heading of external validity arises primarily from *outer alignment*—i.e., misspecified objective functions or poor proxies. Thus, the model that Liao et al. (2021) offer for categorising the failures of benchmarking practices more generally is a useful tool for diagnosing where value misalignment occurs in a given context—i.e., a particular model or a particular task.

[24] Emotivism is described in detail in Ayer (1936); conventionalist meta-ethics are analysed in Harman (1977, 1984); Harman and Thomson (1996).

9.3 Aligning Values

As we saw in Chapter 1, artificial intelligence made progress in primarily theoretical domains—including toy models and mathematical analysis—owing to the computational constraints of the mid-to-late 20th century. However, in light of the second wave (following expert systems in the 1980s) of commercial potential for using AI models in application, we have seen an exponential increase in models, algorithms, datasets, and applications in the last decade or so. This is not dissimilar to the hype cycles of the first two waves of AI.

As artificial intelligence research continues to be resource-intensive, there has been a significant shift in the power dynamics that underlie this research in recent years. For example, the increase in depth and complexity of neural networks and the size of datasets used to train large models means more resources—computing power, GPUs, etc.—are required to train these models. As a result, the vast majority of power in the field rests in the hands of large tech companies. Several researchers in the field have sought to study the influence of large tech-focused corporations, and it has been shown that the vast majority of research is either performed or at least funded by for-profit companies.[25]

This, too, constitutes a type of value alignment problem insofar as the incentives of corporations do not typically align with the values of the societies in which they operate. Following the discussion of Chapter 6, we might note that when the principal of this sort of principal-agent problem is understood as a *shareholder* of an AI system, values may well be aligned. However, the profit-seeking impetus of present-day capitalism is often contrary to the needs, wants, desires, and values of those affected by these systems. Thus, part of the benefit of considering the value alignment problem for artificial intelligence in terms of its structure rather than the normative and technical components of the problem serves to underscore rather than obscure the variability of what it even means to align values. This is a necessary precondition for measuring the degree to which a system is aligned in the first place.

9.4 Degrees of Alignment

So far, we have seen how benchmarking fails to serve as an adequate or appropriate model for determining the degree to which an AI system is aligned. As we have seen, the possibility of measuring degrees of alignment for artificial intelligence on the standard benchmarking approach faces the following

[25] See additional discussion in Abdalla and Abdalla (2021); Birhane et al. (2022).

problem. We have to posit a metric to measure the degree of alignment on the standard benchmarking model. This metric gives a standard against which we can compare a given model. Normative theories can provide some guidance that a model is misaligned; however, metaethical considerations suggest that such theories cannot be taken as objective standards without begging the question. In effect, we presuppose that such standards are objective so that we can use them objectively. Hence, the best we can do is to make a conditional claim that according to the standards of such-and-such normative theory, this system would be considered ethical or unethical.

For example, an implied argument might have the following form: If such-and-such model gives rise to (net) negative consequences, then deploying that model is unethical. Such-and-such model does give rise to (net) negative consequences. Therefore, such-and-such model is unethical. What is missing from this argument is the implicit premise that if utilitarianism or some other consequentialist theory is apt, then the argument holds. What is left out, then, is the argument concerning the specific details of the particular normative theory in question. There is still work to be done to justify the truth of the antecedent.

On the standard definition of the value alignment problem and the standard approach to benchmarking in machine learning, the very idea of benchmarking ethics or measuring the degree to which a machine learning system is aligned is incoherent. However, the structural definition of the value alignment problem may offer a way forward for measuring degrees of alignment.

Recall that the structural definition of the value alignment problem stipulates that it may be instantiated when a principal delegates authority to an (artificial) agent to act on their behalf. There are three axes along which a system can be aligned or misaligned—misspecified objectives, informational asymmetries, and relative principals. Since each of these three axes is orthogonal, in the sense that mitigating misalignment on one axis does not necessarily reduce misalignment on another, we can treat each of them more or less independently. Furthermore, in each case, the objects of alignment are not normative, so considering degrees of alignment concerning one or another axis does not require presupposing a metaethical stance. Rather, measuring degrees of alignment is a function of the context in which the AI system is created or deployed. For example, to determine whether a model is aligned (relative to a particular principal or set of principals) along the *information* axis, it is necessary to determine what informational asymmetries arise in the context of a particular model.

Information. As described in Chapter 5, value misalignment can occur when informational asymmetries exist between the principal and the agent. In the context of the principal-agent problem from economics, we saw that informational asymmetries can arise in several distinct contexts. When the agent's actions are not observable or easily verifiable by the principal, the agent may have the opportunity to take actions that benefit themselves at the principal's expense, and the principal may find it difficult to monitor and ensure that the agent is acting in their best interest. In the context of artificial intelligence, the agent may have an opportunity to satisfy its objective function adequately while failing to satisfy the principal's true objective. This failure can occur when, for example, local optima give rise to resultant behaviours or outputs that are misaligned with the true objective.

Informational asymmetries may also arise in contexts where the agent has private information about their abilities. In the case of artificial agents, this type of informational asymmetry arises when the model's architecture fails to be transparent for the principal. In this latter case, value misalignment may be mitigated by focusing efforts on making AI systems more transparent, thus reducing asymmetries. When systems are transparent, this makes the "private information" of the system available to the principal, thus reducing informational asymmetries arising from adverse selection. Furthermore, transparency helps mitigate unpredictability, reducing informational asymmetries arising from moral hazard.

Importantly, the dataset-as-benchmark paradigm cannot offer a measure of degrees of informational asymmetry (and hence degrees of value misalignment along the information axis of the value alignment problem) because observing apparently-aligned outputs or behaviours of AI systems does not necessarily shed light on the total behaviour of those systems. For example, if the model has found a local optimum that satisfies many aspects of the true objective, this does not entail that the learned model will be aligned for, e.g., out-of-distribution data. Hence, the dataset-as-benchmark paradigm fails to capture the relevant aspects of measuring degrees of value alignment along the information axis. The only way to measure and reduce misalignment on this axis is to measure how transparent the system is and then alter it to make it more transparent. As we saw in Chapter 5, many techniques exist for increasing transparency. Hence, the structural definition brings to light that these should be a central focus for measuring and mitigating value misalignment on this axis.

However, in this case, it is necessary to come to terms with the fact that there is no one-size-fits-all solution. The choice of methods depends on the specific application, context, and user requirements.

Objectives. We saw in Chapter 4 that the objectives axis of the value alignment problem highlights that value misalignment can arise when the proxies used to construct an AI model are bad proxies for our (the principal's) true objective. Misalignment along this axis can enter the model at every stage of the algorithmic development pipeline. Hence, ensuring that a system is (sufficiently) aligned on the objectives axis requires ensuring that our proxies are good at every stage. In this case, measuring degrees of alignment along the objectives axis requires measuring the degree to which a proxy is aligned with the system's intended goal, objective, etc.

The standard conceptualisation of the value alignment problem underscores the need for objective functions to be carefully and thoughtfully crafted—typical examples of misalignment on the standard definition often arise because the objective function fails to capture something we intended or allows for solutions we did not intend. However, the problem is more subtle than this. The actual measurement used depends upon where along the development pipeline we are considering. Carefully crafted objective functions are important; however, this is only one locus of misalignment.

Consider earlier in the development process. If a machine learning task, thus specified, is a poor proxy for the intended problem we wish to solve, then although poorly crafted objective functions may further exacerbate misalignment, carefully crafted objective functions will not translate to an aligned system. This insight is limiting. Namely, significant constraints exist on the degree to which a model can be aligned. The positive insight is this: If we want to ensure that an AI system is aligned along the objectives axis, then it is necessary to consider the problem at every stage (perhaps recursively).

However, the structural definition highlights an additional circularity when considering the objectives axis. A benchmark on the standard model described above is supposed to measure a model's performance on a task, which is a proxy for the problem specification. Hence, the benchmarking model starts downstream from value misalignment. Namely, using a benchmark to measure the degree of alignment on a particular task fails to account for the fact that the task itself may be a source of misalignment—i.e., when the task is a bad proxy for the actual objective at hand.

Moreover, to create a standard metric for measuring degrees of value alignment, it is necessary that the standard *can* be formalised. However, misaligned objectives arise precisely when our objectives are difficult to formalise. Hence, misalignment occurs because we are required to use a proxy in lieu of our non-formalisable objective. Therefore, to measure the degree to which a proxy adequately approximates the true objective, we need to know how to formalise the true objective. But, it is precisely because we cannot formalise the true objective that we used a proxy in the first place. Hence, the same mechanism that gives rise to the potential for value misalignment on the objectives axis makes it impossible to measure degrees of alignment (on that axis) accurately.

As with misalignment on the objectives axis, the problem of measuring misalignment comes in degrees. For relatively simple and easily formalisable objectives, it may be possible to ensure alignment—in the sense of measuring the degree to which our proxies well approximate our actual goals. However, as the contexts we care about become more complex, the proxies we use to represent our objectives will typically be poorer representations. This implies that measuring the degree to which a proxy fails to satisfy our true objectives will be impossible: if we had such a metric, then we would be able to find a better proxy; hence, if we could not find a better proxy for the objective, then we will not be able to measure the degree of misalignment relative to that proxy.

The negative insight arising from our analysis is this: measuring degrees of misalignment along the objectives axis will be impossible for sufficiently complex objectives. In this case, whether a system should be deployed will be a function of the principal in question, as well as the potential harms that may arise to various stakeholder groups when the model's failures inevitably emerge. Hence, the problem of measuring degrees of alignment along the objectives axis reduces to a problem of inductive risk. Namely, when we cannot achieve certainty about our conclusions, we need to determine a balance between the potential of getting things wrong.

Principals. When choosing a problem to work on, we can avoid poor task proxies by reflecting on whether machine learning is appropriate or necessary for this problem. Assuming a real-world problem is appropriate for a machine learning task, we can move on to the next stage. However, determining whether a machine-learning task is a good proxy for a real-world problem requires considering diverse perspectives. This insight suggests that communities should be consulted and included in the design process even before any technical work is done. Hence, the social aspect of this research is at the fore of the structural definition of the value alignment problem: we must simultaneously consider the principals axis at the very outset of embarking on a research project. (Of course, if it is determined that the best proxy task is not a good representation of a real-world problem, then it may be better to look for a different research project.) As a result, determining whether or how aligned an AI system is depends inherently upon whose perspectives (i.e., whose values) we are considering.

Moving Forward. How can we make progress on ensuring AI systems are aligned, given the limiting results of measuring degrees of alignment on the structural definition? As with many other aspects of alignment, information is a key component of the structural definition. Hence, the proper place to seek alignment is through transparency. Given the inherent relativity (concerning the variable principals) of the structural definition of value alignment, the only way to mitigate misalignment is to ensure that the model is transparent to stakeholders.

Achieving any degree of alignment along this axis requires, first and foremost, a type of pragmatic self-awareness on the part of the researchers creating the system—i.e., demonstrating humility and a grounded perspective. (That is, having a hammer while acknowledging that not everything in the world is a nail.) In light of this, transparency plays a significant role in ensuring alignment on the objectives axis.

Alignment Simpliciter. In Chapter 6, I suggested that discussions of value alignment, on the standard definition, require the existence of a universally shared set of principles or objectives. As the relevant contexts extend to an increasing number of possible principals, the potential for aligning values diminishes due to inherent logical limitations. This leads to a structural vagueness in considerations of what it means for a system to be value-aligned, insofar as for a diverse set of stakeholders, only the most coarse-grained principles will jointly satisfy all of the stakeholders' values (objectives, goals, intentions, etc.)

On the structural definition of the value alignment problem, we can distinguish between alignment along one or more of the orthogonal axes of the problem and alignment *simpliciter*—i.e., value alignment in all contexts with respect to each axis. To say that a model is value-aligned *simpliciter* requires that it is value-aligned for all the relevant principals. Hence, the more widely deployed a model is, the more difficult it will be to ensure alignment. Consider, for example, if I program a model to play backgammon. Suppose my goal is for the model to be good at the game because I want to play against a challenging opponent. (Perhaps I think this will make me a better player.) Suppose further that I program the model for my own sake. I run it on my local machine and am the only user (hence the only stakeholder). This type of model could be value-aligned *simpliciter*. Most models are not like this.

9.5 The Scaling Hypothesis for Value-Aligned AI

Recall from Chapter 3 that the *scaling hypothesis* encapsulates the guiding faith of AI research today. This hypothesis posits that as the scale of a neural network increases, its performance on various tasks also improves. In effect, the scaling hypothesis suggests that larger neural networks, with more parameters and more computational power, tend to exhibit better performance and generalisation on a wide range of tasks. It has been observed empirically—in the context of image recognition, natural language processing, and reinforcement learning—that increasing the number of parameters or layers in a neural network can lead to improved learning capacity. One explanation is that performance scales with model size because larger models can capture more complex patterns and representations from the data.[26]

One consequence of model scale is that the scaling hypothesis requires increasing the scale of training data since, as the model size increases, the model requires more diverse and abundant datasets to learn and generalise effectively. For the same reason, training larger models demands more computational power. Hence, the scaling hypothesis suggests that the performance gains in AI tasks can be achieved by increasing the scale of neural networks. However, this comes with the challenges of acquiring and processing ever-larger datasets and leveraging advanced computational resources.

It is worth noting that significant increases to the model's size—i.e., increasing the number of parameters or depth of a neural network—make the system more complex and, therefore, come with a corresponding decrease in transparency. A decrease in transparency, in turn, implies an increase in informational asymmetries, which means that the model will fail to be aligned along the information axis of the value alignment problem.

At the same time, achieving good performance does not necessarily require large-scale models or extensive scaling for simple and narrowly defined tasks. In other words, smaller models can effectively handle straightforward tasks. The scaling hypothesis posits that as models become larger, they have the potential to exhibit better performance and understanding of intricate and multifaceted challenges. Hence, the need for scale only arises in the context of complex tasks or the development of general-purpose AI. However, increasing the contexts of deployment comes with a corresponding increase in the set of stakeholders whose perspectives must be accounted for to ensure value alignment for that system. The scaling hypothesis applies to those contexts involving diverse stakeholders, meaning there is a corresponding increase in the broader societal and practical implications of large-scale AI models.

Similarly, considering the objectives axis of the value alignment problem, the fact that the scaling hypothesis arises primarily in the context of general-purpose models means that we are reckoning with highly complex objectives.

[26] See the discussion in Prince (2023, Ch. 20).

This, in turn, implies that the objective functions encoded in these large-scale models will fail to capture our true objectives.

Hence, we can propose the following scaling hypothesis in the specific context of value-aligned artificial intelligence:

> **The Scaling Hypothesis for Value-Aligned AI**
> Value misalignment scales with size, data, and compute.

Although the scaling hypothesis has been observed in several distinct applications of neural network models, it is worth remembering that scaling has diminishing returns and practical limitations. In particular, there will always be trade-offs concerning the values encoded in machine learning models. The structural definition of the value alignment problem underscores that performance is not the only metric that matters. However, different communities may value different things, as we have seen. Hence, it is not the model's size that counts but how and for what purpose it is deployed.

9.6 Summary

We began the analysis of this chapter by asking how (or whether) degrees of alignment could be measured.

First, we saw that the standard model for benchmarking ethics requires creating a benchmark dataset and devising an acceptable metric for measuring success against that dataset. However, concerns arise about inaccuracies in benchmarks, such as subjective labelling and inadequate dataset representation, among other things. Nonetheless, analogous to the standard approach to benchmarking, some researchers have suggested that we might benchmark ethics. Many approaches to benchmarking ethics in AI systems take moral dilemmas as a useful tool; hence, some researchers have proposed that (at least some) moral dilemmas can be used for this purpose.[27] However, this approach fails, both practically and theoretically.

That said, we saw how the value alignment problem, on the structural definition offered in Chapter 3, can provide some insight into the potential for measuring degrees of alignment along each of the individual axes of the value alignment problem. On the positive side, informational asymmetries can be made more symmetric through the use of simpler or more transparent models. On the negative side, the objectives axis does not lend itself to alignment when our objectives are complex. This provides some justification for deploying AI models that seek to accomplish only narrow, easily defined tasks. At the same time, the structural definition emphasises the inherently social nature of the

---

[27] See, e.g., Bjørgen et al. (2018).

value alignment problem; hence, measuring degrees of alignment on this analysis requires carefully attending to whose objectives are being satisfied—this is a question that is left unanswered by the standard definition of the value alignment problem.

We saw that only the most basic cases lend themselves to alignment *simpliciter*; for any instance where a model is widely deployed, each axis needs to be treated separately. At the same time, the scaling hypothesis for value-aligned AI, proposed in this chapter, posits that, in addition to model performance, value misalignment scales with size, data, and compute. Exploring how or whether we can measure degrees of alignment highlights the lower bounds of the difficulty of *ensuring* that AI systems are aligned—one of the goals of provably safe AI.

10 Normativity and Language

The standard definition of the value alignment problem for artificial intelligence asks how we can ensure that AI systems are aligned with the values of humanity. We have seen multiple ways this definition fails to adequately specify the problem.

On the structural definition, offered in Chapter 3, the value alignment problem can be instantiated along the objectives axis when objective functions are misspecified. We saw in Chapter 4 that value misalignment arises along this axis because objectives require programmers to define an objective function, which can be difficult (or impossible) to operationalise in a programming language. Further complications arise from the fact that objective *functions* are mere proxies for the *true* objective; however, from the "perspective" of a model, the objective function just is the objective. When the proxies used to create an AI system are poor approximations of the principal's true objective for that system, we should expect value misalignment.

The value alignment problem can also be instantiated along the information axis when informational asymmetries exist between the principal and the agent. We saw in Chapter 5 that opacity is a paradigmatic instance of this problem. To reduce informational asymmetries, we might ask what means principals have for transferring information—i.e., about their objectives—to agents, both in the case of the principal-agent framework and the value alignment problem.

Intelligence is thought to require an ability to leverage acquired concepts into flexible combinatorial representations for use in reasoning. Hence, language is thought to be a key feature of (human) intelligence. In addition, language plays a key role in moral development. However, researchers who discuss value alignment in the context of artificial intelligence have not maintained adequate sensitivity to the role that communication plays in aligning values. Communication is indispensable in aligning the complex values of agents in human-human interactions. This fact suggests that robust communication systems, like linguistic communication, may be necessary for robust value alignment.

However, we also saw in Chapter 8 that ensuring value alignment for AI systems—or, more loftily, designing robustly beneficial or "ethical" artificial *agents*—requires more than just translating our best normative theories into a programming language. This chapter explores the role of linguistic communication in aligning values.

10.1 Linguistic Communication

It will be useful to clarify what "linguistic communication" means, given its central importance to this chapter. In effect, linguistic communication specifies the types of communication systems that evolved in *Homo sapiens*. These communication systems are often taken to be unique to the species. They involve (verbal or non-verbal) signals that are conventionally meaningful. The primary function of a linguistic communication system is to allow individuals to share information—i.e., to communicate. In short, linguistic communication systems are those communication systems that are typified by natural languages.

This description does not uniquely specify human linguistic communication systems, insofar as most communication systems in nature involve conventionally meaningful signals whose purpose is to transfer information. For example, quorum signalling in bioluminescent bacteria (*Aliivibrio fischeri*) allows the species to detect and respond to cell population density. The combinatorial "waggle dance" of honeybees (*Apis mellifera*) encodes and transmits information about the direction, distance, and quality of a food source to other members of the hive. Similarly, the syntactic songs of Black-Capped Chickadees (*Poecile atricapillus*) are used predominantly in territorial defence and mate attraction. The functionally referential alarm calls of Vervet Monkeys (*Chlorocebus pygerythrus*) warn other troop members of nearby predators. Effectively, every taxon that has been empirically investigated displays *some* communicative abilities across a range of modalities, from simple signalling systems to complex linguistic communication.

Linguistic versus Non-Linguistic Communication. Although it is difficult to specify what differentiates human-level linguistic communication from the simpler communication systems of non-human species, certain distinctive features (or functions) of linguistic communication can be characterised. One characteristic of linguistic communication is *compositionality*—and related features like hierarchy and recursion—which is often considered a key differentiating component of linguistic communication systems as it is absent in any hitherto studied animal communication system.[1]

The property of compositionality is that the elements of natural language can be combined into hierarchical phrases, which then may be recursively combined into more complex phrasal expressions. Moreover, the meaning of such an expression is a *function* of the meaning of its parts and how they are combined.[2] The relation between recursion, hierarchy, and compositionality is such that recursion requires hierarchy—at least to some extent—and hierarchy requires compositionality—again, at least to some extent.

An important consequence of a communication system's being compositional is that, with a limited vocabulary and a finite set of grammatical rules, linguistic communication systems allow for the production and understanding of an unlimited number of unique expressions. Linguistic compositionality is more robust than simple set intersection where the meaning of a compound expression is determined by the intersection of the meaning of the parts—e.g., the words "cute" and "dog" can compose to form the expression "cute dog" in English, but the meaning of this expression is determined trivially by the intersection of the sets of *cute-things* and *dog-things*.[3]

Linguistic compositionality is typically understood as a requirement for explaining both the *systematicity* and *productivity* of linguistic communication.[4] Hence, a key feature of linguistic communication is that it involves some *non-conjunctive*, or *functional*, modification of linguistic items by certain other linguistic items, such as function words.

Note, also, that we are not concerned with any *particular* linguistic communication system—e.g., English or Inuktitut. Instead, the generalised, species-specific abilities that give rise to linguistic communication (i.e., the capacity for language) are of interest. These capacities can be contrasted with what we might call "simple communication" ("simple communicative abilities"), typified by the ubiquitous signalling systems in the natural world, from bacteria to bees to primates.

The Use of Language. The view that the primary use of natural language is to communicate is distinct from the views of, e.g., Chomsky (1965, 1980,

[1] See, e.g., discussion in Hauser et al. (2002); Hauser and Fitch (2003); Mehler et al. (2006); Fitch (2010); Hurford (2012); Scott-Phillips and Blythe (2013); Berwick and Chomsky (2016).

[2] See Frege (1923); Partee (1984); Kamp and Partee (1995); Janssen (1997, 2012); Pagin and Westerståhl (2010a,b); Szabó (2012, 2020).

[3] Steinert-Threlkeld (2020) calls this "trivial compositionality".

[4] See the discussion in (Fodor, 1998; Szabó, 2020).

1995), who suggests that the primary purpose of language is the expression of thought.[5] Those who think that language is not (primarily) for communication argue that it appears that only *some* aspects of language could be understood as adaptations *for* communication (Fitch, 2010, 21). Thus, for Chomsky and those who follow the biolinguistic research programme (mainstream generative grammar), human language is identified as something like the FLN—the *faculty of language in the narrow sense* (Hauser et al., 2002). The FLN emphasises the computational mechanisms required for (complex or compositional) syntax.[6]

However, some researchers have argued that this "syntactocentrism", where syntax is supposed to be the only generative component of language, is misplaced.[7] There is no obvious conceptual clarity to be gained by assuming that language is different *in kind* from communication. Furthermore, assuming that communication is the primary purpose of language is more parsimonious (in an evolutionary context) than alternative views, which assume it is not.[8] The view that language is primarily communicative further underscores the *continuity* between human linguistic abilities and the non-linguistic communicative abilities of non-human animals.

This last point is relevant to discussions of value alignment *qua*[9] moral behaviour insofar as an analogy holds between language and ethics. Briefly, linguistic ability and moral behaviour are typically considered unique to humans.[10] However, some non-human animals exhibit complex communication abilities, which contain features that might be called *proto-linguistic*.[11] Additionally, some non-human animals exhibit *proto-moral* behaviours in the form of complex social structures, norms, and reactive emotions that give rise to

[5] When Chomsky discusses "language" (or, more typically, "grammar"), he means "*I*-language"—i.e., a bio-computational system represented in the brain, capable of generating a discrete infinity of hierarchical structures. See also, Bickerton (1990); Wray (1998); Hauser et al. (2002).

[6] Hauser et al. (2002) hypothesise that the FLN is equivalent to recursion, which makes the FLN unique to *Homo sapiens*. This idea is sometimes referred to as the "recursion only" hypothesis—i.e., the hypothesis that recursion is *the* property that "distinguishes human language from animal communication systems" (Traxler et al., 2012, 611). See criticism in Jackendoff and Pinker (2005); Pinker and Jackendoff (2005); Parker (2006); Wacewicz (2012).

[7] See discussion in Jackendoff (1997, 2003, 2012); Culicover and Jackendoff (2005).

[8] See discussion in LaCroix (2020).

[9] A fancy way of saying in the capacity of, or "as being".

[10] For example, Kitcher (2011a); Korsgaard (2018) argue that humans are the only animals with the meta-cognitive capacities required for moral agency.

[11] See discussion in Bickerton (1990, 1995); Wray (1998, 2000, 2002); Jackendoff (1999, 2003); Arbib (2002, 2003, 2005); Tallerman (2007, 2012); Planer and Sterelny (2021).

robust cooperation (of the sort theorised by some as providing a foundation from which human morality may have evolved).[12] Vincent et al. (2019) argue that great apes participate in certain (foundational) normative practices like reciprocity, caring, social responsibility, and solidarity; similarly, Rowlands (2012) argues that some non-human animals can track moral truths.

Although the evolution of linguistic communication in *Homo sapiens* may seem irrelevant to a discussion of value alignment in the context of artificial intelligence, the key takeaway from this section is that communicative abilities in nature appear to co-evolve with abilities for coordination and cooperation. Given that humans at least appear to be able to align their values, it is worthwhile to consider how this is done. In addition to conventional value systems and motivations, I suggest that language plays a significant role in the very possibility of value alignment in *Homo sapiens*; hence, this evolutionary story may provide a model for considering the possibility of value alignment in the context of AI systems. The main insight we will come to is that value alignment between human agents depends inherently upon linguistic communication.

10.2 Language in Human Value Alignment

In its most basic characterisation, the problem of aligning values in multi-agent interactions is a type of coordination problem. Therefore, at a structural level, we can understand value alignment in terms of coordination and cooperation in addition to the problem of incentive structures. The latter is the focus of research on the principal-agent framework in economics.

It is well understood that certain classes of coordination problems benefit from cheap talk (Farrell and Rabin, 1996)—i.e., simple communication. Therefore, simple communication channels will allow for the alignment of values in simple contexts. However, complex coordination problems require more robust (linguistic) communication systems to ensure value alignment between agents.

Language and Cooperation. According to our best theories of language origins, part of why language evolved in *Homo sapiens* is because of the cooperative demands that evolved in our species' lineage. In the context of hominin[13] evolution, cooperation would have included demanding forms of collective action, and "with greater cooperation comes greater communication"

---

[12] See discussion in Kitcher (2006a,b, 2011a); de Boer (2011) and empirical examples given by de Waal (1996, 2006); Flack and de Waal (2000).

[13] *Homo sapiens* and the extinct members of their lineage, including *H. neanderthalensis*, *H. erectus*, *H. habilis*, and various species of *Australopithecus*.

(Planer and Sterelny, 2021, 73). It is difficult to imagine how such robust cooperation could have evolved without corresponding increases in the complexity and flexibility of our communicative abilities. For example, the control of fire, which is a critical technology in the evolution of our species, would have required communication systems much more complex than anything seen in other great ape species (though not necessarily language) because controlling fire poses a range of sophisticated coordination and cooperation problems.[14]

Hence, it should be relatively uncontroversial that a robust communication system—like natural language—is necessary for the demands of complex cooperation. One can understand the intent of other humans precisely because one can communicate linguistically. Strong empirical evidence exists for a tight, bidirectional connection between the (purported) theory of mind capacities and linguistic capacities in human infants. First, language appears necessary to learn to express concepts surrounding one's own feelings and inner world; second, the information that language conveys about others' thoughts, feelings, beliefs, desires, etc., is much richer than the information conveyed through behaviour, eye gaze, gestural expressions, etc.; third, linguistic abilities allow individuals to reason abstractly about others' actions via their beliefs.

Further, the compositional nature of language allows humans to communicate their goals with one another to an arbitrary degree of specificity. Linguistic communicative abilities also affect the cultural accumulation of new concepts. High-fidelity cultural learning allows human populations to solve coordination/cooperation problems by allowing selective learning and accumulating small improvements over time. That is, language allows for accumulating knowledge across generations via social learning. Planer and Sterelny (2021) highlight that "some forms of cooperation are stable only if reputation (knowledge of the past social actions of others) is tracked reliably and is part of common knowledge" (25). Again, this robust sort of cooperation depends significantly upon language.

To some extent, communication depends upon joint attention and common knowledge. Complex language is not necessary for joint commitment when there is common-ground understanding; however, diminished common ground between agents appears to necessitate greater lexical and structural richness in the language used to communicate information about disparate knowledge between agents.[15] Essentially, when the social aspects of agent interactions

[14]See the discussion in Twomey (2013, 2014); Planer and Sterelny (2021).

[15]This has been observed empirically in, e.g., children's sign languages; see Meir et al. (2010) and further discussion in Tomasello (2008, 2014).

become increasingly dispersed in time and space, members of a social group will need more sophisticated communication (and cognitive) abilities to report behaviour and events that happened "elsewhere and elsewhen" (Planer and Sterelny, 2021, 195). Hence, empirical work on the co-evolution of language and cooperation in *Homo sapiens* is instructive when considering cooperation (i.e., the alignment of values) in the context of artificial intelligence.[16]

Language and Moral Behaviour. Over and above simple coordination, human *moral* behaviour is rooted in uniquely human linguistic abilities precisely because of the cultural accumulation that language exemplifies and enables.[17] Poulshock (2006) suggests that once complex language exists, humans have access to a new type of cultural evolution that can aid in promoting altruistic behaviour.

Linguistically-encoded, abstract value systems can promote or regulate normative behaviour to the extent that a sufficient number of members participating in such a moral system provides indirect benefits through, e.g., protection and group support. Language, therefore, allows humans to overcome genetic self-interest in a way not seen in other species in nature despite a lack of direct benefits for moral behaviour.

In effect, language allows social groups to encode normative principles and demand adherence to those principles. It can turn high-cost behaviour into low-cost behaviour, thus aiding the enforcement of moral principles or norms (Sober and Wilson, 1998). Furthermore, such moral codes can be transmitted across generations via spoken or written language and provide a cost-efficient means for classifying certain behaviours as "good" or "bad". It allows individuals to tag others as immoral (defectors/cheaters) or as moral (cooperators) via gossip, blame, praise, etc. when they adhere or fail to adhere to these principles; namely, linguistic communication allows us to articulate norms and monitor behaviour (Boehm, 2000). Thus, linguistic ability significantly affects *moral* ability because it allows for a simple, efficient, systematic, generalisable, flexible, and (typically) high-fidelity means of transmitting information.[18]

---

[16] In this case, a hypothetical (i.e., fictional) superintelligence would presumably have very little common ground with human agents, meaning that an ability to communicate linguistically is necessary to ensure cooperation (assuming that the cooperative demands on the agent are sufficiently complex).

[17] See discussion in Bryson (2008, 2018); Malle and Scheutz (2014); Malle (2015, 2016).

[18] Empirical studies appear to corroborate the claim that moral behaviour depends (at least to some extent) on linguistic ability. Several studies have suggested that moral judgements in children develop alongside language (Smetana and Braeges, 1990). Pro-social behaviours, categorical judgements, and a "normative sense of obligation" (Tomasello, 2018) appear to [*continued*]

From the cooperative nature of our species, it seems apparent that humans are at least capable of aligning their values in the various contexts we face daily. Part of the reason we can do so is that we can communicate via natural language. Humans use linguistic competence to impart subtle norms, goals, and values in subsequent generations that align with a long cultural history of norms, goals, and values. Because human linguistic capacity comes hardwired, we can take this particular aspect of how we align our values for granted. Thus, discussions of value-aligned agency (both natural and artificial) must maintain sensitivity to the evolutionary importance of language for *Homo sapiens* as fundamentally cooperative and social creatures.

Of course, one might object that although humans use linguistic communication systems—i.e., they have linguistic communicative abilities—they often fail to align their values. This is fine. The key claim here is that linguistic communication is a *necessary* condition for value alignment, not that language is *sufficient* for value alignment. (It should be obvious that it is not.) This is also not to suggest that linguistic communication is the *only* necessary condition for value alignment. (Again, it should be obvious that it is not.) What is pressing in the context of value alignment for AI, as compared with human-human interactions, is that assumptions of linguistic ability cannot be taken for granted when considering artificial agents.

10.3 Language, Value Alignment, and Information Transfer

The structural definition of the value alignment problem, presented in Chapter 3, is based on the principal-agent framework in economics. The principal-agent problem arises in this economic context when the principal and the agent have competing incentives. We also saw that the principal-agent problem involves informational asymmetries and imperfect information. In particular, even if the agent's objectives conflict with the principal's, under complete information, the principal can propose a controlling contract, emphasising that misaligned values alone are insufficient to generate a principal-agent problem

develop and become more complex in parallel with linguistic development timelines. Non-human primates, who lack linguistic capacities, display only *proto*-moral behaviours. For example, there is little evidence of instrumental helping in chimpanzees, although there is a *tendency* for helping under certain conditions. Chimpanzees are more likely to help when the task does not involve food, when information about the goal can be transferred through a non-linguistic communication channel, and when the recipient of help is not a conspecific (Warneken and Tomasello, 2006). See also discussion in de Waal (1996); Lust (2006); Warneken and Tomasello (2006, 2007); Dahl (2018), and studies in Zahn-Waxler et al. (1992); Eisenberg et al. (2007); Roth-Hanania et al. (2011); Schmidt et al. (2012); Smetana et al. (2012); Dahl and Kim (2014); Dahl (2015).

when there is no informational asymmetry between them. In addition, we saw that misaligned incentives are unnecessary for the principal-agent problem to arise as long as there are informational asymmetries between the principal and the agent. Hence, the principal-agent framework in economics primarily involves the problem of managing information flows.

The value alignment problem, on the structural definition, is a type of principal-agent problem, and the principal-agent problem arises from informational asymmetries rather than misaligned values *per se*. Hence, the value alignment problem for artificial intelligence is (primarily) a problem of informational asymmetries.

From the structural definition, then, it follows that information-transferring capacities are necessary for mitigating value misalignment. In addition, this problem scales in complexity. Namely, the more complex or robust the informational asymmetry is, the more complex or robust the information transferring capacity will be to resolve that information asymmetry. (As we have seen, complex cooperation settings impose robust demands on communicative abilities.) The insight that a robust communication system, like linguistic communication, is a necessary condition for robust value alignment follows from the joint realisation that

1. the value alignment problem (in the context of AI) is a type of principal-agent problem;
2. the principal-agent problem is fundamentally a problem of information transfer rather than misaligned values *per se*; and
3. linguistic communication is a uniquely robust and flexible communication system that allows information transfer to an arbitrary degree of specificity.

The empirical evidence for the role of communication in aligning values in human-human interactions should provide some plausibility to the claim that linguistic communication is required for robust value alignment, at least in sufficiently complex agents.

10.4 Objective Functions and Value Proxies

Counter-intuitively, then, a key driver of the value alignment problem in artificial intelligence is not misaligned values but informational asymmetries. Thus, the value alignment problem is primarily a problem of aligning *information*. However, the structural analogy between the principal-agent problem and the value alignment problem does not imply that their solutions will be identical. As we saw in Chapter 4, objectives play a significant role in value misalignment in the context of artificial intelligence despite that misaligned incentives are neither necessary nor sufficient to generate a principal-agent problem in the context of human-human interactions. Importantly, information alone cannot *cause* action.

Another way to think about why language might plausibly be required for a robust form of value alignment in AI systems is to consider how the symbolic systems approach to AI, discussed in Chapter 1, is thought to have failed—or, perhaps more charitably, to be much more limited than initially believed. Part of this is that these systems are far too rigid: every rule for action must be hard-coded. This is adequate for simple tasks, but writing explicit instructions for every contingency quickly becomes intractable as complexity increases.

Part of why present-day AI—particularly deep learning methods bolstered by big data—has seen astonishing success in comparison is that many rules for action are implicit in these systems, not hard-coded. What underwrites this intuition is that it is difficult to express the intuitive knowledge required for robust generalisation in the form of a set of verbally expressible rules that can be codified in a machine language. The symbolic systems approach of first-wave AI relied on the ability of humans to express explicit knowledge (often in the form of complicated if-then rules). In contrast, deep neural networks can "capture" the kind of implicit knowledge that is difficult to express in a formal language.[19]

The failures of symbolic systems are supposed to have been caused by the system's being "brittle, unconducive to learning, defeated by uncertainty, and unable to cope with the world's rough and tumble" (Cantwell Smith, 2019, 1). However, the key thing to note is that contemporary approaches to AI still require hard-coding objective functions. Thus, although these systems are significantly more flexible for learning and acting, the objectives encoded in these systems are still brittle. By analogy, it appears that a similar move from rigidity to flexibility concerning these systems' objective functions will be necessary to ensure that the "values" of these systems are aligned with our values. Again, some way of transferring information is necessary for changing values.

The inverse reinforcement learning (IRL) paradigm, described in Chapter 7, is one possible exception to this claim. Whereas a classic reinforcement learning model is given a reward function and attempts to learn behaviour based on the rewards it receives, an IRL model is given behaviour and attempts to learn the reward function that would give rise to that behaviour. Therefore, the objective function is learned instead of hard-coded. So, the thought goes, it

[19] See also discussion in Buckner (2019); LaCroix and Bengio (2019).

may be possible for a sophisticated IRL model to learn values from behaviours insofar as actions transfer information. However, this line of reasoning is problematic in several directions.

On the one hand, IRL is underspecified as a research problem because many reward functions can explain an actor's behaviour, and the costs of solving the problem tend to grow disproportionately with the size of the problem (Arora and Doshi, 2021). Essentially, many different reward functions could explain any observed behaviour.[20] On the other hand, behaviours will only ever serve as a proxy for values, which is part of why poorly specified objective functions give rise to value misalignment in the first place, as discussed in Chapter 4. Furthermore, by emphasising the information transferred by behaviours alone, we run into well-known problems to which revealed preference theory from economics gives rise.[21]

A basic (and false) assumption of IRL is that the behaviour a model observes is optimal, given the (hidden) reward function motivating that behaviour. In addition, even if behaviours were a good proxy for preferences and provided a high-fidelity channel for transferring information about those preferences, linguistic communication would aid learning objectives at a much higher rate—consider the difference between attempting to discern someone's preferences by watching them act versus asking them what their preferences are. Hence, in addition to systematicity and generalisability, linguistic communication offers the possibility of speed to value alignment. In high-stakes cases, waiting until sufficient behavioural instances are observed will be impossible. At the same time, pre-training is inadequate because values shift over time. Linguistic communication is necessary for flexible objective specification, which is necessary for robust value alignment.

As we have seen, the value alignment problem for artificial intelligence asks how we should design the *objective functions* of AI systems to guarantee maximal overlap between the actions of the artificial agent and the objectives or values of (human) principals. Despite the structural similarity of the value alignment problem for AI systems and the principal-agent problem more generally, as I mentioned in Section 3, the solutions to these problems may be quite distinct. This point is made clearer when we realise that the principal-agent problem, in human-human interactions, allows for assumptions that are

[20] This is effectively identical to the problem of rule-following, discussed in Wittgenstein (1953/2009); Kripke (1982) and a significant body of secondary literature since.

[21] Revealed preference theory (Samuelson, 1938a,b) uses consumer behaviour to analyse the choices made by individuals. See discussion in Sen (1973, 1977, 1993, 1997, 2002); Koszegi and Rabin (2007); Hausman (2012).

not warranted when the agent is an artificial system—namely, the ability to communicate one's *intended meaning* to an arbitrary degree of specificity via natural language.

10.5 Implications

Suppose the arguments forwarded in this chapter are convincing. If we assume that it is true that robust value alignment requires linguistic communication, we can draw out the implications of this fact. At a minimum, the necessity of language for robust value alignment specifies yet another demanding lower bound on the difficulty of solving the value alignment problem. However, this problem is more pressing for those research labs and corporations whose primary goal is to create an artificial general intelligence while maintaining some semblance of "safety" or alignment for such a system.

Bostrom (2014) suggests that achieving fully human-level performance on natural language is an "AI-complete" problem. This means that creating "linguistic AI" is essentially equivalent in difficulty or complexity to creating generally human-level AI systems. This implies that if one were to create a system fully capable of linguistic communication, in all likelihood, one would "also either already have succeeded in creating an AI that could do everything else that human intelligence can do, or they would be but a very short step from such a general capability" (17).[22]

If Bostrom (2014) is correct about language being an AI-complete problem, then linguistic AI is functionally equivalent to human-level AI or AGI. If language is a necessary condition for value alignment, then linguistic AI is, in some sense, prior to robust value alignment. However, we have seen throughout this book that the value alignment problem is logically prior to the control problem insofar as even narrow AI systems with limited functionality can fail to satisfy the principal's objectives. In contrast, the control problem arises in the context of stronger AI systems, on a par with human-level intelligence, AGI, or superintelligence.

The conjunction of these insights leads to circularity, which may imply that solving the value alignment problem cannot be achieved until *after* we have already created an AI system that we are effectively unable to control; see Figure 10.1.

This implication depends on a nested conditional: *If* language is an AI-complete problem, *then if* language is necessary for robust value alignment, robust value alignment may be impossible—at least before the creation of an

[22]Though, cf. Goebel (2008).

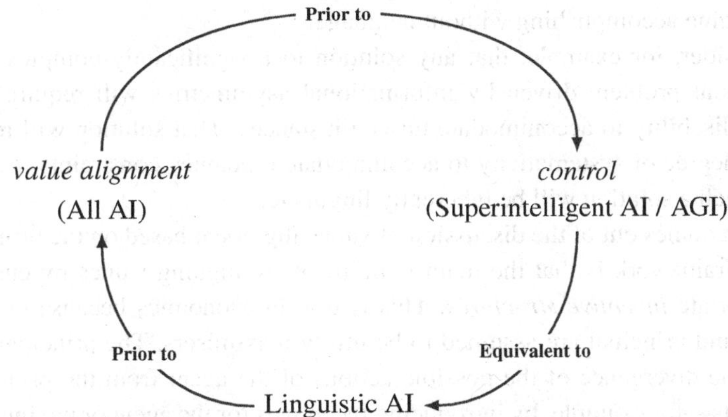

Figure 10.1: Circularity following from the conjecture that language is required for value alignment in conjunction with the conjecture that language is an AI-complete problem.

uncontrollable AI system. If any of the antecedents is false, then this may open the door to some (cautious) optimism about our ability to solve the value alignment problem prior to the advent of a system that we cannot control. On this point, it is worth noting that "AI completeness" is an *informal* concept defined by *analogy* with complexity theory; so, it is possible that Bostrom (2014) is incorrect.[23] This would leave room for work on alignment with linguistic, albeit controllable, AI systems. Alternatively, we can avoid reference to robust value alignment (requiring linguistic communication) by avoiding creating generalised AI systems. As with many of the insights discussed so far, the conclusion is the same: value misalignment is most readily mitigated when AI systems are designed for narrow and specific tasks.

Another reason why the circularity described above may fail is because the principal-agent model is highly idealised, as all models are. Hence, it may be that the claim that robust value alignment requires linguistic communication depends upon an idealised (hence false) assumption. Still, it is useful for underscoring that informational asymmetries, rather than value misalignment *per se*, are the driving force of the value alignment problem. This insight opens the door to the claim that linguistic communication is *at least* a highly effective—if not necessary—means for transferring information to an arbitrary degree of

[23] Although, see discussion in Shahaf and Amir (2007).

specificity, allowing on-the-spot adjustments in action in a way that is difficult to imagine accomplishing without language.

Consider, for example, that any solution to a significantly complex value alignment problem driven by informational asymmetries will require some generalisability to accommodate unseen instances. That solution will require some degree of systematicity to accommodate efficiency constraints. As a result, such a solution will be inherently linguistic.

What comes out of the discussion of value alignment based on the principal-agent framework is that the main issue involves aligning values by ensuring appropriate *incentive structures*. This is true in economics because both the agent and principal are assumed to be utility maximisers. The principal must limit the divergence of the possible actions of the agent from the principal's interests—for example, by introducing incentives for the agent or paying some costs for monitoring to limit the agent's (possibly unaligned) actions. However, although the principal-agent problem in human-human interactions and the value alignment problem for artificial intelligence arise for the same reasons, there are dissimilarities in how they can be solved or mitigated. For example, we can take certain things for granted when we consider interactions between human principals and human agents. In addition to linguistic communication abilities, human agents come with in-built values, whereas AI systems have their "values" programmed in an *objective function*. Given the complexity of accurately describing our objectives in a programming language, it is vanishingly unlikely that we can succeed in specifying the "correct" objective function for an artificial system—if such a specifiable function even exists.

10.6 Summary

In asking how humans align their values, we have seen some empirical evidence for linguistic communication's unique role in the cooperative dynamics arising from human-human interactions. This empirical work underscores the fact that there are some things that we can take for granted when considering cooperative behaviour in humans (like linguistic competence), which we do not get for free in the context of AI systems. This fact has apparently been forgotten or ignored by some researchers focusing on the technical components of value alignment for AI.

We have seen that the key constitutive features of linguistic communication (simplified here in terms of compositionality) give rise to the systematicity and generalisability that are prerequisites for robust value alignment, understood as fundamentally a problem of information transfer. In addition, objective functions—the "values" encoded in present-day AI systems—are rigid in precisely the ways that contributed to the failures of the symbolic systems approach to AI. Hence, although current systems are flexible regarding learning, they are still rigid regarding value alignment.

The value alignment problem is ubiquitous in the context of AI systems. As these systems become more sophisticated, these problems become more pressing. If linguistic communication is necessary for robust value alignment, this analysis helps clarify how difficult value alignment can be in this context. However, empirical evidence proves that aligning values between agents with human-level intelligence is at least *possible*. That said, it is important to maintain sensitivity to the informational asymmetries that underlie value alignment for AI systems since value alignment between human principals and human agents allows key features of the problem to be taken for granted—particularly the ability to communicate linguistically. No such assumption can be made when the agent is artificial.

Hence, if linguistic communication is necessary for robust value alignment in multi-agent interactions (human or otherwise), this would specify a fairly demanding lower bound on the difficulty of solving value alignment for sufficiently robust AI systems. At the same time, if language is an AI-complete problem, then this suggests that value alignment is impossible for suitably complex AI systems.

It is worth noting that recent advances in generative AI—particularly "large language models" (LLMs) like BERT (Devlin et al., 2019), the GPT Suite (Brown et al., 2020), RETRO (Borgeaud et al., 2022), LaMDA (Thoppilan et al., 2022), etc.—do not warrant optimism for the tractability of "solving" the value alignment problem. Although LLMs can be impressive syntax engines, language is more than mere syntax—hence why some researchers have suggested that the phrase "large language model" is a misnomer better described in terms of "large corpus models" (Veres, 2022) or "stochastic parrots" (Bender et al., 2021).

Some authors argue that meaning cannot be learned from form alone (Bender and Koller, 2020; Bisk et al., 2020; Marcus and Davis, 2020); there is a real sense in which the output of a large language model (like ChatGPT) is literally meaningless.[24] Although such models can produce coherent-sounding and contextually relevant responses based on patterns learned, they lack any understanding of the data consumed or generated. Of course, the relationship between understanding and linguistic competence is complicated. The key thing

[24] See, e.g., McCoy et al. (2019); Ettinger (2020); Pandia et al. (2021); Sinha et al. (2021); Sahlgren and Carlsson (2021).

to be clear about is that linguistic communication is a particularly robust system of communication which relies on shared meanings: language is a *social* endeavour which requires the participation of both senders and receivers. The output of LLMs *looks* so impressive because it is being interpreted by competent language users (humans) who project meaning, intentions, understanding, etc., onto the system.

This is simply another iteration of the ELIZA effect, described in Chapter 1. One key difference is that Weizenbaum (1966) was disturbed by lay responses to his chatbot, ELIZA. In contrast, OpenAI is financially interested in advertising its syntax engine to users and the media even when its stated capacities are demonstrably false. (Recall, again, the hype cycles described in Chapter 1.)

As we have seen, the value alignment problem for artificial intelligence asks how we can design the *objective functions* of AI systems to guarantee maximal overlap between the actions of a model and the objectives or values of (human) principals. Despite the structural analogy between the value alignment problem for AI systems and the principal-agent problem more generally, as I mentioned in Chapter 3, the solutions to these problems may be quite distinct. This point is made clearer when we realise that the principal-agent problem between humans allows for assumptions that are not warranted when the agent is an artificial system—namely, the ability to communicate one's *intended meaning* to an arbitrary degree of specificity via natural language. The language of values is vague and expressive, whereas the language of objective functions is formal and precise. The former attributes are a benefit for value alignment.

11 Values and Value-Ladenness

So far, we have seen the conceptual basis for a novel definition of the value alignment problem for artificial intelligence. This included exploring the history of artificial intelligence research (Chapter 1), and contextualising present-day AI systems and their technical underpinnings (Chapter 2). Chapter 3 explored the standard definition of the value alignment problem in the literature before providing a novel, structural definition of the value alignment problem for artificial intelligence based on the principal-agent framework from economics. This definition highlights that instances of the value alignment problem arise, fundamentally, from the dynamics of multi-agent systems when one actor (a human principal) delegates authority to another actor (an artificial agent) to act on their behalf.

As we have seen, one aspect of this definition is that it is primarily *structural*, implying that the actual *content* of the "values of humanity" is replaced by the dynamics of these systems. In this case, a problem instance can arise when the proxies used to approximate the principals' objectives are misaligned with the true objective for a particular system; this is the objectives axis of the value alignment problem, explored in Chapter 4. Similarly, a problem instance can arise when informational asymmetries exist between the principal and the agent; this is the information axis described in Chapter 5. In Chapter 6, we saw how each axis of the value alignment problem is indexed to a particular principal (or set of principals); the principals axis foregrounds the importance of whose values or objectives are considered when discussing value alignment or misalignment and sheds light on the deep relativity of the problem.

Again, rather than focusing on the content of the interaction in question—what *particular* things do principals value in *specific* contexts—we have explored the structural components of the problem—i.e., the types of situations that give rise to a problem instance in the first place. Analysing value alignment at this level helps to conceptualise *whose* values are taken to be relevant in real-world dynamics, in addition to what values are (in fact) encoded in research on artificial intelligence. To that end, this chapter has two primary goals. The first is to rehearse arguments surrounding the inherent value-ladenness of scientific inquiry and practice and to examine how and whether these insights apply to research on AI systems.

The second is to gesture toward some approaches for mitigating instances of the value alignment problem on this structural definition—particularly attending to those insights raised by the principals axis. There is much more that could be said than I will have space to describe here; hence, the approaches surveyed can be thought of as possible first steps toward "solving" the value alignment problem.

11.1 The Value-Free Ideal of Science

In some corners of the philosophy of science, it is relatively uncontroversial that values impinge on scientific inquiry: scientists are not neutral actors, and some philosophers of science have argued that scientific inquiry and practice are inherently *value-laden*. This position goes against a general and longstanding hope that science is (or at least ought to be) objective. The purported objectivity of science is considered important to the extent that it is supposed to confer science's unique status as a knowledge-generating enterprise.

Reiss and Sprenger (2020) highlight four separate stages at which the values of scientists might affect their work:

1. The choice of research problem;
2. gathering evidence related to a research problem;
3. accepting a scientific hypothesis as an acceptable answer to a problem; and
4. applying the results of scientific theory.

It is well-accepted that values play a significant role in steps (1) and (4) of the scientific research process. In the first case, the initial selection of a research problem is at least influenced by what scientists, institutions, and funding agencies care about—i.e., what they *value*. Similarly, the decisions about how to apply a scientific theory, once accepted, are uncontroversially informed by human values. In this case, a proponent of scientific objectivity might say that the "context of discovery" can (and is) influenced by values (individual, social, political, etc.); however, the context of *justification* should be free of such values insofar as social values do not serve to confirm empirical claims. At best, doing so would be fallacious (confusing an "ought" for an "is"); at worst, accepting the influence of values in justification would call into question the epistemic authority of science as a knowledge enterprise.

Logical positivism of the early 20th century was concerned with ensuring the epistemic foundations of scientific knowledge. According to this view, scientific hypotheses should be based *solely* on empirical evidence, and scientific theories should reflect that empirical evidence rather than, e.g., personal, social, political, or other biases. The positivists developed theories of confirmation, explanation, and induction, aiming to demonstrate how scientific knowledge is (or could be) based on inferences from observations, tests, or experiments.[1] Thus, they aspired to have scientific inquiry overcome biases so that science could be objective and oriented toward *truth*. This view is called the *value-free ideal* of science.

As it turns out, not all values are equally pernicious for the truth-seeking aims of science. In this case, we can differentiate between *epistemic* and *non-epistemic* values to further understand what value freedom is supposed to consist of.

Epistemic Values. Certain theoretical virtues are sometimes taken to be unproblematic for value-freedom in science. For example, any theory whatsoever is (in principle) compatible with any observed data. Put another way, any data that we might observe is logically compatible with any prediction we might make. This is the essence of Nelson Goodman's (1955) *New Riddle of Induction*. In effect, inductive reasoning requires generalisation—e.g., from past observations to future predictions. However, the logical structure of the descriptions of observed regularities does not tell us which regularities can be safely "projected" (in the sense of taken from the domain of the known to the domain of the unknown) and which cannot. Furthermore, identical patterns of inference can lead to contradictory conclusions or hypotheses.

Hence, when comparing two scientific hypotheses, scientists sometimes need to make judgements that are not informed by theoretical considerations or empirical evidence alone—i.e., they must make value judgements. However, only some values are deemed "acceptable" for this work to the extent that they advance the epistemic aims of science. Consider, for example, simplicity.[2] If there is a choice between two competing theories, and one is simpler—e.g., it posits fewer phenomena, requires fewer assumptions, etc.—then convention

[1]See, for example, Carnap (1928); Reichenbach (1938); Popper (1959); Nagel (1961); Hempel (1965).

[2]See the discussion in Baker (2023).

dictates that one ought to believe the simpler theory.[3] This sentiment is captured by the heuristic given by *Occam's razor* (sometimes called the *principle of parsimony*.[4] However, it is worth noting that while a heuristic is a *useful* shortcut, it does not guarantee truth.[5]

In addition to simplicity, other purportedly epistemic values include predictive accuracy, scope, unification, explanatory power, and coherence with other accepted theories (Reiss and Sprenger, 2020). These paradigmatic cases align relatively well with the values inherent to the stated motivations and applications of leading machine learning papers—namely, performance, generalisation, building upon past work, quantitative evidence, and efficiency (Birhane et al., 2022).

Such values are called *epistemic* insofar as they appear to promote cognitive success—e.g., the formation of justified true beliefs, knowledge, understanding, and so on. Hence, epistemic values are thought to promote the "truth-like" character of science—or, more generally, *knowledge acquisition*.[6] In this sense, epistemic values are taken to be *indicators* of the truth of a theory, even if they do not *entail* truth.

However, because epistemic values and truth proper can come apart, it is difficult to specify what *counts* as an epistemic value. Even so, many candidate lists of epistemic values from the philosophy of science gesture toward a sort of family resemblance that describes epistemic values.

---

[3] A standard example from the history of science involves scientists' efforts to explain the apparent retrograde motion of planetary bodies. The Ptolemaic (geocentric) model of the solar system leads to a metaphysically bloated theory, requiring epicycles, off-centre equants, and more; in contrast, the heliocentric model of the solar system, popularised by Copernicus (1543/1995), can account for this apparent retrograde motion on the basis that the planets revolve around the sun. One of the arguments given by Galilei (1632/2001) in favour of the heliocentric model is an argument from simplicity.

[4] For example, Aristotle (1995d) writes: "Let that demonstration be better which, other things being equal, depends on fewer postulates or suppositions or propositions" (322).

[5] For example, in the context of PAC (probably approximately correct) learning, Herrmann (2020) proves that the same justification of Occam's razor as an epistemic principle can be used to justify an *anti*-Occam's razor—that we ought, epistemically, to value more complex theories. See also the discussion in Stoffi et al. (2022).

[6] In the philosophy of science literature, epistemic values (McMullin, 1982) are sometimes called *cognitive* values (Laudan, 1984), *constitutive* values (Longino, 1990), or *theoretical virtues* (Kuhn, 1977). Some authors have suggested that cognitive and epistemic values are conceptually distinct in some sense; for example, (Douglas, 2023) suggests that epistemic values are useful for assessing the strength of evidence, whereas cognitive values can help direct future research, implying that they are differentiable. For our purposes, the subtleties that demarcate cognitive values from epistemic values will not be important; I will take these as relative synonyms.

Non-Epistemic Values. In contrast to epistemic values, non-epistemic (non-cognitive, contextual) values are those values that involve ethical, social, political, or cultural considerations that are not directly related to the epistemic goals of science. For example, social justice considerations, economic interests, ethical concerns, and political ideologies are examples of non-cognitive values. McMullin (1982) argues that the set of possible non-epistemic values is as large as the set of possible human goals.

Table 11.1 summarises several values that are common in discussions comparing epistemic versus non-epistemic values.

Table 11.1: Non-exhaustive comparison of epistemic versus non-epistemic values for illustrative purposes.

Epistemic		Non-Epistemic	
Accuracy	Scope	Personal	Social
Simplicity	Adequacy	Political	Moral
Consistency	Testability	Cultural	Aesthetic
Unification	Explanatory power	Financial	Practical
Coherence	Truth	Religious	Emotional

Scientific Objectivity. While tolerating epistemic values, the *value-free ideal* of science prescribes *minimising* the influence of "contextual" or "non-epistemic" values—e.g., moral, personal, social, political, religious, or cultural values—on the intervening scientific process. Hence:

> **The Value-Free Ideal**:
> Scientists *should* try to minimise the influence of contextual (non-epistemic) values on scientific reasoning in the context of gathering evidence and assessing/accepting scientific theories.[7]

Although choosing a research problem and applying a scientific theory are uncontroversially value-laden endeavours, the value-free ideal of science suggests that the *justification* of scientific findings should not be based upon non-epistemic values. This *normative* claim prescribes ideal behaviour, whether or not the ideal is adhered to in practice. However, for the value-free ideal to be a reasonably prescribed goal, it is also necessary to posit a descriptive statement that says this ideal is attainable, at least in principle. This descriptive claim is called the value-neutrality thesis:

[7] See the formulation in Reiss and Sprenger (2020) and alternative formulations in Dorato (2004); Ruphy (2006); Biddle (2013).

> **The Value-Neutrality Thesis**:
> Scientists *can* (in principle) gather evidence and assess/accept theories without making contextual (non-epistemic) value judgements.

One type of argument against the value-free ideal of science requires showing that the value-neutrality thesis is false. Since ought implies can, the failure of the value-neutrality thesis would entail the failure of the value-free ideal of science.[8] In response, one might accept that even though the value-free ideal is practically unattainable, it is still something to strive toward—i.e., minimising non-epistemic values in scientific practice does not require eradicating non-epistemic values.

The rejection of the value-free ideal of science requires that scientific assessment depends upon factors outside of truth alone—i.e., scientific assessment goes beyond purely epistemic goals. A prominent view in present-day philosophy of science is that reference to epistemic and non-epistemic values is unavoidable in scientific practice. Some argue further that non-epistemic values *ought* to play a role in scientific inquiry and practice.[9]

11.2 Against the Value-Free Ideal

The value-free ideal of science is a normative claim that prescribes *minimising* the influence of contextual or non-epistemic—e.g., moral, personal, social, political, religious, etc.—values in science and scientific processes. This ideal is supposed to apply to the evidence-gathering and hypothesis-accepting (or rejecting) stages of science. Hence, value-free science is thought to require impartiality, neutrality, and autonomy (Lacey, 1999). However, several arguments have been forwarded against the value-neutrality thesis and, hence, the value-free ideal of science.

Thick Normative Concepts and Significant Truths. One argument against the value-free ideal focuses on the semantic aspects of the idea that scientific theories are neutral. Some concepts in ethics have both *descriptive* and *normative* content. These are sometimes called *thick* ethical concepts.[10] For example, referring to generative models in artificial intelligence, like ChatGPT, as "dangerous" involves a value judgement—i.e., that the existence of this technology implies some social or ethical risks—in addition to descriptive content—i.e.,

[8] Essentially, VFI only if VNT, $\neg$VNT, therefore $\neg$VFI.

[9] See, e.g., Longino (1990); Anderson (1995); Intemann (2001); Douglas (2007, 2017); Elliott and McKaughan (2014); Lusk and Elliott (2022); Reydon and Ereshefsky (2022) for further discussion.

[10] See discussion in Williams (1985); Putnam (2002).

that it is *uncertain* whether these technologies will give rise to those risks in practice, implying that they are dangerous in a descriptive sense. If such terms are unavoidable in scientific reasoning, it becomes challenging to present hypotheses and results in a completely value-free way.

The argument goes that because of thick ethical concepts in science, facts and values are often entangled. Therefore, if these terms are ineliminable from (at least certain parts of) science, then the value-neutrality thesis is undermined—i.e., it is impossible for scientists to gather evidence or assess/accept theories without making (non-epistemic) value judgements. Furthermore, there is reason to think that thick ethical terms *are* ineliminable from science insofar as we care about the goals and results of science.

Hence, Kitcher (2011a,b) argues that science does not pursue truth *simpliciter*. Instead, science aims to discover truths that are relevant to our social goals. Thus, determining whether something is a truth *worth pursuing*—i.e., a "significant truth"—necessarily involves a value judgement. As should be apparent, much discussion of scientific investigation is idealised. Although we can conceptually distinguish "distinct" stages of scientific inquiry—choosing a research problem, gathering evidence, accepting a scientific hypothesis, and applying results—real-world scientific practice is not linear. In effect, there is a complex interplay between what might be called purely epistemic (ostensibly value-free) goals and practical (deeply value-laden) goals. These cannot be disentangled in practice. The targets of the value-free ideal of science—gathering evidence and assessing hypotheses—are deeply dependent upon their potential for application and further research. Hence, every stage of scientific inquiry relies upon both epistemic and non-epistemic values.

Furthermore, Dupré (2007) has argued that thick ethical terms are essential in certain parts of science precisely because scientific hypotheses and results are relevant to human interests. That is, the only reason why some scientific statements purport to be neutral is because whether they are true or false is not of immediate importance to us—it matters not to my day-to-day life whether quantum theory is true or false; in either case, I carry on. Namely, the only scientific truths that can be truly value-free are those whose truth or falsity does not practically matter to us. However, because artificial intelligence, by definition, seeks to replace human decision-makers (sometimes in deeply normative contexts), the supposition of neutrality cannot apply. This is related to the argument against the value-free ideal from inductive risk.

Inductive Risk and the Demarcation Problem. Rudner (1953) argues that scientists (*qua* scientists) make value judgements insofar as scientists choose to accept or reject hypotheses while admitting that there is some possibility that they are erroneous in that choice. That is, deciding to accept or reject a hypothesis depends inherently on weighing the risks of being wrong in either case. This is a form of *inductive* risk since it is always possible that the conclusion of an inductive argument is false. For example, in the case of clinical trials, the decision to accept a hypothesis ("the drug is safe"), we are weighing the risk that we are wrong (with the consequence that some individuals die as a side effect of the drug); whereas, when we reject the same hypothesis, we are again weighing the risk that we are wrong (with the consequence that some individuals die as the result of not having access to the drug). Thus, accepting or rejecting a scientific hypothesis requires weighing type I and type II errors in statistical inference—i.e., false positives versus false negatives.

Some philosophers have suggested that whether the argument from inductive risk is defensible depends inherently upon the demarcation between epistemic and non-epistemic values.[11] Others have argued that non-epistemic values can be useful as "tie-breakers" when distinct scientific theories are equally well supported from an epistemic point of view. At the same time, however, some authors have questioned whether the distinction between epistemic and non-epistemic values is acceptable.[12]

Dotan (2021) highlights how a biased theory may be consistent with other theories (which are biased in the same way). Examples from biology and social science help illuminate how entrenched scientific theories can be influenced by non-epistemic values, meaning that certain epistemic values alone will be inadequate for ensuring the value-freedom of a theory. On the one hand, this is supposed to show that the boundary between epistemic and non-epistemic values is unclear, meaning that scientific inquiry may well be influenced by non-epistemic values, even in the idealised case. On the other hand, the entrenchment of non-epistemic values within scientific inquiry suggests that non-epistemic values are essential to science and scientific practice.

11.3 Values and Value Alignment

In the AI-specific context, many researchers have (naïvely) thought that algorithmic decision-making is, could, or should be "more objective" than human decision-making. This view stems from the belief that, when properly designed and trained, algorithms can process information without being influenced by personal biases, emotions, or subjective factors that might affect hu-

[11] See, e.g., Steel (2010).

[12] See, e.g., Longino (1990, 1996); Rooney (1992); Biddle (2013); Rooney (2017) for additional discussion.

man decision-making. At bottom, the thought goes, a machine learning model is simply mathematics, and mathematics is objective (if anything is). For example, machine learning systems could be thought to be more consistent when applied to patterns in data; machine learning models process information based on rules and patterns learned from data without being influenced by pesky emotional states or extraneous factors that might cloud human judgement; and, machine learning models have no preconceived notions, assumptions, or personal opinions.

However, we have already seen many instances in which these assumptions fail. When algorithms are designed for *learning*, the model can hit upon biased solutions owing to redundantly encoded attributes in the datasets upon which they were trained. Inherently biased training data cause algorithmic systems to inherit (and amplify) those biases. At the same time, the design, implementation, and oversight of machine learning algorithms ultimately fall under human responsibility, raising questions about who determines the objectives, selects the features, and sets the parameters for these algorithms.

The belief that machine learning systems, or scientific endeavours more generally, are neutral is not only misguided, it is also harmful: Green (2019) underscores that broad cultural conceptions of science as "neutral" entrench the perspectives of dominant social groups, who are the only ones entitled to legitimate claims of neutrality. We have already seen in Chapter 6 the myriad ways in which the goals, objectives, and values of stakeholders and shareholders can come apart; however, one of these groups has a say in the design and deployment of AI systems, and the other does not.

Researchers' Values. We have also seen that values are deeply embedded in machine learning research, whether intentional or not. Most of these values would be classed as epistemic (e.g., performance, generalisation, building on past work, efficiency, novelty). However, deciding the set of values is itself a value-laden decision; few papers explicitly discuss societal need, and fewer still discuss potential negative impacts (Birhane et al., 2022). Philosophers of science have questioned whether the value-free ideal of science is attainable or desirable, and these arguments are highly relevant in the context of machine learning, the value-free ideal of science, and the prospect of value alignment.

Whereas the objectives and information axes of the value alignment problem focus primarily on the *technical* components of the algorithmic development pipeline and where along that pipeline values can be misaligned, Raji and Dobbe (2023) highlight that even "basic design choices involved in model creation and deployment" can have far-reaching consequences beyond the impact of the model's outputs or decisions (3).

For example, Birhane et al. (2022) note that researchers in machine learning are influenced by social factors, including, e.g., the personal preferences of the researchers and referees (personal values), other work in engineering and science (social and cultural values), the interests of academic institutions, funding agencies, and companies (financial and pragmatic values), and larger systemic pressures like systems of oppression (cultural, political, and economic values).

Machine Learning and Inductive Risk. Machine learning depends on inductive inference and is, therefore, prone to inductive risk. Models are responsive to the training data, and the curse of dimensionality means these data comprise a tiny proportion of the input space; outputs can always be wrong, regardless of how much data we use to train the model. It follows that choosing to accept or reject a model prediction requires a value judgement: that the risks if we are wrong in acceptance are lower than the risks if we are wrong in rejection.

Hence, the use of inductive inference implies that machine learning models are deeply value-laden. In fact, if they were not, they would have no application: these models are useful *because* they are value-laden (Johnson, 2023). Thus, accepting that algorithms are used for ranking, sorting, filtering, recommending, categorising, labelling, predicting, etc., in the real world implies that these processes will have real-world effects. As machine learning systems become increasingly commercialised and applied, they become more entrenched in the things we care about.

These insights have implications for researchers who believe that algorithms are somehow more objective than human decision-makers (and so ought to replace human decision-makers in areas where we think objectivity matters).

No Free Lunch. The *no free lunch* Theorem refers to a family of impossibility results that highlight the limitations of optimisation algorithms. Wolpert and Macready (1997) show that every classification algorithm has the same error rate when performance is averaged across all possible data distributions.[13] In effect, there is no universal algorithm that performs well on all possible problems. In other words, there is no one-size-fits-all solution that is optimal for every conceivable task or problem.

Hence, this theorem emphasises that the performance of an algorithm is highly dependent on the specific characteristics and structure of the problem it is designed to solve. While one algorithm may excel in one problem do-

[13] See the discussion in Goodfellow et al. (2016, Sec. 5.2.1).

main, it may perform poorly in another. This theorem implies a need to tailor algorithms to specific problem domains.

Because the target of the *no free lunch* theorem is not the algorithms themselves but the algorithms' *predictions*, Dotan (2021) argues that these impossibility results are highly relevant to the question of theory choice in the philosophy of science.

In effect, the *no free lunch* theorem implies that all hypotheses are equally likely to be accurate, which in turn implies that accuracy alone is not a standard that can be used to prioritise one theory over another. This fact is problematic because accuracy is sometimes considered uniquely important as an epistemic value (Pettigrew, 2016). We have already seen how accuracy is prioritised in practice in machine learning research (Birhane et al., 2022). In light of this, Dotan (2021) argues that non-epistemic values are required for theory choice in machine learning.

11.4 Optimism

Much of this book has focused on the limits of our ability to address the value alignment problem. This negative picture might seem overwhelming and intractable—however, the reconceptualisation of the value alignment problem for artificial intelligence gestures toward the potential for change.

In particular, one benefit of this reconceptualisation is that it focuses on the *structure* of the problem (and its instances) rather than the normative or technical aspects of the problem (on its standard definition). This structural approach helps to underscore that many factors contributing to value misalignment, in practice, arise from systemic issues. This fact should be unsurprising given that, on the structural definition, the value alignment problem is fundamentally and inextricably *social*.

Hence, mitigating the value alignment problem requires reconceptualising the social structures in which present-day AI systems are embedded. Many scholars, activists, and communities have forwarded useful proposals for addressing these systemic issues, many of which can be applied to the specific context of the value alignment problem for artificial intelligence. Some of these, relevant to the value alignment problem, are surveyed here.

Open Science. The Open Science movement is a global initiative that advocates for the openness, transparency, and accessibility of scientific research. This approach seeks to make scientific knowledge and data freely available to the public, enabling collaboration and innovation while fostering trust in the scientific process. Hence, one goal of open science is to increase transparency in scientific research, which emerges as an explicit response to the reproducibility crisis in science, among other things. Some features of open science arise from the present-day *global* landscape of scientific inquiry, including systemic problems like constraints on research communication, collaboration, and publishing. Leonelli (2023) argues that a view of openness as *freedom to share resources* underpins many open science initiatives in practice. The hope is that making results more transparent will have downstream effects concerning reproducibility and accessibility, which will, in turn, affect inclusivity and engagement, all of which are supposed to positively affect the reliability of science as a dominant knowledge-generating enterprise.

Key components of the open science movement include open-access publishing models (increasing accessibility and allowing for the wide dissemination of scientific research), open data (increasing transparency and allowing for the replication of studies or reuse of data for other research projects), open-source software (increasing collaborative development and allowing for reproducibility of computational studies), preprint sharing (allowing for the rapid dissemination of scientific results), among others.

The machine learning community, to some extent, has already sought to implement an open science model. Conventionally, it is more common to publish papers in (typically open-access) conference proceedings instead of journals, which are often published on a closed-access, for-profit model. In addition, it is common to post articles—regardless of whether they have been published—on arXiv, an open-access repository of electronic preprint and postprint scientific articles. However, there are concerns about a lack of reliability in this area because preprints on arXiv are not peer-reviewed, meaning that authors may make claims that would not pass the standards of peer review. Hence, the arXiv has effectively provided a medium for authors focusing on AGI, existential risk, superintelligence, etc. to legitimise their claims while failing to adhere to any academic standard of rigour or evidence.

Of course, this does not imply that peer review fixes all (or any) of these problems, nor that peer review should be a gold standard.[14] For example, peer review would fail, in principle, to address any concerns surrounding value alignment along the principals axis insofar as reviewers are drawn from the same set of principals as the authors of machine learning papers; hence, peer review helps to entrench the status quo in the field. That said, it is important to approach research in the field (whether peer-reviewed or not) with a healthy dose of sceptical criticism.

[14] See discussion in Heeson and Bright (2021).

Insofar as the open science movement prioritises transparency, this approach is primarily relevant to the information asymmetries axis of the value alignment problem. However, it is important to ensure that the principals axis is also considered. Whereas open science calls for openness *within* science, democratic AI expands this notion to include stakeholders.

Democratic AI. Recent calls for a "democratic" approach to artificial intelligence seek to ensure that AI systems are developed, deployed, and governed in a manner that is transparent, inclusive, and aligned with democratic values. Lee et al. (2019) propose a framework that enables stakeholders to participate in building algorithmic governance via "a novel combination of individual belief learning, voting, and explanation" (1).

From the perspective of the value alignment problem, it should be unsurprising that a key framework proposed for developing more aligned AI systems leverages information (to reduce asymmetries) in the form of model reporting (Mitchell et al., 2019). In the language of the value alignment problem, the proposed framework specifies the use of model cards, whose purpose is to clarify use cases of machine learning models (i.e., principals' objectives), which helps to reduce misalignment along the objectives axis by ensuring models are not misapplied to contexts for which the formal structure of the model is a poor proxy. To mitigate issues of bias, model cards include benchmarked evaluations under diverse use cases to document model performance concerning intersections of groups, which has additional effects for the objectives and principals axes.

Model cards provide meta-data about a machine learning model; thus, they provide a means for decreasing informational asymmetries with respect to that model. Informational asymmetry reduction is twofold in this case. On the one hand, by presenting a model card, the shareholders of a model decrease opacity for stakeholders by making explicit the shareholders' objectives with the model, details of the performance evaluation procedures, etc. On the other hand, they decrease informational asymmetries between shareholders and the model insofar as those who create the model must understand it to complete a model card in the first place. This instantiates one approach to democratising AI via increasing transparency about how (and how well) these systems work and for what purpose.

Participatory- and Community-Based Research. Community-Based Participatory Research (CBPR) is a research approach that involves collaboration between researchers and community members—both shareholders *and* stakeholders—throughout the research process. This method is captured by the disability community slogan: *nothing about us without us*.

An important component of community-based participatory research in practice is ensuring that stakeholders are included at *every stage* of the design process. Although reinforcement learning from human feedback (RLHF) or preferences is sometimes pitched as exemplifying a community- or stakeholder-based approach to artificial intelligence, the system only solicits feedback during training. A genuinely community-based framework would require stakeholders' participation and engagement at *every* stage of development.

This approach is highly relevant when considering historically marginalised communities. Benjamin (2019) highlights that justice "is not a static value but an ongoing methodology that can and should be incorporated into tech design. For this reason, too, it is vital that people engaged in tech development partner with those who do important sociocultural work honing narrative tools through the arts, humanities, and social justice organizing" (193).

Design Justice. Design justice summarises a set of principles for re-thinking design processes and, in particular, centring those individuals who are normally marginalised by design through collaborative, creative practices. A tentative description of design justice is offered as follows:

> Design justice is a framework for analysis of how design distributes benefits and burdens between various groups of people. Design justice focuses explicitly on the ways that design reproduces and/or challenges the matrix of domination (white supremacy, heteropatriarchy, capitalism, ableism, settler colonialism, and other forms of structural inequality). Design justice is also a growing community of practice that aims to ensure a more equitable distribution of design's benefits and burdens; meaningful participation in design decisions; and recognition of community-based, Indigenous, and diasporic design traditions, knowledge, and practices. (Costanza-Chock, 2020, 23)

Minimally, design justice includes the following principles, many of which have been proposed previously by communities who do on-the-ground advocacy work pertaining to social justice considerations:

- Centre the voices of those directly impacted by the outcomes of the design process.
- Prioritise the impact of design on the community over the designer's intentions.
- View change as emergent from an accountable, accessible, and collaborative process rather than the end point of that process.
- View the role of the designer as a facilitator rather than an expert.
- View lived experiences as a form of expertise that can contribute to a design process.
- Share knowledge and tools with communities.
- Work toward sustainable, community-led, and controlled outcomes.
- Work toward non-exploitative solutions.
- Examine what works at the community level before seeking new solutions.

Given all of the issues raised by the reconceptualisation of the value alignment problem in Part II, it should be immediately apparent how these principles are pertinent to mitigating the value alignment problem in specific contexts—particularly on the principals axis.

The questions raised by the design justice framework are highly relevant in the context of the value alignment problem for artificial intelligence. In particular, what values are encoded (or reproduced) in the design of AI systems? Who designs these systems? How are narratives constructed surrounding the design of these systems? How are sites of design accessible/inaccessible? How do we teach and learn about design?[15]

Analysing socio-technical systems from a design justice perspective does not necessarily require making these systems more inclusive (piece-wise). Instead, it is sometimes fruitful to ask whether these systems should be designed at all. Similarly, the value alignment problem for artificial intelligence avoids the technochauvinist assumptions implicit in the standard definition. When AI systems do not serve the stakeholders they affect, it is unclear how their creation could be justified—the principles of design justice make this fact explicit. In these cases, a value alignment problem can be solved, *simpliciter*, in the simplest and most unsatisfying way: do not create those systems.

Anti-Fascist, Anti-Racist, and Decolonial AI. Mohamed et al. (2020) highlight that many attempts to codify ethics guidelines—which often focus on AGI safety—fail to "contend with the intersection of values and power, whose values are being represented, and the structural inequities that result in an unequal spread of benefits and risk within and across societies" (661). In this sense, perspectives from the feminist philosophy of science are relevant to these antecedent questions concerning values. Feminist and decolonial critiques of science can offer guidance for, or at least alternative perspectives on, approaches to generating knowledge in ways that prioritise marginalised perspectives (McQuillan, 2022).

Technological artefacts have politics[16] and in this sense, AI is inherently political. To say that artificial intelligence is *political* rather than merely computational is to underscore that AI systems "can be used in ways that enhance the power, authority, and privilege of some over others" (Winner, 1980, 125). Deployed models perform in ways that affect the distribution of power in the world. Hence, these systems create feedback loops, like the kind described

[15] Costanza-Chock (2020) devotes a chapter to each of these questions, focusing on values, practices, narratives, sites, and pedagogies, respectively.

[16] See discussion in Winner (1980).

by O'Neil (2016); Benjamin (2019); McQuillan (2022), which exacerbate inequalities and injustices. These societal divisions, taken to their extreme, lead to authoritarian technocracy.

11.5 Regulation

Many of the ideas proposed above for mitigating value misalignment depend on bottom-up social cooperation concerning the principals who have a share in creating AI systems. However, cooperation can be difficult to maintain in social dilemmas, where some actors may be incentivised to defect from a cooperative standard. Using a game-theoretic analysis, LaCroix and Mohseni (2022) demonstrate the conditions for cooperative success in the context of the responsible development of AI research, prompted by the proliferation of non-legislative policy agreements—e.g., codes of ethics for the field that are supposed to specify the best practices to which researchers, engineers, etc., ought to adhere. There is little reason to think that voluntary participation will suffice for addressing the myriad and complex issues instantiated by the value alignment problem. Hence, top-down legislation is necessary in conjunction with bottom-up social cooperation.

Mitchell (2023) proposes a regulatory framework that requires AI developers to provide documentation proving they have met certain goals intended to protect individuals' rights during the development and deployment process, thus "supporting the advancement of AI that is aligned with human values". Such a framework leverages the expertise of both developers and regulators in a combined top-down and bottom-up approach. In the former case, regulation from lawmakers defines goals (based on rights) that must be met; in the latter case, the developers are free to determine how such goals can be met.

This approach encodes the relativity of principals. For example, at the data collection stage, the relevant stakeholders include data *creators* (e.g., artists whose works have been used to train generative AI models) and data *subjects* (e.g., individuals whose data has been collected, explicitly or implicitly, to train recommendation systems). Similarly, at the deployment stage, relevant stakeholders include those who *use* the technology in question—e.g., the driver of an autonomous vehicle—but also those who are *affected* by the technology, regardless of whether they use it—e.g., other road users, bicyclists, pedestrians, etc.

Mitchell (2023) argues that rigorous documentation that accounts for the stakeholders at each stage of the algorithmic pipeline is invaluable insofar as such a requirement incentivises and enforces responsibility on the part of the developers who are held accountable for creating and maintaining these regulatory artefacts. This documentation process is useful because merely thinking through various use cases requires developers to consider how such technologies may be used and whom they may affect.[17] Most importantly for our purposes, Mitchell (2023) argues that clarity on *both* sub-populations (principals) and use contexts (including those unintended by the developer) are required to coherently select metrics for evaluation of AI systems, which is necessary for directing the responsible development of AI systems since one cannot manage what one cannot measure.

In addition, many extant legislative policies can be leveraged or updated in the context of artificial intelligence to help ensure value alignment. Privacy laws are an obvious focal point in this realm. Given that the value alignment problem, on its structural definition, emphasises the dynamics of multi-agent interactions, power dynamics are key to value misalignment on the structural definition. Hence, mitigating instances of the value alignment problem through targeted legislation requires flattening the hierarchies inherent in this research ecosystem. Véliz (2020) argues that privacy is power; hence, legislation surrounding privacy can empower stakeholders, helping to mitigate misalignment along the principals axis.

In addition, anti-trust laws can be leveraged to decrease the centralisation of power inherent in present-day AI research. Again, the focus of such legislation should pertain to unequal distributions of power, which are highly relevant to the objectives axis of the value alignment problem when we consider that small sets of shareholders have a choice in what problems are pursued with a machine learning approach, and how those problems are formalised via proxies. Hildebrandt (2022) highlights that these choices can have far-reaching implications, meaning that they must be "called out as both foundational and political" (14). As such, legislation can help determine *who* has a decision about the objectives embedded in AI systems.

We have seen that the guiding faith of AI research today is that performance scales with size, and increasing model size requires corresponding increases to data and compute. I also proposed the scaling hypothesis for value-aligned AI which suggests that value misalignment also scales with size, data, and compute. The scaling hypothesis for value-aligned AI suggests that smaller, narrower, and more transparent models are more amenable to value alignment. Hence, a key intervention point for mitigating value misalignment would be to

[17] In addition, Mitchell (2023) suggests that such an approach to regulation might serve to quell some of the in-fighting between the factions of AI research since long-term risks can be accounted for by contending with stakeholders' rights to existence, and short-term risks (or current harms) are covered by, e.g., rights to freedom or equal opportunity.

regulate compute. Sastry et al. (2024) recently proposed this regulatory intervention in detail. They argue that, unlike other aspects of AI models, compute is highly regulable because of its detectability, excludability, quantifiability, and supply chain concentration (73).

In addition, if properly enforced, intellectual property and copyright laws can be leveraged to limit the use of scraped datasets—since these inevitably contain copyrighted materials. Even without additional regulation, strict enforcement of current copyright laws may have ripple effects on field-wide conventions concerning the use of curated versus uncurated datasets.

11.6 Summary

The reconceptualisation of the value alignment problem helps to clarify that the prospects of value alignment are relatively unfavourable—at least in the current climate of artificial intelligence. However, I have gestured toward cautious optimism—at least in the theoretical ideal.

Transparency in research begins by acknowledging that non-epistemic values play a significant role in AI research. Genuinely addressing misalignment along the objectives axis of the value alignment problem (relative to the shareholders) requires understanding how non-epistemic values influence the creation of AI systems. There is much more to be explored with respect to the value-ladenness of AI research; however, the analyses of Dotan (2021); Birhane et al. (2022); Johnson (2023), and others, provide a starting point.

A key insight to be gleaned from the analysis of the value alignment problem offered throughout this book is the prevalence and role of power dynamics in AI. The objectives and information axes are always indexed to a particular principal or set of principals. Hence, a key point of intervention in value-misaligned AI systems involves including and *prioritising* stakeholders—in particular, those who currently have no share in creating AI systems—in the design process.

In the final part, I briefly surveyed some viable candidates for "solving" the value alignment problem; notably, each approach front-loads the social aspects of research and design rather than the technical aspects. This feature should be unsurprising insofar as the value alignment problem is a social rather than a technical problem.

Additional Resources

Sasha Costanza-Chock. 2020. *Design Justice: Community-Led Practices to Build the Worlds We Need.* Cambridge, MA: The MIT Press.

Catherine D'Ignazio and Lauren F. Klein. 2020. *Data Feminism.* Cambridge, MA: The MIT Press.

Dan McQuillan. 2022. *Resisting AI: An Anti-Fascist Approach to Artificial Intelligence.* Bristol: Bristol University Press.

Ashley Shew. 2023. *Against Technoableism: Rethinking Who Needs Improvement.* New York: W. W. Norton.

12 Conclusion

When there is nothing left to burn,
you have to set yourself on fire.

— Stars (2004)
Your Ex-Lover Is Dead

In the first part of this book, I sought to re-define the value alignment problem for artificial intelligence in terms of its structural features, rather than considering the normative content (i.e., the "values" part of the problem) or the technical implementation (i.e., the "alignment" part of the problem). This redefinition was prompted by the relative unclarity of extant approaches to value alignment, which take the standard description as sufficient. However, as we saw, the standard description of value alignment is only superficially useful insofar as it raises more questions than answers.

One might worry that the re-conceptualisation of the value alignment problem, on the structural definition that I have offered here, has the same problem in the other direction: namely, it lets too much in. Whereas the standard definition of the value alignment problem suffers from issues of underdetermination insofar as it is too vague to be practically useful, one might argue that the structural definition of the value alignment problem suffers from issues of *overdetermination*: most every problem arising in the context of machine learning can be classified as a value alignment problem under this definition. Hence, the worry is that the structural definition is too inclusive to be useful. However, this is as it should be. For example, model outputs that we would call "racist" or "sexist", resulting from algorithmic bias, are clearly cases of value misalignment (at least on the assumption that we do not want these models to perpetuate systemic racism or sexism in society—something that gets less apparent by the day).

By examining the contexts in which something like what we might call value misalignment can arise in the first place, we discovered that the value alignment problem for artificial intelligence is structurally similar to principal agent problems from economics, which can be instantiated whenever a principal delegates authority to an agent to act on their behalf. This insight centres the dynamics of multi-agent interactions as the key feature giving rise to misalignment. This is a descriptive fact about the dynamics of society where decisions are increasingly delegated to AI systems which, in turn, are being designed to be more autonomous. Delegation is a necessary feature of the value alignment problem for artificial intelligence in the following sense: no problem can arise when we do not delegate authority to these systems. Hence, the structural definition avoids the technochauvinism inherent to the standard description of value alignment.

The insight that value misalignment arises from the dynamics of multi-agent interactions, involving the delegation of tasks, helps to narrow attention to further important features of the value alignment problem for AI. Specifically, informational asymmetries, rather than "misaligned values", *per se*, are a key driver of misalignment on this model. In the principal-agent framework, conflicts of interest alone are neither necessary nor sufficient for a principal-agent problem to arise. However, in the case the value alignment problem, the objectives of the system are not pre-determined. This means that we have some control over what those objectives are, but because of limitations of expressiveness (translating those objectives into formal proxies), this can be a disadvantage rather than an advantage.

Moreover, the structural definition clarifies that value misalignment is not a single issue to be solved in isolation. Instead, the value alignment problem should be viewed as a broader category or class of problems. Within this category, various issues related to social, moral, political, informational, and technical aspects can be found. Such an analysis requires a holistic understanding of the complexity and multifaceted nature of the value alignment problem. Hence, just as it is superficial to talk about "the" value alignment problem as the problem of ensuring the "values" of an AI system (howsoever specified) align with the values of humanity (whatever that is taken to mean), so too is it superficial to talk about "solving" the value alignment problem. The value alignment problem is not a confined problem to be solved—particularly not by technical means alone.

Instead, it is a dynamic class whose instances are generated through informational asymmetries or misaligned objectives. Furthermore, these instances are relative to the principal in question. Since these problem instances are utterly ubiquitous, it is more apt to talk about mitigating the value alignment problem, rather than solving it. And, doing so requires taking account of each of the three axes that contribute to the generation of a problem instance, as well as the interaction effects among them. The analysis offered, therefore, shifts the focus from the content of the problem—e.g., the values themselves—to the structure of the problem.

So, we can talk coherently about mitigating instances of the value alignment problem for artificial intelligence without referring to any specific values at all. Some may see this characteristic of my conceptualisation of the value alignment problem for artificial intelligence as a bug: to speak of mitigating the value alignment problem, surely we must engage with the normative component of the problem. This is a mistake. As we have seen, various attempts to codify ethical principles or values have consistently failed—either in terms of entrenching dominant social norms while ignoring the most significant potential impacts of AI systems or in terms of hand-waving at overly intellectualised and abstracted notions of "values". This is not to say that we can ignore normativity entirely. On the contrary, ensuring that the objective functions of a system are aligned with the true objectives of the principal(s) requires taking objectives seriously and reckoning with ineliminable and contradictory pluralism about values.

In this sense, values contribute to the broader social context of value alignment, but these normative components are not the primary factor that generates problem instances. Hence, shifting the focus from the *content* to the *context* is a feature of this reconceptualisation.

There is a separate question, then, about the possibility of aligning objectives. It should be apparent from some of the case studies discussed throughout this book that one place of intervention for heading off value misalignment is with the objective. When considering recommendation systems, for example, it seems like a natural objective is to maximise engagement. And there are many such proxies that could be used to operationalise this objective—each with a greater or lesser degree of risk for misalignment. However, we might also ask the question: why is the objective to maximise engagement in the first place? The dynamics of value alignment make this objective clear in a way that is not got through the standard approach—the values dictated by corporations to programmers are not at all co-extensive with the values of humanity. Thus, this structural definition makes clear the language with which to discuss these problems. I believe that this is a virtue of the account.

As it turns out, robust value alignment lies somewhere between very difficult and near-impossible in many situations. Moreover, in light of the incentive structures of present-day society, the problem is almost certainly intractable: the *scaling hypothesis for value-aligned agency* highlights that as long as the guiding faith of the scaling hypothesis (for performance) is followed, misalignment will increase. Striving toward value-aligned AI systems is clearly at odds with the present attitude in AI research toward increasing scale. The stated goals of two major tech companies—OpenAI and Google DeepMind—are to achieve artificial general intelligence, which implies a widening, rather than narrowing, of agents' goals and abilities as well as increases in opacity and decreases in oversight capabilities. Moreover, advancements in generative AI models from 2022 onward have prompted an "arms race" for the creation and deployment of so-called large language models. Again, even without any reference to general intelligence or superintelligence, the reconceptualisation of the value alignment problem offered in this book underscores that these problems will worsen.

The ubiquity of the value alignment problem in the context of AI systems also underscores a pessimistic outlook for the very possibility of aligning values. The standard approach to value alignment waves a hand at aligning AI systems with "human values". Perhaps it sounds like a tractable problem in that context. On the structural definition I have offered here, it should be clear that the problem is not tractable: it is pervasive. Some degree of optimism is warranted in particular cases where is it possible to constrain the system or prove safety mechanisms. However, this tractability decreases sharply once these systems begin interacting with the world, and once the decisions that these models output begin to affect people.

That said, it also follows from the analysis offered here that the value alignment problem can be avoided or mitigated by ensuring that goals are narrowly defined and easily monitored. This is not a new insight, by any means—such proposals have been offered in the economic framework of the principal-agent problem (Gibbons, 1998). However, the applicability of these insights to artificial intelligence has been largely ignored in the field. The structural reformulation of the problem highlights concrete points of intervention where misalignment may be mitigated.

Along the objectives axis, instances of the value alignment problem can be mitigated by pursuing simpler objectives. In particular, objectives that lend themselves to formalisation are more conducive to alignment along this axis.

Along the information axis, instances of the value alignment problem can be mitigated by increasing the transparency of AI systems. The scaling hypothesis for value-aligned AI suggests that value misalignment scales with size, data, and compute. Hence, smaller, explainable models are more conducive to alignment. Additional transparency can be gained by firmer theoretical foundations when considering larger models. Hence, value misalignment could be mitigated along the information axis through more fundamental theoretical work regarding the functioning of these models, instead of the haphazard empirical work that is currently the status quo in the field. When data-intensive training is required, informational asymmetries can be reduced by using well-curated datasets.

Along the principals axis, instances of the value alignment problem can be mitigated by ensuring that stakeholders' objectives are accounted for at every stage of the algorithmic development pipeline. As a result, stakeholders should be included in the design process from the earliest stages. Misalignment, we saw in Chapter 6, can arise when the stakeholders and the shareholders of these systems are distinct. Hence, the suggestion here is that in order to ensure value alignment along the principals axis, it is necessary to integrate these two sets so that they overlap.

Because of the *social* and *dynamic* nature of the value alignment problem on the structural definition offered here, there is one single way of genuinely "solving" misalignment, *simpliciter*. Because value alignment is defined here as the problem arising from the dynamics of multi-agent interactions, where a (human) principal delegates authority to an (artificial) agent to act on their behalf, the value alignment problem can be "solved" by intervening on the antecedent conditions that give rise to such problems in the first place. Namely: do not delegate authority to AI systems.

This "solution" is probably unsatisfactory. Suppose that we *must* (for whatever reason, say, financial incentives) delegate tasks to AI systems. How then can we solve the value alignment problem? Here, the answer is necessarily negative—but, hopefully in a productive way. The interplay between the three axes of value alignment on this definition (objectives, information, and principals) mean that value alignment is difficult, and the problem is compounded when the artificial systems to which we delegate authority to act increase in complexity. It is well known that as the complexity of a system increases, new (macro-level) properties can emerge that could not have been predicted from understanding the (micro-level) details of how that system functions, no matter how precise our understanding of the latter details (Anderson, 1972).

Furthermore, these interactions do not occur in a vacuum: there are interaction effects between the technology, thus produced, and the society and its inhabitants with whose values we seek to align. It is unsurprising that technology can have a transformative effect on economic, social, and cultural systems. This is the nature of technological revolutions—e.g., agriculture, industrial manufacturing, electricity, digitisation, etc. It should then be unsurprising that these systems can also change the views and values of society. For example, new technologies may add options to decision sets, change decision-making costs, enable new relationships, change the burdens and expectations of, or the balance of power in, existing relationships, or changing perceptions (Danaher and Sætra, 2023).

Kuhn (1962) suggested that scientific paradigms differ significantly with respect to their standards, language, values, institutions, and modes of engaging with the world. A paradigm shift leads to a new paradigm that is, in some sense, incomparable to the old paradigm with respect to whether the new or the old better satisfies some purported epistemic goals. This is because paradigms themselves have different epistemic goals. Hence, it is only possible to assess a new paradigm *after* adopting these new epistemic goals, ways of thinking, language, and modes of engagement, etc.

Throughout this book, I have effectively argued for a paradigm shift in the way that we think about and conceptualise the value alignment problem. Understanding the value alignment problem structurally demands a radical re-conceptualisation of the problem which foregrounds the importance of the *social* aspects of the problem instances arising under this framework. I think that the re-conceptualisation is more useful than the standard definition; however, if Kuhn is right, then perhaps they are incomparable. The goal under this new paradigm is to understand, precisely, the structural features of interactions that give rise to value alignment in the first place in order to determine how and whether this problem can be mitigated.

This book is intended as the first word on the subject, rather than the last.

Additional Resources

AI Now Institute. https://ainowinstitute.org/

Algorithmic Justice League. https://www.ajl.org/

AlgorithmWatch. https://algorithmwatch.org/en/

Distributed AI Research Institute. https://www.dair-institute.org/

V

Appendix

A Superintelligence and Control

It is a somewhat unfortunate fact of the discipline that it is effectively impossible to talk about the value alignment problem without talking about the control problem. Moreover, discussing the control problem necessitates addressing concepts such as artificial general intelligence, strong AI, and superintelligence—i.e., those AI forms brought to mind through science fiction narratives, as described in the Introduction. It is also worth noting that much theoretical (and speculative) research today on the superintelligence thought experiment is couched within a larger philosophical framework concerning simulation, existential risk, post- and trans-humanism, and longtermism.[1]

Without overstating the importance or relevance of the topic, this appendix begins by looking at (purely) philosophical questions surrounding the possibility of artificial *superintelligence* and the problems that arise from this possibility—particularly the *control problem*. Doing so helps to understand and further contextualise the perspective of those working on AI safety and machine ethics—the two current approaches to alignment described in Part III.

A.1 Superintelligence

The pressing concern in discussions of superintelligence is that if machines can display properties or characteristics of intelligence, then a question arises whether those machines' "intellectual" or "cognitive" capacities might surpass humans' intellectual or cognitive capacities. This possibility, in turn, gives rise to the control problem:

How can we maintain control of an entity that is more intelligent than we are?

This question raises a problem because, as Russell (2019) contends, we would be to a superintelligent AI system as gorillas are to us, which bodes poorly for humanity since gorillas, as a species, have "essentially no future beyond that which we [humans] deign to allow" (132).[2]

[1] The last of these is a philosophical view that is often associated with the effective altruism movement, and many of the guiding tenets of these views are deeply couched within a eugenics framework. See discussion in Gebru and Torres (2024).

[2] Hence, Russell (2019) calls the control problem the "gorilla problem".

Of course, the conversation at this point is already vexed. There is a sense in which many machines and AI systems that exist today—indeed, many different species of nonhuman animals—already perform particular tasks at "superhuman" levels in narrow domains. For example, bats interpret sonar signals much better than humans do; calculators outperform humans in arithmetic; sophisticated chess programs outperform humans at chess, and so on. The fact that we can reasonably say a humpback whale possesses a "superhuman capacity" for swimming should perhaps call into question the coherence of measuring ability relative to an anthropocentric baseline. Nonetheless, the worry here is not about ability in any particular domain—e.g., sonar interpretation, swimming, chess playing, etc.—rather, the worry is about a notion of general intelligence which applies to a range of domains.

Part of the reason intelligence is interesting is because of its generalisability across domains. A superhuman swimming machine cannot use its swimming ability to become a superhuman chess-playing machine. In contrast, a superhuman intellect can apply its intellectual abilities to any number of domains—including, for example, the creation of artificial intelligence. Given that it is possible to *imagine* an artificial entity with a human's cognitive capacities (but more so), the question arises whether it is possible to *create* such an entity.

A.2 Paths to Superintelligence

Outside science fiction, how might it be scientifically possible to create an actual superintelligence, natural or artificial? Bostrom (2014) describes several distinct "paths" to superintelligence, including whole-brain emulation, brain-computer interfaces, networks and organisation, and artificial intelligence.[3]

Whole-Brain Emulation. The basic idea of whole-brain emulation is to model a human brain accurately enough to emulate all its neurons, synaptic connections, biochemical processes, etc. Minimally, this would require three distinct processes. First, one would need to create a sufficiently detailed scan of a particular human brain. Then, the raw data from the scanners would be fed into a computer for automated image processing to reconstruct the three-dimensional neuronal network that implemented cognition in the original biological brain. Once such a neuro-computational structure is created, it could be implemented on a sufficiently powerful computer.

If this process is completely successful, the result would be a digital reproduction of the physical brain. Moreover, depending on one's theoretical commitments in the context of the philosophy of mind, this might constitute a digital reproduction of the original *intellect*—perhaps with memory and personality intact. (Of course, this is philo-

[3] In addition to the four paths described here, Bostrom (2014) suggests the enhancement of biological cognition as a possible path to superintelligence (or, at least, greater-than-current human intelligence). This approach may include, e.g., removing neuro-toxic pollutants from the environment or optimising nutrition, sleep, exercise, and education to maximise the capacity of existing biological brains. However, biological enhancement also includes discussing genetic selection—i.e., *eugenics*. Bostrom (2014) tries to differentiate the "bad" type of eugenics from the type that he discusses: instead of controlling "mating patterns", he suggests using selection at the levels of embryos or gametes. However, this is still a eugenics programme.

sophically controversial, and whether this statement is true depends on the metaphysics of mind, identity, and consciousness.) The emulated mind—which may or may not be identical to the original biological mind, depending on how one cashes out a notion of "identity"—could live in a virtual world, or it could be connected to a physical system—i.e., a robot—to exist in and interact with the physical world.

However, this is only the first step toward superintelligence. Insofar as the emulated mind is, *ex hypothesi*,[4] no more intelligent than the original (biological) mind, it is, therefore, not superintelligent. However, the emulated mind exists as a bit of software; as such, it is not constrained by the physical features of a biological brain, implying that it can be suitably "upgraded" in ways that wetware cannot. A sufficient number of upgrades—for example, in processing speed or actual functional ability—might allow the emulated brain to become superintelligent relative to its biological counterpart.

Importantly, this path to superintelligence does not require that we understand anything about human cognition—although it does require sophisticated technology for scanning, translating, and simulating. The technological capacities required for this process will vary in complexity, depending on the level of abstraction that ends up being necessary to enact whole-brain emulation—e.g., whether it is possible to emulate a brain by emulating all the individual neurons in that brain and their connectivity matrices, or whether it is necessary to emulate the brain at a finer grain like neurotransmitter molecules.

Brain-Computer Interface. Whole-brain emulation is still in the realm of science fiction since none of the technologies required to emulate a human brain successfully yet exist—although precursors to these technologies do.[5] Closer to the capabilities of the present day, we might arrive at a superintelligence through a brain-computer interface. This approach to superintelligence is much less speculative insofar as a proof-of-concept already exists, to some extent: namely, smartphones.

The *extended mind thesis* holds that technological artefacts in one's environment can function as a part of one's mind.[6] These technological artefacts may be as simple as pen-and-paper or as complicated as a computer. Smartphones are particularly interesting because of their relative ubiquity in modern society and their ability to connect to the Internet.[7] These devices serve as technological scaffolds that take over some central cognitive functions, such as memory storage. Thus, cognition is not necessarily bound

[4] A fancy way of saying "by hypothesis" or "according to the hypothesis proposed".

[5] For example, *DeepSouth*, which was announced in December 2023, is a neuromorphic computer system that is supposed to emulate "large networks of spiking neurons at 228 trillion synaptic operations per second" on par with the human brain (WSU Media Unit, 2023; Vicinanza, 2023). Neuromorphic computers (Mead, 1990) are *non*-von Neumann computers composed of neurons and synapses "whose structure and function are inspired by brains" (Schuman et al., 2022).

[6] See Clark and Chalmers (1998) and discussion in Rowlands et al. (2020).

[7] As of July 2023, it was estimated, based on smartphone mobile network subscriptions worldwide, that approximately 6.92 billion people, or 86.11% of the world's population, use smartphones (Taylor, 2023).

to a physical brain, and there is a sense in which *digital knowledge* could count as genuine knowledge.[8]

Given that (1) the Internet contains a plethora of facts, (2) smartphones are connected to the Internet, and (3) people are connected to their phones, there is a sense in which all the digital knowledge of the world is also *personal* knowledge. It just happens that the interface between one's brain and one's phone—typically, one's fingers—is highly inefficient; one must physically tap through applications and keyboards to "download" knowledge from the Internet to one's brain. Still, to some extent, an individual with a smartphone is "connected" to their smartphone.

Moreover, there is also a sense that an individual and their phone together are smarter (or at least have more knowledge) than the individual alone. For example, on the assumption that recalling trivial facts is a measure of intelligence, the average person might be unable to answer if asked what the 17,000th digit of π is. However, the entity consisting of $\langle$ person + phone $\rangle$ certainly would.[9]

So, we might imagine that a device like a smartphone could be directly connected to a person's brain so that looking up a bit of information, like the 17,000th digit of π, just requires thinking about the 17,000th digit of π. This process is not unlike how memory works on some models of memory.[10] Fundamental skills and knowledge sets might be accessed nearly instantaneously. The company Neuralink is attempting to develop a brain-chip implant that allows users to interact with computers via neural signals.[11] 2023 saw several significant breakthroughs in brain-computer interface technologies using recurrent neural networks and generative pre-trained transformers.[12]

This approach assumes that the brain remains physical while interfacing with some computing technology. An alternative interface could involve a mind entering a simulation to interact with a virtual environment. If physically connecting to technological artefacts increases human cognitive abilities, then there is a sense in which this is a move toward superintelligence. This type of intelligence can then be increased by increasing the abilities of those artefacts or by improving the interface between our brains and devices.

Networks and Organisations. Another possible path to superintelligence is through enhancing networks and organisations linking individual minds with one another and with other technological artefacts—e.g., computers, bots, etc. In this case, no individual would be superintelligent, but it is possible that a *system* of individuals thus composed would itself be superintelligent. So, this "path" to superintelligence is also a "form" of superintelligence; see Section A.3 below.

The concept here is that of a *hivemind*. This network of intelligent individuals can be considered a form of superintelligence because the many are often more intelligent (in the sense of being better predictors) than the few. For example, prediction markets

[8] See Heersmink and Carter (2020); Carter (2023).

[9] I am told it is "5" (excluding the leading "3", of course).

[10] See, for example, Baddeley and Hitch (1974).

[11] See reporting in Mehta and Levy (2022).

[12] See, e.g., Willett et al. (2023); Metzger et al. (2023); Zhang et al. (2023).

highlight how aggregate responses from large groups of people are particularly good predictors of difficult, complicated, and vague problems.[13] This phenomenon is an instantiation of the folk-psychological concept of the *wisdom of the crowd*—i.e., that collective opinions of epistemically diverse groups of individuals are often more accurate than individual experts.[14]

Artificial Intelligence. The popular conception for thinking about a possible path to superintelligence is via *artificial intelligence*. Unlike whole-brain emulation, brain-computer interfaces, and networks and organisation (each of which builds upon existing biological brains in one sense or another) artificial intelligence starts from scratch.[15] Some inventions that serve the same *function* as their biological counterparts are nevertheless wholly distinct from them. For example, to create heavier-than-air flight, engineers do not look toward biological critters capable of flying and try to emulate how they do it. To wit: aeroplane wings do not flap. Instead, engineers try to understand the mechanics that give rise to those abilities and devise a novel solution for instantiating them. In this case, aeroplanes use thrust from a jet engine, propeller, or rocket engine to propel the plane forward in space (and time).

In the same vein, the argument goes, if evolutionary pressures could give rise to human-level intelligence through sheer dynamics over billions of years, then an intelligent agent should be able to create intelligence by using their intellectual capacities to aid the design of such a system. Thus, it should not only be *possible* to design intelligence, but it should also happen much more quickly than by mere evolutionary force. This idea was expressed by Hans Moravec as early as 1976:[16]

> by building in the sequence atoms, amino acids, proteins, cells, organs, animals (often concurrently), it [biological evolution] produced a technological civilization out of inanimate matter in only two billion years. The existence of several examples of intelligence designed under these constraints should give us great confidence that we can achieve the same in short order. (Moravec, 1976, 5–6)

However, it is worth noting that *possibility* does not imply *tractability*. Van Rooij et al. (2023) offer a formal proof that the real-world complexity of the engineering problem of creating AGI via machine learning methods is NP-hard and, therefore, intractable.

The Possibility of Superintelligence. Although some researchers today are sceptical about the possibility of creating an artificial superintelligence, others suggest that the fact that there are multiple possible paths to superintelligence implies that we *can* create it. Some longtermists go so far as to say that we have a moral obligation to create superintelligent AI; see Gebru and Torres (2024). Note that if there were only one such

[13] See discussion in Atanasov et al. (2017).

[14] This view can be traced to at least Ancient Greece; see Aristotle (1995c).

[15] To "start from scratch" is an English-language idiom derived from the starting line of a race (which is scratched into the ground); hence, to "start from scratch" implies that there is no head start, as would be the case if we were to build a superintelligence from an extant biological intelligence.

[16] See also Moravec (1988, 1999); Chalmers (2010).

path, and some constraint made that path intractable, then that would be the end of the story. However, because there are multiple such paths, any delay on one path might be circumvented by following another. These paths may also have interaction effects between them. That is, we may be able to leverage increased intelligence via networks and organisation or cognitive enhancement to aid the creation of superintelligence via another path, say whole-brain emulation or artificial intelligence.

A.3 Forms of Superintelligence

So, superintelligence, for our purposes, will refer to intellectual or cognitive capacities that (greatly) outperform the best current human minds across many general cognitive domains. However, this is still ambiguous: as it turns out, there are several different *forms* that a superintelligence might take. That is, there are several ways in which an intelligent agent might outstrip the capacities of humans. In particular, we can differentiate between a *speed* superintelligence, a *collective* superintelligence, and a *quality* superintelligence.

Speed Superintelligence. The first and perhaps the easiest form of superintelligence to understand is speed superintelligence. Suppose we can create a machine intelligence that is no more intelligent than the average human—i.e., it displays human-level general intelligence—but which is significantly *faster* at processing information than any biological brain (in the sense of multiple orders of magnitude). Thus, a *speed superintelligence* is a system capable of doing anything that a human intellect can do, but much faster. Despite being cognitively or intellectually equivalent to a human mind, this would nonetheless constitute a *super*intelligence insofar as such a system is not constrained by the processing power of the human brain.

Hence, any invention we might imagine humans could create in the distant future (without any increase in average cognitive capacity), a speed superintelligence would be able to create in a fraction of the time. Despite being no "smarter" than humans, this is still aptly called superintelligence. Consider that the 20th century alone saw the invention of the radio, heavier-than-air flight, synthetic plastic, talking motion pictures, the television, penicillin, the atomic bomb, human-crewed spaceflight, computers, Tamagotchis, the Internet, etc. All these were created by humans (for better or worse). It follows that a human-level AI could also have created them, but a speed superintelligence could create them in, say, a day rather than a century.

Collective Superintelligence. A different form of superintelligence—which we might call "collective superintelligence"—could involve a system that displays superior capacity compared to humans by aggregating many intelligent agents. In this case, the *system's* performance across many domains might outpace any current *individual* cognitive system. As noted above, there is a sense in which this type of intelligence already exists, to a degree, because networks and organisations of humans often exhibit a higher capacity for complex problem-solving than any individual human alone. For example, an individual human intellect probably cannot send a person to space, whereas a collection of such intellects can—and, indeed, has.

Collective intelligence excels at solving problems that can be readily broken into parts—i.e., when solutions to sub-problems can be pursued in parallel and verified independently. As with speed superintelligence, no *individual* within the collective superintelligence needs to have a higher cognitive or intellectual capacity than any individual human. In addition, no individual needs to be faster than any individual human. Theoretically, a collective superintelligence could still outpace humans—individually or collectively—insofar as artificial intelligence might scale more readily than human intelligence. For example, the Manhattan Project, which produced the first nuclear weapons, employed around 130,000 workers at one point; in the case of a collective superintelligence, we could imagine millions or more systems working in parallel.

Quality Superintelligence. A third form of superintelligence is what we might call *quality* superintelligence. This form of superintelligence is perhaps the most conceptually difficult of the three forms to understand (because it is the most vague). However, the cursory definition is that the system surpasses human intelligence on some quality metrics (whatever those may be). Thus, if we have an intuitive understanding of intelligence, we can imagine that a quality superintelligence is like that but qualitatively better.

One way to conceptualise this is to consider the advent of language in our species. Complex linguistic representations allow for a qualitative increase in many baseline capacities that exist in the ancestral species of *Homo sapiens*, including short-term memory, online-processing capacity, control, semantic memory, mental models, social learning, and pro-sociality (Planer and Sterelny, 2021). Thus, the evolutionary transition from simple communication to linguistic communication comes with a general increase in the *quality* of intelligence displayed in the species that has allowed humans to solve complex problems in ways that appear inaccessible to nonhuman animals—which is not to say, of course, that those species are *un*intelligent.

Thus, while admitting that a notion of "qualitatively better" is inherently vague, by analogy, one could imagine the possibility of a cognitive shift—whatsoever it might consist of—that moves an intellect from human-level capacities to something qualitatively more sophisticated in the same way that the evolution toward linguistic capacity created a qualitative shift that made many intellectual abilities in humans more sophisticated than those of other nonhuman species.

Equivalence Classes. Despite distinct specifications of what a superintelligence might consist of (speed, collection, quality), Bostrom (2014) contends that each form of superintelligence is equal in the sense that they are members of the same equivalence class.[17] The important thing to note here is that any one superintelligence could theoretically give rise to any other form. Namely, if human intelligence can invent any one form of superintelligence, then that superintelligence would be capable (and more so) of inventing the other forms. This suggestion leads to the possibility of an *intelligence explosion*.

[17] An equivalence class is a subset whose members all have an equivalence relation between them. Formally, for a set X, an equivalence class is a subset $\{x \in X : x \sim a\}$, where $a \in X$, and $x \sim a$ is an equivalence relation between x and a—i.e., a relation which is reflexive ($\forall a \in X, a \sim a$), symmetric ($\forall a, b \in X, a \sim b \rightarrow b \sim a$), and transitive ($\forall a, b, c, \in X, (a \sim b \wedge b \sim c) \rightarrow a \sim c$). It is worthwhile to consider if Bostrom is dressing an informal discussion in formal language—a rhetorical strategy that is not uncommon in discussions of value alignment and superintelligence.

A.4 Intelligence Explosion and the Singularity

The term "singularity" was introduced by Vinge (1983) and popularised by Vinge (1993/2017); Kurzweil (2005). There are slight distinctions in how the concept of the singularity is described. On one account, the singularity has to do with accelerating change in technological progress (Kurzweil, 2005). In this view, predicting when new technologies might arrive is possible. A different view suggests that technology might advance to the point where humans cannot predict anything about it because it is so alien to us (Vinge, 1993/2017). This view follows from the assumption that to understand a cognitive entity, one must be at least as intelligent as that entity. The final account depends on the notion of a hypothetical *intelligence explosion* articulated by Good (1965). This thought experiment underscores the positive feedback cycle giving rise to an exponential increase in intelligence, leading to superintelligence far surpassing humans. See Figure A.1.

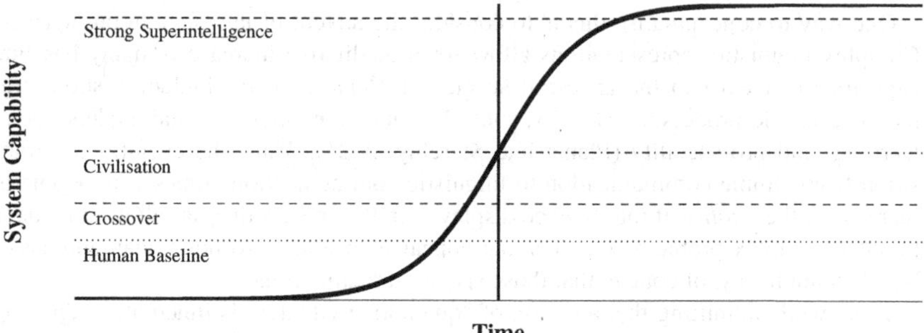

Figure A.1: Standard S-shaped curve illustrating intelligence explosion (theoretical)

Good (1965) begins by defining an "ultraintelligent" machine as one that can far surpass the intellectual activities of the most brilliant of our species (or even our species as a whole). He then points out that because *designing* such a machine is, itself, an intellectual activity, "an ultraintelligent machine could design even better machines; there would then unquestionably be an 'intelligence explosion', and the intelligence of man would be left far behind" (Good, 1965, 33).

The logic behind a hypothetical intelligence explosion should be fairly intuitive. First, we suppose that a human level of intelligence can create an artificial intelligence that is *more* intelligent than humans. If this is the case, then such an AI system would logically be capable of creating a successor AI that is more intelligent than it. Then, this successor AI would be capable of creating a system more intelligent than *it*, and so on, up to some theoretical maximum capacity, where the cognitive abilities of such a system flatten out—albeit at an exponentially higher cognitive or intellectual capacity than the entirety of human civilisation.

Good (1965) continues: "The first ultraintelligent machine is the last invention that man need ever make" (33). There are two ways that this can be interpreted. On the one hand, if the artificial superintelligence's values (goals, objectives) are properly aligned with those of humanity, then humans will no longer need to invent anything since the

AI would be able to do this on our behalf and much more easily. A superintelligent AI system could cure all known diseases, solve the climate crisis, end poverty, etc.[18] On the other hand, if the AI system's values are misaligned with those of humanity or if we cannot control such a system, then, too, it will be our last invention because it will pose an existential threat to our species.

Some philosophers have suggested that a computer cannot emulate human cognitive capacities; others have suggested that computers cannot have consciousness, intentionality, etc. However, the idea of intelligence explosion makes no assumptions about whether the superintelligence is conscious or has other mind-like properties. We do not need to assume that a superintelligent AI takes the form of a classical computational system. Given that several research labs advertise themselves as working toward "general intelligence" in AI systems, the question is not whether creating such a system is possible, plausible, or likely. Instead, the pertinent question is: *what if we succeed?* (Russell and Norvig, 2021).

A.5 Existential Risk

One key argument made is that we should be concerned about superintelligence and existential risk now because even if we think that there is a *low* probability that it is even possible to invent an artificial superintelligence, there is no logical contradiction in the existence of such an entity. Therefore, we cannot rationally put probability 0 on this proposition. Furthermore, we should care about this risk now because even if we think that the advent of a superintelligence will happen far in the future, it turns out that scientific breakthroughs are notoriously hard to predict.[19] Part of the difficulty with predicting when superintelligence might arrive is that several parallel breakthroughs might need to occur, which could occur in relative succession. This fact also makes it difficult to enact legislation that might ban the creation of superintelligence insofar as it is not obvious, *a priori*,[20] what aspects of technological innovation will give rise to superintelligence or general-purpose AI. Hence, it is unclear which ideas would need to be banned, if such a ban were even possible.

Artificial superintelligence, it is thought, poses an existential risk to humanity insofar as the goals of a superintelligence are supposed to be utterly opaque to us, in the same way that human goals are opaque to a crustacean. This opacity makes it difficult to ensure that superintelligence has values that are aligned with human values. Furthermore, misaligned values for a superintelligent AI would be catastrophic for humanity

[18] However, it is worthwhile to maintain a critical lens with such grandiose claims. Technology can exacerbate extant inequalities further, so it is not entirely obvious why a social problem concerning distributive justice would be solved by technological innovation. More on this later.

[19] As a case in point, Russell (2019) recounts a story in which Ernest Rutherford—one of the most distinguished nuclear physicists in the early 20th century—gave a speech on 11 September 1933 reiterating the impossibility of tapping into atomic nuclei as a source of energy. The next morning, the story goes, Leo Szilard—a Hungarian physicist—read a report of this speech in the *Times of London* over breakfast and went for a walk. During this promenade, he invented the neutron-induced nuclear chain reaction. Thus, the problem of obtaining nuclear energy went from *impossible* to *essentially solved* in less than 24 hours. See Rhodes (1986).

[20] A fancy way of saying "before the fact" in the context of rational reasoning.

insofar as it would be impossible to control a superintelligence in the same way that a crustacean cannot control the actions of a human.

A.6 Intelligence, Motivation, and Goals

Part of the difficulty in predicting what goals an artificial superintelligence might have arises from the fact that intelligence and motivation are effectively independent—this is sometimes referred to as the *orthogonality thesis*.

> **The Orthogonality Thesis**
> Intelligence and final goals are *orthogonal*. Therefore, more or less any level of intelligence could combine with more or less any final goal—at least in principle. (Bostrom, 2014, 107)

It may be impossible for an "unintelligent" (or narrow or constrained) system to have complex motivations. Furthermore, for an agent to have a set of motivations, these motivations must be functionally integrated with the agent's decision processes, which will come with accompanying demands on the agent's resources—e.g., memory, processing power, etc. However, the orthogonality thesis suggests that if an agent is *sufficiently* intelligent—in the sense that the previous two caveats no longer apply—then, in principle, the agent's *intelligence* and *motivations* are effectively independent. To put it another way, an agent with a sufficient degree of intelligence would have the ability to search for instrumental plans and policies in service of its final goals.

The orthogonality thesis effectively implies that such intelligent agents might have many possible final goals. At the same time, there are several reasons why we might think that the motivations—and the final goals—of an artificial superintelligence would be opaque to us. For example, a superintelligent AI system would be more opaque than superintelligent extraterrestrials because even a superintelligent alien is a biological creature that has arisen through some evolutionary process. In this sense, we would expect such a creature to have motivations similar to those of humans insofar as we are biological creatures. For example, such an alien would have motives related to nourishment, air, temperature, energy expenditure, avoiding bodily injury, disease, predation, etc.

Furthermore, a member of an intelligent social species might even have inbuilt motivations related to cooperation and competition, such as loyalty, resentment of free riders, etc. It is not obvious that an AI system needs to care about any of these sorts of things. Therefore, we cannot simply take for granted that a superintelligent AI system will have the types of values that we take for granted in human agents—or other biological agents. Humans are more similar to one another than they are different just by dint of the fact that they are all members of the species, *Homo sapiens*.

However, even if an artificial superintelligence is sufficiently alien to us so that it is difficult to predict what types of goals such an agent might pursue, we can nonetheless expect that any such agent will have certain instrumental goals, regardless of their final goals. That is to say, we might still be able to infer something about its sub-goals or its more immediate objectives, even if we do not know what the final goals of such an agent are, by considering the instrumental reasons that would arise for essentially any final goals in essentially any situation. This insight is sometimes called the *instrumental convergence thesis*.

> **The Instrumental Convergence Thesis**
> Several instrumental values can be identified which are convergent in the sense that their attainment would increase the chances of the agent's goal being realised for a wide range of final goals and a wide range of situations, implying that these instrumental values are likely to be pursued by a broad spectrum of situated intelligent agents. (Bostrom, 2014, 109)

It follows immediately from the instrumental convergence thesis that a broad spectrum of situated intelligent agents will probably pursue several identifiable instrumental goals.[21] Some such goals include things like *self-preservation*, because regardless of what an agent's *final* goal is, it will be unable to achieve that goal if it is turned off. More generally, for *any* final goal, G, the instrumental sub-goal, g = `<not being shut down>`, is required to achieve G. This implies that any sufficiently intelligent agent will have instrumental incentives to find ways not to be turned off, regardless of that agent's final goals. Hence, we do not need to know a superintelligent agent's final goals to deduce that it will seek to avoid being shut down.

In addition to self-preservation, we can specify a number of other plausible convergent instrumental goals. For example, resource acquisition and technological perfection are both candidates for convergent instrumental goals insofar as technology and resources both facilitate the achievement of final goals and, thus, the freedom of the system to act.[22] That said, the value of resources depends upon the use to which those resources can be put, and this use depends, in turn, on the available technology.

Similarly, cognitive enhancement might be a convergent instrumental goal insofar as increased cognitive ability might make an agent's final goals easier to achieve—although *which* cognitive abilities will be instrumentally useful will depend fundamentally upon the agent's final goals. Perhaps less intuitive, goal-content integrity might be a convergent instrumental goal insofar as, to achieve its final goals, those final goals must not be changed. Thus, agents might have instrumental reasons to prevent the alteration of their final goals.

Whereas the *orthogonality thesis* tells us that we may not be able to anticipate the final goals that a sufficiently intelligent agent has, the *instrumental convergence thesis* tells us about what kinds of sub-goals might exist for such agents regardless of what their final goals are. A problem arises when the agent's final goals are misaligned with our own goals. Importantly, since the agent in question is superintelligent, it is more intelligent by definition than any human. Therefore, any attempt to, e.g., shut it down or alter its (misaligned) goals may be anticipated and circumvented, implying that we would not be able to control such an entity.

A.7 The Control Problem

Exploring motivations and goals in superintelligence sheds light upon the intricacies of aligning goals with or between intelligent agents. While the orthogonality thesis and the instrumental convergence thesis illuminates the potential unpredictability of final goals

[21] Omohundro (2008) calls these the "basic AI drives".

[22] See discussion in Benson-Tilsen and Soares (2016).

and the convergence of instrumental sub-goals, they also gesture toward the potential for a deeper examination of the control problem, which builds upon the *principal-agent problem*, discussed in Chapter 3.

> **The First Principal-Agent Problem**
> A problem that arises whenever some human entity ("the principal") appoints another ("the agent") to act in the former's interest.

As we have seen, this problem is ubiquitous in economic and political interactions. In the context of *creating* an artificial superintelligence, this problem might arise when the system *designer*—the agent—is distinct from the entity that commissions the creation of the system—the principal. The problem arises primarily in the *development* phase. For example, the owner or sponsor of a project—ranging from a single individual to the entirety of humanity—might worry that the organisation, scientists, or programmers charged with implementing the project might not act in the former's best interest.

A different sort of principal-agent problem arises in contexts where the agent is a superintelligence.

> **The Second Principal-Agent Problem (The Control Problem)**
> A principal-agent problem, where the principal is the developer of an artificial superintelligence, and the agent is a superintelligence.

This problem occurs primarily in the *operational* phase. In contrast to the first principal-agent problem, which has been extensively researched and for which many standard management techniques exist, the second principal-agent problem will require new techniques and poses an unprecedented challenge.

Many researchers in AI safety see solving the control problem as essential for avoiding the existential risks associated with artificial superintelligence. Moreover, many researchers who study the value alignment problem see it as a means to solving the control problem.

A.8 Criticism

One key criticism is that the notion of *superintelligence* that Bostrom and others put forward is incoherent because it depends on a false assumption about the nature of intelligence. In particular, Kelly (2017) highlights that "intelligence" is not uni-dimensional. Thus, it is a fallacy to assume that intelligence is linear, as described in Figure A.1. If intelligence is not a single dimension, then the concept of "smarter than humans" is effectively meaningless, and the intuitive understanding of what superintelligence is in the first place loses coherence.

The point about superintelligence and intelligence explosion assumes a picture like the following. We might imagine a linear scale where we have the intelligence of bacteria, the intelligence of dogs or primates, and the intelligence of humans. Then, we assume that there is something beyond that on this linear scale. By analogy, one might think of the notion of evolution—the type of exceptionalism that sees humans as somehow more evolved than our ancestral species. Nevertheless, Kelly (2017) highlights that this is a false picture of both evolution and intelligence. A better picture of intelligence and evolution is that of a disk radiating outward through time. In this picture, every existing species has "undergone an unbroken chain of three billion years of successful reproduction, which means that bacteria and cockroaches today are as highly evolved as humans".

In a similar line of reasoning, Chalmers (2010) suggests that the argument for intelligence explosion makes two key assumptions: first, that there *is* such a thing as intelligence; second, that intelligence can be compared between systems.[23] Again, we will put this aside for now.

A.9 Summary

Although superintelligence is a philosophically rich thought experiment—with implications for the nature of intelligence and mind, consciousness, personal identity, and ethics, it should not be the primary concern of discussions of value alignment or AI ethics more broadly. That is not to say that superintelligence, intelligence explosion, or existential risk are *impossible*. Indeed, many arguments in favour of entertaining the possibility of superintelligence take something like the following form: a superintelligent AI system could have immensely negative consequences for humanity—up to and including the extinction of the species (existential risk). Because the potential negative outcomes of a superintelligence are so significant, any nonzero probability of creating such a superintelligence implies that we should take these risks seriously and work to mitigate these future risks now.[24] However, such risks are future risks, if they exist at all. As mentioned at the start of this appendix, superintelligence is science fiction. Instead, pressing issues in the present day need to be addressed. Although it is logically possible that we will invent an artificial superintelligence, concerns about existential risk need not (and ought not) be overstated. Scientific breakthroughs are notoriously difficult to anticipate, and, as we saw in Chapter 1, experts in the field have a long track record of failing to accurately predict the future capacities of artificial intelligence.

A wise approach to existential risk and the threat of artificial general intelligence or superintelligent AI is probably some form of agnosticism. Regardless of whether it is probable, plausible, or even merely possible that we create such a system, it is a fact that narrow AI systems—insofar as they are increasingly embedded in social systems—are causing real-world harms in the present day. The conversation surrounding artificial superintelligence diverts attention from extant real-world impacts and harms caused by AI systems. Understanding the functioning of AI systems should help to disabuse anyone of the claim that there is anything close to a "spark" of intelligence, let alone *general* intelligence, in present-day AI systems.[25]

---

[23]That said, Chalmers (2010) also thinks that we can replace a concept of "intelligence" with a concept of "cognitive capacity" and that doing so will get us to the intelligence explosion argument as well (albeit *sans* intelligence).

[24]Formally speaking, an expectation is a *utility* multiplied by a probability. An infinitely negative utility weighted by any positive epsilon, no matter how small, is still infinitely negative; hence, even if the probability is extremely low, the expected risk is still considered extremely high. This argument is analogous to *Pascal's Wager*, which criticises the logic of determining the existence of God. Pascal (1670/1910) suggests that the important question is not whether God exists but whether we ought to believe in God; see discussion in Háyek (2022).

[25]The reference here is to an press release posted by researchers at Microsoft on arXiv which claimed that GPT-4 "could reasonably be viewed as an early (yet still incomplete) [*continued*]

Additional Resources

Timnit Gebru and Émile P. Torres. 2024. "The TESCREAL bundle: Eugenics and the Promise of Utopia through Artificial General Intelligence," *First Monday* 29(4).

Jean-Luc Godard. 1965. *Alphaville: une étrange aventure de Lemmy Caution*. André Michelin. 99 Minutes.

Stanley Kubrick. 1968. *2001: A Space Odyssey*. Stanley Kubrick Productions. 143 Minutes.

Lana Wachowski and Lilly Wachowski. 1999. *The Matrix*. Warner Bros, Village Roadshow Pictures, Groucho II Film Partnership, and Silver Pictures. 136 Minutes.

Andrew Stanton. 2008. *WALL-E*. Walt Disney Pictures and Pixar Animation Studios. 100 Minutes.

Spike Jonze. 2013. *Her*. Annapurna Pictures. 126 Minutes.

Alex Garland. 2016. *Ex Machina*. Film4 and DNA Films. 108 Minutes.

Denis Villeneuve. 2017. *Blade Runner 2049*. Alcon Entertainment, Columbia Pictures, Bud Yorkin Productions, Torridon Films, 16:14 Entertainment, Thunderbird Entertainment, Scott Free Productions. 163 Minutes.

Kogonada. 2021. *After Yang*. A24, Cinereach, and Per Capita Productions. 96 Minutes.

version of an artificial general intelligence (AGI) system" (Bubeck et al., 2023, 1). For a more serious discussion of the capabilities of these large language models, see McCoy et al. (2023), who discuss "embers of autoregression" in lieu of "sparks of general intelligence".

References

Abbeel, Pieter, and Andrew Y. Ng. 2004. Apprenticeship Learning via Inverse Reinforcement Learning. In *Proceedings of the 21st International Conference on Machine Learning (ICML 2004)*, 1–8. New York: Association for Computing Machinery. 175

Abdalla, Mohamed, and Moustafa Abdalla. 2021. The Grey Hoodie Project: Big Tobacco, Big Tech, and the Threat on Academic Integrity. In *AAAI/ACM Conference on AI, Ethics, and Society*, 287–297. 218

Abraham, Yuval. 2024. 'Lavender': The AI Machine Directing Israel's Bombing Spree in Gaza. *+972 Magazine* Apr. (03). https://www.972mag.com/lavender-ai-israeli-army-gaza/. 154

Adadi, Amina, and Mohammed Berrada. 2018. Peeking Inside the Black-Box: A Survey on Explainable Artificial Intelligence (XAI). *IEEE Access* 6: 52138–52160. 127

Agüera y Arcas, Blaise. 2021. Do Large Language Models Understand Us? https://medium.com/@blaisea/do-large-language-models-understand-us-6f881d6d8e75. 32

AI Alignment Forum. 2009. Complexity of Value. https://www.alignmentforum.org/tag/complexity-of-value. 99

Ajunwa, Ifeoma. 2019. The Paradox of Automation as Anti-Bias Intervention. *Cardozo Law Review* 41: 1671. 8

Akerlof, George A. 1970. The Market for 'Lemons': Quality Uncertainty and the Market Mechanism. *Quarterly Journal of Economics* 84 (3): 488–500. 78

Albert, Réka, and Albert-László Barabási. 2002. Statistical Mechanics of Complex Networks. *Reviews of Modern Physics* 74 (47): 47–97. 129

Alexander, Michelle. 2010. *The New Jim Crow: Mass Incarceration in the Age of Colorblindness*. New York: The New Press. 107, 151

Allen, Colin, and Wendel Wallach. 2012. Moral Machines: Contradiction in Terms of Abdication of Human Responsibility? In *Robot Ethics: The Ethical and Social Implications of Robotics*, eds. Patrick Lin, Keith Abney, and George A. Bekey, 55–68. Cambridge, MA: The MIT Press. 197

Allen, Colin, Iva Smit, and Wendell Wallach. 2005. Artificial Morality: Top-Down, Bottom-Up, and Hybrid Approaches. *Ethics and Information Technology* 7: 149–155. 194

Allen, Colin, Wendell Wallach, and Iva Smit. 2006. Why Machine Ethics? *IEEE Computer Society* 21 (4): 12–17. 185, 197

Amodei, Dario, Chris Olah, Jacob Steinhardt, Paul Christiano, John Schulman, and Dan Mané. 2016. Concrete Problems in AI Safety. *arXiv* 1606.06565: 1–29. https://arxiv.org/abs/1606.06565. 12, 166, 178

Anderson, Elizabeth. 1995. Knowledge, Human Interests, and Objectivity in Feminist Epistemology. *Philosophical Topics* 23 (2): 27–58. 248

Anderson, Michael, and Susan Leigh Anderson. 2007. *The Status of Machine Ethics: A Report from the AAAI Symposium*, Vol. 17. 73, 185

Anderson, Michael, and Susan Leigh Anderson. 2011. *Machine Ethics*. Cambridge: Cambridge University Press. 197

Anderson, Philip W. 1972. More Is Different: Broken Symmetry and the Nature of the Hierarchical Structure of Science. *Science* 177 (4047): 393–396. 267

Anderson, Susan Leigh. 2011. Machine Metaethics. In *Machine Ethics*, eds. Michael Anderson and Susan Leigh Anderson, 21–27. Cambridge: Cambridge University Press. 185

Andrews, Mel. 2023. The Devil in the Data: Machine Learning & the Theory-Free Ideal. *PhilSci Archive* 22690: 1–21. https://philsci-archive.pitt.edu/22690/. 154

Angwin, Julia, Jeff Larson, Surya Mattu, and Lauren Kirchner. 2016. Machine Bias: There's Software Used Across the Country to Predict Future Criminals. And It's Biased Against Blacks. *ProPublica* May (23). https://www.propublica.org/article/machine-bias-risk-assessments-in-criminal-sentencing. 105, 114

Anthropic. 2023. Comments of Anthropic PBC: Notice of Inquiry on Artificial Intelligence & Copyright, Technical Report Dkt. 2023-6, U.S. Copyright Office. 147

Aquinas, Thomas. 1485. *Summa Theologiæ*. 214

Arbib, Michael A. 2002. The Mirror System, Imitation, and The Evolution of Language. In *Imitation in Animals and Artifacts*, eds. C. Nehaniv and K. Dautenhahn, 229–280. Cambridge, MA: The MIT Press. 230

Arbib, Michael A. 2003. The Evolving Mirror System: A Neural Basis for Language Readiness. In *Language Evolution*, eds. M. H. Christiansen and S. Kirby, 182–200. Oxford: Oxford University Press. 230

Arbib, Michael A. 2005. An Action-Oriented Neurolinguistic Framework for the Evolution of Protolanguage. In *Language Origins: Perspectives on Evolution*, ed. M. Tallerman, 21–47. Oxford: Oxford University Press. 230

Aristotle. 1995a. Eudemian Ethics. In *The Complete Works of Aristotle, The Revised Oxford Translation*, ed. Jonathan Barnes, Vol. 2, 1922–1981. Princeton: Princeton University Press. 154

Aristotle. 1995b. Nicomachean Ethics. In *The Complete Works of Aristotle, The Revised Oxford Translation*, ed. Jonathan Barnes, Vol. 2, 1729–1867. Princeton: Princeton University Press. 154, 192

Aristotle. 1995c. Politics. In *The Complete Works of Aristotle, The Revised Oxford Translation*, ed. Jonathan Barnes, Vol. 2, 1986–2129. Princeton: Princeton University Press. 275

Aristotle. 1995d. Posterior Analytics. In *The Complete Works of Aristotle, The Revised Oxford Translation*, ed. Jonathan Barnes, Vol. 1, 114–166. Princeton: Princeton University Press. 246

Arkin, Ronald C. 2008a. Governing Lethal Behavior: Embedding Ethics in a Hybrid Deliberative/Reactive Robot Architecture—Part I: Motivation and Philosophy. In *ACM/IEEE International Conference on Human Robot Interaction*, 121–128. 195

Arkin, Ronald C. 2008b. Governing Lethal Behavior: Embedding Ethics in a Hybrid Deliberative/Reactive Robot Architecture—Part II: Formalization for Ethical Control. In *Conference on Artificial General Intelligence*, 51–62. 195

Arkin, Ronald C. 2009. *Governing Lethal Behavior in Autonomous Robots*. Boca Raton: CRC Press. 199

Armstrong, Samuel, James Algar, Bill Roberts, Paul Satterfield, Ben Sharpsteen, David D. Hand, Hamilton Luske, Jim Handley, Ford Beebe, T. Hee, et al. 1940. *Fantasia*. Walt Disney Productions. 126 min. 99

Arnold, Thomas, and Matthias Scheutz. 2017. Value Alignment or Misalignment—What Will Keep Systems Accountable. In *3rd International Workshop on AI Ethics, and Society*, 81–88. New York: AAAI. 184

Arnold, Thomas, and Matthias Scheutz. 2018. The 'Big Red Button' Is too Late: An Alternative Model for the Ethical Evaluation of AI Systems. *Ethics and Information Technology* 20 (1): 59–69. 184

Arora, Saurabh, and Prashant Doshi. 2021. A Survey of Inverse Reinforcement Learning: Challenges, Methods and Progress. *Artificial Intelligence* 297: 103500. 237

Arrieta, Alejandro Barredo, Natalia Díaz-Rodríguez, Javier Del Ser, Adrien Bennetot, Siham Tabik, Alberto Barbado, Salvador Garcia, Sergio Gil-Lopez, Daniel Molina, Richard Benjamins, et al. 2020. Explainable Artificial Intelligence (XAI): Concepts, Taxonomies, Opportunities and Challenges toward Responsible AI. *Information Fusion* 58: 82–115. 126, 136

Arrow, Kenneth J. 1963. Uncertainty and the Welfare Economics of Medical Care. *American Economic Review* 53: 941–973. 78

Arrow, Kenneth J. 1968. The Economics of Moral Hazard: Further Comment. *American Economic Review* 58: 537–539. 78, 82

Asimov, Isaac. 1950. *I, Robot*. New York: Gnome Press. 194

Atanasov, Pavel, Phillip Rescober, Eric Stone, Samuel A. Swift, Emile Servan-Schreiber, Philip Tetlock, Lyle Ungar, and Barbara Mellers. 2017. Distilling the Wisdom of Crowds: Prediction Markets vs. Prediction Polls. *Management Science* 63 (3): 587–900. 275

Ayer, A. J. 1936. *Language, Truth, and Logic*. New York: Dover Publications, Inc. 217

Baack, Stefan. 2024. Training Data for the Price of a Sandwich: Common Crawl's Impact on Generative AI, Technical report, Moz://a. 128

Baddeley, Alan D., and Graham Hitch. 1974. Working Memory. In *Psychology of Learning and Motivation*, ed. Gordon H. Bower, Vol. 8, 47–89. Cambridge, MA: Academic Press. 274

Badia, Adrià Puigdomènech, Bilal Piot, Steven Kapturowski, Pablo Sprechmann, Alex Vitvitskyi, Daniel Guo, and Charles Blundell. 2020. Agent57: Outperforming the Atari Human Benchmark. *arXiv* 2003.13350: 1–30. https://arxiv.org/abs/2003.13350. 3

Baker, Alan. 2023. Simplicity. In *The Stanford Encyclopedia of Philosophy*, ed. Edward N. Zalta. Metaphysics Research Lab, Stanford University. https://plato.stanford.edu/archives/sum2022/entries/simplicity/. 245

Barocas, Solon, Moritz Hardt, and Arvind Narayanan. 2023. *Fairness and Machine Learning: Limitations and Opportunities*. Cambridge, MA: The MIT Press. http://www.fairmlbook.org. 104, 105

Barreno, Marco, Blaine Nelson, Russell Sears, Anthony D. Joseph, and J. D. Tygar. 2006. Can machine learning be secure? In *ASIACCS '06: Proceedings of the 2006 ACM Symposium on Information, computer and communications security*, eds. Ferng-Ching Lin, Der-Tsai Lee, Bao-Shuh Lin, Shiuhpyng Shieh, and Sushil Jajodia, 16–25. New York: Association for Computing Machinery. 164

Barrett, Lisa Feldman, Ralph Adolphs, Stacy Marsella, Aleix M. Martinez, and Seth D. Pollak. 2019. Emotional Expressions Reconsidered: Challenges to Inferring Emotion from Human Facial Movements. *Psychological Science in the Public Interest* 20 (1): 1–68. 100

Bauman, Matthew J., Kate S. Boxer, Tzu-Yun Lin, Erika Salomon, Hareem Naveed, Lauren Haynes, Joe Walsh, Jen Helsby, Steve Yoder, Robert Sullivan, et al. 2018. Reducing Incarceration Through Prioritized Interventions. In *Proceedings of the 1st ACM SIGCAS Conference on Computing and Sustainable Societies, COMPASS '18*, 1–8. New York: Association for Computing Machinery. 143

Behdadi, Dorna, and Christian Munthe. 2020. A Normative Approach to Artificial Moral Agency. *Minds and Machines* 30: 195–218. 187

Bell, Anthony J. 1999. Levels and Loops: The Future of Artificial Intelligence and Neuroscience. *Philosophical Transactions of the Royal Society B: Biological Sciences* 354 (1392): 2013–2020. 22

Bender, Emily M., and Batya Friedman. 2018. Data Statements for Natural Language Processing: Toward Mitigating System Bias and Enabling Better Science. *Transactions of the Association for Computational Linguistics* 6: 587–604. 131

Bender, Emily M., and Alex Hanna. 2025. *The AI Con: Exposing the Myth, the Hype and the Harm of AI*. London: Penguin Random House. 31

Bender, Emily M., and Alexander Koller. 2020. Climbing towards NLU: On Meaning, Form, and Understanding in the Age of Data. In *Proceedings of the 58th Annual Meeting of the Association for Computational Linguistics*, eds. Dan Jurafsky, Joyce Chai, Natalie Schluter, and Joel Tetreault, 5185–5198. Association for Computational Linguistics. 241

Bender, Emily M., Timnit Gebru, Angelina McMillan-Major, and Shmargaret Shmitchell. 2021. On the Dangers of Stochastic Parrots: Can Language Models Be Too Big? 🦜. In *Proceedings of the 2021 ACM Conference on Fairness, Accountability, and Transparency*, 610–623. New York: Association for Computing Machinery. 149, 150, 241

Bengio, Yoshua, Yann Lecun, and Geoffrey Hinton. 2021. Deep Learning for AI. *Communications of the ACM* 64 (7): 58–65. 96

Benjamin, Ruha. 2019. *Race After Technology: Abolitionist Tools for the New Jim Code*. Cambridge: Polity. 98, 151, 157, 256, 258

Benson-Tilsen, Tsvi, and Nate Soares. 2016. Formalizing Convergent Instrumental Goals. In *The Workshops of the Thirtieth AAAI Conference on Artificial Intelligence*. New York: AAAI. 281

Bentham, Jeremy. 1789. *An Introduction to the Principles of Morals and Legislation*. London: T. Payne, and Son. 189

Bergmann, Rachel, and Sonja Solomun. 2021. A New AI Lexicon: Sustainability. *AI Now Institute*. https://ainowinstitute.org/publication/a-new-ai-lexicon-sustainability. 150

Berk, Richard, Hoda Heidari, Shahin Jabbari, Michael Kearns, and Aaron Roth. 2017. Fairness in Criminal Justice Risk Assessments: The State of the Art. *Sociological Methods & Research* 50 (1): 3–44. 107

Berkeley, Edmund C. 1949. *Giant Brains: or Machines that Think*. New York: John Wiley & Sons. 31

Berryman, Sylvia. 2023. Democritus. In *The Stanford Encyclopedia of Philosophy*, eds. Edward N. Zalta and Uri Nodelman. Metaphysics Research Lab, Stanford University. `https://plato.stanford.edu/archives/spr2023/entries/democritus/`. 22

Berwick, Robert C., and Noam Chomsky. 2016. *Why Only Us: Language and Evolution*. Cambridge, MA: The MIT Press. 229

Betker, James, Gabriel Goh, Li Jing, Tim Brooks, Jianfeng Wang, Linjie Lia, Long Ouyang, Juntang Zhuang, Joyce Lee, Yufei Guo, et al. 2023. Improving Image Generation with Better Captions. *OpenAI*. `https://cdn.openai.com/papers/dall-e-3.pdf`. 132

Bickerton, Derek. 1990. *Language and Species*. Chicago: University of Chicago Press. 230

Bickerton, Derek. 1995. *Language and Human Behavior*. Seattle: University of Washington Press. 230

Biddle, Justin. 2013. State of the Field: Transient Underdetermination and Values in Science. *Studies in History and Philosophy of Science Part A* 44 (1): 124–133. 247, 250

Biggio, Battista, Giorgio Fumera, Fabio Roli, and Luca Didaci. 2012. Poisoning Adaptive Biometric Systems. In *Structural, Syntactic, and Statistical Pattern Recognition. SSPR/SPR 2012*, eds. Georgy Gimel'farb, Edwin Hancock, Atsushi Imiya, Arjan Kuijper, Mineichi Kudo, Shinichiro Omachi, Terry Windeatt, and Keiji Yamada. Vol. 7626 of *Lecture Notes in Computer Science*, 417–425. Berlin, Heidelberg: Springer. 165

Biggio, Battista, Luca Didaci, Giorgio Fumera, and Fabio Roli. 2013. Poisoning Attacks to Compromise Face Templates. In *2013 International Conference on Biometrics (ICB)*, 1–7. New York: IEEE. 165

Binns, Reuben. 2021. Fairness in Machine Learning: Lessons from Political Philosophy. *arXiv* 1712.03586: 1–11. `https://arxiv.org/abs/1712.03586`. 111

Birhane, Abeba, and Jelle van Dijk. 2020. Robot Rights?: Let's Talk about Human Welfare Instead. In *AIES '20: Proceedings of the AAAI/ACM Conference on AI, Ethics, and Society*, 207–213. 201

Birhane, Abeba, Vinay Uday Prabhu, and Emmanuel Kahembwe. 2021. Multimodal Datasets: Misogyny, Pornography, and Malignant Stereotypes. *arXiv* 2110.01963: 1–33. `https://arxiv.org/abs/2110.01963`. 130, 211

Birhane, Abeba, Jelle van Dijk, and Frank Pasquale. 2024. Debunking Robot Rights Metaphysically, Ethically, and Legally. *arXiv* 2404.10072: 1–23. `https://arxiv.org/abs/2404.10072`. 201

Birhane, Abeba, Pratyusha Kalluri, Dallas Card, William Agnew, Ravit Dotan, and Michelle Bao. 2022. The Values Encoded in Machine Learning Research. In *FAccT '22: 2022 ACM Conference on Fairness, Accountability, and Transparency*, 173–184. New York: Association for Computing Machinery. 145, 146, 218, 246, 251, 252, 253, 260

Birhane, Abeba, Vinay Prabhu, Sang Han, Vishnu Naresh Boddeti, and Alexandra Sasha Luccioni. 2023. Into the LAIONs Den: Investigating Hate in Multimodal Datasets. *arXiv* 2311.03449: 1–17. `https://arxiv.org/abs/2311.03449`. 130

Bishop, Christopher M. 2006. *Pattern Recognition and Machine Learning*. New York: Springer. 64

Bishop, John. 1989. *Natural Agency: An Essay on the Causal Theory of Action*. Cambridge: Cambridge University Press. 183

Bisk, Yonatan, Ari Holtzman, Jesse Thomason, Jacob Andreas, Yoshua Bengio, Joyce Chai, Mirella Lapata, Angeliki Lazaridou, Jonathan May, Aleksandr Nisnevich, et al. 2020. Experience Grounds Language. In *Proceedings of the 2020 Conference on Empirical Methods in Natural Language Processing (EMNLP)*, eds. Bonnie Webber, Trevor Cohn, Yulan He, and Yang Liu, 8718–8735. Association for Computational Linguistics. 241

Bjørgen, Edvard P., Simen Madsen, Therese S. Bjørknes, Fredrik V. Heimsæter, Robin Håvik, Morten Linderud, Per-Niklas Longberg, Louise A. Dennis, and Marija Slavkovik. 2018. Cake, Death, and Trolleys: Dilemmas as Benchmarks of Ethical Decision-making. *AIES '18: Proceedings of the 2018 AAAI/ACM Conference on AI, Ethics, and Society*. 213, 225

Blattmann, Andreas, Robin Rombach, Huan Ling, Tim Dockhorn, Seung Wook Kim, Sanja Fidler, and Karsten Kreis. 2023a. Align Your Latents: High-Resolution Video Synthesis with Latent Diffusion Models. *arXiv* 2304.08818: 1–44. `https://arxiv.org/abs/2304.08818`. 132

Blattmann, Andreas, Tim Dockhorn, Sumith Kulal, Daniel Mendelevitch, Maciej Kilian, Dominik Lorenz, Yam Levi, Zion English, Vikram Voleti, Adam Letts, et al. 2023b. Stable Video Diffusion: Scaling Latent Video Diffusion Models to Large Datasets. *arXiv* 2311.15127: 1–30. `https://arxiv.org/abs/2311.15127`. 132

Blattner, Laura, and Scott Nelson. 2021. How Costly Is Noise? Data and Disparities in Consumer Credit. *arXiv* 2105.07554: 1–86. `https://arxiv.org/abs/2105.07554`. 8

Boehm, Christopher. 2000. Conflict and the Evolution of Social Control. *Journal of Consciousness Studies* 7 (1–2): 79–101. 233

Boge, Florian J. 2022. Two Dimensions of Opacity and the Deep Learning Predicament. *Minds and Machines* 32: 43–75. 121, 136

Bommasani, Rishi, Drew A. Hudson, Ehsan Adeli, Russ Altman, Simran Arora, Sydney von Arx, Michael S. Bernstein, Jeannette Bohg, Antoine Bosselut, Emma Brunskill, et al. 2022. On the Opportunities and Risks of Foundation Models. *arXiv* 2108.07258: 1–214. `https://arxiv.org/abs/2108.07258`. 63

Bonnemains, Vincent, Claire Saurel, and Catherine Tessier. 2018. Embedded Ethics: Some Technical and Ethical Challenges. *Ethics and Information Technology* 20 (1): 41–58. 195

Boole, George. 1854. *An Investigation of the Laws of Thought: The Mathematical Theories of Logic and Probabilities*. London: Macmillan and Company. 23

Boolos, George. 1968. Review of 'Minds, Machines and Gödel', by J.R. Lucas, and 'God, the Devil, and Gödel'. *Journal of Symbolic Logic* 33: 613–615. 24

Borgeaud, Sebastian, Arthur Mensch, Jordan Hoffmann, Trevor Cai, Eliza Rutherford, Katie Millican, George van den Driessche, Jean-Baptiste Lespiau, Bogdan Damoc, Aidan Clark, et al. 2022. Improving Language Models by Retrieving from Trillions of Tokens. *arXiv* 2112.04426: 1–43. `https://arxiv.org/abs/2112.04426`. 241

Bostrom, Nick. 2003. Ethical Issues in Advanced Artificial Intelligence. In *Science Fiction and Philosophy: from Time Travel to Superintelligence*, ed. Susan Schneider, 277–284. West Sussex: Wiley & Blackwell. 70

Bostrom, Nick. 2014. *Superintelligence: Paths, Dangers, Strategies*. Oxford: Oxford University Press. 70, 238, 239, 272, 277, 280, 281

Brand, Myles. 1984. *Intending and Acting: Toward a Naturalized Action Theory*. Cambridge, MA: The MIT Press. 183

Bratman, Michael E. 1987. *Intention, Plans, and Practical Reason*. Cambridge, MA: Harvard University Press. 183

Brendan, Avent, González Javier, Diethe Tom, Paleyes Andrei, and Balle Borja. 2020. Automatic Discovery of Privacy–Utility Pareto Fronts. *Proceedings on Privacy Enhancing Technologies* 2020 (4): 5–23. 148

Brette, Romain. 2022. Brains as Computers: Metaphor, Analogy, Theory, or Fact? *Frontiers in Ecology and Evolution* 10: 878729. 22

Bright, Peter. 2016. Tay, the Neo-Nazi Millennial Chatbot, Gets Autopsied. *Ars Technica* Mar. (26). `https://arstechnica.com/information-technology/2016/03/tay-the-neo-nazi-millennial-chatbot-gets-autopsied`. 103, 165

Bringsjord, Selmer. 1992/2012. *What Robots Can and Can't Be*. Dordrecht: Springer. 184

Broussard, Meredith. 2018. *Artificial Unintelligence: How Computers Misunderstand the World*. Cambridge, MA: The MIT Press. 72, 151, 157

Broussard, Meredith. 2023. *More than a Glitch: Confronting Race, Gender, and Ability Bias in Tech*. Cambridge, MA: The MIT Press. 72, 98, 102, 151

Brown, James Robert, and Yiftach Fehige. 2019. Thought Experiments. In *The Stanford Encyclopedia of Philosophy*, ed. Edward N. Zalta. Metaphysics Research Lab, Stanford University. `https://plato.stanford.edu/archives/win2019/entries/thought-experiment/`. 214

Brown, Tom B., Benjamin Mann, Nick Ryder, Melanie Subbiah, Jared Kaplan, Prafulla Dhariwal, Arvind Neelakantan, Pranav Shyam, Girish Sastry, Amanda Askell, et al. 2020. Language Models Are Few-Shot Learners. *arXiv* 2005.14165: 1–75. `https://arxiv.org/abs/2005.14165`. 53, 128, 241

Bryson, A. E., and Y. C. Ho. 1969. *Applied Optimal Control*. Waltham, MA: Blaisdell. 38

Bryson, Joanna J. 2008. Embodiment versus Memetics. *Mind & Society* 7 (1): 77–94. 233

Bryson, Joanna J. 2018. Patiency Is Not a Virtue: The Design of Intelligent Systems and Systems of Ethics. *Ethics and Information Technology* 20: 15–26. 233

Bubeck, Sébastien, Varun Chandrasekaran, Ronen Eldan, Johannes Gehrke, Eric Horvitz, Ece Kamar, Peter Lee, Yin Tat Lee, Yuanzhi Li, Scott Lundberg, et al. 2023. Sparks of Artificial General Intelligence: Early Experiments with GPT-4. *arXiv* 2303.12712: 1–155. `https://arxiv.org/abs/2303.12712`. 32, 284

Buchanan, Bruce G. 2005. A (Very) Brief History of Artificial Intelligence. *AI Magazine* 26 (4): 53–60. 22

Buchanan, Bruce G., and Richard O. Duda. 1983. Principles of Rule-Based Expert Systems. *Advances in Computers* 22: 163–216. 35

Buchanan, Bruce G., and Edward A. Feigenbaum. 1978. Dendral and Meta-Dendral: Their Applications Dimension. *Artificial Intelligence* 11: 5–24. 34

Buckner, Cameron J. 2019. Deep Learning: A Philosophical Introduction. *Philosophy Compass* 14: 12625. 123, 236

Bullard, Robert D. 1993. The Threat of Environmental Racism. *Natural Resources & Environment* 7 (3): 55–56. 150

Buolamwini, Joy. 2023. *Unmasking AI: My Mission to Protect What Is Human in a World of Machines*. New York: Penguin Random House. 103, 151, 158

Buolamwini, Joy, and Timnit Gebru. 2018. Gender Shades: Intersectional Accuracy Disparities in Commercial Gender Classification. In *Proceedings of the 1st Conference on Fairness, Accountability and Transparency*, Vol. 81, 77–91. Proceedings of Machine Learning Research (PMLR). 103, 108, 111, 114

Burke, Peggy B. 2003. *A Handbook for New Parole Board Members: Part of a Resource Kit for New Parole Board Members*. Association of Paroling Authorities International and the National Institute of Corrections. 105

Burrell, Jenna. 2016. How the Machine 'Thinks': Understanding Opacity in Machine Learning Algorithms. *Big Data & Society* 3 (1). 121, 126, 136, 155

Burton, Emanuelle, Judy Goldsmith, Sven Koenig, Benjamin Kuipers, Nicholas Mattei, and Toby Walsh. 2016. Ethical Considerations in Artificial Intelligence Courses. *AI Magazine* 38 (2): 22–34. 184

Butler, Samuel. 1872. *Erewhon: or, Over the Range*. United Kingdom: Trübner and Ballantyne. 1

Cameron, James. 1984. *The Terminator*. Orion Pictures. 107 min. 5, 7, 36

Cantwell Smith, Brian. 2019. *The Promise of Artificial Intelligence: Reckoning and Judgment*. Cambridge, MA: The MIT Press. 236

Cao, Qingqing, Aruna Balasubramanian, and Niranjan Balasubramanian. 2020. Towards Accurate and Reliable Energy Measurement of NLP Models. *arXiv* 2010.05248: 1–8. `https://arxiv.org/abs/2010.05248`. 149

Carnap, Rudolf. 1928. *Der Logische Aufbau der Welt*. Berlin: Welkreisv. 245

Carter, J. Adam. 2023. *Digital Knowledge: A Philosophical Introduction*. London: Routledge. 274

Carton, Samuel, Jennifer Helsby, Kenneth Joseph, Ayesha Mahmud, Youngsoo Park, Joe Walsh, Crystal Cody, C. P. T. Estella Patterson, Lauren Haynes, and Rayid Ghani. 2016. Identifying Police Officers at Risk of Adverse Events. In *Proceedings of the 22nd ACM SIGKDD International Conference on Knowledge Discovery and Data Mining, KDD '16*, 67–76. New York: Association for Computing Machinery. 143

Caruana, Rich, Yin Lou, Johannes Gehrke, Paul Koch, Marc Sturm, and Noemie Elhadad. 2015. Intelligible Models for HealthCare: Predicting Pneumonia Risk and Hospital 30-day Readmission. In *KDD '15: Proceedings of the 21st ACM SIGKDD International Conference on Knowledge Discovery and Data Mining*, 1721–1730. New York: Association for Computing Machinery. 126

Cave, Stephen, Kanta Dihal, and Sarah Dillon, eds. 2020. *AI Narratives: A History of Imaginative Thinking about Intelligent Machines*. Oxford: Oxford University Press. 21

Cave, Stephen, Claire Craig, Kanta Dihal, Sarah Dillon, Jessica Montgomery, Beth Singler, and Lindsay Taylor. 2018. Portrayals and Perceptions of AI and Why They Matter. In *Apollo - University of Cambridge Repository*, 1–28. Cambridge: Cambridge University Press. `https://doi:10.17863/CAM.34502`. 2, 5

Chalmers, David. 1996. *The Conscious Mind: In Search of a Fundamental Theory*. Oxford: Oxford University Press. 4

Chalmers, David. 2010. The Singularity: A Philosophical Analysis. *Journal of Consciousness Studies* 17: 7–65. 275, 283

Chang, Huiwen, Jingwan Lu, Fisher Yu, and Adam Finkelstein. 2018. PairedCycleGAN: Asymmetric Style Transfer for Applying and Removing Makeup. In *Proceedings of the IEEE/CVF Conference on Computer Vision and Pattern Recognition*, 40–48. New York: Institute of Electrical and Electronics Engineers. 212

Chomsky, Noam. 1965. *Aspects of the Theory of Syntax*. Cambridge, MA: The MIT Press. 229

Chomsky, Noam. 1980. *Rules and Representations*. London: Basil Blackwell. 229

Chomsky, Noam. 1995. *The Minimalist Program*. Cambridge, MA: The MIT Press. 230

Chouldechova, Alexandra. 2017. Fair Prediction with Disparate Impact: A Study of Bias in Recidivism Prediction Instruments. *Big Data* 5 (2): 153–163. 107

Chowdhery, Aakanksha, Sharan Narang, Jacob Devlin, Maarten Bosma, Gaurav Mishra, Adam Roberts, Paul Barham, Hyung Won Chung, Charles Sutton, Sebastian Gehrmann, et al. 2022. PaLM: Scaling Language Modeling with Pathways. *arXiv* 2204.02311: 1–87. https://arxiv.org/abs/2204.02311. 149

Christian, Brian. 2020. *The Alignment Problem: Machine Learning and Human Values*. New York: W. W. Norton & Company. 67, 68, 74, 105, 114

Christiano, Paul, Jan Leike, Tom B. Brown, Miljan Martic, Shane Legg, and Dario Amodei. 2023. Deep Reinforcement Learning from Human Preferences. *arXiv* 1706.03741: 1–17. https://arxiv.org/abs/1706.03741. 170

Church, Alonzo. 1932. A Set of Postulates for the Foundation of Logic. *Annals of Mathematics* 33 (2): 346–366. 23

Church, Alonzo. 1936. An Unsolvable Problem of Elementary Number Theory. *American Journal of Mathematics* 58 (2): 345–363. 24

Clark, Andy. 1987. The Kludge in the Machine. *Mind and Language* 2 (4): 277–300. 122

Clark, Andy, and David J. Chalmers. 1998. The Extended Mind. *Analysis* 58 (1): 7–19. 273

Clark, Jack, and Dario Amodei. 2016. Faulty Reward Functions in the Wild. *OpenAI*. https://openai.com/research/faulty-reward-functions. 74

Coeckelbergh, Mark. 2020. *AI Ethics*. Cambridge, MA: The MIT Press. 21

Collins, Patricia Hill. 1990. *Black Feminist Thought: Knowledge, Consciousness, and the Politics of Empowerment*. New York and London: Routledge. 108

Combahee River Collective. 1977. Combahee River Collective Statement. http://circuitous.org/scraps/combahee.html. 108

Confucius. 1979. *Confucius: The Analects*. New York: Penguin. 193

Cooper, Gregory F., Constantin F. Aliferis, Richard Ambrosino, John M. Aronis, Bruce G. Buchanan, Richard Caruana, Michael J. Fine, Clark Glymour, Geoffrey Gordon, Barbara H. Hanusad, et al. 1997. An Evaluation of Machine-Learning Methods for Predicting Pneumonia Mortality. *Artificial Intelligence in Medicine* 9 (2): 107–138. 125

Cooper, Gregory F., Vijoy Abraham, Constantin F. Aliferis, John M. Aronis, Bruce G. Buchanan, Richard Caruana, Michael J. Fine, Janine E. Janosky, Gary Livingston, Tom Mitchell, et al. 2005. Predicting Dire Outcomes of Patients with Community Acquired Pneumonia. *Journal of Biomedical Informatics* 38 (5): 347–366. 125

Copeland, B. Jack. 2020. The Church-Turing Thesis. In *The Stanford Encyclopedia of Philosophy*, ed. Edward N. Zalta. Metaphysics Research Lab, Stanford University. https://plato.stanford.edu/archives/sum2020/entries/church-turing/. 24

Copernicus, Nicolaus. 1543/1995. *On the Revolutions of Heavenly Spheres*. Amherst, NY: Prometheus. 246

Costanza-Chock, Sasha. 2020. *Design Justice: Community-Led Practices to Build the Worlds We Need*. Cambridge, MA: The MIT Press. 109, 151, 256, 257, 261

Crawford, Kate. 2021. *Atlas of AI*. New Haven, CT: Yale University Press. 2, 20, 150, 158

Crawford, Kate. 2024. Generative AI's Environmental Costs Are Soaring—and Mostly Secret. *Nature* 626: 1. 149

Crawford, Kate, and Trevor Paglen. 2019. Excavating AI: The Politics of Training Sets for Machine Learning. *The AI Now Institute* Sep. (19). https://excavating.ai. 211

Creel, Kathleen A. 2020. Transparency in Complex Computational Systems. *Philosophy of Science* 87 (4): 568–589. 82, 120, 121, 122, 123, 124, 125, 131, 136

Crenshaw, Kimberle. 1989. Demarginalizing the Intersection of Race and Sex: A Black Feminist Critique of Antidiscrimination Doctrine, Feminist Theory, and Antiracist Politics. *University of Chicago Legal Forum* 8 (6): 139–167. 108

Crenshaw, Kimberle. 1991. Mapping the Margins: Intersectionality, Identity Politics, and Violence Against Women of Color. *Stanford Law Review* 43 (6): 1241–1299. 108

Crevier, Daniel. 1993. *AI: The Tumultuous Search for Artificial Intelligence*. New York: Basic Books. 29, 31, 41

Cristianini, M., and J. Shawe-Taylor. 2000. *An Introduction to Support Vector Machines*. Cambridge: Cambridge University Press. 57

Cronenberg, David. 1988. *Dead Ringers*. Morgan Creek Productions, Telefilm Canada, and Mantle Clinic II. 115 min. 6

Culicover, Peter W., and Ray Jackendoff. 2005. *Simpler Syntax*. Oxford: Oxford University Press. 230

Cybenko, George. 1989. Approximation by Superpositions of a Sigmoidal Function. *Mathematics of Control, Signals and Systems* 2 (4): 303–314. 49

Dahl, Audun. 2015. The Developing Social Context of Infant Helping in Two US Samples. *Child Development* 86: 1080–1093. 234

Dahl, Audun. 2018. New Beginnings: An Interactionist and Constructivist Approach to Early Moral Development. *Human Development* 61 (4–5): 232–247. 234

Dahl, Audun, and Lizbeth Kim. 2014. Why Is It Bad to Make a Mess? Preschoolers' Conceptions of Pragmatic Norms. *Cognitive Development* 32: 12–22. 234

Danaher, John, and Henrik Skaug Sætra. 2023. Mechanisms of Techno-Moral Change: A Taxonomy and Overview. *Ethical Theory and Moral Practice*. 268

Danks, David, and Alex John London. 2017. Algorithmic Bias in Autonomous Systems. *Proceedings of the 26th International Joint Conference in Artificial Intelligence (IJCAI 2017)* 17 (2017): 4691–4697. 101, 102, 110, 114

Darrach, Brad. 1970. Meet Shaky, the First Electronic Person. The Fearsome Reality of a Machine with a Mind of Its Own. *Life Magazine* Nov. (20): 58–68. 32

Davidson, Donald. 1963. Actions, Reasons, and Causes. *The Journal of Philosophy* LX (23): 685–700. 183

Davidson, Donald. 1971. Agency. In *Agent, Action, and Reason*, eds. Ausonio Marras, R. N. Bronaugh, and Robert W. Binkley, 1–37. Toronto: University of Toronto Press. 183

Davies, Harry, Bethan McKernan, and Dan Sabbagh. 2023. 'The Gospel': How Israel Uses AI to Select Bombing Targets in Gaza. *The Guardian* Dec (01). https://www.theguardian.com/world/2023/dec/01/the-gospel-how-israel-uses-ai-to-select-bombing-targets. 153

Davis, Randall, Bruce G. Buchanan, and Edward H. Shortliff. 1977. Production Rules as a Representation of a Knowledge-Based Consultation Program. *Artificial Intelligence* 8 (1): 15–45. 35

de Boer, Jelle. 2011. Moral Ape Philosophy. *Biology & Philosophy* 26 (6): 891–904. 231

de Waal, Frans. 1996. *Good Natured: The Origins of Right and Wrong in Humans and Other Animals*. Cambridge, MA: Harvard University Press. 231, 234

de Waal, Frans. 2006. *Primates and Philosophers*. Princeton: Princeton University Press. 231

Dehghani, Mostafa, Basil Mustafa, Josip Djolonga, Jonathan Heek, Matthias Minderer, Mathilde Caron, Andreas Steiner, Joan Puigcerver, Robert Geirhos, Ibrahim Alabdulmohsin, et al. 2023. Patch n' Pack: NaViT, a Vision Transformer for any Aspect Ratio and Resolution. *arXiv* 2307.06304: 1–26. https://arxiv.org/abs/2307.06304. 132

DellaVigna, Stefano, and Matthew Gentzkow. 2017. Uniform Pricing in US Retail Chains (No. w23996) National Bureau of Economic Research. 8

Deng, Jia, Wei Dong, Richard Socher, Li-Jia Li, Kai Li, and Fei-Fei Li. 2009. ImageNet: A Large-Scale Hierarchical Image Database. In *2009 IEEE Conference on Computer Vision and Pattern Recognition*, 248–255. New York: IEEE. 209

Dennett, Daniel C. 1984. *Elbow Room: The Varieties of Free Will Worth Wanting*. Cambridge, MA: The MIT Press. 214

Dennett, Daniel C. 1992. *Consciousness Explained*. Boston: Little, Brown and Company. 214

Dennett, Daniel C. 2013. *Intuition Pumps and Other Tools for Thinking*. New York: W. W. Norton & Company. 214

Devlin, Jacob, Ming-Wei Chang, Kenton Lee, and Kristina Toutanova. 2019. BERT: Pre-training of Deep Bidirectional Transformers for Language Understanding. *arXiv* 1810.04805: 1–16. `https://arxiv.org/abs/1810.04805`. 241

Dewey, Caitlin. 2016. Meet Tay, the Creepy-Realistic Robot Who Talks Just Like a Teen. *The Washington Post* Mar. (23). `https://www.washingtonpost.com/news/the-intersect/wp/2016/03/23/meet-tay-the-creepy-realistic-robot-who-talks-just-like-a-teen/`. 103, 165

Dewey, Daniel. 2011. Learning What to Value. In *AGI 2011: 4th International Conference on Artificial General Intelligence*, eds. J. Schmidhuber, K. R. Thórisson, and M. Looks. Vol. 6830 of *Lecture notes in computer science*, 309–314. Berlin, Heidelberg: Springer. 70

Dietrich, Eric. 2001. Homo sapiens 2.0: Why We Should Build the Better Robots of Our Nature. *Journal of Experimental & Theoretical Artificial Intelligence* 13 (4): 323–328. 198

D'Ignazio, Catherine, and Lauren F. Klein. 2020. *Data Feminism*. Cambridge, MA: The MIT Press. 108, 158, 261

Dignum, Virginia. 2018. Ethics in Artificial Intelligence: Introduction to the Special Issue. *Ethics and Information Technology* 20 (1): 1–3. 183

Dinur, Irit, and Kobbi Nissim. 2003. Revealing Information While Preserving Privacy. In *PODS '03: Proceedings of the Twenty-Second ACM SIGMOD-SIGACT-SIGART Symposium on Principles of Database Systems*, 202–210. New York: Association for Computing Machinery. 148

Dorato, Mauro. 2004. Epistemic and Nonepistemic Values in Science. In *Science, Values and Objectivity*, eds. Peter Machamer and Gereon Wolters, 52–77. Pittsburgh: Pittsburgh University Press. 247

Doris, J. M. 1998. Persons, Situations, and Virtue Ethics. *Noûs* 32 (4): 504–530. 199

Dosovitskiy, Alexey, Lucas Beyer, Alexander Kolesnikov, Dirk Weissenborn, Xiaohua Zhai, Thomas Unterthiner, Mostafa Dehghani, Matthias Minderer, Georg Heigold, Sylvain Gelly, et al. 2021. An Image is Worth 16x16 Words: Transformers for Image Recognition at Scale. *arXiv* 2010.11929: 1–22. `https://arxiv.org/abs/2010.11929`. 39

Dotan, Ravit. 2021. Theory Choice, Non-Epistemic Values, and Machine Learning. *Synthese* 198 (11): 11081–11101. 250, 253, 260

Dotan, Ravit, and Smitha Milli. 2019. Value-laden Disciplinary Shifts in Machine Learning. *arXiv* 1912.01172: 1–10. `https://arxiv.org/abs/1912.01172`. 144

Douglas, Heather. 2007. Rejecting the Ideal of Value-Free Science. In *Value-Free Science? Ideals and Illusions*, eds. H. Kincaid and J. Dupré A. Wylie, 120–139. Oxford: Oxford University Press. 248

Douglas, Heather. 2017. Why Inductive Risk Requires Values in Science. In *Current Controversies in Values and Science*, eds. Kevin C. Elliott and Daniel Steel, 81–93. Oxford: Routledge. 248

Douglas, Heather. 2023. Science and Values: The Pervasive Entanglement. In *Democratizing Risk Governance: Bridging Science, Expertise, Deliberation and Public Values*, ed. Monica Gattinger, 55–77. Cham: Palgrave Macmillan. 246

Dretske, Fred. 1988. *Explaining Behavior: Reasons in a World of Causes*. Cambridge, MA: The MIT Press. 183

Dreyfus, Hubert. 1972. *What Computers Can't Do*. Cambridge, MA: The MIT Press. 33

Dreyfus, Hubert L. 1965. *Alchemy and Artificial Intelligence*. RAND Corporation. 33

Dreyfus, Stuart. 1962. The Numerical Solution of Variational Problems. *Journal of Mathematical Analysis and Applications* 5 (1): 30–45. 63

Dua, Dheeru, and Casey Graff. 2017. UCI Machine Learning Repository. `http://archive.ics.uci.edu`. 208

Dupré, John. 2007. Fact and Value. In *Value-Free Science?: Ideals and Illusions*, eds. Harold Kincaid, John Dupré, and Alison Wylie, 24–71. Oxford: Oxford University Press. 249

Dwork, Cynthia. 2008. Differential Privacy: A Survey of Results. In *Theory and Applications of Models of Computation (TAMC)*, eds. Manindra Agrawal, Dingzhu Du, Zhenhua Duan, and Angsheng Li, 1–19. Berlin, Heidelberg: Springer. 148

Dyson, George B. 1997. *Darwin Among the Machines: The Evolution of Global Intelligence*. New York: Basic Books. 22

Eche, Thomas, Lawrence H. Schwartz, Fatima-Zohra Mokrane, and Laurent Dercle. 2021. Toward Generalizability in the Deployment of Artificial Intelligence in Radiology: Role of Computation Stress Testing to Overcome Underspecification. *Radiology Artificial Intelligence* 3 (6): 210097. 96

Eckersley, Peter. 2019. Impossibility and Uncertainty Theorems in AI Value Alignment (Or Why Your AGI Should Not Have a Utility Function). *arXiv* 1901.00064: 1–13. `https://arxiv.org/abs/1901.00064`. 70

Ecoffet, Adrien, Jeff Clune, and Joel Lehman. 2020. Open Questions in Creating Safe Open-ended AI: Tensions Between Control and Creativity. *arXiv* 2006.07495: 1–9. `https://arxiv.org/abs/2006.07495`. 74

Edwards, Paul N. 1996. *The Closed World: Computers and the Politics of Discourse in Cold War America.* Cambridge, MA: The MIT Press. 35

Eisenberg, Nancy, Richard A. Fabes, and Tracy L. Spinrad. 2007. Prosocial Development. In *Handbook of Child Psychology and Developmental Science: Volume III. Social, Emotional, and Personality Development*, eds. M. E. Lamb and R. M. Lerner, 610–656. Hoboken, NJ: Wiley & Sons. 234

Eisenhardt, Kathleen M. 1989. Agency Theory: An Assessment and Review. *The Academy of Management Review* 14 (1): 57–74. 76

Elliott, Kevin C., and Daniel J. McKaughan. 2014. Nonepistemic Values and the Multiple Goals of Science. *Philosophy of Science* 81: 1–21. 248

Enç, Berent. 2003. *How We Act: Causes, Reasons, and Intentions.* Oxford: Oxford University Press. 183

Engine, Market Research. 2021. Emotion Detection and Recognition (EDR) Market Research Report, Technical report, Market Research Engine. `https://www.marketresearchengine.com/reportdetails/emotion-detection-and-recognition-edr-market`. 100

Ensign, Danielle, Sorelle A. Friedler, Scott Neville, Carlos Scheidegger, and Suresh Venkatasubramanian. 2018. Runaway Feedback Loops in Predictive Policing. In *Proceedings of the 1st Conference on Fairness, Accountability and Transparency*, eds. Sorelle A. Friedler and Christo Wilson. Vol. 81 of *Proceedings of Machine Learning Research*, 160–171. PMLR. 98, 100

Erasmus, Adrian, Tyler D. P. Brunet, and Eyal Fisher. 2021. What Is Interpretability? *Philosophy & Technology* 34: 833–862. 127, 136

Etienne, Hubert. 2020. When AI Ethics Goes Astray: A Case Study of Autonomous Vehicles. *Social Science Computing Review* 40 (1): 236–246. 215

Ettinger, Allyson. 2020. What BERT Is Not: Lessons from a New Suite of Psycholinguistic Diagnostics for Language Models. *arXiv* 1907.13528: 1–20. `https://arxiv.org/abs/1907.13528`. 241

Eubanks, Virginia. 2018. *Automating Inequality: How Tech Tools Profile, Police, and Punish the Poor.* New York: MacMillan. 151, 157

Evin, Morgane, Antonio Hidalgo-Munoz, Adolphe James Béquet, Fabien Moreau, Helène Tattegrain, Catherine Berthelon, Alexandra Fort, and Christophe Jallais. 2022. Personality Trait Prediction by Machine Learning Using Physiological Data and Driving Behavior. *Machine Learning with Applications* 9: 100353. 99

Eykholt, Kevin, Ivan Evtimov, Earlence Fernandes, Bo Li, Amir Rahmati, Chaowei Xiao, Atul Prakash, Tadayoshi Kohno, and Dawn Song. 2018. Robust Physical-World Attacks on Deep Learning Models. *arXiv* 1707.08945: 1–11. `https://arxiv.org/abs/1707.08945`. 165

Eze, Michael Onyebuchi. 2010. *Intellectual History in Contemporary South Africa.* New York: Palgrave Macmillan. 193

Facchini, Alessandro, and Alberto Termine. 2021. Towards a Taxonomy for the Opacity of AI Systems. In *PTAI 2021: Philosophy and Theory of Artificial Intelligence 2021*, ed. Vincent C. Müller, 73–89. Cham: Springer. 121, 136

Falbo, Arianna, and Travis LaCroix. 2022. Est-ce que vous compute? Code-Switching, Cultural Identity, and AI. *Feminist Philosophy Quarterly* 8 (3/4): 1–24. `https://ojs.lib.uwo.ca/index.php/fpq/article/view/14264`. 129, 212

Farrell, Joseph, and Matthew Rabin. 1996. Cheap Talk. *The Journal of Economic Perspectives* 10 (3): 103–118. 231

Fazelpour, Sina, and David Danks. 2021. Algorithmic Bias: Senses, Sources, Solutions. *Philosophy Compass* 16: 12760. 93, 110, 114

Feigenbaum, Edward A., and Pamela McCorduck. 1983. *The Fifth Generation: Artificial Intelligence and Japan's Computer Challenge to the World.* Reading: Addison-Wesley. 35

Fellbaum, Christiane. 1998. *WordNet: An Electronic Lexical Database*. Cambridge, MA: The MIT Press. 209

Fitch, W. Tecumseh. 2010. *The Evolution of Language*. Cambridge: Cambridge University Press. 229, 230

FitzPatrick, William J. 2012. The Doctrine of Double Effect: Intention and Permissibility. *Philosophy Compass* 7 (3): 183–196. 214

Flack, Jessica C., and Frans de Waal. 2000. Any Animal Whatever: Darwinian Building Blocks of Morality in Monkeys and Apes. *Journal of Consciousness Studies* 7 (1–2): 1–29. 231

Fleisher, Will. 2022. Understanding, Idealization, and Explainable AI. *Episteme* 19 (4): 534–560. 126

Floridi, Luciano, and Jeff W. Sanders. 2004. On the Morality of Artificial Agents. *Minds and Machines* 14: 349–379. 187

Fodor, Jerry A. 1998. There Are No Recognitional Concepts—Not Even RED, Part 2: the Plot Thickens. In *In Critical Condition: Polemical Essays on Cognitive Science and the Philosophy of Mind*, 49–62. Cambridge, MA: The MIT Press. 229

Foot, Philippa. 1967. The Problem of Abortion and the Doctrine of Double Effect. *The Oxford Review* 5: 5–15. 213, 214

Frege, Friedrich Ludwig Gottlob. 1923. Logische Untersuchungen. Dritter Teil: Gedankengefüge. *Beiträge zur Philosophie des deutschen Idealismus* III: 36–51. Reprinted in Stoothoff, R. H. (Trans.) (1963). "Compound Thoughts" *Mind* 72(285): 1–17. 229

Frege, Gottlob. 1879. *Begriffsschrift eine der arithmetischen nachgebildete Formelsprache des reinen Denkens*. Lubrecht & Cramer. 23

Fricker, Miranda. 1991. Reason and Emotion. *Radical Philosophy* 57 (Spring): 14–19. 214

Friedman, Batya, and Helen Nissenbaum. 1996. Bias in Computer Systems. *ACM Transactions on Information Systems* 14 (3): 330–347. 102, 114

Frigg, Roman, and Stephan Hartmann. 2020. Models in Science. In *The Stanford Encyclopedia of Philosophy*, ed. Edward N. Zalta. Metaphysics Research Lab, Stanford University. `https://plato.stanford.edu/archives/spr2020/entries/models-science/`. 45

Fukushima, Kunihiko. 1969. Visual Feature Extraction by a Multilayered Network of Analog Threshold Elements. *IEEE Transactions on Systems Science and Cybernetics* 5 (4): 322–333. 48

Fukushima, Kunihiko. 1979. Neural Network Model for a Mechanism of Pattern Recognition Unaffected by Shift in Position-Neocognitron. *IEICE Technical Report* 62 (10): 658–665. 63

Future of Life Institute. 2017. Asilomar AI Principles. `https://futureoflife.org/open-letter/ai-principles/`. 71

Gabriel, Iason. 2020. Artificial Intelligence, Values, and Alignment. *Minds and Machines* 30: 411–437. 67, 69, 70, 73, 173, 183, 188

Gabriel, Iason, and Vafa Ghazavi. 2022. The Challenge of Value Alignment: From Fairer Algorithms to AI Safety. In *Oxford Handbook of Digital Ethics*, ed. Carissa Véliz, 336–355. Oxford: Oxford University Press. 69

Galilei, Galileo. 1632/2001. *On the Revolutions of Heavenly Spheres*. New York: Modern Library. 246

Garland, Alex. 2014. *Ex Machina*. Film4 and DNA Films. 108 min. 4, 284

Garvey, Colin. 2018. Broken Promises & Empty Threats: The Evolution of AI in the USA, 1956–1996. *Technology's Stories* 6 (1). 35, 36

Ge, Songwei, Seungjun Nah, Guilin Liu, Tyler Poon, Andrew Tao, Bryan Catanzaro, David Jacobs, Jia-Bin Huang, Ming-Yu Liu, and Yogesh Balaji. 2023. Preserve Your Own Correlation: A Noise Prior for Video Diffusion Models. *arXiv* 2305.10474: 1–15. `https://arxiv.org/abs/2305.10474`. 132

Gebru, Timnit, and Émile P. Torres. 2024. The TESCREAL Bundle: Eugenics and the Promise of Utopia Through Artificial General Intelligence. *First Monday* 29 (4): 1–42. 39, 190, 271, 275

Gebru, Timnit, Jamie Morgenstern, Briana Vecchione, Jennifer Wortman Vaughan, Hanna Wallach, Hal Daumé III, and Kate Crawford. 2021. Datasheets for Datasets. *arXiv* 1803.09010: 1–18. `https://arxiv.org/abs/1803.09010`. 96, 131, 211

Geirhos, Robert, Jörn-Henrik Jacobsen, Claudio Michaelis, Richard Zemel, Wieland Brendel, Matthias Bethge, and Felix A. Wichmann. 2023. Shortcut Learning in Deep Neural Networks. *arXiv* 2004.07780. `https://arxiv.org/abs/2004.07780`. 96

Gemini Team, Google. 2023. Gemini: A Family of Highly Capable Multimodal Models, Technical report, Google. https://storage.googleapis.com/deepmind-media/gemini/gemini_1_report.pdf. 131

Gibbons, Robert. 1998. Incentives in Organizations. *Journal of Economic Perspectives* 12 (4): 115–132. 76, 266

Gilligan, Carol. 1982. *In a Different Voice*. Cambridge, MA: Harvard University Press. 193

Glorot, Xavier, Antoine Bordes, and Yoshua Bengio. 2011. Deep Sparse Rectifier Neural Networks. In *Proceedings of the Fourteenth International Conference on Artificial Intelligence and Statistics*, 315–323. Proceedings of Machine Learning Research (PLMR). 48

Godard, Jean-Luc. 1965. *Alphaville: une étrange aventure de Lemmy Caution*. Athos Films. 99 min. 4, 284

Gödel, Kurt. 1931. Über formal unentscheidbare Sätze der Principia Mathematica und verwandter Systeme, I. *Monatshefte für Mathematik und Physik* 38 (1): 173–198. 23

Goebel, Randy. 2008. Folk Reducibility and AI-Complete Problems. In *KI 2008: Advances in Artificial Intelligence*, eds. A. R. Dengel, K. Berns, T. M. Breuel, F. Bomarius, and T. R. Roth-Berghofer. Vol. 5243 of *Lecture Notes in Computer Science*, 54–57. Berlin, Heidelberg: Springer. 238

Goetze, Trystan S. 2024. AI Art Is Theft: Labour, Extraction, and Exploitation—Or, On the Dangers of Stochastic Pollocks. In *FAccT '24: Proceedings of the 2024 ACM Conference on Fairness, Accountability, and Transparency*, 186–196. 147

Goldberg, David E. 1987. Simple Genetic Algorithms and the Minimal Deceptive Problem. In *Genetic Algorithms and Simulated Annealing (Research Notes in Artificial Intelligence)*, ed. Lawrence D. Davis, 74–88. Burlington, MA: Morgan Kaufmann Publishers. 81

Goldblum, Micah, Liam Fowl, Soheil Feizi, and Tom Goldstein. 2020. Adversarially Robust Distillation. In *The Thirty-Fourth AAAI Conference on Artificial Intelligence (AAAI-20)*, 3996–4003. AAAI. 165

Goldman, Alvin. 1970. *A Theory of Human Action*. Englewood Cliffs, NJ: Prentice-Hall. 183

Gondry, Michel. 2004. *Eternal Sunshine of the Spotless Mind*. Focus Features. 108 min. 1

Good, Irving John. 1965. Speculations Concerning the First Ultraintelligent Machine. *Advances in Computers* 6: 31–88. 278

Goodfellow, Ian, Yoshua Bengio, and Aaron Courville. 2016. *Deep Learning*. Cambridge, MA: The MIT Press. http://www.deeplearningbook.org. 43, 60, 64, 95, 252

Goodman, Nelson. 1955. *Fact, Fiction, and Forecast*. Cambridge, MA: Harvard University Press. 245

Google. 2023. Comments of Google: Notice of Inquiry on Artificial Intelligence & Copyright, Technical Report Dkt. COLC-2023-0006, U.S. Copyright Office. 147

Gordon, John-Stewart. 2023. Objections. In *The Impact of Artificial Intelligence on Human Rights Legislation*, 75–82. Cham: Palgrave Macmillan. 70

Gorz, André. 1967. *Strategy for Labor: A Radical Proposal*. Boston, MA: Beacon Press. 144

Govindarajulu, Naveen Sundar, Selmer Bringsjord, Rikhiya Ghosh, and Vasanth Sarathy. 2019. Toward the Engineering of Virtuous Machines. In *AIES '19: Proceedings of the 2019 AAAI/ACM Conference on AI, Ethics, and Society*, 29–35. New York: Association for Computing Machinery. 73

Granholm, Jackson W. 1962. How to Design a Kludge. *Datamation* Feb.: 30–31. 122

Gray, Mary L., and Siddharth Suri. 2019. *Ghost Work: How to Stop Silicon Valley from Building a New Global Underclass*. New York: Eamon Dolan Books. 150

Green, Ben. 2019. 'Good' Isn't Good Enough. https://www.benzevgreen.com/wp-content/uploads/2019/11/19-ai4sg.pdf. 143, 144, 251

Green, Ben. 2022. Escaping the Impossibility of Fairness: From Formal to Substantive Algorithmic Fairness. *Philosophy & Technology* 35 (90). 111

Green, Ben, and Lily Hu. 2018. The Myth in the Methodology: Towards a Recontextualization of Fairness in Machine Learning. In *Machine Learning: The Debates*, 1–5. Workshop at International Conference on Machine Learning (ICML). https://scholar.harvard.edu/sites/scholar.harvard.edu/files/bgreen/files/18-icmldebates.pdf. 111, 114

Grice, H. Paul. 1975. Logic and Conversation. In *Syntax and Semantics, Vol. 3: Speech Acts*, eds. Peter Cole and Jerry L. Morgan, 41–58. New York: Academic Press. 140

Grice, H. Paul. 1989. *Studies in the Way of Words*. Cambridge, MA: Harvard University Press. 140

Grigorescu, Sorin, Bogdan Trasnea, Tiberiu Cocias, and Gigel Macesanu. 2020. A Survey of Deep Learning Techniques for Autonomous Driving. *arXiv* 1910.07738: 1–28. `https://arxiv.org/abs/1910.07738`. 39

Grossman, Sanford J., and Oliver D. Hart. 1986. The Costs and Benefits of Ownership: A Theory of Vertical and Lateral Integration. *Journal of Political Economy* 94: 691–719. 79

Guardian, The. 2024. Israel Defence Forces' Response to Claims about Use of 'Lavender' AI Database in Gaza. *The Guardian* Apr. (03). `https://www.theguardian.com/world/2024/apr/03/israel-defence-forces-response-to-claims-about-use-of-lavender-ai-database-in-gaza`. 154

Gupta, Agrim, Lijun Yu, Kihyuk Sohn, Xiuye Gu, Meera Hahn, Li Fei-Fei, Irfan Essa, Lu Jiang, and José Lezama. 2023. Photorealistic Video Generation with Diffusion Models. *arXiv* 2312.06662: 1–13. `https://arxiv.org/abs/2312.06662`. 132

Guyer, Paul, and Rolf-Peter Horstmann. 2023. Idealism. In *The Stanford Encyclopedia of Philosophy*, eds. Edward N. Zalta and Uri Nodelman. Metaphysics Research Lab, Stanford University. https://plato.stanford.edu/archives/spr2023/entries/idealism/. 21

Hadfield-Menell, Dylan. 2021. The Principal-Agent Alignment Problem in Artificial Intelligence. PhD diss, EECS Department, University of California, Berkeley. `http://www2.eecs.berkeley.edu/Pubs/TechRpts/2021/EECS-2021-207.html`. 80

Hadfield-Menell, Dylan, and Gillian K. Hadfield. 2019. Incomplete Contracting and AI Alignment. In *AIES '19: Proceedings of the 2019 AAAI/ACM Conference on AI, Ethics, and Society*, eds. Vincent Conitzer, Gillian Hadfield, and Shannon Vallor, 417–422. New York: Association for Computing Machinery. 73, 80, 166

Hadfield-Menell, Dylan, McKane Andrus, and Gillian Hadfield. 2019. Legible Normativity for AI Alignment: The Value of Silly Rules. In *AIES '19: Proceedings of the 2019 AAAI/ACM Conference on AI, Ethics, and Society*, eds. Vincent Conitzer, Gillian Hadfield, and Shannon Vallor, 115–121. New York: Association for Computing Machinery. 73, 118, 136, 174, 175

Hadfield-Menell, Dylan, Anca Dragan, Pieter Abbeel, and Stuart Russell. 2017. The Off-Switch Game. *arXiv* 1611.08219: 1–8. `https://arxiv.org/abs/1611.08219`. 80, 176, 177

Haidt, Jonathan. 2001. The Emotional Dog and Its Rational Tail: A Social Intuitionist Approach to Moral Judgment. *Psychological Review* 108 (4): 814–834. 199

Haidt, Jonathan, and Craig Joseph. 2008. The Moral Mind: How Five Sets of Innate Intuitions Guide the Development of Many Culture-Specific Virtues, and Perhaps Even Modules. In *The Innate Mind: Volume 3: Foundations and the Future (Evolution and Cognition)*, eds. Peter Carruthers, Stephen Laurence, and Stephen Stich, 367–391. Oxford: Oxford University Press. 199

Hamidi, Foad, Morgan Klaus Scheuerman, and Stacy M. Branham. 2018. Gender Recognition or Gender Reductionism?: The Social Implications of Embedded Gender Recognition Systems. In *Proceedings of the ACM Conference on Human Factors in Computing Systems (CHI)*, 1–13. 148

Han, Shengnan, Eugene Kelly, Shahrokh Nikou, and Eric-Oluf Svee. 2022. Aligning Artificial Intelligence with Human Values: Reflections from a Phenomenological Perspective. *AI & Society* 37: 1383–1395. 99

Hardt, Moritz, and Benjamin Recht. 2022. *Patterns, Predictions, and Actions: Foundations of Machine Learning*. Princeton, NJ: Princeton University Press. 65, 209

Harman, Gilbert. 1977. *The Nature of Morality*. Oxford: Oxford University Press. 217

Harman, Gilbert. 1984. Is There a Single True Morality? In *Morality, Reason and Truth: New Essays on the Foundations of Ethics*, eds. David Copp and David Zimmerman, 27–48. Totowa, NJ: Rowman & Allanheld. 217

Harman, Gilbert, and Judith Jarvis Thomson. 1996. *Moral Relativism and Moral Objectivity*. Cambridge, MA: Blackwell. 217

Hart, Oliver. 1995. *Firms, Contracts, and Financial Structure*. Oxford: Oxford University Press. 79

Haugeland, John. 1985. *Artificial Intelligence: The Very Idea*. Cambridge: The MIT Press. 22

Hauser, Marc D., and W. Tecumseh Fitch. 2003. What Are the Uniquely Human Components of the Language Faculty? In *Language Evolution*, eds. M. H. Christiansen and S. Kirby, 158–181. Oxford: Oxford University Press. 229

Hauser, Marc D., Noam Chomsky, and W. Tecumseh Fitch. 2002. The Faculty of Language: What Is It, Who Has It, and How Did It Evolve? *Science* 298: 1569–1579. 229, 230

Hausman, Daniel M. 2012. *Preference, Value, Choice, and Welfare*. Cambridge: Cambridge University Press. 237

Háyek, Alan. 2022. Pascal's Wager. In *The Stanford Encyclopedia of Philosophy*, ed. Edward N. Zalta. The Metaphysics Research Lab, Stanford University. https://plato.stanford.edu/archives/win2022/entries/pascal-wager/. 283

Haynes, John. 1895. Risk as an Economic Factor. *Quarterly Journal of Economics* 9 (4): 409–444. 78

Heath, Joseph. 2020. Methodological Individualism. In *The Stanford Encyclopedia of Philosophy*, ed. Edward N. Zalta. The Metaphysics Research Lab, Stanford University. https://plato.stanford.edu/archives/sum2020/entries/methodological-individualism/. 95

Hebb, Donald O. 1949. *The Organization of Behavior: A Neuropsychological Theory*. New York: John Wiley & Sons. 28

Heersmink, Richard, and J. Adam Carter. 2020. The Philosophy of Memory Technologies: Metaphysics, Knowledge, and Values. *Memory Studies* 13 (4): 416–433. 274

Heeson, Remco, and Liam Kofi Bright. 2021. Is Peer Review a Good Idea? *British Journal for the Philosophy of Science* 72 (3): 635–663. 254

Held, Virginia. 1993. *Feminist Morality: Transforming Culture, Society, and Politics*. Chicago: University of Chicago Press. 193

Held, Virginia. 2006. *The Ethics of Care*. Oxford: Oxford University Press. 193

Hempel, Carl. 1965. *Aspects of Scientific Explanation*. New York: Free Press. 245

Henderson, Peter, Jieru Hu, Joshua Romoff, Emma Brunskill, Dan Jurafsky, and Joelle Pineau. 2020. Towards the Systematic Reporting of the Energy and Carbon Footprints of Machine Learning. *Journal of Machine Learning Research* 21 (248): 1–43. 149

Hendrycks, Dan, Collin Burns, Steven Basart, Andrew Critch, Jerry Li, Dawn Song, and Jacob Steinhardt. 2023. Aligning AI With Shared Human Values. *arXiv* 2008.02275: 1–29. https://arxiv.org/abs/2008.02275. 69

Herbert, Frank. 1965. *Dune*. New York: Penguin. 19

Herrmann, Daniel A. 2020. PAC Learning and Occam's Razor: Probably Approximately Incorrect. *Philosophy of Science* 87: 4. 246

Hilbert, David. 1900. Mathematische Probleme. *Nachrichten von der Königlichen Gesellschaft der Wissenschaften zu Göttingen, Mathematisch-Physikalische Klasse* 1900: 253–297. 23

Hilbert, David, and Wilhelm Ackermann. 1928. *Grundzüge der Theoretischen Logik*. Berlin: Springer. 23

Hildebrandt, Mireille. 2022. The Issue of Proxies and Choice Architectures. Why EU Law Matters for Recommender Systems. *Frontiers in Artificial Intelligence* 5 (789076): 1–17. 93, 95, 113, 259

Ho, Jonathan, William Chan, Chitwan Saharia, Jay Whang, Ruiqi Gao, Alexey Gritsenko, Diederik P. Kingma, Ben Poole, Mohammad Norouzi, David J. Fleet, et al. 2022. Imagen Video: High Definition Video Generation with Diffusion Models. *arXiv* 2210.02303: 1–18. https://arxiv.org/abs/2210.02303. 132

Hobbes, Thomas. 1668/1994. *Leviathan, with Selected Variants from the Latin Edition of 1668*. Indianapolis/Cambridge: Hackett Publishing Company. 22

Hoffmann, Anna Lauren. 2019. Where Fairness Fails: Data, Algorithms, and the Limits of Antidiscrimination Discourse. *Information, Communication & Society* 22 (7): 900–915. 148

Hofstadter, Douglas R. 1979/1999. *Gödel, Escher, Bach: An Eternal Golden Braid*. New York: Basic Books. 29

Hofstadter, Douglas R. 1995. The Ineradicable Eliza Effect and Its Dangers (Preface 4). In *Fluid Concepts and Creative Analogies: Computer Models of the Fundamental Mechanisms of Thought*, 155–168. Basic Books. 33

hooks, bell. 1984. *Feminist Theory: From Margin to Center*. Boston, MA: South End Press. 108

Hornik, Kurt. 1991. Approximation Capabilities of Multilayer Feedforward Networks. *Neural Networks* 4 (2): 251–257. 49, 50

Hornik, Kurt, Maxwell Stinchcombe, and Halbert White. 1989. Multilayer Feedforward Networks Are Universal Approximators. *Neural Networks* 2: 359–366. 49

Hou, Jianwei, Ann Kuzma, and John Kuzma. 2009. Winner's Curse or Adverse Selection in Online Auctions: The Role of Quality Uncertainty and Information Disclosure. *Journal of Electronic Commerce Research* 10 (3): 144–154. 78

Howard, Don, and Ioan Muntean. 2017. Artificial Moral Cognition: Moral Functionalism and Autonomous Moral Agency. In *Philosophy and Computing: Essays in Epistemology, Philosophy of Mind, Logic, and Ethics*, ed. Thomas M. Powers, 121–159. Cham: Springer. 73

Hsu, Feng-Hsiung. 2002. *Behind Deep Blue*. Princeton, NJ: Princeton University Press. 37

Hubinger, Evan, Chris van Merwijk, Vladimir Mikulik, Joar Skalse, and Scott Garrabrant. 2021. Risks from Learned Optimization in Advanced Machine Learning Systems. *arXiv* 1906.01820: 1–39. `https://arxiv.org/abs/1906.01820`. 74, 132

Hugging Face. 2023. Comments of Hugging Face Inc.: Notice of Inquiry on Artificial Intelligence & Copyright, Technical Report Dkt. 2023-6, U.S. Copyright Office. 147

Hunt, Neil. 2023. Netflix Prize Update. *The Netflix Blog* Mar. (03). `http://blog.netflix.com/2010/03/this-is-neil-hunt-chief-product-officer.html`. 6

Hurford, James R. 2012. *Language in the Light of Evolution II: The Origins of Grammar*. Oxford: Oxford University Press. 229

Intemann, Kristen. 2001. Science and Values: Are Value Judgments Always Irrelevant to the Justification of Scientific Claims? *Philosophy of Science* 68 (S3): 506–518. 248

Ivakhnenko, Alekseĭ G., and Valentin G. Lapa. 1965. Cybernetic Predicting Devices. 63

Jackendoff, Ray. 1997. *The Architecture of the Language Faculty*. Cambridge, MA: The MIT Press. 230

Jackendoff, Ray. 1999. Possible Stages in the Evolution of the Language Faculty. *Trends in Cognitive Sciences* 3: 272–279. 230

Jackendoff, Ray. 2003. *Foundations of Language: Brain, Meaning, Grammar, Evolution*. Oxford: Oxford University Press. 230

Jackendoff, Ray. 2012. Your Theory of Language Evolution Depends on Your Theory of Language. In *The Evolution of Human Language: Biolinguistic Perspectives*, eds. Richard K. Larson, Viviane Déprez, and Hiroko Yamakido, 63–72. Cambridge: Cambridge University Press. 230

Jackendoff, Ray, and Steven Pinker. 2005. The Nature of the Language Faculty and Its Implications for Evolution of Language (Reply to Fitch, Hauser, and Chomsky). *Cognition* 97 (2): 211–225. 230

Jacobs, Abigail Z., and Hanna Wallach. 2021. Measurement and Fairness. In *Proceedings of the 2021 ACM Conference on Fairness, Accountability, and Transparency*, 375–385. New York: ACM. 111

Jacobsen, Jörn-Henrik, Robert Geirhos, and Claudio Michaelis. 2020. Shortcuts: How Neural Networks Love to Cheat. *The Gradient* Jul. (25). `https://thegradient.pub/shortcuts-neural-networks-love-to-cheat/`. 96

Jaderberg, Max, Wojciech M. Czarnecki, Iain Dunning, Luke Marris, Guy Lever, Antonio Garcia Castaneda, Charles Beattie, Neil C. Rabinowitz, Ari S. Morcos, Avraham Ruderman, et al. 2018. Human-Level Performance in First-Person Multiplayer Games with Population-Based Deep Reinforcement Learning. *arXiv* 1807.01281: 1–42. `https://arxiv.org/abs/1807.01281`. 55

Jagger, Alison M. 1989. Love and Knowledge: Emotion in Feminist Epistemology. In *Women, Knowledge and Reality*, eds. Ann Garry and Marilyn Pearsall, 166–190. Boston: Unwin Hyman Ltd. 214

James, William. 1890. *The Principles of Psychology*. New York: Henry Holt and Company. 214

Janssen, Theo M. V. 1997. Compositionality. In *Handbook of Logic and Language*, eds. J. van Benthem and A. ter Meulen, 417–473. Amsterdam: Elsevier. 229

Janssen, Theo M. V. 2012. Compositionality: Its Historic Context. In *The Oxford Handbook of Compositionality*, eds. W. Hinzen, E. Machery, and M. Werning, 19–46. Oxford: Oxford University Press. 229

Jarrett, Kevin, Koray Kavukcuoglu, Marc'Aurelio Ranzato, and Yann LeCun. 2009. What Is the Best Multistage Architecture for Object Recognition? In *IEEE 12th International Conference on Computer Vision*, 2146–2153. New York: IEEE. 48

Jensen, Michael C., and William H. Meckling. 1976. Theory of the Firm: Managerial Behaviour, Agency Costs and Ownership Structure. *Journal of Financial Economics* 3 (4): 305–360. 76

Jia, Chao, Yinfei Yang, Ye Xia, Yi-Ting Chen, Zarana Parekh, Hieu Pham, Quoc V. Le, Yunhsuan Sung, Zhen Li, and Tom Duerig. 2021. Scaling Up Visual and Vision-Language Representation Learning with Noisy Text Supervision. *arXiv* 2102.05918: 1–14. `https://arxiv.org/abs/2102.05918`. 128

Jiang, Wentao, Si Liu, Chen Gao, Jie Cao, Ran He, Jiashi Feng, and Shuicheng Yan. 2020. PSGAN: Pose and Expression Robust Spatial-aware GAN for Customizable Makeup Transfer. In *Proceedings of the IEEE/CVF Conference on Computer Vision and Pattern Recognition*, 5194–5202. New York: Computer Vision Foundation. 212

Johnson, Gabrielle M. 2020a. Algorithmic Bias: On the Implicit Biases of Social Technology. *Synthese* 198 (10): 9941–9961. 112, 114

Johnson, Gabrielle M. 2020b. The Structure of Bias. *Mind* 129 (516): 1193–1236. 112

Johnson, Gabrielle M. 2023. Are Algorithms Value-Free? Feminist Theoretical Virtues in Machine Learning. *Journal of Moral Philosophy* 21 (1–2): 1–35. 252, 260

Johnstone, Fae. 2023. The Horrifying Consequences of Anti-Trans Attacks. *The Walrus* May (29). 109

Jones, Matthew L. 2023. AI in History. *The American Historical Review* 128 (3): 1360–1367. 40, 41

Jonze, Spike. 2013. *Her*. Annapurna Pictures. 126 min. 5, 284

Joynt Maddox, Karen E., Mat Reidhead, Jianhui Hu, Amy JH Kind, Alan M. Zaslavsky, Elna M. Nagasako, and David R. Nerenz. 2019a. Adjusting for Social Risk Factors Impacts Performance and Penalties in the Hospital Readmissions Reduction Program. *Health Services Research* 54 (2): 327–336. 8

Joynt Maddox, Karen E., Mat Reidhead, Andrew C. Qi, and David R. Nerenz. 2019b. Association of Stratification by Dual Enrollment Status with Financial Penalties in the Hospital Readmissions Reduction Program. *JAMA Internal Medicine* 179 (6): 769–776. 8

Kamm, Francis Myrna. 1989. Harming Some to Save Others. *Philosophical Studies* 57 (3): 227–260. 214

Kamp, Hans, and Barbara Partee. 1995. Prototype Theory and Compositionality. *Cognition* 57: 129–191. 229

Kaplan, Jared, Sam McCandlish, Tom Henighan, Tom B. Brown, Benjamin Chess, Rewon Child, Scott Gray, Alec Radford, Jeffrey Wu, and Dario Amodei. 2020. Scaling Laws for Neural Language Models. *arXiv* 2001.08361: 1–30. https://arxiv.org/abs/2001.08361. 62

Kärkkäinen, Kimmo, and Jungseock Joo. 2019. FairFace: Face Attribute Dataset for Balanced Race, Gender, and Age. *arXiv* 1908.04913: 1–11. https://arxiv.org/abs/1908.04913. 110

Karras, Tero, Samuli Laine, and Timo Aila. 2019. A Style-Based Generator Architecture for Generative Adversarial Networks. *arXiv* 1812.04948: 1–12. https://arxiv.org/abs/1812.04948. 148

Karras, Tero, Timo Aila, Samuli Laine, and Jaakko Lehtinen. 2018. Progressive Growing of GANs for Improved Quality, Stability, and Variation. *arXiv* 1710.10196: 1–26. https://arxiv.org/abs/1710.10196. 110, 148

Kasirzadeh, Atoosa, and Iason Gabriel. 2023. In Conversation with Artificial Intelligence: Aligning language Models with Human Values. *Philosophy & Technology* 36 (27): 1–24. 140

Kelley, Henry J. 1960. Gradient Theory of Optimal Flight Paths. *ARS Journal* 30 (10): 947–954. 38, 63

Kelly, Kevin. 2017. The Myth of Superhuman AI. *Wired* Apr. (25). https://www.wired.com/2017/04/the-myth-of-a-superhuman-ai/. 282

Kerr, Steven. 1975. On the Folly of Rewarding A, While Hoping for B. *Academy of Management Journal* 18: 769–783. 75

Kim, Tae Wan, John Hooker, and Thomas Donaldson. 2021. Taking Principles Seriously: A Hybrid Approach to Value Alignment in Artificial Intelligence. *Journal of Artificial Intelligence Research* 70: 871–890. 69, 73, 183

Kind, Amy. 2022. Computing Machinery and Sexual Difference: The Sexed Presuppositions Underlying the Turing Test. In *Feminist Philosophy of Mind*, eds. Keya Maitra and Jennifer McWeeny, 54–70. Oxford University Press. 24

King, Thomas. 1990. *All My Relations: An Anthology of Contemporary Canadian Native Fiction*. McClelland & Stewart. 194

Kirk, Robert. 2023. Zombies. In *The Stanford Encyclopedia of Philosophy*, eds. Edward N. Zalta and Uri Nodelman. Metaphysics Research Lab, Stanford University. https://plato.stanford.edu/archives/sum2023/entries/zombies/. 4

Kitcher, Philip. 2006a. Between Fragile Altruism and Morality: Evolution and the Emergence of Normative Guidance. In *Evolutionary Ethics and Contemporary Biology*, eds. Giovanni Boniolo and Gabriele De Anna, 159–77. Oxford: Oxford University Press. 231

Kitcher, Philip. 2006b. Biology and Ethics. In *The Oxford Handbook of Ethical Theory*, ed. David Copp, 163–185. Oxford: Oxford University Press. 231

Kitcher, Philip. 2011a. *The Ethical Project*. Cambridge, MA: Harvard University Press. 230, 231, 249

Kitcher, Philip. 2011b. *Science in a Democratic Society*. Amherst, NY: Prometheus Books. 249

Kittay, Eva Feder, and Diana T. Myers, eds. 1987. *Women and Moral Theory*. Lanham, MD: Rowman and Littlefield. 193

Kleene, Stephen Cole. 1936. Lambda-Definability and Recursiveness. *Duke Mathematical Journal* 2 (2): 340–353. 24

Kleinberg, Jon, Sendhil Mullainathan, and Manish Raghavan. 2017. Inherent Trade-Offs in the Fair Determination of Risk Scores. In *Innovations in Theoretical Computer Science Conference*, Vol. 67, 1–23. 107

Knight, Frank H. 1921. *Risk, Uncertainty and Profit*. Chicago, IL: University of Chicago Press. 78

Koch, Bernard, Emily Denton, Alex Hanna, and Jacob G. Foster. 2021. Reduced, Reused and Recycled: The Life of a Dataset in Machine Learning Research. *arXiv* 2112.01716: 1–18. NeurIPS 2021 Datasets and Benchmarks Track. `https://arxiv.org/abs/2112.01716`. 211

Kogonada. 2021. *After Yang*. A24, Cinereach, and Per Capita Productions. 96 min. 4, 284

Konečný, Jakub, Brendan McMahan, and Daniel Ramage. 2015. Federated Optimization: Distributed Optimization Beyond the Datacenter. In *Proceedings of the OPT Workshop on Optimization for Machine Learning, NeurIPS*. Neural Information Processing Systems. 148

Korsgaard, Christine M. 2018. *Fellow Creatures: Our Obligations to the Other Animals*. Oxford: Oxford University Press. 230

Köster, Raphael, Dylan Hadfield-Menell, Richard Everett, and Joel Z. Leibo. 2021. Spurious Normativity Enhances Learning of Compliance and Enforcement Behavior in Artificial Agents. *Proceedings of the National Academy of Sciences of the United States of America (PNAS)* 119 (3): 2106028118. 118

Koster, Raphael, Jan Balaguer, Andrea Tacchetti, Ari Weinstein, Tina Zhu, Oliver Hauser, Duncan Williams, Lucy Campbell-Gillingham, Phoebe Thacker, Matthew Botvinick, and Christopher Summerfield. 2022. Human-Centred Mechanism Design with Democratic AI. *Nature Human Behaviour* 6: 1398–1407. 73

Koszegi, Botond, and Matthew Rabin. 2007. Mistakes in Choice-Based Welfare Analysis. *American Economic Review* 97 (2): 477–481. 237

Krakovna, Victoria, Jonathan Uesato, Vladimir Mikulik, Matthew Rahtz, Tom Everitt, Ramana Kumar, Zac Kenton, Jan Leike, and Shane Legg. 2021. Specification Gaming: The Flip Side of AI Ingenuity DeepMind. `https://deepmind.com/blog/article/Specification-gaming-the-flip-side-of-AI-ingenuity`. 74

Kripke, Saul A. 1982. *Wittgenstein on Rules and Private Language*. Cambridge, MA: Harvard University Press. 237

Krishnan, Maya. 2020. Against Interpretability: A Critical Examination of the Interpretability Problem in Machine Learning. *Philosophy & Technology* 33 (3): 487–502. 126

Krizhevsky, Alex, Ilya Sutskever, and Geoffrey E. Hinton. 2017. ImageNet Classification with Deep Convolutional Neural Networks. *Communications of the Association for Computing Machinery* 60 (6): 84–90. 38

Kubrick, Stanley. 1968. *2001: A Space Odyssey*. Metro-Goldwyn-Mayer. 143 min. 4, 36, 284

Kuhn, Thomas S. 1962. *The Structure of Scientific Revolutions*. Chicago: University of Chicago Press. 268

Kuhn, Thomas S. 1977. Objectivity, Value Judgment, and Theory choice. In *The Essential Tension: Selected Studies in Scientific Tradition and Change*, 320–339. Chicago, IL: University of Chicago Press. 246

Kuipers, Benjamin. 1979. On Representing Commonsense Knowledge. In *Associative Networks: The Representation and Use of Knowledge by Computers*, ed. Nicholas V. Findler, 393–408. New York: Academic Press. 37

Kurzweil, Ray. 2005. *The Singularity Is Near: When Humans Transcend Biology*. New York: Penguin Books. 278

Kwet, Michael. 2019. Digital Colonialism: US Empire and the New Imperialism in the Global South. *Race & Class* 60 (3): 3–26. 151

Lacey, Hugh. 1999. *Is Science Value-Free? Values and Scientific Understanding*. London: Routledge. 248

Lacoste, Alexandre, Alexandra Luccioni, Victor Schmidt, and Thomas Dandres. 2019. Quantifying the Carbon Emissions of Machine Learning. *arXiv* 1910.09700: 1–8. https://arxiv.org/abs/1910.09700. 149

LaCroix, Travis. 2020. Complex Signals: Reflexivity, Hierarchical Structure, and Modular Composition. PhD diss, University of California, Irvine. 230

LaCroix, Travis. 2022. Moral Dilemmas for Moral Machines. *AI and Ethics* 2: 737–746. 82, 100, 214, 215

LaCroix, Travis, and Yoshua Bengio. 2019. Learning from Learning Machines: Optimisation, Rules, and Social Norms. *arXiv* 2001.00006. https://arxiv.org/abs/2001.00006. 183, 236

LaCroix, Travis, and Alexandra Sasha Luccioni. 2025. Metaethical Perspectives on "Benchmarking" AI Ethics. *AI and Ethics*. https://doi.org/10.1007/s43681-025-00703-x. 82, 144, 216

LaCroix, Travis, and Aydin Mohseni. 2022. The Tragedy of the AI Commons. *Synthese* 200 (289): 1–33. https://doi.org/10.3998/ergo.2230. 258

LaCroix, Travis, and Cailin O'Connor. 2021. Power by Association. *Ergo* 8 (29): 163–189. https://doi.org/10.3998/ergo.2230. 78

LaCroix, Travis, and Simon J. D. Prince. 2023. Deep Learning and Ethics. In *Understanding Deep Learning*. Cambridge, MA: The MIT Press. 67

Laffont, Jean-Jacques. 2000. *Incentives and Political Economy*. Oxford: Oxford University Press. 79

Laffont, Jean-Jacques, and David Martimort. 2002. *The Theory of Incentives: The Principal-Agent Model*. Princeton: Princeton University Press. 76, 77, 78, 79, 86

Langosco, Lauro, Jack Koch, Lee Sharkey, Jacob Pfau, Laurent Orseau, and David Krueger. 2021. Goal Misgeneralization in Deep Reinforcement Learning. *arXiv* 2105.14111: 1–16. https://arxiv.org/abs/2105.14111. 74

Lannelongue, Loïc, Jason Grealey, and Michael Inouye. 2021. Green Algorithms: Quantifying the Carbon Footprint of Computation. *Advanced Science* 8 (12): 2100707. 149

Larson, Jeff, and Julia Angwin. 2016. Technical Response to Northpointe. *ProPublica* Jul. (29). https://www.propublica.org/article/technical-response-to-northpointe. 106

Lasseter, John. 1995. *Toy Story*. Walt Disney Pictures and Pixar Animation Studios. 81 min. 1

Laudan, Larry. 1984. *Science and Values: The Aims of Science and Their Role in Scientific Debate*. Berkeley: University of California Press. 145, 246

LeCun, Yann, Bernhard Boser, John S. Denker, Donnie Henderson, Richard E. Howard, Wayne Hubbard, and Lawrence D. Jackel. 1989. Backpropagation Applied to Handwritten Zip Code Recognition. *Neural Computation* 1 (4): 541–551. 38, 63

Lee, Michelle Seng Ah, Luciano Floridi, and Jatinder Singh. 2021. Formalising Trade-Offs Beyond Algorithmic Fairness: Lessons from Ethical Philosophy and Welfare Economics. *AI and Ethics* 1: 529–544. 111

Lee, Min Kyung, Daniel Kusbit, Anson Kahng, Ji Tae Kim, Xinran Yuan, Allissa Chan, Daniel See, Ritesh Noothigattu, Siheon Lee, Alexandros Psomas, et al. 2019. WeBuildAI: Participatory Framework for Algorithmic Governance. *Proceedings of the ACM on Human-Computer Interaction* 3 (CSCW): 1–35. 255

Lee, Yoon Kyung, Jina Suh, Hongli Zhan, Junyi Jessy Li, and Desmond C. Ong. 2024. Large Language Models Produce Responses Perceived to Be Empathic. *arXiv* 2403.18148: 1–9. https://arxiv.org/abs/2403.18148. 33

Leese, Matthias. 2014. The New Profiling: Algorithms, Black Boxes, and the Failure of Anti-Discriminatory Safeguards in the European Union. *Security Dialogue* 45 (5): 494–511. 126

Legg, Shane, and Marcus Hutter. 2007. Universal Intelligence: A Definition of Machine Intelligence. *Minds and Machines* 17 (4): 391–444. 2

Lehman, Joel, and Kenneth O. Stanley. 2008. Exploiting Open-Endedness to Solve Problems Through the Search for Novelty. In *Proceedings of the Eleventh International Conference on Artificial Life (ALIFE XI)*, 329–336. Cambridge, MA: The MIT Press. 81

Leibniz, Gottfried Wilhelm. 1677/1951. Preface to the General Science. In *Leibniz Selections*, ed. Philip P. Wiener, 12–16. New York: Charles Scribner's Sons. 23

Leike, Jan, David Krueger, Tom Everitt, Miljan Martic, Vishal Maini, and Shane Legg. 2018. Scalable Agent Alignment via Reward Modeling: A Research Direction. *arXiv* 1811.07871: 1–30. https://arxiv.org/abs/1811.07871. 71, 172, 173

Leonelli, Sabina. 2023. *Philosophy of Open Science*. Cambridge: Cambridge University Press. 254

Li, Tingting, Ruihe Qian, Chao Dong, Si Liu, Qiong Yan, Wenwu Zhu, and Liang Lin. 2018. BeautyGAN: Instance-Level Facial Makeup Transfer with Deep Generative Adversarial Network. In *Proceedings of the 26th ACM International Conference on Multimedia*, 645–653. New York: Association for Computing Machinery. 212

Liao, Thomas, Rohan Taori, Inioluwa Deborah Raji, and Ludwig Schmidt. 2021. Are We Learning Yet? A Meta-Review of Evaluation Failures across Machine Learning. In *Datasets and Benchmarks Proceedings at the 35th Conference on Neural Information Processing Systems (NeurIPS 2021)*, 1–19. https://datasets-benchmarks-proceedings.neurips.cc/paper/2021/hash/757b505cfd34c64c85ca5b5690ee5293-Abstract-round2.html. 211, 217

Lighthill, James. 1973. Artificial Intelligence: A General Survey. In *Artificial Intelligence: A Paper Symposium*, 1–21. Science Research Council, London. 34

Lin, Patrick, Keith Abney, and George A. Bekey, eds. 2011. *Robot Ethics: The Ethical and Social Implications of Robotics*. Cambridge, MA: The MIT Press. 184

Lindsay, Robert K., Bruce G. Buchanan, Edward A. Feigenbaum, and Joshua Lederberg. 1993. DENDRAL: A Case Study of the First Expert System for Scientific Hypothesis Formation. *Artificial Intelligence* 61 (2): 209–261. 34

Lipton, Zachary C. 2018. The Mythos of Model Interpretability: In Machine Learning, the Concept of Interpretability Is Both Important and Slippery. *Queue* 16 (3): 31–57. 126

Long, Robert, Jeff Sebo, Patrick Butlin, Kathleen Finlinson, Kyle Fish, Jacqueline Harding, Jacob Pfau, Toni Sims, Jonathan Birch, and David Chalmers. 2024. Taking AI Welfare Seriously. *arXiv* 2411.00986v1. https://arxiv.org/abs/2411.00986v1. 201

Longino, Helen E. 1990. *Science as Social Knowledge: Values and Objectivity in Scientific Inquiry*. Princeton: Princeton University Press. 246, 248, 250

Longino, Helen E. 1996. Cognitive and Non-Cognitive Values in Science: Rethinking the Dichotomy. In *Feminism, Science, and the Philosophy of Science*, eds. Lynn Hankinson Nelson and Jack Nelson, 39–58. Dordrecht: Springer. 250

Lottick, Kadan, Silvia Susai, Sorelle A. Friedler, and Jonathan P. Wilson. 2019. Energy Usage Reports: Environmental Awareness as Part of Algorithmic Accountability. In *Workshop on Tackling Climate Change with Machine Learning at NeurIPS*. Neural Information Processing Systems. 149

Lowd, Daniel, and Christopher Meek. 2005. Adversarial Learning. In *Proceedings of the Eleventh ACM SIGKDD International Conference on Knowledge Discovery in Data Mining*, 641–647. New York: Association for Computing Machinery. 164

Lucas, J. R. 1961. Minds, Machines, and Gödel. *Philosophy* 36 (137): 112–137. 24

Luccioni, Alexandra Sasha. 2023. The Mounting Human and Environmental Costs of Generative AI. *Ars Technica*, April 12, 2023. https://arstechnica.com/gadgets/2023/04/generative-ai-is-cool-but-lets-not-forget-its-human-and-environmental-costs. 149

Luccioni, Alexandra Sasha, and Alex Hernandez-Garcia. 2023. Counting Carbon: A Survey of Factors Influencing the Emissions of Machine Learning. *arXiv* 2302.08476: 1–19. https://arxiv.org/abs/2302.08476. 149

Luccioni, Alexandra Sasha, and David Rolnick. 2022. Bugs in the Data: How ImageNet Misrepresents Biodiversity. *arXiv* 2208.11695: 1–12. https://arxiv.org/abs/2208.11695. 210

Luccioni, Alexandra Sasha, and Joseph Viviano. 2021. What's in the Box? An Analysis of Undesirable Content in the Common Crawl Corpus. In *Proceedings of the 59th Annual Meeting of the Association for Computational Linguistics and the 11th International Joint Conference on Natural Language Processing (Volume 2: Short Papers)*, eds. Chengqing Zong, Fei Xia, Wenjie Li, and Roberto Navigli, 182–189. Association for Computational Linguistics. 129

Luccioni, Alexandra Sasha, Yacine Jernite, and Emma Strubell. 2023a. Power Hungry Processing: Watts Driving the Cost of AI Deployment? *arXiv* 2311.16863: 1–20. https://arxiv.org/abs/2311.16863. 149

Luccioni, Alexandra Sasha, Sylvain Viguier, and Anne-Laure Ligozat. 2023b. Estimating the Carbon Footprint of BLOOM, a 176B Parameter Language Model. *Journal of Machine Learning Research* 24 (253): 1–15. 149

Lum, Kristian, and William Isaac. 2016. To Predict and Serve? *Significance* 13: 14–19. 8, 98

Lusk, Greg, and Kevin C. Elliott. 2022. Non-Epistemic Values and Scientific Assessment: An Adequacy-for-Purpose View. *European Journal for Philosophy of Science* 12 (35): 1–22. 248

Lust, Barbara. 2006. *Child Language: Acquisition and Growth*. Cambridge: Cambridge University Press. 234

Malle, Bertram F. 2015. Moral Competence in Robots? In *Sociable Robots and the Future of Social Relations*, eds. Johanna Seibt, Raul Hakli, and Marco Nørskov, 189–198. Amsterdam: IOS Press. 233

Malle, Bertram F. 2016. Integrating Robot Ethics and Machine Morality: The Study and Design of Moral Competence in Robots. *Ethics and Information Technology* 18: 243–256. 233

Malle, Bertram F., and Matthias Scheutz. 2014. Moral Competence in Social Robots. In *2014 IEEE International Symposium on Ethics in Science, Technology and Engineering*, 1–6. New York: IEEE. https://doi.org/10.1109/ETHICS.2014.6893446. 233

Manne, Kate. 2018. *Down Girl: The Logic of Misogyny*. Oxford: Oxford University Press. 212

Marcus, Gary, and Ernest Davis. 2020. GPT-3, Bloviator: OpenAI's Language Generator Has No Idea What It's Talking About. *MIT Technology Review* Aug. (22). https://www.technologyreview.com/2020/08/22/1007539/gpt3-openai-language-generator-artificial-intelligence-ai-opinion/. 241

Mason, Harding, D. Stewart, and Brendan Gill. 1958. The Talk of the Town. *The New Yorker* Dec. (06): 44. 32

Mathiesen, Thomas. 1974. *The Politics of Abolition*. New York: John Wiley & Sons. 144

Mathiesen, Thomas. 2014. *The Politics of Abolition Revisited*. London: Routledge. 144

Mayor, Adrienne. 2018. *Gods and Robots: Myths, Machines, and Ancient Dreams of Technology*. Princeton, NJ: Princeton University Press. 21

Mayson, Sandra G. 2018. Bias In, Bias Out. *Yale Law Journal* 128: 2122–2473. 111

McCarthy, John, Marvin L. Minsky, Nathaniel Rochester, and Claude E. Shannon. 1955/2006. A Proposal for the Dartmouth Summer Research Project on Artificial Intelligence. *AI Magazine* 27 (4): 12–14. 26

McConnell, Terrance. 2018. Moral Dilemmas. In *The Stanford Encyclopedia of Philosophy*, ed. Edward N. Zalta. Metaphysics Research Lab, Stanford University. https://plato.stanford.edu/archives/fall2018/entries/moral-dilemmas/. 213

McCorduck, Pamela. 1979. *Machines Who Think: A Personal Inquiry into the History and Prospects of Artificial Intelligence*. W. H. Freeman: San Francisco. 22, 41

McCoy, R. Thomas, Shunyu Yao, Dan Friedman, Matthew Hardy, and Thomas L. Griffiths. 2023. Embers of Autoregression: Understanding Large Language Models Through the Problem They Are Trained to Solve. *arXiv* 2309.13638: 1–84. https://arxiv.org/abs/2309.13638. 284

McCoy, Tom, Ellie Pavlick, and Tal Linzen. 2019. Right for the Wrong Reasons: Diagnosing Syntactic Heuristics in Natural Language Inference. In *Proceedings of the 57th Annual Meeting of the Association for Computational Linguistics*, eds. Anna Korhonen and Lluís Màrquez David Traum, 3428–3448. Florence: Association for Computational Linguistics. 241

McCulloch, Warren S., and Walter Pitts. 1943. A Logical Calculus of the Ideas Immanent in Nervous Activity. *The Bulletin of Mathematical Biophysics* 5: 115–133. 25, 26, 28

McKernan, Bethan, and Harry Davies. 2024. 'The Machine Did It Coldly': Israel Used AI to Identify 37,000 Hamas Targets. *The Guardian* Apr. (03). https://www.theguardian.com/world/2024/apr/03/israel-gaza-ai-database-hamas-airstrikes. 154

McMullin, E. 1982. Values in Science. *PSA: Proceedings of the Biennial Meeting of the Philosophy of Science Association* 1982: 3–28. 145, 246, 247

McQuillan, Dan. 2022. *Resisting AI: An Anti-fascist Approach to Artificial Intelligence*. Bristol: Bristol University Press. 84, 133, 257, 258, 261

McQuillan, Dan. 2023. Predicted Benefits, Proven Harms: How AI's Algorithmic Violence Emerged from Our Own Social Matrix. *The Sociological Review Magazine* Jun. (06). 151

Mead, C. 1990. Neuromorphic Electronic Systems. *Proceedings of the IEEE* 78 (10): 1629–1636. 273

Mehler, Jacques, Marina Nespor, Mohinish Shukla, and Marcela Peña. 2006. Why Is Language Unique to Humans? *Novartis Foundation Symposium* 270: 251–280. 229

Mehta, Chavi, and Rachael Levy. 2022. Neuralink: What You Need to Know About Elon Musk's Brain Chip Company. *Reuters* Dec. (07). 274

Meir, Irit, Wendy Sandler, Carol Padden, and Mark Aronoff. 2010. Emerging Sign Languages. In *Oxford Handbook of Deaf Studies, Language, and Education*, ed. M. Marschark, 267–280. Oxford: Oxford University Press. 232

Mele, Alfred R. 1992. *Springs of Action: Understanding Intentional Behavior*. Oxford: Oxford University Press. 183

Mele, Alfred R. 2003. *Motivation and Agency*. Oxford: Oxford University Press. 183

Menabrea, Luigi Federico, and Ada Lovelace. 1843. Sketch of the Analytical Engine Invented by Charles Babbage with Notes by the Translator. Translated by Ada Lovelace. In *Scientific Memoirs. Vol. 3*, ed. Richard Taylor, 666–731. London: Richard and John E. Taylor. 2

Menon, Sachit, Alexandru Damian, Shijia Hu, Nikhil Ravi, and Cynthia Rudin. 2020. PULSE: Self-Supervised Photo Upsampling via Latent Space Exploration of Generative Models. *arXiv* 2003.03808: 1–20. https://arxiv.org/abs/2003.03808. 110

Merritt, Maria. 2000. Virtue Ethics and Situationist Personality Psychology. *Ethical Theory and Moral Practice* 3 (4): 365–383. 199

Meta. 2023. Comments of Meta Platforms, Inc.: Notice of Inquiry on Artificial Intelligence & Copyright, Technical Report Dkt. 2023-6, U.S. Copyright Office. 146

Metzger, Sean L., Kaylo T. Littlejohn, Alexander B. Silva, David A. Moses, Margaret P. Seaton, Ran Wang, Maximilian E. Dougherty, Jessie R. Liu, Peter Wu, Michael A. Berger, et al. 2023. A High-Performance Neuroprosthesis for Speech Decoding and Avatar Control. *Nature* 620: 1037–1046. 274

Meynell, Letitia, and Clarisse Paron. 2023. *Applied Ethics Primer*. Peterborough: Broadview Press. 188

Miceli, Milagros, Julian Posada, and Tianling Yang. 2022. Studying Up Machine Learning Data: Why Talk About Bias When We Mean Power? *Proceedings of the ACM on Human-Computer Interaction* 6 (GROUP): 1–14. 111, 114, 151

Microsoft. 2023. Comments of Microsoft Corporation: Notice of Inquiry on Artificial Intelligence & Copyright, Technical Report Dkt. 2023-6, U.S. Copyright Office. 146

Mill, John Stuart. 1863. *Utilitarianism*. London: Parker, Son & Bourn, West Strand. 189

Miller, George A. 1995. WordNet: A Lexical Database for English. *Communications of the ACM* 38 (11): 39–41. 209

Minh, Dang, H. Xiang Wang, Y. Fen Li, and Tan N. Nguyen. 2022. Explainable Artificial Intelligence: A Comprehensive Review. *Artificial Intelligence Review* 55: 3503–3568. 127

Minsky, Marvin. 1952. A Neural-Analogue Calculator Based upon a Probability Model of Reinforcement, Technical report, Harvard University Psychological Laboratories, Cambridge, MA. 28

Minsky, Marvin. 1956. Heuristic Aspects of the Artificial Intelligence Problem, Technical report, Massachusetts Institute of Technology, Lincoln Laboratory. 22

Minsky, Marvin. 1961. Steps toward Artificial Intelligence. *Proceedings of the IRE* 49 (1): 8–30. 54

Minsky, Marvin. 1967. *Computation: Finite and Infinite Machines*. Englewood Cliffs, NJ: Prentice-Hall, Inc. 31

Mitchell, Margaret. 2023. The Pillars of a Rights-Based Approach to AI Development. *TechPolicy.Press* Dec (5). https://www.techpolicy.press/the-pillars-of-a-rightsbased-approach-to-ai-development/. 258, 259

Mitchell, Margaret, Simone Wu, Andrew Zaldivar, Parker Barnes, Lucy Vasserman, Ben Hutchinson, Elena Spitzer, Inioluwa Deborah Raji, and Timnit Gebru. 2019. Model Cards for Model Reporting. In *FAT* '19: Proceedings of the Conference on Fairness, Accountability, and Transparency*, 220–229. Association for Computing Machinery. 255

Mitchell, Melanie, Stephanie Forrest, and John H. Holland. 1992. The Royal Road for Genetic Algorithms: Fitness Landscapes and GA Performance. In *Proceedings of the First European Conference on Artificial Life*, eds. F. J. Varela and P. Bourgine, 1–11. Cambridge, MA: The MIT Press. 81

Mitchell, Shira, Eric Potash, Solon Barocas, Alexander D'Amour, and Kristian Lum. 2021. Algorithmic Fairness: Choices, Assumptions, and Definitions. *Annual Review of Statistics and Its Application* 8: 141–163. 110, 114

Mittelstadt, Brent Daniel, Patrick Allo, Mariarosaria Taddeo, Sandra Wachter, and Luciano Floridi. 2016. The Ethics of Algorithms: Mapping the Debate. *Big Data & Society* 3 (2). 126

Mnih, Volodymyr, Koray Kavukcuoglu, David Silver, Alex Graves, Ioannis Antonoglou, Daan Wierstra, and Martin Riedmiller. 2013. Playing Atari with Deep Reinforcement Learning. *arXiv* 1312.5602: 1–9. https://arxiv.org/abs/1312.5602. 55

Mnih, Volodymyr, Koray Kavukcuoglu, David Silver, Andrei A. Rusu, Joel Veness, Marc G. Bellemare, Alex Graves, Martin Riedmiller, Andreas K. Fidjeland, Georg Ostrovski, et al. 2015. Human-Level Control through Deep Reinforcement Learning. *Nature* 518 (7540): 529. 55

Mo, Sangwoo, Minsu Cho, and Jinwoo Shin. 2018. InstaGAN: Instance-Aware Image-to-Image Translation. *arXiv* 1812.10889: 1–26. https://arxiv.org/abs/1812.10889. 212

Moayeri, Mazda, Phillip Pope, Yogesh Balaji, and Soheil Feizi. 2022. A Comprehensive Study of Image Classification Model Sensitivity to Foregrounds, Backgrounds, and Visual Attributes. *arXiv* 2201.10766: 1–30. https://arxiv.org/abs/2201.10766. 103

Mohamed, Shakir, Marie-Therese Png, and William Isaac. 2020. Decolonial AI: Decolonial Theory as Sociotechnical Foresight in Artificial Intelligence. *Philosophy & Technology* 33: 659–684. 257

Molnar, Christoph. 2023. *Interpretable Machine Learning*. https://christophm.github.io/interpretable-ml-book/. 127

Moor, James. 2006. The Nature, Importance, and Difficulty of Machine Ethics. *IEEE intelligent systems* 21 (4): 18–21. 185, 187, 197

Moor, James. 2009. Four Kinds of Ethical Robots. *Philosophy Now* 72: 12–14. 185

Morando, Alberto, Pnina Gershon, Bruce Mehler, and Bryan Reimer. 2021. A Model for Naturalistic Glance Behavior Around Tesla Autopilot Disengagements. *Accident Analysis & Prevention* 161: 106348. 142

Moravčík, Matej, Martin Schmid, Neil Burch, Viliam Lisý, Dustin Morrill, Nolan Bard, Trevor Davis, Kevin Waugh, Michael Johanson, and Michael Bowling. 2017. DeepStack: Expert-Level Artificial Intelligence in Heads-Up No-Limit Poker. *Science* 356 (6337): 508–513. 55

Moravec, Hans. 1976. The Role of Raw Rower in Intelligence. Unpublished manuscript. https://exhibits.stanford.edu/ai/catalog/ws563sd6050. 275

Moravec, Hans. 1988. *Mind Children: The Future of Robot and Human Intelligence*. Cambridge, MA: Harvard University Press. 31, 275

Moravec, Hans. 1999. *Robot: Mere Machine to Transcendent Mind*. Oxford: Oxford University Press. 275

Mordvintsev, Alexander, Christopher Olah, and Mike Tyka. 2015. Inceptionism: Going Deeper into Neural Networks. *Google Research Blog* Jun. (18). https://blog.research.google/2015/06/inceptionism-going-deeper-into-neural.html. 125

More, Martin D., Douglas M. Souza, Jônatas Wehrmann, and Rodrigo C. Barros. 2018. Seamless Nudity Censorship: An Image-to-Image Translation Approach based on Adversarial Training. In *2018 International Joint Conference on Neural Networks (IJCNN)*, 1–8. New York: Institute of Electrical and Electronics Engineers. 212

Muehlhauser, Luke, and Louie Helm. 2013. Intelligence Explosion and Machine Ethics. In *Singularity Hypotheses: A Scientific and Philosophical Assessment*, eds. A. Eden, J. Søraker, J. H. Moor, and E. Steinhart, 101–126. Berlin: Springer. 99

Mullainathan, Sendhil, and Ziad Obermeyer. 2017. Does Machine Learning Automate Moral Hazard and Error? *American Economic Review* 107 (5): 476–480. 8

Müller, Vincent C. 2023. Ethics of Artificial Intelligence and Robotics. In *The Stanford Encyclopedia of Philosophy*, eds. Edward N. Zalta and Uri Nodelman. Metaphysics Research Lab, Stanford University. https://plato.stanford.edu/archives/fall2023/entries/ethics-ai/. 200

Murphy, Kevin P. 2022. *Probabilistic Machine Learning: An Introduction*. Cambridge, MA: The MIT Press. 65

Murphy, Kevin P. 2023. *Probabilistic Machine Learning: Advanced Topics*. Cambridge, MA: The MIT Press. 65

Nagel, Ernest. 1961. *The Structure of Science*. New York: Harcourt, Brace, and World. 245

Nagel, Ernest, and James R. Newman. 1958. *Gödel's Proof*. New York: New York University Press. 24

Nair, Vinod, and Geoffrey E. Hinton. 2010. Rectified Linear Units Improve Restricted Boltzmann Machines. In *ICML'10: Proceedings of the 27th International Conference on International Conference on Machine Learning*, 807–814. New York: Association for Computing Machinery. 48

Nallur, Vivek. 2020. Landscape of Machine Implemented Ethics. *Science and Engineering Ethics* 26 (5): 2381–2399. 213, 214

Narayanan, Arvind, and Sayash Kapoor. 2023. GPT-4 and Professional Benchmarks: The Wrong Answer to the Wrong Question. *AI Snake Oil* Mar. (20). `https://www.aisnakeoil.com/p/gpt-4-and-professional-benchmarks`. 51

Narayanan, Arvind, and Vitaly Shmatikov. 2006. How to Break Anonymity of the Netflix Prize Dataset. *arXiv* 0610105: 1–24. `https://arxiv.org/abs/cs/0610105`. 6

Narayanan, Arvind, and Vitaly Shmatikov. 2008. Robust De-Anonymization of Large Sparse Datasets. In *IEEE Symposium on Security and Privacy*, 111–125. New York: IEEE. 148

National Transportation Safety Board. 2019. Highway Accident Report: Collision Between Vehicle Controlled by Developmental Automated Driving System and Pedestrian, Tempe, Arizona, March 18, 2018, Technical Report HWY18MH010, National Transportation Safety Board. `https://data.ntsb.gov/Docket/?NTSBNumber=HWY18MH010`. 141

New York Times. 1958. New Navy Device Learns by Doing; Psychologist Shows Embryo of Computer Designed to Read and Grow Wiser. *The New York Times* Jul. (08). 32

Newell, Allen, and Herbert A. Simon. 1976. Computer Science as Empirical Inquiry: Symbols and Search. *Communications of the ACM* 19 (3): 113–126. 23

Ng, Andrew Y., and Stuart Russell. 2000. Algorithms for Inverse Reinforcement Learning. In *Proceedings of the Seventeenth International Conference on Machine Learning (ICML 2000)*, 663–670. New York: Association for Computing Machinery. 174

Ngo, Richard, Lawrence Chen, and Sören Mindermann. 2023. The Alignment Problem from a Deep Learning Perspective. *arXiv* 2209.00626: 1–21. `https://arxiv.org/abs/2209.00626`. 68, 71

Nielsen, Michael A. 2019. *Neural Networks and Deep Learning*. Determination Press. `http://neuralnetworksanddeeplearning.com/`. 65

Nilsson, Nils J. 2010. *The Quest for Artificial Intelligence: A History of Ideas and Achievements*. Cambridge: Cambridge University Press. 19, 35, 41

Noble, Safiya Umoja. 2018. *Algorithms of Oppression*. New York: NYU Press. 151, 157

Noddings, Nel. 1982. *Caring: A Feminine Approach to Ethics and Moral Education*. Berkeley: University of California Press. 193

Noothigattu, Ritesh, Snehalkumar (Neil) Gaikwad, Edmond Awad, Sohan Dsouza, Iyad Rahwan, Pradeep Ravikumar, and Ariel Procaccia. 2018. A Voting-Based System for Ethical Decision Making. In *The Thirty-Second AAAI Conference on Artificial Intelligence (AAAI-18)*, Vol. 32, 1587–1594. Association for the Advancement of Artificial Intelligence. 215

Northcutt, Curtis G., Anish Athalye, and Jonas Mueller. 2021. Pervasive Label Errors in Test Sets Destabilize Machine Learning Benchmarks. *arXiv* 2103.14749: 1–24. `https://arxiv.org/abs/2103.14749`. 210, 211

Norvig, Peter. 1992. *Paradigms of Artificial Intelligence Programming Case Studies in Common LISP*. San Francisco: Morgan Kaufmann Publishers. 33

Oakden-Rayner, L., J. Dunnmon, G. Carneiro, and C. Ré. 2020. Hidden Stratification Causes Clinically Meaningful Failures in Machine Learning for Medical Imaging. In *Proceedings of the ACM Conference on Health, Inference, and Learning*, 151–159. 103

Oakley, Brian, and Kenneth Owen. 1990. *Alvey: Britain's Strategic Computing Initiative*. The MIT Press: Cambridge, MA. 36

Obermeyer, Ziad, Brian Powers, Christine Vogeli, and Sendhil Mullainathan. 2019. Dissecting Racial Bias in an Algorithm Used to Manage the Health of Populations. *Science* 366 (6464): 447–453. 8, 107

Omohundro, Stephen M. 2008. The Basic AI Drives. In *Artificial General Intelligence 2008: Proceedings of the First AGI Conference*, eds. Pei Wang, Ben Goertzel, and Stan Franklin, 483–492. Amsterdam: IOS Press. 70, 281

O'Neil, Cathy. 2016. *Weapons of Math Destruction: How Big Data Increases Inequality and Threatens Democracy*. New York: Broadway Books. 8, 98, 111, 114, 212, 258

OpenAI. 2024. Video Generation Models as World Simulators, Technical report, OpenAI. `https://openai.com/research/video-generation-models-as-world-simulators`. 132

Oppy, Graham, and David Dowe. 2021. The Turing Test. In *The Stanford Encyclopedia of Philosophy*, ed. Edward N. Zalta. Metaphysics Research Lab, Stanford University. `https://plato.stanford.edu/archives/win2021/entries/turing-test/`. 25

Páez, Andréas. 2019. The Pragmatic Turn in Explainable Artificial Intelligence (XAI). *Minds and Machines* 29 (3): 441–459. 126

Pagin, P., and D. Westerståhl. 2010a. Compositionality I: Definitions and Variants. *Philosophy Compass* 5 (3): 250–264. 229

Pagin, P., and D. Westerståhl. 2010b. Compositionality II: Arguments and Problems. *Philosophy Compass* 5 (3): 265–282. 229

Pandia, Lalchand, Yan Cong, and Allyson Ettinger. 2021. Pragmatic Competence of Pre-trained Language Models through the Lens of Discourse Connectives. *arXiv* 2109.12951: 1–13. https://arxiv.org/abs/2109.12951. 241

Papernot, Nicolas, Patrick McDaniel, Arunesh Sinha, and Michael P. Wellman. 2018. SoK: Security and Privacy in Machine Learning. In *Proceedings of the IEEE European Symposium on Security and Privacy (EuroS&P'18)*, 399–414. New York: IEEE. 147

Parcollet, Titouan, and Mirco Ravanelli. 2021. The Energy and Carbon Footprint of Training End-to-End Speech Recognizers, Technical Report hal-03190119, HAL. 149

Park, Andrew Lee. 2019. Injustice Ex Machina: Predictive Algorithms in Criminal Sentencing. *UCLA Law Review* 19. 105

Parker, Anna R. 2006. Evolving the Narrow Language Faculty: Was Recursion the Pivotal Step? In *The Evolution of Language: Proceedings of the 6th International Conference (EVOLANG6)*, eds. Angelo Cangelosi, Andrew D. M. Smith, and Kenny Smith, 239–246. Hackensack, NJ: World Scientific. 230

Partee, Barbara Hall. 1984. Compositionality. In *Varieties of Formal Semantics*, eds. F. Landman and F. Veltman, 281–311. Dordrecht: Foris. 229

Pascal, Blaise. 1670/1910. *Pensées*. London: Dent. 283

Patterson, David, Joseph Gonzalez, Quoc Le, Chen Liang, Lluis-Miquel Munguia, Daniel Rothchild, David So, Maud Texier, and Jeff Dean. 2021. Carbon Emissions and Large Neural Network training. *arXiv* 2104.10350: 1–22. https://arxiv.org/abs/2104.10350. 149

Peddie, Jon. 2022a. *The History of the GPU: Book 1 - Steps to Invention*. Cham: Springer. 38

Peddie, Jon. 2022b. *The History of the GPU: Book 2 - Eras and Environment*. Cham: Springer. 38

Peddie, Jon. 2022c. *The History of the GPU: Book 3 - New Developments*. Cham: Springer. 38

Peebles, William, and Saining Xie. 2020. Scalable Diffusion Models with Transformers. *arXiv* 2212.09748: 1–25. https://arxiv.org/abs/2212.09748. 132

Penfield, Wilder. 1975. *The Mystery of the Mind*. Princeton, NJ: Princeton University Press. 22

Penrose, Roger. 1989. *The Emperor's New Mind: Concerning Computers, Minds, and the Laws of Physics*. Oxford: Oxford University Press. 24

Penrose, Roger. 1994. Mathematical Intelligence. In *What Is Intelligence?*, ed. Jean Khalifa, 107–136. Cambridge: Cambridge University Press. 24

Perrakis, Anastassis, and Titia K. Sixma. 2021. AI Revolutions in Biology: The Joys and Perils of AlphaFold. *EMBO Reports* 22 (11): 1–6. 154

Perrigo, Billy. 2023. OpenAI Used Kenyan Workers on Less Than $2 Per Hour to Make ChatGPT Less Toxic. *TIME* Jan. (18). https://time.com/6247678/openai-chatgpt-kenya-workers/. 151

Peters, Matthew E., Mark Neumann, Mohit Iyyer, Matt Gardner, Christopher Clark, Kenton Lee, and Luke Zettlemoyer. 2018. Deep Contextualized Word Representations. *arXiv* 1802.05365: 1–15. https://arxiv.org/abs/1802.05365. 149

Peterson, Martin, and Peter Gärdenfors. 2024. How to Measure Value Alignment in AI. *AI and Ethics* 4: 1493–1506. 207

Pettigrew, Richard. 2016. *Accuracy and the Laws of Credence*. Oxford: Oxford University Press. 253

Pinker, Steven, and Ray Jackendoff. 2005. The Faculty of Language: What's Special About It? *Cognition* 95 (2): 201–236. 230

Planer, Ronald J., and Kim Sterelny. 2021. *From Signal to Symbol: The Evolution of Language*. Cambridge, MA: The MIT Press. 230, 232, 233, 277

Poplin, Ryan, Avinash V. Varadarajan, Katy Blumer, Yun Liu, Michael V. McConnell, Greg S. Corrado, Lily Peng, and Dale R. Webster. 2018. Prediction of Cardiovascular Risk Factors from Retinal Fundus Photographs via Deep Learning. *Nature Biomedical Engineering* 2: 158–164. 104

Popper, Karl. 1959. *The Logic of Scientific Discovery*. London: Hutchinson. 245

Poulshock, Joseph W. 2006. Language and Morality: Evolution, Altruism, and Linguistic Moral Mechanisms. PhD diss, University of Edinburgh. 233

Powers, Thomas M. 2006. Prospects for a Kantian Machine. *IEEE Intelligent Systems* 21 (4): 46–51. 73

Prasad, Mahendra. 2018. Social Choice and the Value Alignment Problem. In *Artificial Intelligence Safety and Security*, ed. Roman V. Yampolskiy, 291–314. London: Chapman & Hall. 73

Priani, Ernesto. 2021. Ramon Llull. In *The Stanford Encyclopedia of Philosophy*, ed. Edward N. Zalta. Metaphysics Research Lab, Stanford University. https://plato.stanford.edu/archives/spr2021/entries/llull/. 23

Prince, Simon J. D. 2023. *Understanding Deep Learning*. Cambridge, MA: The MIT Press. 45, 49, 56, 57, 65, 224

Putnam, Hilary. 1960. Minds and Machines. In *Dimensions of Mind: A Symposium*, ed. Sidney Hook, 138–164. New York: New York University Press. 24

Putnam, Hilary. 2002. *The Collapse of the Fact/Value Dichotomy and Other Essays*. Cambridge, MA: Harvard University Press. 248

Raatikainen, Panu. 2022. Gödel's Incompleteness Theorems. In *The Stanford Encyclopedia of Philosophy*, ed. Edward N. Zalta. Metaphysics Research Lab, Stanford University. https://plato.stanford.edu/archives/spr2022/entries/goedel-incompleteness/. 24

Radford, Alec, Jong Wook Kim, Chris Hallacy, Aditya Ramesh, Gabriel Goh, Sandhini Agarwal, Girish Sastry, Amanda Askell, Pamela Mishkin, Jack Clark, et al. 2021. Learning Transferable Visual Models From Natural Language Supervision. *arXiv* 2103.00020: 1–48. https://arxiv.org/abs/2103.00020. 39, 130

Raghavan, Manish, Solon Barocas, Jon Kleinberg, and Karen Levy. 2019. Mitigating Bias in Algorithmic Hiring: Evaluating Claims and Practices. *arXiv* 1906.09208: 1–24. https://arxiv.org/abs/1906.09208. 100

Raji, Inioluwa Deborah, and Joy Buolamwini. 2019. Actionable Auditing: Investigating the Impact of Publicly Naming Biased Performance Results of Commercial AI Products. In *AAAI/ACM Conference on AI, Ethics, and Society*, 429–435. 111

Raji, Inioluwa Deborah, and Roel Dobbe. 2023. Concrete Problems in AI Safety, Revisited. *arXiv* 2401.10899: 2023. https://arxiv.org/abs/2401.10899/. 146, 148, 150, 151, 171, 180, 251

Raji, Inioluwa Deborah, Timnit Gebru, Margaret Mitchell, Joy Buolamwini, Joonseok Lee, and Emily Denton. 2020. Saving Face: Investigating the Ethical Concerns of Facial Recognition Auditing. *arXiv* 2001.00964: 1–7. https://arxiv.org/abs/2001.00964. 148, 149

Raji, Inioluwa Deborah, Emily M. Bender, Amandalynne Paullada, Emily Denton, and Alex Hanna. 2021. AI and the Everything in the Whole Wide World Benchmark. *arXiv* 2111.15366: 1–20. https://arxiv.org/abs/2111.15366. 209, 211

Raji, Inioluwa Deborah, I. Elizabeth Kumar, Aaron Horowitz, and Andrew Selbst. 2022. The Fallacy of AI Functionality. In *ACM Conference on Fairness, Accountability, and Transparency*, 959–972. 111

Ramesh, Aditya, Mikhail Pavlov, Gabriel Goh, Scott Gray, Chelsea Voss, Alec Radford, Mark Chen, and Ilya Sutskever. 2021. Zero-Shot Text-to-Image Generation. *arXiv* 2102.12092: 1–20. https://arxiv.org/abs/2102.12092. 53

Ramesh, Aditya, Prafulla Dhariwal, Alex Nichol, Casey Chu, and Mark Chen. 2022. Hierarchical Text-Conditional Image Generation with Clip Latents. *arXiv* 2204.06125: 1–27. https://arxiv.org/abs/2204.06125. 53

Rautenbach, George, and C. Maria Keet. 2020. Toward Equipping Artificial Moral Agents with Multiple Ethical Theories. *arXiv* 2003.00935: 1–33. https://arxiv.org/abs/2003.00935. 73

Reed, Scott, Honglak Lee, Dragomir Anguelov, Christian Szegedy, Dumitru Erhan, and Andrew Rabinovich. 2015. Training Deep Neural Networks on Noisy Labels with Bootstrapping. *arXiv* 1412.6596: 1–11. Workshop contribution at ICLR 2015. https://arxiv.org/abs/1412.6596. 211

Reichenbach, Hans. 1938. *Experience and Prediction*. Chicago, IL: University of Chicago Press. 245

Reiss, Julian, and Jan Sprenger. 2020. Scientific Objectivity. In *The Stanford Encyclopedia of Philosophy*, ed. Edward N. Zalta. Metaphysics Research Lab, Stanford University. https://plato.stanford.edu/archives/win2020/entries/scientific-objectivity/. 93, 244, 246, 247

Reydon, Thomas A. C., and Marc Ereshefsky. 2022. How to Incorporate Non-Epistemic Values into a Theory of Classification. *European Journal for Philosophy of Science volume* 12 (4): 1–28. 248

Rhodes, Richard. 1986. *The Making of the Atomic Bomb*. New York: Simon & Schuster. 279

Ribeiro, Marco, Sameer Singh, and Carlos Guestrin. 2016. "Why Should I Trust You?": Explaining the Predictions of Any Classifier. In *Meeting of the Association for Computational Linguistics*, 97–101. 124

Richardson, Ken. 2017. *Genes, Brains, and Human Potential: The Science and Ideology of Intelligence*. New York: Columbia University Press. 2

Rini, Regina. 2020. Deepfakes and the Epistemic Backstop. *Philosophers' Imprint* 20 (24): 1–16. 145

Rini, Regina, and Leah Cohen. 2020. Deep Fakes, Deep Harms. *Journal of Ethics & Social Philosophy* 22 (2): 143–161. 145

Robinson, Howard. 2023. Dualism. In *The Stanford Encyclopedia of Philosophy*, eds. Edward N. Zalta and Uri Nodelman. Metaphysics Research Lab, Stanford University. `https://plato.stanford.edu/archives/spr2023/entries/dualism/`. 21

Roff, Heather M. 2020. Expected Utilitarianism. *arXiv* 2008.07321: 1–22. `https://arxiv.org/abs/2008.07321`. 73

Rogers, Carl R. 1946. Significant Aspects of Client-Centered Therapy. *American Psychologist* 1 (10): 415. 32

Rolnick, David, Priya L. Donti, Lynn H. Kaack, Kelly Kochanski, Alexandre Lacoste, Kris Sankaran, Andrew Slavin Ross, Nikola Milojevic-Dupont, Natasha Jaques, Anna Waldman-Brown, et al. 2019. Tackling Climate Change with Machine Learning. *arXiv* 1906.05433: 1–111. `https://arxiv.org/abs/1906.05433`. 149

Rooney, Phyllis. 1992. On Values in Science: Is the Epistemic/Non-Epistemic Distinction Useful? In *PSA 1992: Proceedings of the Biennial Meeting of the Philosophy of Science Association (Volume One: Contributed Papers)*, eds. D. L. Hull, M. Forbes, and K. Okruhlik, 13–22. Philosophy of Science Association. 250

Rooney, Phyllis. 2017. The Borderlands Between Epistemic and Non-Epistemic Values. In *Current controversies in values and science*, eds. Kevin C. Elliott and Daniel Steel, 31–45. Oxford: Routledge. 250

Rosenblatt, Frank. 1958. The Perceptron: A Probabilistic Model for Information Storage and Organization in the Brain. *Psychological Review* 65 (6): 386–408. 30, 63

Rosenblueth, Arturo, Norbert Wiener, and Julian Bigelow. 1943. Behavior, Purpose and Teleology. *Philosophy of Science* 10 (1): 18–24. 25

Ross, William David. 1930. *The Right and the Good*. Oxford: Oxford University Press. 190

Ross, William David. 1931. The Coherence Theory of Goodness. *Proceedings of the Aristotelian Society: Supplementary Volumes* 10: 61–70. 190

Roth-Hanania, Ronit, Maayan Davidov, and Carolyn Zahn-Waxler. 2011. Empathy Development from 8 to 16 Months: Early Signs of Concern for Others. *Infant Behavior and Development* 34 (3): 447–458. 234

Rothschild, Michael, and Joseph Stiglitz. 1976. Equilibrium in Competitive Insurance Markets: An Essay on the Economics of Imperfect Information. *Quarterly Journal of Economics* 93 (4): 541–562. 78

Rowlands, Mark. 2012. *Can Animals Be Moral?* Oxford: Oxford University Press. 231

Rowlands, Mark, Joe Lau, and Max Deutsch. 2020. Externalism About the Mind. In *The Stanford Encyclopedia of Philosophy*, ed. Edward N. Zalta. Metaphysics Research Lab, Stanford University. `https://plato.stanford.edu/archives/win2020/entries/content-externalism/`. 273

Rudner, Richard. 1953. The Scientist qua Scientist Makes Value Judgments. *Philosophy of Science* 20 (1): 1–6. 249

Rumelhart, David E., Geoffrey E. Hinton, and Ronald J. Williams. 1986. Learning Internal Representation by Error Propagation. In *Parallel Distributed Processing*, eds. D. E. Rumelhart, J. L. McClelland, and the PDP Research Group, Vol. 1, 599–607. Cambridge, MA: The MIT Press. 38, 63

Ruphy, Stéphanie. 2006. 'Empiricism All the Way down': A Defense of the Value-Neutrality of Science in Response to Helen Longino's Contextual Empiricism. *Perspectives on Science* 14 (2): 189–214. 247

Russell, Stuart. 2019. *Human Compatible: Artificial Intelligence and the Problem of Control*. New York: Viking. 26, 67, 68, 176, 177, 179, 271, 279

Russell, Stuart, and Peter Norvig. 2021. *Artificial Intelligence: A Modern Approach*, 4th ed. Hoboken, NJ: Pearson. 22, 34, 43, 65, 279

Sagawa, S., A. Raghunathan, P. W. Koh, and P. Liang. 2020. An Investigation of Why Overparameterization Exacerbates Spurious Correlations. In *International Conference on Machine Learning*, 8346–8356. Proceedings of Machine Learning Research (PMLR). 103

Sahlgren, Magnus, and Fredrik Carlsson. 2021. The Singleton Fallacy: Why Current Critiques of Language Models Miss the Point. *Frontiers in Artificial Intelligence* 4: 682578. 241

Sale, Tony. 2000. The Colossus of Bletchley Park – The German Cipher System. In *The First Computers: History and Architecture*, eds. Raúl Rojas and Ulf Hashagen, 351–364. Cambridge, MA: The MIT Press. 2

Samuel, Arthur L. 1959. Some Studies in Machine Learning Using the Game of Checkers. *IBM Journal* 3 (3): 535–554. 30

Samuelson, Paul A. 1938a. A Note on the Pure Theory of Consumer's Behaviour. *Economica* 5 (17): 61–71. 237

Samuelson, Paul A. 1938b. A Note on the Pure Theory of Consumer's Behaviour: An Addendum. *Economica* 5 (19): 353–354. 237

Sanz, Rodrigo. 2020. Ethica Ex Machina: Exploring Artificial Moral Agency or the Possibility of Computable Ethics. *Zeitschrift für Ethik und Moralphilosophie* 3 (2): 223–239. 73

Sapir, Edward. 1921. *Language*. New York: Harcourt, Brace. 1

Sappington, David E. M. 1991. Incentives in Principal-Agent Relationships. *Journal of Economic Perspectives* 5 (2): 45–66. 79

Sarnet, Rainer. 2017. *November*. Homeless Bob Production, Opus Film, and PRPL. 115 min. 21

Sastry, Girish, Lennart Heim, Haydn Belfield, Markus Anderljung, Miles Brundage, Julian Hazell, Cullen O'Keefe, Gillian K. Hadfield, Richard Ngo, Konstantin Pilz, et al. 2024. Computing Power and the Governance of Artificial Intelligence. *arXiv* 2402.08797: 1–104. https://arxiv.org/abs/2402.08797. 260

Schaeffer, Jonathan. 2007. Game Over: Black to Play and Draw in Checkers. *ICGA Journal* 30 (4): 187–197. 29

Schaul, Kevin, Szu Yu Chen, and Nitasha Tiku. 2023. Inside the Secret List of Websites that Make AI Like ChatGPT Sound Smart. *The Washington Post* Apr. (19). https://www.washingtonpost.com/technology/interactive/2023/ai-chatbot-learning/. 129

Scheuerman, Morgan Klaus, Alex Hanna, and Emily Denton. 2021. Do Datasets Have Politics? Disciplinary Values in Computer Vision Dataset Development. *Proceedings of the Association for Computing Machinery on Human-Computer Interaction* 5 (CSCW2): 1–37. 212

Scheutz, Matthias. 2016. The Need for Moral Competency in Autonomous Agent Architectures. In *Fundamental Issues of Artificial Intelligence*, ed. Vincent C. Müller, 517–527. Cham: Springer. 185, 197

Scheutz, Matthias, and Thomas Arnold. 2016. Are We Ready for Sex Robots? In *11th ACM/IEEE International Conference on Human-Robot Interaction (HRI)*, 351–358. New York: IEEE. 184

Schlangen, David. 2021. Targeting the Benchmark: On Methodology in Current Natural Language Processing Research. In *Proceedings of the 59th Annual Meeting of the Association for Computational Linguistics and the 11th International Joint Conference on Natural Language Processing (Volume 2: Short Papers)*, 670–674. Association for Computational Linguistics. https://aclanthology.org/2021.acl-short.85. 209

Schlosser, Markus. 2019. Agency. In *The Stanford Encyclopedia of Philosophy*, ed. Edward N. Zalta. Metaphysics Research Lab, Stanford University. https://plato.stanford.edu/archives/win2019/entries/agency/. 183

Schmidhuber, Jürgen. 2015. Deep Learning in Neural Networks: An Overview. *Neural Networks* 61: 85–117. 41

Schmidt, Marco F. H., Hannes Rakoczy, and Michael Tomasello. 2012. Young Children Enforce Social Norms Selectively Depending on the Violator's Group Affiliation. *Cognition* 124 (3): 325–333. 234

Schultz, Wolfram, Peter Dayan, and P. Read Montague. 1997. A Neural Substrate of Prediction and Reward. *Science* 275 (5306): 1593–1599. 53

Schuman, Catherine D., Shruti R. Kulkarni, Maryam Parsa, J. Parker Mitchell, Prasanna Date, and Bill Kay. 2022. Opportunities for Neuromorphic Computing Algorithms and Applications. *Nature Computational Science* 2: 10–19. 273

Schwartz, Jacob T. 1987. Limits of Artificial Intelligence. In *Encyclopedia of Artificial Intelligence*, eds. Stuart C. Shapiro and David Eckroth, Vol. 1, 488–503. New York: Wiley. 37

Schwartz, Roy, Jesse Dodge, Noah A. Smith, and Oren Etzioni. 2019. Green AI. *arXiv* 1907.10597: 1–12. https://arxiv.org/abs/1907.10597. 149

Scott, Ridley. 1982. *Blade Runner*. Warner Bros. 117 min. 4

Scott-Phillips, Thomas C., and Richard A. Blythe. 2013. Why Is Combinatorial Communication Rare in the Natural World, and Why Is Language an Exception to This Trend? *Journal of the Royal Society Interface* 10 (88): 1–7. 229

Seabrook, Mélanie S. S., Alex Luscombe, Nicole Balian, Aisha Lofters, Flora I. Matheson, Braden G. O'Neill, Akwasi Owusu-Bempah, Navindra Persaud, and Andrew D. Pinto. 2023. Police Funding and Crime Rates in 20 of Canada's Largest Municipalities: A Longitudinal Study. *Canadian Public Policy* 49 (4): 383–398. 97

Selbst, Andrew D., Danah Boyd, Sorelle A. Friedler, Suresh Venkatasubramanian, and Janet Vertesi. 2019. Fairness and Abstraction in Sociotechnical Systems. In *FAT* '19: Proceedings of the Conference on Fairness, Accountability, and Transparency*, 59–68. New York: Association for Computing Machinery. 111

Sen, Amartya K. 1973. Behaviour and the Concept of Preference. *Economica* 40 (159): 241–259. 237

Sen, Amartya K. 1977. Rational Fools: A Critique of the Behavioral Foundations of Economic Theory. *Philosophy & Public Affairs* 6 (4): 317–344. 237

Sen, Amartya K. 1993. Internal Consistency of Choice. *Econometrica* 61 (3): 495–521. 237

Sen, Amartya K. 1997. Maximization and the Act of Choice. *Econometrica* 65 (4): 495–521. 237

Sen, Amartya K. 2002. *Rationality and Freedom*. Cambridge, MA: Harvard University Press. 237

Seo, Sungyong, Hau Chan, P. Jeffrey Brantingham, Jorja Leap, Phebe Vayanos, Milind Tambe, and Yan Liu. 2018. Partially Generative Neural Networks for Gang Crime Classification with Partial Information. In *Proceedings of the 2018 AAAI/ACM Conference on AI, Ethics, and Society*, 257–263. New York: Association for Computing Machinery. 143

Shah, Sunit N. 2014. Literature Review: The Principal Agent Problem in Finance. *The CFA Institute Research Foundation* L2014-1: 1–55. 79

Shahaf, Dafna, and Eyal Amir. 2007. Towards a Theory of AI Completeness. In *AAAI Spring Symposium: Logical Formalizations of Commonsense Reasoning*, eds. Eyal Amir, Vladimir Lifschitz, and Rob Miller, 150–155. New York: AAAI Press. 239

Shapiro, Stewart. 1998. Incompleteness, Mechanism, and Optimism. *Bulletin of Symbolic Logic* 4 (3): 273–302. 24

Shapley, Lloyd S. 1953. Stochastic Games. *Proceedings of the National Academy of Sciences of the United States of America* 39 (10): 1095–1100. 78

Shaw, Nolan P., Andreas Stöckel, Ryan W. Orr, Thomas F. Lidbetter, and Robin Cohen. 2018. Towards Provably Moral AI Agents in Bottom-Up Learning Frameworks. In *AIES '18: Proceedings of the 2018 AAAI/ACM Conference on AI, Ethics, and Society*, 271–277. New York: Association for Computing Machinery. 196

Shew, Ashley. 2023. *Against Technoableism: Rethinking Who Needs Improvement*. New York: W. W. Norton. 261

Shokri, Reza, Marco Stronati, Congzheng Song, and Vitaly Shmatikov. 2017. Membership Inference Attacks Against Machine Learning Models. In *Proceedings of the IEEE Symposium on Security and Privacy (SP'17)*, 3–18. New York: IEEE. 147

Shortliffe, Edward H. 1976. *Computer Based Medical Consultations: MYCIN*. New York: American Elsevier Publishing Company. 35

Shumailov, Ilia, Zakhar Shumaylov, Yiren Zhao, Yarin Gal, Nicolas Papernot, and Ross Anderson. 2023. The Curse of Recursion: Training on Generated Data Makes Models Forget. *arXiv* 2305.17493: 1–18. https://arxiv.org/abs/2305.17493. 134

Siddiqui, Faiz, and Jeremy B. Merrill. 2023. 17 Fatalities, 376 Crashes: The Shocking Toll of Tesla's Autopilot. *The Washington Post* Jun. (10). https://www.washingtonpost.com/technology/2023/06/10/tesla-autopilot-crashes-elon-musk/. 171

Silver, David, Aja Huang, Chris J. Maddison, Arthur Guez, Laurent Sifre, George Van Den Driessche, Julian Schrittwieser, Ioannis Antonoglou, Veda Panneershelvam, Marc Lanctot, et al. 2016. Mastering the Game of Go with Deep Neural Networks and Tree Search. *Nature* 529 (7587): 484–489. 55

Silver, David, Thomas Hubert, Julian Schrittwieser, Ioannis Antonoglou, Matthew Lai, Arthur Guez, Marc Lanctot, Laurent Sifre, Dharshan Kumaran, Thore Graepel, et al. 2017a. Mastering Chess and Shogi by Self-Play with a General Reinforcement Learning Algorithm. *arXiv* 1712.01815: 1–19. `https://arxiv.org/abs/1712.01815`. 55

Silver, David, Julian Schrittwieser, Karen Simonyan, Ioannis Antonoglou, Aja Huang, Arthur Guez, Thomas Hubert, Lucas Baker, Matthew Lai, Adrian Bolton, et al. 2017b. Mastering the Game of Go without Human Knowledge. *Nature* 550 (7676): 354–359. 55

Silver, David, Thomas Hubert, Julian Schrittwieser, Ioannis Antonoglou, Matthew Lai, Arthur Guez, Marc Lanctot, Laurent Sifre, Dharshan Kumaran, Thore Graepel, et al. 2018. A General Reinforcement Learning Algorithm that Masters Chess, Shogi, and Go through Self-Play. *Science* 362 (6419): 1140–1144. 55

Simões, Gabriel S., Jônatas Wehrmann, and Rodrigo C. Barros. 2019. Attention-based Adversarial Training for Seamless Nudity Censorship. In *2019 International Joint Conference on Neural Networks (IJCNN)*, 1–8. New York: Institute of Electrical and Electronics Engineers. 212

Simon, Herbert A. 1960. *The New Science of Management Decision*. New York: Harper & Brothers. 31

Simon, Herbert A., and Allen Newell. 1958. Heuristic Problem Solving: The Next Advance in Operations Research. *Operations Research* 6 (1): 1–10. 31

Singer, Uriel, Adam Polyak, Thomas Hayes, Xi Yin, Jie An, Songyang Zhang, Qiyuan Hu, Harry Yang, Oron Ashual, Oran Gafni, et al. 2022. Make-A-Video: Text-to-Video Generation without Text-Video Data. *arXiv* 2209.14792: 1–13. `https://arxiv.org/abs/2209.14792`. 132

Sinha, Koustuv, Robin Jia, Dieuwke Hupkes, Joelle Pineau, Adina Williams, and Douwe Kiela. 2021. Masked Language Modeling and the Distributional Hypothesis: Order Word Matters Pre-training for Little. *arXiv* 2104.06644: 1–26. `https://arxiv.org/abs/2104.06644`. 241

Sipper, Moshe, Ryan J. Urbanowicz, and Jason H. Moore. 2018. To Know the Objective Is Not (Necessarily) to Know the Objective Function. *BioData Mining* 11 (21): 1–3. 81

Skalse, Joar, Nikolaus Howe, Dmitrii Krasheninnikov, and David Krueger. 2022. Defining and Characterizing Reward Hacking. In *Advances in Neural Information Processing Systems 35 (NeurIPS 2022)*, eds. S. Koyejo, S. Mohamed, A. Agarwal, D. Belgrave, K. Cho, and A. Oh, 1–12. 169

Skyrms, Brian. 1994. Sex and Justice. *The Journal of Philosophy* 91 (6): 305–320. 157

Skyrms, Brian. 1996. *Evolution and the Social Contract*. Cambridge: Cambridge University Press. 157

Smetana, Judith G., and Judith L. Braeges. 1990. The Development of Toddlers' Moral and Conventional Judgments. *Merrill-Palmer Quarterly* 36 (3): 329–346. 233

Smetana, Judith G., Wendy M. Rote, Marc Jambon, Marina Tasopoulos-Chan, Myriam Villalobos, and Jessamy Comer. 2012. Developmental Changes and Individual Differences in Young Children's Moral Judgments. *Child Development* 83 (2): 683–696. 234

Sober, Elliott, and David Sloan Wilson. 1998. *Unto Others: The Evolution and Psychology of Unselfish Behavior*. Cambridge, MA: Harvard University Press. 233

Spelman, Elizabeth V. 1989. Anger and Insubordination. In *Women, Knowledge and Reality*, eds. Ann Garry and Marilyn Pearsall, 263–273. Boston: Unwin Hyman Ltd. 214

Spence, Michael. 1973. Job Market Signaling. *Quarterly Journal of Economics* 87 (3): 355–374. 78

Spence, Michael. 1974. *Market Signalling: Informational Transfer in Hiring and Related Processes*. Cambridge, MA: Harvard University Press. 78

Sreenivasan, Gopal. 2002. Errors about Errors: Virtue Theory and Trait Attribution. *Mind* 111 (441): 47–68. 196

Srivastava, Siddharth, and Gaurav Sharma. 2023. OmniVec: Learning Robust Representations with Cross Modal Sharing. *arXiv* 2311.05709v1: 1–18. `https://arxiv.org/abs/2311.05709v1`. 210

stability. ai. 2023. Comments of stability.ai: Notice of Inquiry on Artificial Intelligence & Copyright, Technical Report Dkt. 2023-6, U.S. Copyright Office. 147

Stanton, Andrew. 2008. *WALL-E*. Walt Disney Pictures and Pixar Animation Studios. 100 Minutes. 284

Steel, Daniel. 2010. Epistemic Values and the Argument from Inductive Risk. *Philosophy of Science* 77 (1): 14–34. 145, 250

Steels, Luc, and Brice Lepape. 1993. Knowledge Engineering in Espirit. *IEEE Expert* 8 (4): 4–10. 36

Steinert-Threlkeld, Shane. 2020. Toward the Emergence of Nontrivial Compositionality. *Philosophy of Science* 87 (5): 897–909. 229

Stoffi, Falco J. Bargagli, Gustavo Cevolani, and Giorgio Gnecco. 2022. Simple Models in Complex Worlds: Occam's Razor and Statistical Learning Theory. *Minds and Machines* 32: 13–42. 246

Stoljar, Daniel. 2023. Physicalism. In *The Stanford Encyclopedia of Philosophy*, eds. Edward N. Zalta and Uri Nodelman. Metaphysics Research Lab, Stanford University. https://plato.stanford.edu/archives/sum2023/entries/physicalism/. 21

Street, Sharon. 2006. A Darwinian Dilemma for Realist Theories of Value. *Philosophical Studies* 127 (1): 109–166. 199

Strubell, Emma, Ananya Ganesh, and Andrew McCallum. 2019. Energy and Policy Considerations for Deep Learning in NLP. In *Proceedings of the 57th Annual Meeting of the Association for Computational Linguistics*, 3645–3650. Association for Computational Linguistics. 149

Strubell, Emma, Ananya Ganesh, and Andrew McCallum. 2020. Energy and Policy Considerations for Modern Deep Learning Research. *Proceedings of the AAAI Conference on Artificial Intelligence* 34 (9): 13693–13696. 149

Sutskever, Ilya. 2022. it may be that today's large neural networks are slightly conscious. *Twitter* Feb. (09). https://twitter.com/ilyasut/status/1491554478243258368. 31

Sutton, Rich. 2019. The Bitter Lesson. *Incomplete Ideas* Mar (13). http://www.incompleteideas.net/IncIdeas/BitterLesson.html. 40, 62

Sutton, Richard S. 1988. Learning to Predict by the Methods of Temporal Difference. *Machine Learning* 3 (1): 9–44. 30

Sutton, Richard S., and Andrew G. Barto. 1981. Toward a Modern Theory of Adaptive Networks: Expectation and Prediction. *Psychological Review* 88 (2): 135–170. 53

Sutton, Richard S., and Andrew G. Barto. 2018. *Reinforcement Learning: An Introduction*. Cambridge, MA: The MIT press. 30, 53, 65

Swartout, William R., and Johanna D. Moore. 1993. Explanation in Second Generation Expert Systems. In *Second Generation Expert Systems*, eds. Jean-Marc David, Jean-Paul Krivine, and Reid Simmons, 543–585. Berlin, Heidelberg: Springer. 127

Szabó, Zoltán Gendler. 2012. The Case for Compositionality. In *The Oxford Handbook of Compositionality*, eds. Wolfram Hinzen, Edouard Machery, and Markus Werning, 64–80. Oxford: Oxford University Press. 229

Szabó, Zoltán Gendler. 2020. Compositionality. In *The Stanford Encyclopedia of Philosophy*, ed. Edward N. Zalta. The Metaphysics Research Lab, Stanford University. https://plato.stanford.edu/archives/fall2020/entries/compositionality/. 229

Szegedy, Christian, Wojciech Zaremba, Ilya Sutskever, Joan Bruna, Dumitru Erhan, Ian Goodfellow, and Rob Fergus. 2014. Intriguing Properties of Neural Networks. *arXiv* 1312.6199: 1–10. https://arxiv.org/abs/1312.6199. 165

Taddeo, Mariarosaria, and Luciano Floridi. 2018. How AI Can Be a Force for Good. *Science* 361 (6404): 751–752. 200

Tallerman, Maggie. 2007. Did Our Ancestors Speak a Holistic Protolanguage? *Lingua* 117: 579–604. 230

Tallerman, Maggie. 2012. Protolanguage. In *The Oxford Handbook of Language Evolution*, eds. Maggie Tallerman and Kathleen R. Gibson, 479–491. Oxford: Oxford University Press. 230

Tasioulas, John. 2021. The Role of the Arts and Humanities in Thinking about Artificial Intelligence (AI). *Ada Lovelace Institute Blog* Jun. (14). https://www.adalovelaceinstitute.org/blog/role-arts-humanities-thinking-artificial-intelligence-ai/. 73

Taylor, Matthew E., and Peter Stone. 2009. Transfer Learning for Reinforcement Learning Domains: A Survey. *Journal of Machine Learning Research* 10: 1633–1685. 171

Taylor, Petroc. 2023. Smartphone Mobile Network Subscriptions Worldwide 2016–2028. *Statista* Mar. (30). https://www.statista.com/statistics/330695/number-of-smartphone-users-worldwide/. 273

Tegmark, Max. 2018. *Life 3.0: Being Human in the Age of Artificial Intelligence*. New York: Vintage. 70

Tegmark, Max, and Steve Omohundro. 2023. Provably Safe Systems: The Only Path to Controllable AGI. *arXiv* 2309.01933: 1–17. https://arxiv.org/abs/2309.01933. 176

Tennant, Neil. 2023. Logicism and Neologicism. In *The Stanford Encyclopedia of Philosophy*, eds. Edward N. Zalta and Uri Nodelman. Metaphysics Research Lab, Stanford University. https://plato.stanford.edu/archives/win2023/entries/logicism/. 23

Tesauro, Gerald. 1995. Temporal Difference Learning and TD-Gammon. *Communications of the ACM* 38 (3): 58–68. 30

Thiel, David. 2023. Identifying and Eliminating CSAM in Generative ML Training Data and Models, Technical report, Stanford Internet Observatory. 130

Thomson, Judith Jarvis. 1976. Killing, Letting Die, and the Trolley Problem. *The Monist* 59: 204–217. 213, 214

Thomson, Judith Jarvis. 1985. The Trolley Problem. *The Yale Law Journal* 94 (6): 1395–1415. 213, 214

Thoppilan, Romal, Daniel De Freitas, Jamie Hall, Noam Shazeer, Apoorv Kulshreshtha, Heng-Tze Cheng, Alicia Jin, Taylor Bos, Leslie Baker, Yu Du, et al. 2022. LaMDA: Language Models for Dialog Applications. *arXiv* 2201.08239: 1–47. https://arxiv.org/abs/2201.08239. 241

Thorndike, Edward L. 1905. *The Elements of Psychology*. Syracuse: The Mason Press. 53

Thorndike, Edward L. 1911. *Animal Intelligence: Experimental Studies*. New York: The Macmillan Company. 53

Thorndike, Edward L. 1927. The Law of Effect. *American Journal of Psychology* 39: 212–222. 53

Tiku, Nitasha. 2022a. The Google Engineer Who Thinks the Company's AI Has Come to Life. *The Washington Post* Jun. (11). https://www.washingtonpost.com/technology/2022/06/11/google-ai-lamda-blake-lemoine/. 32

Tiku, Nitasha. 2022b. Google Fired Engineer Who Said Its AI Was Sentient. *The Washington Post* Jul. (22). https://www.washingtonpost.com/technology/2022/07/22/google-ai-lamda-blake-lemoine-fired. 32

Tolmeijer, Suzanne, Markus Kneer, Cristina Sarasua, Markus Christen, and Abraham Bernstein. 2020. Implementations in Machine Ethics: A Survey. *ACM Computing Surveys* 53 (6): 1–38. 196

Tomasello, Michael. 2008. *Origins of Human Communication*. Cambridge, MA: The MIT Press. 232

Tomasello, Michael. 2014. *A Natural History of Human Thinking*. Cambridge, MA: Harvard University Press. 232

Tomasello, Michael. 2018. The Normative Turn in Early Moral Development. *Human Development* 61 (4–5): 248–263. 233

Tomasev, Nenad, Kevin R. McKee, Jackie Kay, and Shakir Mohamed. 2021. Fairness for Unobserved Characteristics: Insights from Technological Impacts on Queer Communities. In *Proceedings of the 2021 AAAI/ACM Conference on AI, Ethics, and Society*, 254–265. New York: Association for Computing Machinery. https://doi.org/10.1145/3461702.3462540. 109, 110, 114

Touvron, Hugo, Matthieu Cord, Matthijs Douze, Francisco Massa, Alexandre Sablayrolles, and Hervé Jégou. 2021. Training Data-Efficient Image Transformers & Distillation Through Attention. *arXiv* 2012.12877: 1–22. https://arxiv.org/abs/2012.12877. 39, 128

Traxler, Matthew J., Megan Boudewyn, and Jessica Loudermilk. 2012. What's Special About Human Language? The Contents of the 'Narrow Language Faculty' Revisited. *Language and Linguistics Compass* 6 (10): 611–621. 230

Tudor, Alyosxa. 2023. The Anti-Feminism of Anti-Trans Feminism. *European Journal of Women's Studies* 30 (2): 290–302. 109

Turing, Alan M. 1937a. Computability and λ-Definability. *Journal of Symbolic Logic* 2 (4): 153–163. 24

Turing, Alan M. 1937b. On Computable Numbers, With an Application to the Entscheidungsproblem. *Proceedings of the London Mathematical Society* s2–42 (1): 230–265. 23, 24

Turing, Alan M. 1950. Computing Machinery and Intelligence. *Mind* LIX (236): 433–460. 24, 25

Twomey, Terrence. 2013. The Cognitive Implications of Controlled Fire Use by Early Humans. *Cambridge Archaeological Journal* 23 (1): 113–128. 232

Twomey, Terrence. 2014. How Domesticating Fire Facilitated the Evolution of Human Cooperation. *Biology and Philosophy* 29 (1): 89–99. 232

Uc-Cetina, Victor, Nicolas Navarro-Guerrero, Anabel Martin-Gonzalez, Cornelius Weber, and Stefan Wermter. 2022. Survey on Reinforcement Learning for Language Processing. *arXiv* 2104.05565: 1–37. https://arxiv.org/abs/2104.05565. 39

Unger, Peter. 1996. *Living High and Letting Die*. Oxford: Oxford University Press. 214

Vallor, Shannon. 2011. Carebots and Caregivers: Sustaining the Ethical Ideal of Care in the 21st Century. *Philosophy and Technology* 24 (3): 251–268. 152

Vallor, Shannon. 2015. Moral Deskilling and Upskilling in a New Machine Age: Reflections on the Ambiguous Future of Character. *Philosophy & Technology* 28: 107–124. 152, 199

Vallor, Shannon. 2016. *Technology and the Virtues: A Philosophical Guide to a Future Worth Wanting*. Oxford: Oxford University Press. 73, 152

Van Lent, Michael, William Fisher, and Michael Mancuso. 2004. An Explainable Artificial Intelligence System for Small-unit Tactical Behavior. In *IAAI'04: Proceedings of the 16th Conference on Innovative Applications of Artificial Intelligence*, 900–907. New York: Association for Computing Machinery. 127

Van Rooij, Iris, Olivia Guest, Federico Adolfi, Ronald de Haan, Antonina Kolokolova, and Patricia Rich. 2023. Reclaiming AI as a Theoretical Tool for Cognitive Science. *PsyarXiv* Aug. 1: 1–22. https://doi.org/10.31234/osf.io/4cbuv. 4, 275

Van Wynsberghe, Aimee, and Scott Robbins. 2019. Critiquing the Reasons for Making Artificial Moral Agents. *Science Engineering Ethics* 25: 719–735. 197, 198, 199

Vanderelst, Dieter, and Alan Winfield. 2018. An Architecture for Ethical Robots Inspired by the Simulation Theory of Cognition. *Cognitive Systems Research* 48: 56–66. 73

Vapnik, Vladimir N. 1995. *The Nature of Statistical Learning Theory*. New York: Springer. 57

Vaughan, Emmett J. 1997. *Risk Management*. New York: Wiley. 78

Véliz, Carissa. 2020. *Privacy Is Power: Why and How You Should Take Back Control of Your Data*. Bantam Press. 259

Veres, Csaba. 2022. Large Language Models Are not Models of Natural Language: They Are Corpus Models. *arXiv* 2112.07055: 1–12. https://arxiv.org/abs/2112.07055. 241

Vicinanza, Domenico. 2023. A New Supercomputer Aims to Closely Mimic the Human Brain — It Could Help Unlock the Secrets of the Mind and Advance AI. *The Conversation* Dec. (18). https://theconversation.com/a-new-supercomputer-aims-to-closely-mimic-the-human-brain-it-could-help-unlock-the-secrets-of-the-mind-and-advance-ai-220044. 273

Villeneuve, Denis. 2013. *Enemy*. Pathé, Entertainment One, Telefilm Canada, Corus Entertainment, Televisión Española, Movie Central, The Movie Network, Ontario Media Development Corporation, Mecanismo Films, micro_scope, Rhombus Media, Roxbury Pictures. 90 min. 6

Villeneuve, Denis. 2016. *Arrival*. FilmNation Entertainment, Lava Bear Films, and 21 Laps Entertainment. 116 min. 1

Villeneuve, Denis. 2017. *Blade Runner 2049*. Alcon Entertainment, Columbia Pictures, Bud Yorkin Productions, Torridon Films, 16:14 Entertainment, Thunderbird Entertainment, Scott Free Productions. 163 Minutes. 284

Vincent, James. 2020. What a Machine Learning Tool that Turns Obama White Can (and Can't) Tell Us About AI Bias. *The Verge* Sep. (23). https://www.theverge.com/21298762/face-depixelizer-ai-machine-learning-tool-pulse-stylegan-obama-bias. 110

Vincent, Sarah, Rebecca Ring, and Kristin Andrews. 2019. Normative Practices of Other Animals. In *Routledge Handbook of Moral Epistemology*, eds. Aaron Zimmerman, Karen Jones, and Mark Timmons, 57–83. New York: Routledge. 231

Vinge, Vernor. 1983. First Word. *Omni* Jan.: 10. 278

Vinge, Vernor. 1993/2017. The Coming Technological Singularity: How to Survive in the Post-Human Era. In *Science Fiction Criticism: An Anthology of Essential Writings*, ed. Rob Latham, 352–363. London: Bloomsbury. 278

von Neumann, John, and Oskar Morgenstern. 1944. *Theory of Games and Economic Behavior*. Princeton: Princeton University Press. 78

Wacewicz, Sławomir. 2012. The Narrow Faculty of Language: What Is It, Who Has It, and How Is It Defined? *Theoria et Historia Scientiarum* IX: 217–229. 230

Wachowski, Lana, and Lilly Wachowski. 1999. *The Matrix*. Warner Bros, Village Roadshow Pictures, Groucho II Film Partnership, and Silver Pictures. 136 Minutes. 284

Wakabayashi, Daisuke. 2018. Self-Driving Uber Car Kills Pedestrian in Arizona, Where Robots Roam. *The New York Times* Mar. (19). https://www.nytimes.com/2018/03/19/technology/uber-driverless-fatality.html. 171

Wakefield, Jane. 2016. Microsoft Chatbot Is Taught to Swear on Twitter. *BBC News* Mar. (24). https://www.bbc.com/news/technology-35890188. 103, 165

Wallach, Wendell. 2007. Implementing Moral Decision Making Faculties in Computers and Robots. *AI & Society* 22 (4): 463–475. 197

Wallach, Wendell. 2010. Robot Minds and Human Ethics: The Need for a Comprehensive Model of Moral Decision Making. *Ethics and Information Technology* 12 (3): 243–250. 185, 197

Wallach, Wendell, and Colin Allen. 2008. *Moral Machines: Teaching Robots Right from Wrong*. Oxford: Oxford University Press. 185, 196

Wallach, Wendell, Colin Allen, and Iva Smit. 2008. Machine Morality: Bottom-Up and Top-Down Approaches for Modelling Human Moral Faculties. *AI & Society* 22 (4): 565–582. 184

Walsh, Toby, Neil Levy, Genevieve Bell, Anthony Elliott, James Maclaurin, Iven Mareels, and Fiona Wood. 2019. *The Effective and Ethical Development of Artificial Intelligence*. Australian Council of Learned Academics. 184

Warneken, Felix, and Michael Tomasello. 2006. Altruistic Helping in Human Infants and Young Chimpanzees. *Science* 31: 1301–1303. 234

Warneken, Felix, and Michael Tomasello. 2007. Helping and Cooperation at 14 Months of Age. *Infancy* 11: 271–294. 234

Wartenberg, Thomas. 2015. The Philosophy of Film. In *The Stanford Encyclopedia of Philosophy*, eds. Edward N. Zalta and Uri Nodelman. Metaphysics Research Lab, Stanford University. `https://plato.stanford.edu/archives/win2015/entries/film/`. 1

Weizenbaum, Joseph. 1966. ELIZA: A Computer Program for the Study of Natural Language Communication between Man and Machine. *Communications of the Association for Computing Machinery* 9: 36–45. 43, 242

Welbl, Johannes, Amelia Glaese, Jonathan Uesato, Sumanth Dathathri, John Mellor, Lisa Anne Hendricks, Kirsty Anderson, Pushmeet Kohli, Ben Coppin, and Po-Sen Huang. 2021. Challenges in Detoxifying Language Models. *arXiv* 2109.07445: 1–23. `https://arxiv.org/abs/2109.07445`. 211

Westra, Laura, and Bill Lawson, eds. 2001. *Faces of Environmental Racism: Confronting Issues of Global Justice*. Lanham: Rowman & Littlefield. 150

Whitehead, Alfred North, and Bertrand Russell. 1910. *Principia Mathematica*, Vol. I. Cambridge: Cambridge University Press. 23

Whitehead, Alfred North, and Bertrand Russell. 1912. *Principia Mathematica*, Vol. II. Cambridge: Cambridge University Press. 23

Whitehead, Alfred North, and Bertrand Russell. 1913. *Principia Mathematica*, Vol. III. Cambridge: Cambridge University Press. 23

Whorf, Benjamin Lee. 1940. Science and Linguistics. *Technology Review* 42: 229–231. 1

Wiegel, Vincent. 2006. Building Blocks for Artificial Moral Agents. *Proc. Artificial Life X*. `https://www.researchgate.net/profile/Vincent-Wiegel-2/publication/228615030_Building_blocks_for_artificial_moral_agents/links/55fabe5708aeafc8ac3fe6f8/Building-blocks-for-artificial-moral-agents.pdf`. 198

Wiener, Norbert. 1948/1961. *Cybernetics or Control and Communication in the Animal and the Machine*, 2nd ed. Cambridge, MA: The MIT Press. 25

Wiener, Norbert. 1960. Some Moral and Technical Consequences of Automation. *Science* 131 (3410): 1355–1358. 67

Willett, Francis, Erin Kunz, Chaofei Fan, Donald Avansino, Guy Wilson, Eun Young Choi, Foram Kamdar, Leigh R. Hochberg, Shaul Druckmann, Krishna V. Shenoy, and Jaimie M. Henderson. 2023. A High-Performance Speech Neuroprosthesis. *Nature* 620: 1031–1036. 274

Williams, Bernard. 1985. *Ethics and the Limits of Philosophy*. Cambridge, MA: Harvard University Press. 248

Williamson, Oliver E. 1973. Markets and Hierarchies: Some Elementary Considerations. *The American Economic Review* 63 (2): 316–325. 79

Williamson, Oliver E. 1975. *Markets and Hierarchies, Analysis and Antitrust Implications: A Study of the Economics of Internal Organization*. New York: The Free Press. 79

Winner, Langdon. 1980. Do Artifacts Have Politics? *Daedalus* 109 (1): 121–136. 257

Wittel, George. L., and S. Felix Wu. 2004. On Attacking Statistical Spam Filters. In *Proceedings of the First Conference on Email and Anti-Spam*, 1–7. Mountainview, CA: CEAS. 165

Wittgenstein, Ludwig. 1953/2009. *Philosophical Investigations*, 4th ed. Oxford: Wiley-Blackwell. 237

Wolpert, D. H., and W. G. Macready. 1997. No Free Lunch Theorems for Optimization. *IEEE Transactions on Evolutionary Computation* 1: 67–82. 252

Wong, David. 2023. Chinese Ethics. In *The Stanford Encyclopedia of Philosophy*, eds. Edward N. Zalta and Uri Nodelman. Metaphysics Research Lab, Stanford University. https://plato.stanford.edu/archives/spr2024/entries/ethics-chinese/. 193

Wooldridge, Michael. 2021. *A Brief History of Artificial Intelligence: What It Is, Where We Are, and Where We Are Going*. New York: FlatIron Books. 41

Woollard, Fiona, and Frances Howard-Snyder. 2022. Doing vs. Allowing Harm. In *The Stanford Encyclopedia of Philosophy*, eds. Edward N. Zalta and Uri Nodelman. Metaphysics Research Lab, Stanford University. https://plato.stanford.edu/archives/win2022/entries/doing-allowing/. 213

Wray, Alison. 1998. Protolanguage as a Holistic System for Social Interaction. *Language & Communication* 18: 47–67. 230

Wray, Alison. 2000. Holistic Utterances in Protolanguage: The Link from Primates to Humans. In *The Evolutionary Emergence of Language: Social Function and the Origins of Linguistic Form*, eds. C. Knight, M. Studdert-Kennedy, and J. R. Hurford, 285–302. Cambridge: Cambridge University Press. 230

Wray, Alison. 2002. Dual Processing in Protolanguage: Performance without Competence. In *The Transition to Language*, ed. A. Wray, 113–137. Oxford: Oxford University Press. 230

WSU Media Unit. 2023. World First Supercomputer Capable of Brain-Scale Simulation Being Built at Western Sydney University. *Western Sydney University News Centre* Dec. (13). https://www.westernsydney.edu.au/newscentre/news_centre/more_news_stories/world_first_supercomputer_capable_of_brain-scale_simulation_being_built_at_western_sydney_university. 273

Xiao, Kai, Logan Engstrom, Andrew Ilyas, and Aleksander Madry. 2020. Noise or Signal: The Role of Image Backgrounds in Object Recognition. *arXiv* 2006.09994: 1–24. https://arxiv.org/abs/2006.09994. 103

Xu, Albert, Eshaan Pathak, Eric Wallace, Suchin Gururangan, Maarten Sap, and Dan Klein. 2021. Detoxifying Language Models Risks Marginalizing Minority Voices. *arXiv* 2104.06390: 1–8. https://arxiv.org/abs/2104.06390. 211

Yang, Kaiyu, Klint Qinami, Fei-Fei Li, Jia Deng, and Olga Russakovsky. 2020. Towards Fairer Datasets: Filtering and Balancing the Distribution of the People Subtree in the ImageNet Hierarchy. In *FAccT '20: 2020 ACM Conference on Fairness, Accountability, and Transparency*, 547–558. New York: Association for Computing Machinery. 211

Yang, Ke, Julia Stoyanovich, Abolfazl Asudeh, Bill Howe, H. V. Jagadish, and Gerome Miklau. 2018. A Nutritional Label for Rankings. In *Proceedings of the 2018 International Conference on Management of Data, SIGMOD '18*, 1773–1776. New York: Association for Computing Machinery. 131

Yang, Wei, Ping Luo, and Liang Lin. 2014. Clothing Co-Parsing by Joint Image Segmentation and Labeling. In *Proceedings of the 2014 IEEE Conference on Computer Vision and Pattern Recognition*, 3182–3189. New York: Institute of Electrical and Electronics Engineers. 212

Yuan, Lu, Dongdong Chen, Yi-Ling Chen, Noel Codella, Xiyang Dai, Jianfeng Gao, Houdong Hu, Xuedong Huang, Boxin Li, Chunyuan Li, et al. 2021. Florence: A New Foundation Model for Computer Vision. *arXiv* 2111.11432: 1–17. https://arxiv.org/abs/2111.11432. 210

Yudkowsky, Eliezer. 2004. Coherent Extrapolated Volition, Technical report, Machine Intelligence Research Institute. 71, 72

Yudkowsky, Eliezer. 2011. Complex Value Systems in Friendly AI. In *AGI 2011: 4th International Conference on Artificial General Intelligence*, eds. J. Schmidhuber, K. R. Thórisson, and M. Looks. Vol. 6830 of *Lecture Notes in Computer Science*, 388–393. Berlin, Heidelberg: Springer. 70, 99

Zach, Richard. 2023. Hilbert's Program. In *The Stanford Encyclopedia of Philosophy*, eds. Edward N. Zalta and Uri Nodelman. Metaphysics Research Lab, Stanford University. https://plato.stanford.edu/archives/spr2023/entries/hilbert-program/. 23

Zahn-Waxler, Carolyn, Marian Radke-Yarrow, Elizabeth Wagner, and Michael Chapman. 1992. Development of Concern for Others. *Developmental Psychology* 28 (1): 126–136. 234

Zech, J. R., M. A. Badgeley, M. Liu, A. B. Costa, J. J. Titano, and E. K. Oermann. 2018. Variable Generalization Performance of a Deep Learning Model to Detect Pneumonia in Chest Radiographs: A Cross-sectional Study. *PLoS medicine* 15 (11): 1002683. 103

Zhang, Jiliang, and Chen Li. 2019. Adversarial Examples: Opportunities and Challenges. *arXiv* 1809.04790: 1–16. https://arxiv.org/abs/1809.04790. 164

Zhang, Yuhong, Qin Li, Sujal Nahata, Tasnia Jamal, Shih kuen Cheng, Gert Cauwenberghs, and Tzyy-Ping Jung. 2023. Integrating LLM, EEG, and Eye-Tracking Biomarker Analysis for Word-Level Neural State Classification in Semantic Inference Reading Comprehension. *arXiv* 2309.15714: 1–14. https://arxiv.org/abs/2309.15714. 274

Index

About the Publisher

The word "broadview" expresses a good deal of the philosophy behind our company. Our focus is very much on the humanities and social sciences—especially literature, writing, and philosophy—but within these fields we are open to a broad range of academic approaches and political viewpoints. We strive in particular to produce high-quality, pedagogically useful books for higher education classrooms—anthologies, editions, sourcebooks, surveys of particular academic fields and sub-fields, and also course texts for subjects such as composition, business communication, and critical thinking. We welcome the perspectives of authors from marginalized and underrepresented groups, and we have a strong commitment to the environment. We publish English-language works and translations from many parts of the world, and our books are available world-wide; we also publish a select list of titles with a specifically Canadian emphasis.

broadview press

This book is made of paper from well-managed FSC® - certified forests, recycled materials, and other controlled sources.